MY LIFE BETWEEN JAPAN AND AMERICA

*Other Books by Edwin O. Reischauer:*

The Japanese, 1977

Toward the 21st Century: Education for a Changing World, 1973

East Asia: Tradition and Transformation, with J. K. Fairbank and A. M. Craig, 1973

Japan, the Story of a Nation, 1970 (rev. ed., 1981)

Beyond Vietnam: The United States and Asia, 1967

East Asia: The Modern Transformation, with J. K. Fairbank and A. M. Craig, 1965

East Asia: The Great Tradition, with J. K. Fairbank, 1960

Ennin's Travels in T'ang China, 1955

Ennin's Diary; The Record of a Pilgrimage to China in Search of the Law, 1955

Wanted: An Asian Policy, 1955

Translations from Early Japanese Literature, with Joseph Yamagiwa, 1951

The United States and Japan, 1950 (rev. eds., 1957, 1965)

Japan Past and Present, 1946 (rev. ed., 1963)

Edwin O. Reischauer, 1981. *(© John Goodman 1981)*

# MY LIFE BETWEEN
# JAPAN AND AMERICA

## EDWIN O. REISCHAUER

*A Cornelia & Michael Bessie Book*

HARPER & ROW, PUBLISHERS, New York
*Cambridge, Philadelphia, San Francisco, London*
*Mexico City, São Paulo, Singapore, Sydney*

FIRST EDITION

*Designer: Sidney Feinberg*

This book is set in 10-point Avanta by The Haddon Craftsmen, Inc., ComCom Division, Allentown, Pennsylvania, and printed and bound by R. R. Donnelley, Harrisonburg, Virginia.

Library of Congress Cataloging-in-Publication Data

Reischauer, Edwin O. (Edwin Oldfather), 1910–
  My life between Japan and America.
  "A Cornelia and Michael Bessie book."
  Includes index.
  1. Reischauer, Edwin O. (Edwin Oldfather), 1910–
2. Ambassadors—United States—Biography.
3. Ambassadors—Japan—Biography.  4. United States—
Foreign relations—Japan.  5. Japan—Foreign relations—
United States.  I. Title.
E840.8.R45A37  1986      327.2′092′4   [B]      85–45652
ISBN 0–06–039054–9

88 89 90 RRD 10 9 8 7 6 5 4

# Contents

# Acknowledgments

I wish to express my deep appreciation for the invaluable editorial guidance Simon Michael Bessie and his associate editor Brooke Drysdale Samuels contributed to this book. An author, I find, has difficulty in distinguishing what is important and interesting to others in the undergrowth that envelopes his own career. Without the ruthless slashing of the axes of my two editors and their careful pruning, the account of my life would have remained a tangled part of the forest and would not have been shaped into a tree that could stand alone.

My gratitude at a different level goes to Nancy Deptula, Jill Conway and Ella Rutledge for invaluable help checking names, titles and dates and for vast amounts of typing. Jill Conway in particular deserves my heartfelt thanks for endless hours of secretarial drudgery.

My final and greatest thanks are due the hundreds—even thousands—of persons who participated with me in my life work. Some like Serge Elisséeff and John Fairbank played major roles. Others are merely among the hundreds who assisted me in my tasks or who are continuing this work as I myself drop out. With the exception of my immediate family, none of these persons was asked to check the manuscript for corrections or advice, so none of the errors and misinterpretations can be blamed on them. But all are part of the story, for without their cooperation and support little that I have done in my life would have been accomplished.

# Preface: A Twig Is Bent

A S AN American boy born and raised in Japan, I attended a school for foreign students in Tokyo which eventually became known as The American School in Japan. It covered the twelve years of elementary and secondary education, and in my day averaged around one hundred and thirty students. In roughly descending order of numbers, the students were Americans, Japanese, Canadians, Chinese, English, Europeans, Asians, white and red Russians, and Latin Americans.

Faced by this motley crew of children, visiting dignitaries invariably felt called upon to expatiate on the importance of international understanding. They would wax eloquent about building bridges across the sea, and I would visualize the progressively longer underpinnings of these structures as they marched across the continental shelf and then plunged down to the ocean abyss. An even more popular figure of speech was "hands across the sea."

All this inspired nothing but hilarity among my comrades and me, perhaps because we found the idea of international understanding absurdly self-evident. And yet the need for international understanding and cooperation became the central focus of my life, determined, I am sure, by my birth and childhood in Japan.

Even as a youth I viewed the appalling ignorance and lack of interest about Japan in other lands with dismay. For most Americans, Japan might as well have been on the other side of the moon, and for the few who were aware of it, the chief picture was of cherry blossoms, geisha, and Mt. Fuji. Even these they knew only incorrectly, having silly misconceptions about geisha and calling Mt. Fuji "Fujiyama" instead of the correct "Fuji-san." My comrades and I despised Western tourists who straggled through Japan confirming their own misconceptions, and we had a deep antipathy for Occidentals from other Asian lands, who tended to regard the Japanese as upstarts, arrogant in their monkeylike mimicry of Western technology and military power and lacking in appropriately servile respect for the white race. Even our own parents seemed at times embarrassingly insensitive to Japanese ways. Quite unconsciously we had acquired the habit of looking at things two different ways—from the Japanese angle of vision as well as from our own national viewpoint. This proved to be the key to my career and, extended worldwide, is the only hope I can see for world peace and human survival.

When I drifted into the study of history during college, it was quite natural for me to concentrate on the then almost nonexistent field of Japanese history, and the broader field—including China and Korea—of what came to be known as East Asian studies. It became my ambition to help create in America a greater awareness of that part of the world, which embraces more than a quarter of the population of the globe and an equal proportion of its historical experience. East Asia, it seemed to me, deserved some study and at least a small foothold in our university curriculums. In the early 1930s, however, when I started my serious study of East Asia at Harvard University, even such modest objectives seemed visionary. There was little taught in American universities to prepare one for a career in such a field, and two years of study in Europe revealed that there was not much more instruction about Japan and East Asia there.

In the meantime, the clouds of war were gathering over the Pacific. They blew up in part from the worldwide depression of the 1930s, which helped to produce not only the Nazism of Germany but a turn toward dictatorial rule and military expansion in Japan. Japan was mounting a challenge to European imperialism and American naval supremacy in the Pacific. It was also inundating Asia with a flood of cheap, shoddy Japanese manufactures, which threatened the near monopoly the European nations held in their colonies and spheres of influence. Japan and the West seemed like two trains hurtling at each other on the same track, each sure it had the right of way.

Half-trained persons like myself in an unrecognized field of study could do nothing about the unfolding tragedy. Ignorant and unconcerned, the American government and people were quite unwilling to take Japanese interests and attitudes seriously. I could see that if the approaching war and future ones were to be avoided, people would have to learn to look at problems from both points of view. One person naturally could accomplish little in so large a task, but my future life work seemed to be clearly cut out for me.

The storm that was brewing between the United States and Japan finally broke in the lightninglike Japanese attack on Pearl Harbor on December 7, 1941, and it raged on for almost four years, all the way from the broad expanses of the North Pacific to the borders of India. Ironically enough, it was only when we became absorbed in the war that Americans began to develop an interest in Japan. Our leaders realized the necessity of learning a great deal more about the Japanese and their language, and Americans began to study Japan and its East Asian neighbors. The toehold a few of us had gained at Harvard and other American universities as scholars of East Asia grew into a broad and rapidly expanding beachhead. As one of the earliest professional scholars in East Asian studies, I found myself carried along like a surfer, riding the forward edge of a great wave. In my half century of contact with Harvard, I have had the satisfaction of seeing Japanese and East Asian studies grow from precarious infancy to healthy maturity. I have also seen the whole nation shift from disdainful disinterest in Japan and other trans-Pacific countries to keen awareness of them and a deep respect.

As interest in Japan increased, I became accepted as one of its chief interpreters in the United States, and in Japan after the war I became an even better known interpreter of the two countries to each other. I turned, in fact, into an inveterate pontificator on the theme of international understanding through greater mutual knowledge. I took care to avoid the images of bridges and hands across the sea, but the message was the same.

Since specialists on Japan were so few at the beginning of the war, I was drawn away from my concentration on ancient Chinese and Japanese history to more immediately useful work in Washington, and at the war's end to planning for the future of Japan. These experiences undoubtedly contributed to my being selected as the American Ambassador to Japan in the 1960s. The transformation from being a scholar of ancient history to serving for five and a half years in a key ambassadorial post reminded me of the professed confusion of Chuang-tzu, the ancient Chinese philosopher, between his being a man who had dreamed that he had been a butterfly or a butterfly who was now dreaming that he was a man. Despite great trepidation, I took the ambassadorial post because it gave me an unparalleled chance to help strengthen understanding and appreciation between Japan and America. I was determined to help lay the foundations for a real partnership between them as a major step toward world peace.

◆§

This, in short, has been the career of the youthful scoffer at "hands across the seas." It took place during the period of Japan's amazing growth from a still backward developing nation to a position among the global leaders. During this time, Japan also moved from a sort of spiritual isolationism to a cautious effort to play an appropriate international role, while the United States shifted from supercilious disinterest, through frantic concern over a seemingly superhuman enemy, to fulsome appreciation and respect for Japan and close cooperation with it as probably its most important partner and ally. It is these themes that form the framework of my story, in which my own life serves merely as illustrative detail and a way to put some flesh of living reality on the bare bones of great historic trends.

My childhood fell during World War I, when the arrogance of nineteenth-century Western domination still hung heavy over Asia. My early years of political consciousness came in the 1920s, when Japan was bidding for true equality with the West and Japanese-American rivalry in the Pacific was mounting. While I was entering on my studies of East Asian history during the 1930s, Japan returned to the path of imperial conquest, throwing down the gauntlet to America and Europe. Then, following the terrible war and the American Occupation of Japan, there was a period of uneasy collaboration between the two. In the sixties I had a chance as the American Ambassador to Japan to try to strengthen that relationship and I did my best to turn it into a full and equal partnership. And now, as I fade from the scene, I have the satisfaction of seeing the partnership I championed firmly established as a matter of vital importance to both countries. American interest in Japan has grown to proportions far greater than I had ever imagined possible. Japanese-American relations are now those between the two greatest industrialized trading nations in the world, between the two leading democracies, and, most significantly, between the strongest country of the West and the leading nation of non-Western cultural background.

In writing down my memories, I have for the most part had no diary or other extensive written materials to draw on. Unlike the Japanese, who are inveterate diary writers, I have never been moved to record my daily life. Only for my years as Ambassador to Japan do I have weekly letters to my family and fairly extensive memoranda addressed to myself for certain periods. The remainder of my story depends on sheer memory, which is notoriously selective and unreliable.

I offer an incident that occurred at the Harvard Commencement festivities in 1947 as a warning. I was sitting with one of our graduate students, Marion Levy, now a distinguished senior professor at Princeton, listening to General George C. Marshall, then Secretary of State. He was delivering the post-Commencement address in which he set forth publicly for the first time the famous Marshall Plan that changed the course of history. During the speech, as I remember the occasion, I commented to Levy on the great significance of the Secretary's remarks. Levy's memory is that I leaned over and said, "Marshall sure isn't saying very much, is he?"

# PART ONE
# GROWING UP
# IN JAPAN
# 1910-1927

A. K. and Helen Reischauer with their three B.I.J.s:
Edwin (left), Felicia and Robert, 1917.

# 1

# On Being a B.I.J.

In MY youth, American children born in Japan, especially those of missionary parentage, were called B.I.J.'s. We were very proud of the distinction and felt superior to our less fortunate comrades. We tended to know a great deal more about living in Japan than they did and to speak better Japanese. We were as much at home with chopsticks as with forks, and rice became the staple of my diet in place of potatoes and bread—a trait I have passed on to my children and they in turn to my grandchildren. Our elders envied us our more accurate pronunciation of Japanese and attributed to us a sort of mystique—an inherent comprehension of the subtleties of the Orient.

Even Japanese, then as well as now, seem to feel that being born in Japan confers a sort of key to understanding the country. During the 1930s, when the police were becoming increasingly suspicious of all foreigners as potential spies and one was constantly subjected to police interrogation while traveling, my birth in Japan served as a form of passport. A policeman, after dutifully questioning me on my identity, what I was doing, and where I was going, all of which was already recorded in his notebook, would then frequently ask me about my attitude toward the Japanese government or the current aggression Japan was engaged in on the continent. These were embarrassing questions, since I had no sympathy for Japanese imperialism, but I found that I could always evade an answer by simply starting out with, "Well, you know, I was born in Japan . . ." Invariably the policeman would accept this as ample evidence of my understanding of the Japanese point of view and would pass on to less sensitive matters.

There was, of course, something to this mystique of being a B.I.J. I never had to discover Japan, and nothing about it has ever seemed strange or exotic to me. It was rather trips to America in my youth that produced such feelings. I remember at the age of five looking down from the deck of our ship docking in San Francisco and being astounded at the sight of white men working as stevedores and black men mixed among them. At that time almost the only Westerners in Japan were missionaries, teachers, diplomats, businessmen, and occasional tourists. I had never seen a white man doing manual labor, unless one counts the occasional forlorn Russian refugee who would trudge the streets of Tokyo selling cloth from a large pack on his shoulder. A black man was an even more exotic sight, since there were no blacks at all in Japan in those days. Even now I find much in the great diversity of our country that is surprising or even exotic. I cannot say the same about tremendously homogeneous Japan. I have often thanked my lucky stars that my metier has been to try to understand and explain Japan, not the vastly more complex and mystifying society of America.

Things as they existed in Japan seemed to me what was natural and normal. The four regular seasons, the lush fields, the pervasive greenness, the ever present mountains, and the often spectacularly beautiful seacoast were for me the geographic norm. All Japanese art, as well as the Chinese and Korean art that lie behind it, has always appealed to me. My present home in Massachusetts I actually designed on the basis of a neighbor's house, but Japanese often describe it as being an adaptation of contemporary Japanese domestic architecture. If so, this is the result of Japanese artistic canons I have unconsciously absorbed since youth, not because of any conscious imitation.

The sights, the sounds, and the smells of Japan were familiar parts of my environment from birth. At night one heard the clapping of two sticks together as the watchmen for fires passed through the streets, and during the day, the distinctive calls and horns of peddlers of food. Most memorable was the sound of the little curved horn and the cry of "Tofu, Tofu" from the sellers of that nutritious and delectable food, which fortunately has at last made its way to much of America. Then there was the clatter of the wooden clogs, or *geta,* which are no longer worn in cities. They made a deafening roar when throngs walked on paved areas, and after we returned at the end of the summer from the unpaved paths of our summer home in the mountains or from trips to America, this sound always meant to me, "I am back home in Tokyo." Such sounds are now unfortunately only memories of a distant, almost unimaginable past.

The smells of Japan were equally distinctive. Some emanating from noodle shops or other little eating establishments or from food-vending pushcarts were enticing. Others were repulsive, though accepted by me as part of my natural habitat. I am thinking particularly of the odor of the large wooden buckets in which farmers living within reach of the city would haul by hand or oxcart the human waste of the city to manure their fields. They would ladle the waste from large bowls in the toilets of houses through small outside apertures, creating an almost unbearable stench, which they then would spread out more permanently over the countryside.

Many city houses still lack flush toilets, but the work of collecting this so-called night soil is now efficiently done almost without odor by big trucks equipped with suction tubes. This once familiar smell therefore has disappeared and also the medical problems night soil caused. The application of human waste to vegetables transmitted intestinal worms from person to person. We had to undergo an annual deworming, which consisted of taking a strong medicine that killed the worms and left their human hosts temporarily wishing they too were dead. The worms in their agony were known to try to escape through their host's mouth—an ordeal that my brother once experienced.

◦§

Westerners born in other Asian countries have had a sense of rapport with their lands of birth similar to that we B.I.J.'s felt for Japan. This was true of the "China Born," as they were called in China, as well as the "Korea Kids." Everyone has read about the young Britishers born under the British Raj, who considered India their home and had to discover England when traumatically sent back there for their schooling.

Being born in Japan, however, was very different in one way. Japan was then one of the few independent nations of Asia and the only one that stood on a footing of political equality with the West. In 1894 it had gotten the British to agree to end within five years the system of extraterritoriality, whereby Westerners living in Japan were tried by their own courts. This was a major part of the so-called unequal treaties which had been fastened on Japan shortly after Commodore Matthew C. Perry, with his superior American fleet, had forced the Japanese in 1854 to open their ports to intercourse with the West. In 1894–95 Japan had defeated China with surprising ease and acquired from it the island colony of Taiwan. Then in 1904–05 Japan had astounded the world by defeating the mighty Russian Empire, winning a foothold in South Manchuria in China and five years later absorbing the whole of the ancient kingdom of Korea. Japan was beginning to approach the highest European standards of the day, which were defined by military power and imperialism. Its victory over Russia was the first defeat in modern times of a Western nation by a non-Western one and had earth-shaking consequences. It stirred up the first tremors of nationalism throughout much of the rest of Asia.

In most of Asia the dominance and superior status of Occidentals was taken for granted, but not in Japan, which was a country clearly ruled by and for its own people. Westerners were merely guests living there on Japanese tolerance. Despite this, many Westerners even in Japan retained their nineteenth-century assumptions of Occidental cultural superiority. I can remember their tendency to make fun of Japanese peculiarities, particularly the not always successful efforts of Japanese to imitate Western ways. There was much hilarity over Japanese errors in English pronunciation and grammar on the part of people who made far greater mistakes themselves in speaking Japanese or arrogantly refused to try to learn the language at all. Amusing errors in signs in English, such as the sign over a tailor shop which read "Ladies Have Fits Upstairs," were highly prized collector's items. The fundamental attitude that I encountered in my own home, however, was one of deep respect for the Japanese and complete acceptance of the fact that we were living in Japan on Japanese terms.

Not far from our home was an old feudal mansion with a massive gate, unfortunately destroyed in the great earthquake of 1923. In my childhood the Crown Prince, the present Emperor, resided there, before being moved to the official Crown Prince's Palace, the small imitation of Versailles that is now a national guest house. One day when I was riding my bicycle past the front of this old feudal gate on my way to see a friend, a policeman yanked me off my bike by my sailor collar, because the Crown Prince was about to come out. In most of Asia at that time such an incident would have been unthinkable. But to me the event was entirely natural. In America the great people were Americans, and people lived by American custom. In Japan the great people were Japanese, and we lived by Japanese custom. That was the way it was and the way it ought to be.

Like any boy, I grew up proud of my home town and proud of the country I lived in. In a way I even shared in the Japanese sense of nationalism. I was still too young to be aware of the humiliating brush-off Japan received from President Wilson, backed by the British, when it requested that a clause on racial equality be included in the Versailles Peace Treaty at the end of World War I. Racial prejudice against Orientals on the west coast of America and in Canada and Australia accounted for the callous American and British refusal. The first political issue of which I was keenly aware was the infamous exclusion act passed by the American Congress in 1924. The Japanese felt insulted to have a "Gentleman's Agreement," whereby Tokyo had voluntarily prevented Japanese workers from emigrating to the United States, changed into an absolute exclusion of Japanese immigrants on racial grounds. At the age of thirteen I was as indignant over this act as any Japanese nationalist could have been.

My sympathy for Japanese nationalism spilled unconsciously over into a general Asian nationalism. The empires of the Western powers seemed to me unjust, and I was incensed by the way Westerners living in other parts of Asia looked down on the "natives." I found it infuriating that they regarded the Japanese as being uppity for trying to run things their own way in their own country, and I resented their denouncing of the Japanese for wishing to join in the game of imperialism, which the Europeans seemed to think was their own special prerogative.

Being born in Japan freed me from the start from the racial prejudice against Japanese and other Asians then almost universal among Westerners. I remember how indignant I was when on a trip back to the United States at the age of thirteen all the steerage passengers on the ship were lined up on deck in San

Francisco and those who looked Chinese were unceremoniously yanked out of line by the American immigration officers on the suspicion that they might be ethnic Chinese posing as Filipinos. When I lived in China in the late 1930s, I found it distinctly uncomfortable to be in a place where extraterritoriality and custom gave me a special status of superiority. Later, in Hong Kong, I was irritated to see ER, standing for Elizabeth Regina, on the belt buckles of the Chinese policemen. When my first wife died in the 1950s, it seemed completely natural to me to marry a Japanese woman, Haru Matsukata. She happened to have, like me, a mixed Japanese-American cultural background, and for both of us it has always taken a conscious effort to realize that we had an interracial marriage. After our marriage, when our family visited pre-independence Singapore, a friend took us to a big old club of local fame as a sight worth seeing; but, as we drove up to the entrance, he suddenly realized that Haru, as an Oriental, would not be allowed to enter. I would have been furious had it not been so absurd. It was all too reminiscent of the fabled signs in a Shanghai park that once denied entry to Chinese and dogs.

Whether or not there is any truth in the mystique about being a B.I.J., my Japanese birth did inculcate in me certain attitudes that were very uncommon among Westerners at that time but which were to prove of immense value to me in my career. As I have said, I was free from racial prejudice, had a strong dislike for Western imperialism, and had a corresponding enthusiasm for Asian nationalism. Such attitudes are common enough today, but other Westerners have come to them only slowly and through painful experiences. I imbibed them from birth. In a sense, I was a generation or two ahead of my time—a useful headstart in facing the problems of our rapidly changing world.

# 2

# A Small Boy in Japan

I WAS born in Tokyo on October 15, 1910. Together with several million other babies, my birth was heralded by the appearance of Halley's comet. The year 1910 is counted in Japan as the forty-third year of Meiji, the first modern Emperor.

My parents had arrived in Japan as missionaries in 1905, just after the signing in Portsmouth, New Hampshire, of the treaty concluding the Russo-Japanese War. Not realizing how close to financial collapse Japan had come, the Japanese people were highly indignant when, despite Japan's victory, the treaty brought them no cash indemnity from Russia. Defeat, they felt, had been snatched from the jaws of victory. They blamed this in part on President Theodore Roosevelt, who, in an act of friendship for Japan, had engineered the treaty. For the moment, the United States was almost as unpopular with the public as was their own government. But not then nor even during the nervous buildup to World War II was there ever the slightest personal threat to Americans in Japan.

My parents took up residence in a missionary house on the campus of Meiji Gakuin, one of Japan's first modern private schools for boys, in what was then Shiba Ward in Tokyo but is now part of Minato Ward. Founded in 1863, the school had been developed jointly by two American missionary societies, those of the Northern Presbyterian Church, to which my parents belonged, and the comparably Calvinist Dutch Reformed Church.

The Meiji Gakuin campus had five missionary residences, three of them together in a corner of the grounds. The central one, in which I was born, was sunny but flimsy, and might be characterized architecturally as typical Meiji-foreign. All three, like all Japanese residences of the time, were freezing cold in winter, having no central heating systems. We fought off the chill as best we could with heavy long underwear, sweaters, and coal-burning stoves and fireplaces. Unlike the Japanese, who used daily hot baths to warm themselves up, we still lived in the American age of the Saturday night bath. But for that weekly bath we had a glorious, deep, Japanese-style wooden bathtub, heated by a charcoal burner fitted into it. The only problem was that untutored visitors from America might pull the plug on the bath water, letting it out, and thus inviting the charcoal fire to ignite the whole house.

The Meiji Gakuin campus was a beautiful place in my childhood. The foreign residences and the Japanese-style home of the Japanese president were surrounded by fine gardens, and the entire campus was covered with grass and ringed by trees, which in places were virtual forests to small children. Time has played havoc with the campus of Meiji Gakuin University, as it is now called. There seem to be a hundred students for each remaining tree. Factory-style, high-rise buildings have replaced the quaint old halls. All is so changed that I prefer not to visit the school but to retain the picture in my memory of how it once looked.

I was the second child in our family. My brother, three and a half years my senior, had the manly name of Robert Karl, but I received what always seemed to me the somewhat sissy name of Edwin, from which I escaped in later years to Eddie and then to Ed. As a middle name I was given my mother's maiden surname of Oldfather, which, distinguished though it may be, proved a heavy burden for a young boy.

The family was completed in the autumn of 1914 by the birth of my sister Felicia. Unfortunately she was born deaf because of a case of German measles my mother contracted during her pregnancy—a connection not known in those days. As a result, Felicia spent most of her childhood back in the United States attending schools for the deaf; since I was the closest to her in age, I developed a special rapport with her and probably greater skills of communication than any of the other members of the family.

An integral and important part of the family consisted of the two women servants we always had. The term used for them in those days was *jochu,* or "maids," which in recent years has been considered demeaning and has been replaced for the few servants who remain by such more acceptable terms as "helpers" *(o-tetsudai).*

Whatever the word used, however, the maids were treated in our home with respect and as equals. They came from Christian backgrounds and were addressed with honorifics in what was even then an outmoded style. Haru ("Spring"), the same name as my wife's, was called O-Haru-san, and Kiku ("Chrysanthemum") was O-Kiku-san. Later came O-Kiyo-san as a replacement for her older sister, O-Kiku-san, who was getting married. I never knew their family names. During my early days as Ambassador, however, a newspaper located O-Kiku-san, then widowed, and brought her to the Embassy for a visit, made artificial by the presence of the mass media and strangely unreal by forty years of divergent experiences.

O-Kiyo-san was a bright young woman, and my parents, in what was probably an excess of American egalitarianism for those days in Japan, arranged for her to continue her high school education. Since girls' high schools at the time were largely the preserve of the upper and middle classes, and class consciousness still ran strong in Japan, the strain of adjusting to the snobbishness of her classmates proved too great for her, and she had a complete mental breakdown. This story is hardly imaginable in the egalitarian society of contemporary Japan.

O-Haru-san and O-Kiku-san played a large role in my early years and, no doubt, helped shape my personality and sense of values. No English lullaby sticks in my mind, but I remember with perfect clarity the lullaby they would sing me, which began *"Nenneko botchan,"* or "sleepy little boy." I spent much of my time hanging around them in the kitchen and seem to have begun my verbal life bilingually. As a small child, Japanese came to me as naturally as English, though what I spoke might best be called kitchen Japanese. I would forget much of it during periodic year-long trips to the United States, and, when I started school, I remained an illiterate in Japanese with the vocabulary of a small child. Still, I felt perfectly at home in it, and it sufficed for my purposes. Somewhere I did pick up a command of the two *kana* syllabaries by which Japanese can be written phonetically syllable by syllable, and I also learned a smattering of Chinese characters, largely from the destination markers on streetcars.

I learned a great deal more than language from the maids, however. The story of Momotaro, the boy born from a peach who set off with his faithful monkey, dog, and pheasant to subjugate the island of demons, was as familiar to me as Little Red Riding Hood. So also were the story of Urashimataro, the Japanese Rip van Winkle, who visited the Sea King's Palace, and many more. The dark places in the corners of the rooms of our house, which was lit in the early days by gas, were peopled by Japanese, not Western, goblins. All this was as much a part of my life as the games of cowboys and Indians, which my brother and I enacted with the aid of our beloved hobby-horse.

The maids had a deep influence on me in ways that are hard to define. Perhaps I owe to them my typically Japanese tendency to be more self-conscious about the impression I make on others than judgmental on how they impress me. Most important was the appreciation of the traditional samurai values which I believe I absorbed from O-Haru-san. She was a daughter of a samurai of the Tosa domain, which played a prominent role in the Meiji Restoration and subsequently in the latter part of the nineteenth century provided leaders for the popular movement demanding democratic reforms. Her family, like most samurai families, failed to make a successful transition from feudalism to the more egalitarian system of the Meiji period, and she had been raised without a formal education, being like me master of only the phonetic *kana*. She had been forced to go into domestic service, but she had retained her samurai pride, honesty, strength of will, and sense of loyalty.

O-Haru-san was a person of great natural ability. She was artistically gifted but found little opportunity to express her talent except in the beautiful pie crust flowers with which she would adorn her pies. She was of course a fine cook, and she ran her kitchen with Prussian efficiency. As a quasi-mother, paralleling my own mother in inner strength and bravery, she gave me much for which I shall always be grateful.

While the maids loomed large in my life, Japanese friends of my own age played little part. A major problem was that Westerners back in those days stood out in Japan much more than they do today. Japanese thought of them all as being red-haired and blue-eyed and looked on them as appearing very exotic. Red hair was considered the color of animals, and today "Japan through blue eyes" is the conventional phrase for a Westerner's view of Japan. Even in the parts of Tokyo where Westerners are now so common as to draw no attention, they were openly stared at by adults and would draw a trailing crowd of urchins shouting *"Ijin pappa, neko pappa."* I have never met a Japanese who knew what that meant—they obviously heard it far less often than I—but *ijin* means "barbarian" and *neko* is "cat," and I believe the phrase was meant to suggest that the speech of Westerners sounded like the yowling of cats. Children also often shouted *"Gudobai* (goodbye)" at us. There is probably deep psychological meaning in the fact that after World War II the corresponding cry became *"Haro* (Hello)."

The Japanese children of our neighborhood were not considered "suitable" playmates for me in those class-conscious days, and the children of my parents' Japanese colleagues lived scattered around the city at great distances. My contacts with my Japanese peers was largely limited to the few who attended our English-speaking school, the elite who played tennis with us at the summer resort, and a boy whom I tutored in English for a while. At the age of about twelve I was a very inept language teacher. I would glance desperately around the room for something to serve as an object of conversation, usually ending up with the colors of a magnificent stuffed Japanese crane which, in its glass case, occupied one corner of the room. Needless to say, no lasting friendship developed from these lessons, nor did they continue very long.

Lacking many Japanese friends of my own age, I was thrown back largely on the companionship of other missionary children, but there were few of them around. My parents represented the beginning of a new wave of missionaries, coming after a hiatus of some years. One older boy on the Meiji Gakuin campus, however, was James ("Jimmy") Landis. His father was a gifted but erratic scholar, who had acquired a Ph.D. and a sweet, motherly wife in Germany. Jimmy was like his father—brilliant but unpredictable. He caused an interfamily crisis when he was caught hanging my terrified brother down a well by his heels. He had also embittered relations between the foreign children on the hill at Meiji Gakuin and the surrounding Japanese children by engaging in exchanges of insults in Japanese and stone-throwing battles. His talents and weaknesses were to become more obvious in later years when, after serving as dean of the Harvard Law School and chairman of the Securities and Exchange Commission, he was convicted of tax evasion and subsequently drowned in his pool, possibly a suicide.

Whether or not Jimmy Landis was to blame, I had little luck in my repeated efforts to join the neighborhood Japanese children in their games. Not accepted as a playmate by them, I was usually forced to find companionship from my brother. Frequently we were the only Western children around, and he became my chief childhood companion. He naturally used his age advantage to browbeat me unmercifully. This, together with his special aura of being the firstborn, his better looks, and greater charm of personality, kept me in my place. To the servants he was the *waka-danna-sama,* a term for the "young master," or heir, in merchant families. To satisfy my wishes for a corresponding title, the maids created for me the term *ko-danna-sama,* or the "little master."

We spent long weekends with only each other for companionship. In time we developed complicated war games, which for a whole Saturday would occupy all the bedrooms on the second floor and entail the maneuvering of literally thousands of soldiers. The battle strategies might be based on the trench warfare of World War I, the movements of armies in approximately eighteenth-century style, or feudal castle warfare. Our generals, which included a small bronze elephant and a bust of Wagner, developed their own personalities and reputations, which somehow we preserved despite the fact that the ultimate outcome of battle was determined by the throw of the dice.

Even with a brother and on occasion some other friends, my childhood in Japan involved a great deal of solitude. This I filled largely with reading. We had fallen heir to a number of copies of a British publication called *The Boys Own Paper*, which had been assembled into yearly volumes entitled *The Boys Own Annual*. The stories were mostly about English schoolboy life or tales of the Western Front in World War I, but there were some about adventures in the American West or Australia and occasional accounts of the Boer War or colonial battling on the Northwest Frontier of India. *The National Geographic* was another standby, but I wandered further afield. My parents had a set of Shakespeare's plays, each bound separately as a small red leather booklet. I had read these from end to end by the time I was thirteen, but I cannot imagine now what I could have gotten from them.

# 3

# American Roots: A Missionary Heritage

Despite my Japanese background, I was always keenly aware I was an American and knew I would always be considered a foreigner in Japan. In some ways this made things easier. I never had any doubts about my own identity. American children raised abroad frequently have a keener sense of their nationality than do their American-born peers. In the United States, foreign countries often seem unreal in their remoteness, while ethnic variations within American society become confused with national distinctions. I have known many Americans who became aware of their own nationalism only when they first traveled abroad.

American family roots, of course, lead back to a variety of ethnic heritages. My family name is typically Germanic—a real Sauerkraut name, as my first parents-in-law used to say. The name stems from Upper Austria, where there is a small island of Protestants north of the beautiful lakes and mountains of the Salzkammergut area, just east of Salzburg. It is a pretty region of apple orchards and large, square, whitewashed farmhouses surrounding courtyards. The Reischauer name appears to have died out in Austria itself, but during a visit to this area in my student days, I found the baptismal records of my grandfather and grandmother in a Protestant church in a village called Scharten near the town of Efferding.

It was from there in 1853 that my great-grandfather, Matthias Reischauer, and his family left for the United States, entering through New Orleans and going up the Mississippi by flatboat to southern Illinois. Here they settled near Jonesboro with other Austrian and German Protestant families in a farming community at a place they called Kornthal, or "Grain Valley." Matthias brought with him to America a son named Rupert, born in 1841, who was my grandfather, and whose anglicized name Robert was passed on to my brother.

My grandfather served in the Northern Army in the Civil War, until he was medically discharged in 1864. His early death in 1888, when my father was still only nine, greatly influenced my father's thinking and was important in inducing him to enter the ministry. I, of course, never knew my grandfather. But my grandmother, Maria Gattermeier, who was also born in 1841 in the same Scharten parish, lived to the age of eighty-four. She never spoke anything but German, however, while I at the time knew not a word of the language.

My father, August Karl, was born on September 4, 1879, and had a typical nineteenth-century farm upbringing. His earliest schooling was in German, but he later switched to what was called Union Academy in the nearby town of Anna. There he came under the influence of its Presbyterian leaders, and on their advice continued his studies at a small Presbyterian college, Hanover, which stands on a beautiful high bluff in southeastern Indiana, overlooking the majestic Ohio River. Feeling that the Lutheran faith in which he had been raised was overly conservative, my father joined the Presbyterian Church and went on from college to McCormick Theological Seminary in Chicago. Graduating there in 1905, he chose the foreign mission field, as was common among the better theological students in his generation. For reasons I never knew, his first choice was Brazil and Japan his second. Since there was no opening in Brazil at the time but a teaching position at Meiji Gakuin, he went to Japan. My lifelong connection with Japan, therefore, was something of a happenstance.

My mother, Helen Sidwell Oldfather by birth, was like my father the child of a Civil War veteran. Her father, Jeremiah, was the great-grandson of a Protestant German, Friedrich Altvater, who with nineteen other men led their families from Berlin in about 1769 to seek greater religious freedom in America.* The group landed in Baltimore, then moved on to Pennsylvania, where in 1784 they founded the town of Berlin in the southwestern part of the state. About 1811 one of Friedrich's sons, Henry, moved on to Montgomery County in southwestern Ohio, where he translated his family name to Oldfather. It was there that my maternal grandfather was born in 1841.

Jeremiah Oldfather fought through the whole Civil War as a member of an Ohio regiment, leaving behind many harrowing tales of adventure and suffering. I suspect that it was these experiences which induced him after graduation from Miami University in Ohio to go on to Lane Seminary and enter the ministry. He elected to go to the mission field, and left in 1872 as a Presbyterian missionary bound for the extremely dangerous country of Persia, the modern Iran.

Jeremiah took with him his bride, Felicia Narcissa Rice, whose name had originally been Reis and stemmed from German-speaking Switzerland or the Palatinate. Reis landholdings were first recorded south of Pittsburgh in 1755. Here the family established what was known as Rice's Fort, which underwent an Indian attack in 1782. Members of the family moved on to Kentucky and Indiana, where my grandmother was born in 1848. She was orphaned at nine, while her father was a candidate for Congress, but I have an oval portrait of her and her mother, who is holding a Bible and looking very stern.

Felicia Rice Oldfather lived to the age of ninety-three and was the only one of my grandparents I knew well. In fact among her twelve grandchildren, I had a particularly close relationship with her. While I was still a small boy, she spent a year with us in Japan, taking the place of my mother, who was back in the United States getting my sister started in a school for the deaf. Throughout her life she was a voracious reader, and she had decided opinions on most subjects. Despite her own and her husband's Germanic backgrounds, she conveyed the feeling to the whole family that we were of Scottish descent, presumably because of our Presbyterian affiliations.

In Persia, Jeremiah and Felicia Oldfather spent eighteen years in the Turkish-speaking Azerbaijan area in the extreme northwest of that country, largely in the towns of Tabriz and Urumiah (now called Rezaiyeh). The trip to this remote region was hazardous, and life there was harsh, not without dangers for Christian missionaries. The people were unfriendly and the missionaries led lonely, isolated lives. Family lore is full of tales of marauding Kurds lurking in the mountains and deadly scorpions lurking in bedroom slippers.

My grandparents' children were all born in Persia but, as the problem of their education began to loom, the family decided to abandon the mission field in

*For information on this branch of the family, I am indebted to an unpublished pamphlet by my cousin Dorothy Adams Moore on the "Oldfather-Adams Genealogy."

EOR pulled in ricksha by brother Bob and friends.

A. K. Reischauer with EOR
(left), Bob and a Japanese
student, in the garden
on the Meiji Gakuin campus
in 1914–15.

The "young masters" (EOR standing) with the family. O-Haru-san (extreme left), O-Kiku-san (middle) and O-Kiyo-san (right).

Off for college.

1890. My grandfather became the pastor in the small college community of Hanover in southern Indiana, where he died dramatically in 1910 at the age of sixty-nine while giving his farewell sermon. It was in Hanover that my parents met. My mother had always been educated with her older sister and as a result graduated from Hanover College at the surprisingly young age of eighteen. She was already a teacher of Latin at the secondary school attached to the college when my father, only a few months her junior but years behind academically because of his start in the German language, turned up as a freshman.

The family obviously made the transition back to life in the United States with success; yet I have always been struck by the paucity of Iranian influences and the lack of a feeling for the country that they brought back with them after spending eighteen years in Persia. This stands in sharp contrast with the feel for Japan which my early years in that country gave me.

To return to my own position as a missionary kid, I have known many persons who have been psychologically marred or at least embarrassed by such a background. For them, the gap between their childhood in a backward corner of the world and their later life in America may have been too great to bridge, or perhaps it was the conflict between an austerely religious childhood and the looseness of modern American society that left them confused. Missionaries have also been looked down on in recent years in certain academic circles. They have been seen as bigots, who, protected by superior Western military might, forced their constricting beliefs on innocent, happy natives or bought "rice Christians" through niggardly financial aid parceled out to cynical but impoverished recipients. Missionary work has often been regarded as the epitome of "cultural imperialism" and a particularly invidious form of Western aggression.

There is, of course, some truth to these characterizations, particularly in China, which is the major source for this interpretation. But basically it gives a very misleading picture of the missionary movement as a whole. Missionaries are usually motivated by the noble desire to share with others what they value most. We do not hear of the cultural imperialism of the early Christian missionaries who helped civilize North and East Europe, nor of the Buddhist missionaries who expanded their religion through South, Central, and East Asia. In a sense, missionaries are no different from proponents of the green revolution or world literacy. In fact, they are much like teachers anywhere. Those of us in Asian studies in the United States often quite rightly refer to our missionary zeal for spreading our subject.

Unlike China, the missionary movement in Korea became identified with the nationalistic fight against Japanese domination and now against military dictatorship. In Japan, the Christian Church has had little of the aura of cultural imperialism it acquired in China. It was taken up principally by young samurai intellectuals seeking liberal educational, social and political alternatives to the somewhat authoritarian patterns of the government. It is no accident that Christians have played major roles not just in education but also in the fields of social services, the labor movement, the organization of tenant farmers, and the founding of the Socialist Party. Though never numbering as much as 1 percent of the population, Christians have tended to be people of education, looked up to with respect, and enjoying far more than their share of positions of leadership.

It never once occurred to me to follow my parents in Christian missionary work, and I easily slipped into a very different attitude toward organized religion than they had, but I have always respected their beliefs and have taken pride in their accomplishments. Without doubt, I drew many of my ideals as well as personal traits from my missionary background.

Frugality was one of those traits. We had to be careful with money to the point of parsimony. We were poor compared to the families of businessmen, diplomats, and the prominent Japanese with whom we came in contact. In our case, in particular, the education of my sister and her future care called for careful husbanding of our meager missionary income. My parents made clear to my brother and me that any family savings would have to go to Felicia and we should expect no inheritance. Every penny counted and I learned to pinch each one twice. In my youth no Japanese was allowed to leave even a single grain of rice in his bowl; to this day I still feel compelled to eat every grain of rice on my plate. Here the missionary and Japanese influences merged. But in fact, compared to most people we were not really poor, nor did we feel so. We had servants, a home, garden, a summer place such as only the rich in Japan could afford. My parents held respected positions in society. And we traveled widely around the world, even if by second class.

My mother and father were loving, attentive parents, and we did much together as a family, such as reading aloud in the evenings. My mother imbued my brother and me with a strong sense of what we would now call women's rights, as well as social justice for the less privileged. Both our parents also tried to give us as normal an American boyhood as possible and succeeded in doing so to a surprising degree. My mother in particular saw to it that my brother and I had chores to perform around the house, somewhat to the dismay of the servants, who saw the "young masters" in a different light.

My father provided us with an admirable role model. He may have lacked some of my mother's social graces and was known to fall asleep when he found himself stuck with a boring dinner guest, but he was very much a gentleman in all the best senses of the word. He was always firm in his principles and convictions, and was a good companion to us boys. The many long hikes we took together in the mountains in summer and on weekends still stand out in my mind as high points of my youth.

Initially, my father taught theology and Greek at the Seminary of Meiji Gakuin and English in other parts of the school, but he soon became interested in studying Buddhism, arguing that there was no point in trying to convert Japanese to Christianity unless one understood the religion they already had. My brother and I came to take great pride in his scholarly achievements. His first book had been an essay entitled *Personal Immortality*, but in 1917 he published a volume called *Studies in Japanese Buddhism*, which for many years was considered an authoritative source and won him the honorary degree of Doctor of Divinity at New York University. He continued his Buddhist studies by translating the *Essentials of Salvation (Ojoyoshu)* by the Buddhist monk Genshin (942–1017), which was an important text for the popular faith movement that emerged in eleventh-century Japan, and he also wrote several other books.

In his prime, my father was active in the Asiatic Society of Japan. The British Minister and later Ambassador traditionally served as the largely honorary president of the society. No American diplomat, I believe, was ever so honored. They appear to have been either too little interested or in later years too busy, as in my case. Under the president of the society, there frequently were three vice-presidents—a Britisher, an American, and a Japanese. For some years these three were Anesaki Masaharu,* the learned Tokyo University professor of Sanskrit; Sir George Sansom, the talented British diplomat and virtual founder of modern Japanese studies in the West; and my father. It is probably no accident that my brother and I became scholars in the Japanese field. After my brother had already won his Ph.D., I happened to give my maiden scholarly presentation before the Asiatic Society of Japan in 1936. On this occasion Sir George jokingly asked my father whether he was trying to found a dynasty of Japanese scholars.

Another of my father's activities was to try to create a strong, unified Christian university for men. In the early days after the opening of Japan, Christian schools, as important training facilities in the English language, played a large role in education for both boys and girls; but as the government began to perfect its national educational system, the boys' schools sank into second-rate status. It was my father's feeling that, if the Christian schools could pool their resources, they could create at least one first-rate Christian university. But each major denomination had its own school, and the rivalries between them proved too strong to be overcome. The Christian girls' schools, however, were eager to form a joint university. Together with the famous Christian leader and diplomat Dr. Nitobe Inazo, whose picture now graces the 5,000-yen note, and the woman educator

---

*The Japanese, like the Chinese and Koreans, place the family name first. I have normally followed this practice, except, of course, for Americans of Japanese descent.

Dr. Yasui Tetsu, my father established in 1918 the Tokyo Women's University (Tokyo Joshi Daigaku, usually called in English the Tokyo Women's Christian College). Today, it is regarded as probably Japan's leading women's university, both academically and socially, and I know its creation always gave my father his most gratifying sense of accomplishment.

My mother from the start was active in the Women's Christian Temperance Union and settlement work for the poor, but her main achievement was the founding of Japan's first school for the deaf that used the oral method of instruction. She had become interested in the problem because of Felicia's handicap, and took training courses in the United States while getting Felicia started in school there. Then in 1920, with the aid of Miss Lois Kramer of the German Reformed Church and some Japanese colleagues, she started a small school called the Japan Deaf Oral School (Nippon Rowa Gakko). In my youth, the children and teachers of the tiny school always came to our home for their annual Christmas party; during the 1960s my wife and I revived the tradition by having the greatly expanded school come for its Christmas party to the American Embassy, where the children of the Embassy officers aided us in entertaining them. Today, the Deaf Oral School is the only private school for the deaf in Japan, but it is considered one of the best in the country and is certainly one of the most heartwarming places one can visit in all Tokyo.

Through their work, both of my parents gained the respect and love of many Japanese, some of which rubbed off on me. I have always had every reason to be proud of both of them, and of their achievements as missionaries. Their work in founding schools in fact seems much more tangible and lasting than anything I have ever been able to do myself.

# 4

# Early School Days

MY PARENTS' first furlough came in 1912–13. Their return trip to Japan was by way of Europe and the Trans-Siberian Railway; since I was to repeat this trip in 1935, I must be one of the very few living Americans who have traveled the Trans-Siberian both before and after the Russian Revolution. A second emergency furlough came in 1915–16, because of my mother's health, which never was robust, and the need to put my sister into a school for the deaf.

As a result, I was in the United States in September 1916 when I was about to turn six, and entered a public school in Champagne, Illinois, where my mother's elder sister, Miriam (Myra for short), was married to Charles Ryan Adams, the local Presbyterian minister.

In December, my father, brother, and I together with my grandmother returned to Japan. There I was put in the Tokyo Grammar School, which was situated in the Tsukiji ("filled land") section of Tokyo. Because of the small classes in the school, it was soon discovered that I was already able to read, so I was promoted to second grade. This put me more than a year ahead of my age cohort, which was to be a mixed blessing the rest of my school days.

I attended school in Tsukiji in the second and fifth grades, but during my third and fourth years, my mother, who had returned from America, kept my brother and me at home and taught us herself by what was known as the Palmer Method. One reason for this was probably the current worldwide influenza epidemic.

I have few memories of the intellectual side of my schooling in Tsukiji, except for a vigorous dispute I had with my teacher in second grade over some principle of mathematics. I do not even remember my teachers except for a tall, deep-voiced Russian, who spoke no English but apparently got good results from us as we lustily sang "The Volga Boatman" in Russian.

The most memorable part of my Tsukiji school days was the commuting trip there of about an hour each way. Travel in the city was primarily by streetcar, and the trip to Tsukiji involved at least one transfer as well as walks at both ends. At the Tsukiji end we walked from what is now popularly known as the Ginza shopping area, crossing on the way two or three bridges which were frequented by begging lepers.

The Tokyo streetcars we rode looked something like the Toonerville trolley, with open platforms at each end. For a transfer, one was given a longish ticket with a map of the city's streetcar network on it, punched at the points of transfer and ultimate destination. Armed with this documentation, we loved to play a game we called "skipping cars." Wherever streetcars would slow down or pile up, we could, if lucky, leap from our streetcar and jump aboard the one ahead. The game was to see how many cars we could skip in this way. Japanese conductors were considerably more indulgent to unruly foreign boys than to the more strictly disciplined Japanese children.

I learned the map of Tokyo from its streetcar and commuting railroad systems, as was probably the case for most residents of Tokyo in those days. As a result, I find myself somewhat disoriented by the Tokyo of today, which depends on a very different system. Since the end of World War II a series of new place names and a new transport system of subways and elevated roads have obliterated much of the Tokyo I knew as a boy. The city has been largely destroyed twice in my lifetime, once in the earthquake of 1923 and again in the American bombing of 1945, but it is the redrawing of its transportation map and the changing of its place names that often make me feel a stranger in my own home town.

In 1920, between my fifth- and sixth-grade years, the Tokyo Foreign School, as it was then called, moved from Tsukiji to the newly filled-in area of Shibaura, and in the process changed its name to The American School in Japan. This was the first of five moves, each somewhat farther to the west, which were eventually to bring the school to its present site in the western suburbs of Tokyo, about seventeen miles due west of Tsukiji. In 1920, Shibaura was not the mass of large factories and buildings it is today; it was a desolate area of sun-cracked mud, almost devoid of structures of any kind. In this wilderness, our new school, which had a different color—white, red, and green—for each story, stood out like some strangely shaped national flag.

At about the time of the move to Shibaura, the school added Japanese classes to the curriculum, but since they did not count in our academic ratings, we, or at least I, did not take them very seriously. But the classes did increase my stock of Chinese characters to add to the two phonetic syllabaries *(kana)* I already knew. We used the standard national readers, which were changed from time to time. Japanese identify their age cohort by the series in use when they started school. My series included a poem that began *"Ka, ka, karasu ga naite iku* (Caw, caw, the crows fly crying)": when I was seriously ill in Tokyo in 1983 and had been unconscious for more than a week, that poem was the first thing I was able to articulate understandably in either English or Japanese.

The three years the school was at Shibaura passed pleasantly for me. The school prospered and the student body grew to an all-time high for my days of 186. I had good teachers—a Miss Pearl Keehn from Burlington, Iowa, for fifth and sixth grade, and a Miss Ruth Seleen of Spokane, Washington, for seventh and eighth. (Each teacher taught two classes.) The older boys had a baseball team on which lanky Gordon Bowles was the catcher and clean-up batter. He came by his height honestly, for his Quaker missionary father was humorously called by the Japanese *"Sangai-sama* (Mr. Three Stories)." Gordon was the only American in his graduating class of 1921, the others being two English boys, a Japanese girl, and two Russians who were photographed for the school annual in their respective uniforms as soldiers in the red and white Russian armies. Gordon became a well-known anthropologist, specializing in the peoples of the Himalayas, and was active in Japanese-American relations until after his retirement from Syracuse University.

~§

An important part of my school years consisted of the long summers we spent at our summer home in Karuizawa, 3,000 feet high in the mountains eighty miles northwest of Tokyo. Karuizawa had been founded as a summer resort by missionaries in the late nineteenth century, but some rich, aristocratic Japanese and a few of the embassies also had establishments there. My parents, together with their close friend and colleague, Miss Matilda London of Philadelphia, had jointly built a cottage in Karuizawa before I was born. Miss Lila Halsey, another single missionary lady, usually summered with us. Both of them taught at Joshi Gakuin, a prestigious missionary girls school in Tokyo. Miss London we children called Aunt Ti; the Japanese principal of the school, a Miss Mitani, whose much younger brother, Mitani Takanobu, I was to come to know decades later as the Grand Chamberlain of the Imperial Court, was another of our make-believe aunts, but Miss Halsey somewhat puckishly insisted that we had enough aunts and she would be our Cousin Lila.

Our house, built with walls and roof of cedar bark, was in the Happy Valley section, a place name that pops up all over Asia wherever Britishers resided in the nineteenth century. Karuizawa was small in those days, consisting of a little Japanese village, once a post station on a through highway, a modern railway station with a few houses more than a mile away, and a scattering of summer homes.

Our cottage stood at the beginning of a steep rise up to the ridge that formed the eastern edge of the broad pocket in the mountains in which Karuizawa nestles. By rigorously topping the trees in front of the house each year, my father preserved a fine open view from our home out over the whole of Karuizawa. On the right to the west stood out in all its grandeur the huge, rounded, purple mass of Mt. Asama, Japan's most active volcano, only eight miles away and rising to 8,179 feet. It had erupted violently in 1783, devastating the whole region and leaving the Karuizawa area buried several feet deep in scoria. This perforated, cinderlike volcanic stone is so light that it floats in water. It makes the whole area useless for agriculture but gives a substructure to the soil that prevents the buildup of mud, despite the frequent rains and spectacular thunderstorms that sweep through the mountains.

Mt. Asama almost constantly belched forth smoke and usually had a spring eruption that would throw stones the size of pigeon eggs as far as our house. But quiescent or in eruption, it always made a spectacular backdrop for our view out over Karuizawa, particularly the majestic sunsets which unfolded from behind it. Lightning storms could have no more impressive setting than Mt. Asama afforded them, and I am sure my lifelong love of thunder and lightning goes back to the magnificent electric storms we would watch progress across the valley between us and the great volcano.

During my childhood, we spent every summer we were in Japan at Karuizawa, and the trip there from Tokyo was always an adventure. It was about a five-hour train ride in soot-filled carriages. At almost every station, vendors walked along the platform, singing out the wares they had to sell. There were always *o-bento,* or Japanese box lunches, tea in charming little earthenware pots, and other edibles. At Isobe, a famous sweet cracker called *Isobesembei* was sold, and Yokogawa at the base of the mountains and Karuizawa at the top were famous for their buckwheat noodles, or *soba*.

As the train drew near to the edge of the Kanto Plain, the track grew steeper. Then at Yokogawa electric cog locomotives were hitched on at the center and rear to shove the train up an incredible 7 percent incline through twenty-six tunnels to Karuizawa. We would stand on the platform of the first car, which had no engine in front, to witness this marvelous feat, gulping in the wonderfully cool, fresh air, until we finally emerged high up at Karuizawa.

We hiked all over the mountains of the Karuizawa area and in later years I made an annual ascent of Asama, eruptions permitting; but the chief focus of our childhood activities was the tennis courts. My partner was a Canadian, Herb Norman. Under his fuller name of E. Herbert Norman, he was to become well known as a gifted scholar of modern Japanese history, an outstanding Canadian diplomat, and a tragic controversial figure in world politics, of whom I shall write more later. Herb, being a year older than I, always beat me for the junior singles title, but teamed together we were invincible in doubles. In my memory our partnership on the courts of Karuizawa lasted for years, though it actually continued only until the summer of 1922, when I was still short of my twelfth birthday. I was not to see Herb again until my student days in Europe.

Summers in Karuizawa were not just a break in the year but seemed a whole lifetime in themselves. I have far more memories of the minutiae of life there than I do of the much longer periods of time spent in Tokyo. Although I have been to Karuizawa only two or three times briefly since I was sixteen, it remains crystal clear in my mind's eye. Many changes have come since then and I hate to think of it as it is now. The whole broad mountain basin and surrounding areas have filled up with people, houses, sports facilities, and traffic. But there is still no sound in the world more soothing to me than the patter of rain on the cedar bark roof of our house. Even though our old cottage still stands, for me the phrase "You can't go home again" applies best to Karuizawa.

⊷

I was in Karuizawa when the Great Kanto Earthquake struck on September 1, 1923. Until then, people generally measured time as being before or after "the war," meaning World War I. For the residents of Tokyo and the Kanto area, things now became defined as occurring before or after "the earthquake." The earthquake, together with the great fires that resulted from overturned cooking *hibachi*, took over 100,000 lives and devastated Tokyo, Yokohama, and surrounding areas. Except for the central core of steel and concrete buildings, most of downtown Tokyo and the working-class districts to the east, as well as Yokohama and much of the area between the two cities, were burned out; but the slightly hilly and more wooded western side of Tokyo—the so-called Yamanote or "Hand of the Mountain" district where we lived—was spared from fire. Karuizawa was about a hundred miles from the earthquake's epicenter, but even there it was a fearsome thing. Several houses collapsed and one person was killed.

It had been raining on the morning of September 1 in Karuizawa, and a group of friends and I were playing cards on the floor of our living room when the earthquake struck. We dashed outside and watched as the stone and tile chimney of the cottage toppled over.

Some of my friends had much more exciting experiences. One claimed that he had been pinned down in a fallen house in Kamakura, a seaside resort near Tokyo, but that a tidal wave had lifted the timbers, allowing him to swim free. However true his story, a tidal wave did occur there and almost engulfed my future wife, who was also summering in Kamakura.

In Karuizawa we had no idea of the extent of the catastrophe at first since all communications had been knocked out. News spread that fires in the direction of Tokyo could be seen from the Toge, or "Pass." This was the point in the chain of hills against which our house nestled where the old highway leading from this area to the feudal capital of Edo (the later Tokyo) crossed the main divide between the Japan Sea and Pacific Ocean sides of Japan and started its descent down to the Kanto Plain. The road remained well preserved from Karuizawa up to the Toge, but had long before disappeared beyond that point. My father, brother, and I set out at once for the Toge, but by the time we reached it, a thick fog had settled in, reducing visibility to a few feet. We only learned the next day of the terrible significance of the fires that had been visible from eighty miles away.

My father, Aunt Ti, and the maids soon left to do what they could about restoring things in Tokyo. My brother and I volunteered to give assistance to the hordes of refugees that began to stream through Karuizawa by train, jamming every carriage and even crowding the roofs. I spent two or three nights at the railway station, giving out small bottles of cow's milk to mothers with babies. Each trainload was a stinking mass of suffering humanity and of gaunt faces in shock.

The Shibaura school, standing on its shaky mud base, was damaged beyond repair. For a while the school operated, much reduced in numbers, in Karuizawa, but then moved back to Tokyo as the chill of winter approached. It found quarters in the former residence of the parents of Gordon Bowles on the campus of the Friends Girls' School in Mita, near Keio University.

The school had shrunk to less than a hundred students, and for the first time in several years Americans constituted less than half the total. But under adversity, morale was high. Baseball was our only sport that year, and we practiced right through the winter. As the baby of the team at thirteen, I was put in left field where a large mound of charcoal bags left little ground to be covered. My brother was the star pitcher, and a Mexican boy played second. Most of the rest were Japanese, including the older brother of the first girl to stir my interest in the other sex, though I was much too shy even to ask her to dance. The high point of the year was a baseball series with our arch rivals, the Canadian Academy of Kobe, in which we triumphed gloriously.

The earthquake, however, hung heavily on our minds throughout the year. Scenes of devastation surrounded us on all sides, and there were literally hundreds of aftershocks which lasted all year long. Some of them were quite severe, but since all the vulnerable structures had already collapsed, the tremors did little damage. Nevertheless, we slept that whole winter with our clothes beside our beds so that we could snatch them up if we were forced to run outdoors in the middle of the night.

My fear of earthquakes lingered on for years. Eight years later, when I lived in Perkins Hall, a brick graduate student dormitory at Harvard, I would inevitably react in momentary terror whenever a truck hit a pothole in the street outside, shaking the building. It must have been close to thirty years that the fear of earthquakes hung over me, and it is still felt by many residents of Tokyo. Devastating earthquakes have hit the city about every sixty years, and today, slightly over sixty years since the Great Kanto Earthquake, there is much speculation about what another one would mean to the great node of some twenty million people that now centers around Tokyo.

# 5

# High School

Early in the summer of 1924, our family returned to the United States on furlough. In those days, travel meant relaxation for adults and fun for children. There were no grueling overnight flights to leave one's inner clocks awry, no sudden upsetting changes of environment. The trip from Japan to the eastern part of the United States took about three weeks.

My father and mother had sponsoring churches in Chicago and Detroit;

while they stayed on for a few days in Chicago, my brother and I went down to the old family farm in southern Illinois, where the slight southern drawl of the area and the strange idiom of the hired hand caught our fancy. By the time our parents arrived, we had, to their consternation, mastered the use of "ain't," "Pass them thar taters," and the like.

After spending some time at the summer camp of my Uncle Charley and Aunt Myra on a lake in Michigan, we all proceeded by car to Springfield, Ohio, where Uncle Charley now had his church. From there my brother set off for Oberlin College in northern Ohio and my parents departed for the Presbyterian Mission Board headquarters in New York and various speaking engagements. I was left as a sort of foster son with my uncle and aunt. They could not have been nicer to me and their two youngest children, who were still living at home, were like siblings to me, but I was miserable and fell ill for a prolonged period in midwinter. At fourteen I found it very difficult to make the shift from my life in Tokyo and the cozy atmosphere of the tiny American School to an undistinguished American city of around seventy thousand which had one large senior high school to serve the whole city. I was lost in its factorylike atmosphere, with bells clanging out the change of classes, lockers for my books, and a move from room to room for each new class. Though accustomed to an international and interracial mix of students, I was unprepared for the intellectual and social variety of a big American public high school. My only consolation was a basketball team, which a neighbor boy and I organized at the local YMCA.

Summer finally came, however, and after a long visit at the camp in Michigan, my parents and I returned to Japan in time for the start of the school year in the autumn of 1925. After my dismal year in America, I was delighted to be back in my familiar haunts and with my old friends. Among them I had the kudos of knowing all the latest popular songs and other lore about life in America.

The next two years, my junior and senior years in high school, were in many ways the high point of my youth. An upperclassman myself and free from the overshadowing presence of my brother, I was now king of the walk. By the time my class graduated, there was only one other boy in it, and he had no interest in sports or other extracurricular activities. This gave me ample opportunity to be the captain of every sports team and head of almost everything else. It was a very exhilarating time.

Our family moved in the autumn of 1925 about ten miles out into the suburbs to a newly built house on the campus of Tokyo Women's University. This necessitated a trip of an hour or more each way by electric trains and streetcars, but I rather enjoyed the commuting, which was the normal way of life for most residents of Tokyo.

My studies I remember as being very routine, and I performed lackadaisically. Sports occupied most of my interest—baseball, basketball, tennis, and soccer. For a baseball diamond we shared with numerous other schools the Yoyogi Parade Grounds of the Imperial Army's First Division, located beside the beautiful Meiji Shrine. Often during a practice session or game activities had to be briefly suspended while a platoon of soldiers with fixed bayonets threw themselves down on the ground back of second base, shot off several rounds of blank ammunition, and then with a tremendous shout stormed and successfully captured home plate. The parade grounds were a full two-mile walk from the school; this walk on top of all the exercise and usually followed by a bowl or two of *soba* noodles on my way home normally left me much too groggy to absorb my Latin homework, much to my mother's distress.

Girls had also become another diversion from my studies. I had been taught to dance my freshman year by older girls who lacked sufficient partners, and gained the reputation of being a real smoothie. During my junior and senior years we were all wild about dancing, using the extra time after lunch to dance in the gymnasium and dancing madly the whole time at parties. In our partners and dates we hadn't the slightest consciousness of nationality or race. The pairing was strictly according to personal preferences.

Besides sports and girls, I had two other extracurricular activities. One was a jazz band. I directed it and played the piano with what little skill I retained from my childhood lessons. Our relatively good saxophonist, Rindge "Spuds" Ushijima, was a large, fat boy, but that was not the reason for his nickname. It was derived from the fact that his father had emigrated from Japan to California in 1888 and acquired such large tracts of potato fields near Stockton, California, that he came to be known under his American name of George Shima as the Japanese "potato king." Despite Spuds's musical talents, our band was terrible. The only song we did at all well was "Baby Face," which was then very popular. Its lyrics and some other more risqué ones—"And she's got so much of the skin you love to touch"—made my mother fear that I was destined for no good end.

My other extracurricular activity was the publication of the *Chochin* (or *Lantern*), the first genuine annual The American School ever had. Previously a *Black and Orange Annual,* named for the school's colors, had appeared sporadically, but it was a trifling endeavor. The *Chochin* was largely the creation of myself as editor and Phil Garman—later a university expert on labor problems —as business manager. The name was a simple steal from *The Lantern* of some college in Ohio, though the connotations of *chochin* and "lantern" are quite different. For a purely student-run undertaking in a tiny school, the *Chochin* was not bad; its traditions and name are still kept alive at The American School today, though in much more grandiose form.

My class of 1927 graduated seven strong, down from thirteen a year or two earlier. My last summer in Karuizawa was in many ways the best. I felt myself to be at the top of the heap and ready for new worlds to conquer. Near summer's end, a group of us boarded the *Taiyo Maru* to proceed to various American colleges. The *Taiyo Maru* happened to figure twice in history. The second time was in 1941 when she carried the last Japanese spies to Hawaii and brought back the last written reports on Pearl Harbor. The earlier time was after World War I, when she was part of the German war booty assigned Japan. The original German builders had made some miscalculation in her construction, which produced a slight list that had to be corrected. This may have been the source of the ubiquitous stories circulating among Westerners during the 1920s and 1930s about the alleged inability of the Japanese to do anything but copy. It was claimed that they would meticulously reproduce dents caused by accidents to models in shipment or purposeful errors introduced into blueprints by tricky Europeans, with the result that the ships they built turned turtle and the airplanes they manufactured came crashing down. There never was a word of truth in any of the many forms this story took, but it was religiously believed by most Westerners, especially American military men.

As can be imagined, we all had a wonderful time on the *Taiyo Maru* in the late summer of 1927. In San Francisco we were met by "Spuds" Ushijima and other friends, and spent a few days in Berkeley. Then we started east together by train. I said goodbye to my current girlfriend while watching a full moon through the train window somewhere in Iowa. I would never see her again. After a few days at my Aunt Myra's home in Springfield, Ohio, I proceeded to join my brother at Oberlin.

I felt that I was putting Japan completely behind me. My recent year in the United States and the influence of The American School had made me much more thoroughly American than I had been as a small boy, and I was determined to become a typical American college man. It never occurred to me that my untypical attitudes and childhood experiences would affect my own later choice of career.

# PART TWO
# STUDYING
# AROUND THE WORLD
# 1927-1938

Newly married to Adrienne Danton at their home in Kyoto, 1936.

# 6
# College Years at Oberlin

W<small>HEN</small> I entered Oberlin in September 1927, I had spent only three scattered years in the United States and the rest of my life in Japan. The next six years—first at Oberlin, then in graduate school at Harvard—were important in establishing my self-image as an American who happened to be born in Japan rather than a resident of Japan who happened to be an American citizen. These years were also crucial in setting my life course, and here my childhood background won out.

At first I was simply eager to fit into life in the United States and avoid appearing different from my peers. I took care not to do anything that would call attention to my birth and upbringing and found no difficulty in doing this. When traveling, I concealed my place of birth to avoid bothersome questions. This was particularly important in crossing the Canadian border, where the usual question asked by border guards to establish one's nationality was "Where were you born?" I used a series of fictitious birthplaces, such as Springfield, Ohio, Jonesboro, Illinois, and Berkeley, California, which I assumed I knew more about than the questioner.

The college environment helped cut my umbilical cord with Japan. An American college town is a curious phenomenon—rural, remote, and parochial. Oberlin was no exception. The flat northern Ohio landscape was in no way reminiscent of Japan. All American children knew that if they dug a hole deep enough they would reach China on the other side of the world, but Japan was in no one's mind. The college did not offer any instruction on Japan, and like most contemporary college students, we never read the newspapers, which had virtually no news about Japan in any case. For four years I did not have a bit of Japanese food or hear a word of Japanese, except for an occasional greeting exchanged with one of the two or three Japanese students in the School of Theology.

My only contact with Japan was through letters from my parents, which took close to a month for transmission. Because I was still only sixteen when I left home, my parents had insisted that we write each other once a week, however perfunctory the letters might be. This proved a good way to keep in touch, and we continued the routine the rest of their lives. Except for these letters and a little financial aid, I was entirely on my own. Since I was now seven thousand miles away and communication by mail was slow, my parents realized there was little point in trying to guide me, so they wisely made no effort to do so. I had my aunt's home in Springfield to go to for Christmas vacations. Here I would see my sister, who spent all her vacations there during her years of study at the Clarke School for the Deaf in Northampton, Massachusetts. My parents provided me with the $25 monthly supplement to their salaries they received for me from the mission board and told me I could call on my aunt in Springfield for whatever other funds I needed. Fortunately, I never required any extra money after my freshman year, being able to acquire what I needed through scholarships, work, and summer jobs. The $25 supplement continued until I turned twenty-one, shortly after I had entered graduate school at Harvard.

I had chosen to go to Oberlin simply because my brother was there, but it proved a good place for me. It had high academic standards and was relatively small. There were only about three hundred students in each undergraduate class; including the famous conservatory of music and the graduate School of Theology, the total student body was less than two thousand. My adjustment to life in the United States was therefore much easier than it might have been at a larger and more impersonal institution.

Founded in 1833, Oberlin prided itself on having been coeducational and open to blacks from the start. Despite this background, however, it was distinctly a WASP institution and not much more enlightened on race relations than the rest of America. The 1920s were a bad time in that respect. I remember a large Ku Klux Klan parade in Springfield the year I spent there, and the college tolerated having its occasional black athletes put up in separate hotels when sports teams went out of town.

Oberlin had few residential facilities for its male students, who mostly lived in groups in private residences. Another freshman and I were taken into my brother's group of seniors, which, though occupying only the two upper floors of a private residence, operated under the grandiose name of "The Castle." We were treated somewhat in the style of the younger boys in *Tom Brown's School Days,* but we were pleased to be living in a house with several "big men on campus," a category that included my brother.

I ate my meals at Delta Lodge, a dining club of about fifty male students. Because of an insufficiency of jobs, I could earn my board only one of two semesters each year. I started in the lowliest job of washing pots and pans and scrubbing the kitchen floor, work which I found terribly difficult because of my previous life with servants; eventually I rose to the simple job of washing glasses and cutlery, which my workmate, Tommy Okino of Japanese descent from Hilo,

Hawaii, had reduced to a few easy operations. In later life he demonstrated the same efficiency as a prestigious judge in Honolulu.

The Castle group naturally changed character over the years, but by our senior year we had built it back again into a group of eight leading seniors, including the football, track, and tennis captains, the editor of the school paper and annual, and the president of the Men's Honor Court, the major organ of student government for men. Two of our group were from the American School in Shanghai. One was C. Martin Wilbur, who had been with me during my last two summers in Karuizawa and had been one of our group on the *Taiyo Maru*. Later he became a professor of modern Chinese history at Columbia. The other was Jack Service, who under his full name of John S. Service was to become a well-known member of the American Foreign Service and a leading China expert, but was among those who had their careers blighted by the McCarthyist madness after World War II. Backed by his wife, our classmate, Cary Schultz, he rode through those years of adversity with great courage and subsequently made a new career for himself at the University of California in Berkeley.

৺ঌ

My parents came to the United States the summer after my freshman year to attend my brother's graduation from Oberlin. After some time at my Uncle Charley's camp in Michigan, we drove down to my father's old farm in southern Illinois, which was operated by his older brother, my Uncle Ed. From there my parents left for Japan, accompanied by Bob, who was returning to Tokyo to teach history and serve as coach at The American School. I stayed on working for a month on the farm. It still operated basically by horsepower, giving me a glimpse back into the nineteenth century. Uncle Ed was a quiet, gentle man, whom I admired greatly. I could not have been of much help to him, and I think he vastly overpaid me when he gave me $10 for my month's labor. But when he died, he left me $2,000 in an insurance policy, the only inheritance I ever received. The next two summers I worked as a counselor at the University of Michigan Fresh Air Camp, a charity institution run for underprivileged boys from the Detroit area.

At college, sports initially loomed much larger than study for me. I played left field and leadoff batter on the freshman baseball team and was a regular starter on the freshman basketball team. My sophomore year I had to choose between the varsity tennis and baseball teams during the spring term, settling on tennis and serving as captain my last two years. My basketball career sputtered when I failed to make the varsity team, but I played intramural basketball on the class and Delta Lodge teams. In the autumn I played varsity soccer. The sport was all but unknown in America at that time, and our team, made up largely of players with foreign backgrounds like mine, was relatively good.

My social life at Oberlin was satisfactory, but intellectual matters interested me at first much less than either sports or girls. In fact, it was not until my last two years that my studies were even in the running. My freshman-year grades were only average; I was bored by the courses in advanced English composition and French and despised the course in zoology. The fact that I was usually the last to arrive at laboratory sessions and the first to leave probably did not help.

I enjoyed my courses in history and decided to follow in my brother's foot-steps by majoring in that subject. Gradually my grades picked up, and I discovered that I had a special aptitude for taking examinations. It was easy for me to organize and marshal facts on the spur of the moment; therefore all I needed to do to win an A in almost any subject was to cram my head before an examination with the necessary names, dates, and figures. This I did by staying up late the night before an examination and then getting up early the next morning, imprinting the information on my mind just long enough for use in the examination. Unfortunately, all this data usually faded away again as fast as I had learned it. But the system worked, and in the second half of my junior year I had a grade record which I was surreptitiously told was the highest in Oberlin history for a single semester. This won me a full scholarship my senior year.

Relatively few of the Oberlin professors left much impression on me. I had only one course with the outstanding member of the History Department, Frederick B. Artz, who was away at Harvard as a visiting professor much of the time I was at Oberlin. Probably the professor who most influenced me was Oscar Jaszi, of the Department of Political Science, which was my minor field of concentration. Jaszi was a Hungarian Jew who after World War I had been in the Socialist cabinet that was driven out by the Hungarian dictator Horthy. He had a passionate devotion to the search for world peace, which greatly influenced my own thinking. Among the courses he offered was one named "International Irenics," to the mystification of everyone, in which he reviewed the various concepts and plans for peace in Western thought.

It was definitely because of Jaszi's influence that I founded in my senior year an Oberlin Peace Society. The Great Depression had already struck, but in isolated Oberlin we were scarcely aware of it. Jaszi's eloquence, however, and his personal involvement made the problems of world peace come alive for us. A good number of students joined the Peace Society, and branches were formed in two or three other colleges. However, there was nothing for us to do in Oberlin to further the cause of peace, except to resolve never to participate in war ourselves —a resolution which for most of us would be washed away by the events of the next few years.

Because of my natural interest in Asia, I took whatever Oberlin had to offer in that area, which was precious little. A political science course called "Problems of the Pacific" was given by a professor with no special knowledge of the subject; not surprisingly, it proved very superficial. We learned a lot about disputes over cable rights on the island of Yap, but nothing about the basic dynamics of the problems of East Asia. The only other course on Asia was even more disappointing. It was offered by an Englishman in the School of Theology on the Mughal age of India. The man was a poor teacher and had no concept of the abysmal ignorance of his students. He lost us at once with a detailed discussion of the Sunni-Shiite split in Islam, and we all remained intellectually wandering in the desert the remainder of the semester.

The one substantial piece of work I did on Asia was a 213-page paper on "American Japanese Relations Before 1860." Professor Moore, the chairman of the Department of History, called to my attention a prize offered for an essay on Japanese-American relations and suggested that, since no one else was competing, I could easily win this prize by submitting a suitable paper. I set about the task with great energy but no guidance. Superficially the results looked quite impressive, but the contents were simply a rehash of other books. Despite the obvious weaknesses of the paper, I was awarded the prize, which I believe was for the princely sum of $200.

Oberlin provided me with four very happy years and a chance to solidify my childhood background into a real interest in Asia and international relations. But my specific objectives remained vague, and I was far from settled on a life career.

# 7

# Graduate Study at Harvard

As MY graduation from Oberlin drew near, plans for the immediate future became pressing. A business career never once entered my mind. Nor did I ponder how best to make a living. It was simply not a family tradition to go into anything but the professions, and I had been raised to think that the purpose of life was to make one's maximum contribution to society, however humble that might be. My developing interests at Oberlin suggested that this might be in connection with Asia and international relations, but my specific plans still remained amorphous.

In the autumn of 1930 Professor Moore proposed my name for the prestigious three-year Rhodes Scholarship at Oxford University, and I was chosen one of two official nominees from the state of Ohio; but in the six-state regional competition that followed, I lost out for one of the four scholarships. My failure, according to Professor Moore, was due to the fact that, at twenty, I was considered too young. And, more important, I had no good rationale for studying at Oxford since I wished to specialize in Japan and East Asia, and Oxford had nothing on Japan and only a very weak program on Chinese offered by a retired missionary. Professor Moore had also put my name up for an internship at the League of Nations in Geneva. This he considered definitely in the bag, but unfortunately, the bag burst wide open. The world depression necessitated financial retrenchment, and the program was canceled.

With the roads to Oxford and Geneva blocked, I took up a third option, which was to go to Harvard for graduate work in East Asian studies. This decision, I see in retrospect, was a rather daring one. There was actually no field of East Asian studies nor any regular job opportunities, academic or otherwise. It took a great act of faith and reckless disregard of the financial consequences to strike out in this direction, but I had no doubts or hesitation. Such is the courage of youth.

There were few universities in the United States where study of East Asia was possible. Most schools had no more than a few scattered courses. The leading places were probably Columbia, Harvard, and the University of California at Berkeley. Among these, Harvard possessed a special advantage in that it had the Harvard Yenching Institute, which offered a few fellowships for East Asian studies. My brother had been granted a reasonably adequate one for 1930–31 and got it renewed for 1931–32. Fresh out of college myself, I won a more marginal grant of $600 for 1931–32 and had it renewed at the same level for the following year.

I should say a word about the Harvard Yenching Institute, for I was to be associated with it most of the rest of my life. It was founded on the basis of a grant from the estate of Charles M. Hall, the inventor of the electrical process for reducing bauxite ore to aluminum. A misprint in the original brochure about the company he founded had accidentally simplified the original English spelling of "aluminium" to its present American form. Hall, who died in 1914, had been a loyal Congregationalist and in his will left generous sums to institutions with Congregational backgrounds. Among these were Oberlin, his alma mater, and a category described as being for educational purposes in "Japan, Continental Asia, Turkey and the Balkan States in Europe." He probably had in mind such Congregational schools as Doshisha in Kyoto, Roberts College in Istanbul, the American University in Beirut, and various Christian colleges in China and India. The use of the term "Continental Asia" may have been designed to exclude the Philippines, then under American colonial rule.

The Asian aspect of Hall's will finally took shape in 1928 as the Harvard Yenching Institute. It was designed largely by two extraordinary educational entrepreneurs, Wallace B. Donham, then dean of the Harvard Business School, and J. Leighton Stuart, the president of a missionary school, Yenching University in Peking, and later a postwar American Ambassador to China. They decided that, under the joint names of their two universities, the new Institute would concentrate on the development of Chinese historical and cultural studies at the Christian colleges of China, since these schools were woefully weak in both fields. Yenching University was to be a center for graduate training in the field, while Harvard would create a center of Chinese studies to help set the standards for the whole undertaking and train scholars and teachers for it. At Yenching, a monumental project for indexing the major classics of China was energetically pursued under the leadership of the distinguished scholar William Hung, who was to end his career as a refugee at Harvard. A Chinese-Japanese library was started at Harvard and, under the able administration of Alfred Kaiming Chiu, grew into one of the leading research libraries in the world in the Chinese and Japanese languages. In the early years, generous grants were given to a few prominent Western scholars who were engaged in research activities in China, Central Asia, and Indo-China. Smaller fellowships were assigned to Western students for study at Harvard of China and, in the case of my brother and myself, Japan. It is a curious fact that, despite the overwhelming original emphasis of the Institute on China, the four directors the Institute had until 1986 were all basically in the Japanese field.

I enrolled in the Harvard Graduate School of Arts and Sciences in the autumn of 1931. Since my brother that summer had married his college sweetheart, Jean Anderson, and had moved into a small university-owned apartment at Holden Green, I took his place as the roommate of his former Oberlin classmate, Arthur Hogue, in Perkins Hall, an old graduate student dormitory on Oxford Street. Hogue and I gradually developed a close friendship, and he even tolerated my maddening habit of studying Chinese every evening from eight until midnight with my radio blaring jazz beside me. Bob and Jean were kind enough to let me have dinner with them every night. This assured me of at least one hearty meal a day and good companionship. It was hard on Jean, however. She did not mind so much the extra mouth to feed as the fact that Bob and I would engage in endless discussions of our studies, principally the Chinese language and Japanese history, leaving her in frustrated silence. Except for my contacts with Bob, Jean, and Hogue, my graduate days at Harvard were mostly a monastic experience of unremitting study.

Harvard during its last two years under the leadership of President Lowell was still a very aristocratic, parochially New England institution. The feeling I received was of a school heavily centered on the undergraduate college, which was populated largely by preppies, as we would now call them. Only a few bright New York Jews and middle westerners were tolerated but not really welcomed. The snobbish student clubs were still important, even though the house system had been instituted a few years earlier. The graduate schools were seen as peripheral adornments, catering to outlanders in order to meet broader national needs. For all their national renown, they were in the penumbra of the true Harvard aura. Radcliffe was only a somewhat embarrassing excrescence. I realized that I was merely a second-class citizen in a Harvard society of this sort; nonetheless it was exhilarating to be part of the scholastic community. I felt that we students of the graduate schools formed an elite of scholarship. After some decades of looking at Harvard graduate students from the other side of the fence, I cringe at my youthful self-satisfaction.

Harvard, though one of the three foremost centers for East Asian studies in the nation, had only a meager offering and few students. My brother and I were the only ones trying to specialize in Japanese studies. Since there was no department for the study of East Asia, I entered the History Department and won an M.A. degree the next June. One course highly recommended for all history M.A. candidates was "Government 6: History of Political Theory," given by Charles Howard McIlwain. He was an interesting lecturer and a delightful person, who had an engaging way of stroking his bald pate from the rear as he ruminated over his statements. Unfortunately, he had a poor sense of timing. The first semester ended with him lecturing on the classic age, and he would not have reached the eighteenth and nineteenth centuries without a mad dash in the last two weeks of the spring semester.

The only course in Japanese was too elementary for me, so I started my East Asian studies with the introductory Chinese language course and a half course of reading in Chinese history. The regular instructor of Chinese, with whom my brother was taking the second-year language course, was a dignified Chinese gentleman named Mei Kuang-ti. I was assigned, however, to James R. Ware, an advanced student and a holder of a Harvard Yenching fellowship, who had returned unexpectedly from China and was made a teaching fellow. I was his only student.

Ware's knowledge of Chinese, especially its pronunciation, left much to be desired, and I got off to a shaky start without an inkling of the tonal system which is needed for speaking Chinese or comprehending it by ear. Of course, at that time this was par for the course for the scattered few trying to learn Chinese in the West. The object was to learn to read Chinese, not speak it, and some of the leading Sinologists of Europe prided themselves on having been in China little if at all. Sinology had grown up in the spirit of Egyptology, and treated Chinese as if it were a dead language.

During the first semester we used an inferior textbook of *baihua*, the contemporary spoken form of standard northern Chinese. Then at the start of the second semester, Ware announced that he was too busy finishing his Ph.D. thesis to meet with me for classes but that he had selected a text which fitted my interests and suggested I work on it by myself. It was the section on Japan from a third-century Chinese history, the *Weizhi*. This is a very important text, being the earliest account of the inhabitants of the Japanese islands, but it naturally was in classical Chinese, not the *baihua* I had been studying. Since it was on an obscure topic, scholars even today are not entirely agreed on what all of it means; for me, it was like switching from a third-grade primer to *Beowulf*.

The only dictionary at my disposal compounded my problems. It was a 1909 revision of an 1874 work by S. Wells Williams and so organized as to confuse rather than enlighten. For even the simplest of Chinese characters, it would give a bewildering array of meanings, with no indication as to which were primary meanings and which unusual usages. I was forced to prepare a 3- by 5-inch card for each character in the text, with the Chinese character brushed in my clumsy calligraphy on one side and Williams's multiple translations typed on the other. These I arranged in the order of the text with their translation side up, then puzzled over the almost infinite possibilities of translation until I hit upon one that seemed to make some sense in the context. In this way I slowly made an alleged translation, which I submitted to Ware at the end of the semester. I cannot imagine a way to start classical Chinese that would require so much labor for such small returns, but I did become familiar with a lot of Chinese characters, and this contributed to my learning to read written Japanese. I never did take any regular courses in the Japanese language, but since Japanese utilizes Chinese characters as the basis of its writing system, I was able to combine my knowledge of spoken Japanese with the characters I learned through Chinese to develop a reading knowledge of Japanese.

In the summer of 1932, between my two graduate years at Harvard, a seminar on Chinese studies was held at Harvard, sponsored by the American Council of Learned Societies and financed by the humanities division of the Rockefeller Foundation. Mortimer Graves of the Council had enthusiastically embraced the development of non-Western studies in American universities, and David Stevens, in charge of the humanities division at the Rockefeller Foundation, was backing him up financially. It is not generally realized how much the fields of East Asian and other non-Western studies owe to the enthusiasm of Mortimer Graves and the foresight of David Stevens. No one had informed me of this summer seminar until it was too late to apply for formal admission, much less for a fellowship, but I attended it faithfully as an auditor at my own expense. This was my first real immersion in East Asian studies. It was also my first chance to get to know Langdon Warner, who was the modest though inspiring dean of Japanese art studies in the United States.

At the seminar I met Hugh Borton and Charles Burton Fahs, both already committed to Japanese studies. Burton was working on a Ph.D. in political science at Northwestern University with the financial backing of the Rockefeller Foundation. Hugh and his wife "Buddie" were Quakers, who had taught at the Friends Girls' School in Tokyo, the one-time home of The American School in Japan, and, inspired by the scholarship and charisma of Sir George Sansom of the British Embassy, had gone to Columbia to pursue Japanese studies. They, together with myself and two or three others, were to form the total body of professional Japanese specialists outside of government service until the outbreak of war with Japan in 1941.

My brother and Jean left Harvard at the end of my first year to return to Japan, where he wrote his Ph.D. thesis on "Alien Land Tenure in Japan," a subject that did not interest him in the slightest but was the only one on which he could find a thesis supervisor at Harvard. This left me as the only student in the Japanese field, if I could be called a student given that I had as yet taken no course in the subject.

◦§

Except for my course in Chinese, my first year at Harvard had not been very different from that of any other M.A. candidate in history, and my career plans remained uncertain. I had vague thoughts that, if I earned a Ph.D., I might someday be invited back to teach in the History Department at Oberlin and could then introduce a course in East Asian history there. During my second year at Harvard, however, my career was steered by others into a more specific and ambitious course.

Serge Elisséeff, probably at that time the leading professional scholar in the Japanese field in the Western world, had been brought from the University of Paris for a year as a visiting professor at Harvard to allow the trustees of the Harvard Yenching Institute to look him over as a candidate for permanent directorship of the Institute.

Elisséeff's grandfather, a Russian peasant, had established a great fortune through a wine-importing firm and well-known department stores in St. Petersburg and Moscow, but the young Elisséeff, in revolt against the family's mercantile tradition and wealth, turned to the arts and scholarship. He also rebelled at the Sinological tradition of treating East Asian languages and cultures as if they belonged to a dead tradition, and went in 1908 to Japan, where he managed to win entrance into Tokyo Imperial University, the present Tokyo University.

With the indulgence of his professors and the use of a number of outside tutors, he successfully overcame his language handicap, graduating in June 1912 near the top of his class in the field of Japanese literature. Graduation ceremonies at Tokyo Imperial University were at that time attended by the Japanese Emperor. Elisséeff always jokingly claimed that it was the Meiji Emperor's shock at seeing his Occidental face among the graduates—the first such face in history—that caused his death only a few weeks later.

Not long after Elisséeff's return to Russia, the Revolution wiped out his fortune and his prospects. In the late summer of 1920, he fled to Finland and then to France with his wife Vera and their two small sons. Eventually he won French citizenship and a position at the Sorbonne. Paris at the time was the acknowledged center of Sinological studies in the West, but he proved willing to come to Harvard.

Elisséeff was a devoted and inspiring teacher and one of the most charming persons I have ever known. During a quarter century of working closely together, he never once spoke unkindly or in irritation to me. He was a marvelous conversationalist and grand raconteur—sometimes to the point of excess. His most outstanding characteristics, however, were his insistence on high scholarly standards and his devotion to his students. He, if anyone, deserves the title of the father of Japanese studies in the United States.

During my second year at Harvard I took another course in Chinese with Ware, but now, with Elisséeff at Harvard, there was also work in the Japanese field that I could take. The central course of my curriculum that year was the one he offered on premodern Japanese history. History was not his forte, but he conscientiously boned up on masses of factual material from Japanese scholarly works and encyclopedias, which he presented to his students in huge semidigested chunks. He did not offer much analysis, but he gave us a good foundation of factual information for our later studies.

I also took a reading course under the guidance of Elisséeff and a young Japanese scholar, Kishimoto Hideo, who was the son-in-law of Anesaki Masaharu, the famous student of Sanskrit and Japanese religions (and my father's associate at the Asiatic Society of Japan). Kishimoto was taking a Ph.D. in Sanskrit at Harvard and became a close lifetime friend. He later went on to be professor of Sanskrit at Tokyo University, the head and rebuilder of the university's great library after World War II, and for a while a well-known author for his popular book on his ten-year fight against cancer.

In the spring of 1933, I was unexpectedly approached by Elisséeff with a proposal that was to set the course of my life. He laid out for me a five-year program of study abroad—two in Paris and three in Japan and China—after which I would join the Department of Far Eastern Languages, which he and Ware intended to set up at Harvard. (Today it is known as the Department of

East Asian Languages and Civilizations.) Naturally I leaped at the opportunity. Elisséeff envisioned himself and Ware at the center of classical Chinese and Japanese studies at Harvard, and me straddling the two fields, representing the eastward extension of the classical East Asian area. Later a fourth person was added to represent the westward extension of Chinese civilization into Central Asia. This was Francis W. Cleaves, whom I first met after his return to Harvard from studying in China, in 1940.

The instruction available at that time at Harvard and especially Elisséeft s plans for my future turned me decisively away from my college interest in international affairs toward early history. It seems ironic that just when my career was being deflected from the modern world to ancient times, incidents were taking place which inevitably would pull me back to contemporary affairs. When I left Japan in 1927, the country was at the height of the so-called period of Taisho Democracy, showing good promise of becoming a peaceful member of the world trading community and a staunch democracy of the British parliamentary type. The great world depression, however, combined with conflicts over leadership among the successors to the original builders of modern Japan, diverted the country down a different, more perilous course. The very month I started my graduate studies at Harvard, Japan in the euphemistically named Manchurian Incident started again on its conquests on the Asian mainland, which were to lead eventually to World War II.

# 8

# A Student in Paris

IN EARLY June 1935 I set out enthusiastically for Paris. It must be the dream of every young American to be footloose in Europe—Paris in the springtime and all that. I was hardly footloose, having been dispatched by my mentor for a serious course of study, but the allure of Europe and Paris in particular was nonetheless strong. Europe, though sorely wounded in the First World War, had not yet suffered the even greater disaster of World War II or undergone the physical transformation of postwar affluence and the homogenizing cultural blight of modern mass communications and jet travel. English was still by no means the universal second language. In fact, I found my French and

German of more general use to me in every country I visited in Europe except, of course, for England itself.

My two years in Paris were a sort of golden age for me, although this was not because of the excellence of the teaching. Paris may have been the Mecca of Sinology, but the instruction was spotty and, in Japanese studies, undeniably weak. Accidental blessings of the feeble state of Japanese studies everywhere in the Occident were that the term "Japanology" never became fully established, nor did a chasm open up between premodern and modern Japanese studies, as happened in the case of classical Sinology and the study of modern China.

The chief value of my two years in Europe was the new angle of vision they gave me on the contemporary problems of Japan and China as well as on my classic studies of East Asia. Most American scholars in the East Asian field have a bipolar view of their subject, looking at China or Japan from a strictly American point of view. Europe gave me the advantage of another perspective. The lands of Northern Europe are of a size and age more comparable to Japan, and the past hangs heavy throughout Europe, as it does in China and Japan. At that time, internal unrest and international rivalries were severe in Europe, as they were in East Asia, but not in the United States, where the depression made Americans retreat further into the isolationism that had followed World War I. I have always felt that my ability to look at East Asia from two very different parts of the Occident permitted me a broader view of the area than most of my colleagues had, just as my study of both China and Japan—a luxury denied most students in this age of growing specialization—has given me a sharper perspective.

I sailed to France third class and on my arrival in Paris in mid-June immediately set about exploring the city by foot, covering its whole central portion. This became my routine for every new city I visited, and I still believe it is the best way to learn one's way around an old city and get a feel for it. I was determined to immerse myself as much as possible in the European way of life. However, this was more easily said than done. My very clothing made me stand out as an American, which, inappropriately in my case, meant "rich American" to most Europeans. My fellowship had been substantially increased for my travels, but just when I was embarking on them the United States went off the gold standard and the value of my dollars plummeted. For a while I was a very poor American indeed, until the Harvard Yenching Institute increased my grant in partial compensation. But, rich or poor, my clothes screamed "American" among the somberly clad Frenchmen. The chief offenders were my light-colored topcoat and two-toned black and white shoes. The shoes I had dyed to a shabby but uniform black and my topcoat to a dark blue. In the process the topcoat shrank badly, which gave me a scarecrow appearance, but I was satisfied to be no longer sartorially recognizable as an American.

Language was a more difficult problem. I had learned enough French and

German to pass my reading examinations at Harvard, which were then required for a Ph.D. degree. I had taken three years of high school and college French, and had had the foresight to take an introductory course in German my senior year at Oberlin. From these beginnings I had developed a reading knowledge of these two languages on my own, but I literally could not speak a word of either, as I immediately realized on arriving in France.

Elisséeff had arranged for me to go to a little town some thirty miles south of Paris called Étampes, where I was to stay at the home of a family named Lignier for language lessons. Monsieur Lignier was a retired *lycée* instructor, badly crippled by gout, who supplemented his small retirement income by teaching French to foreign boarders. He was a fine teacher. Not a single word other than French was ever spoken in the house, and after six weeks of hard work I was prepared to pursue my studies in Paris without any great difficulty. Madame Lignier was a vivacious little woman, and both she and her husband became real friends. The French are a notably offish people, particularly with foreigners; aside from the Elisséeffs', theirs was the only home I ever entered during my two years in France.

There was a special personal reason why my first year in Europe was a golden time for me. I was falling in love with a girl who was taking a course at the university in Paris that summer and then was spending the rest of the academic year in Vienna as an exchange student. Elinor Adrienne Danton had a background somewhat like mine. Her father, despite his noted French name, was of mixed German-speaking Alsatian and Viennese descent. He had been a poor boy but had won a Ph.D. in German literature at Columbia. Her mother, who was of old American stock from New Jersey, had also obtained a Ph.D. in German literature, which was quite unusual for women in those days. The young Danton couple were teaching German literature in a college in Oregon when the clouds of World War I made the future of German teaching in the United States seem bleak. Wisely they took up an invitation for both of them to teach German at Qinghua University in Peking, where they remained for ten years, from 1916 to 1927. He wrote books on the Chinese people and Chinese-American cultural relations and she a book on Western etiquette for Chinese. Adrienne thus spent her formative years, from the ages of five to sixteen, in China, learning to speak standard Chinese with a beautiful accent. The Dantons left China in 1927 to teach at Oberlin, where Adrienne was a year behind me in college. I scarcely knew her there, but she went on to Radcliffe in 1932 to take an M.A. in fine arts, and it was in Cambridge that we had come to know each other.

I went from Étampes to Paris each weekend while she was there, and she introduced me to the museums, art, and architecture of the city and its environs. We danced in the streets on the *quatorze juillet*, as is traditional on Bastille Day, and one day while sitting in the Luxembourg Gardens, realized we were engaged.

Adrienne's summer school ended in late July, and I arranged for her to come out to Étampes for a week before she left for Heidelberg to study German in preparation for her year in Vienna. I had let Madame Lignier believe that "my friend" was a man. ("Mon ami" is aurally indistinguishable from "mon amie.") The dear Madame was startled when a girl arrived but was soon enraptured to see young love blossoming in her own home. Adrienne and I spent an idyllic week exploring the medieval structures and ruins of the area. I shall never forget the glorious view we had of our favorite cathedral, Chartres, as we approached it through the wheat fields on a tiny railway line, long since abandoned, but then running directly from Étampes to Chartres. When Adrienne finally left for Germany, we started a daily correspondence, which was to last the next two years. Combining love and our studies, I always wrote in French and she in German. The results undoubtedly were clumsy and maudlin to the extreme; when she died twenty years later, I thought it best to burn the letters.

Adrienne was a wonderful person, cheerful, effervescent, and bubbling with *joie de vivre*. At the same time, she was endlessly thoughtful of others, and this combination of qualities made her immediately beloved by anyone she met. She was also a person of strong principles and incredible bravery in the face of great physical suffering. When she saw fit, she could give me a good tongue lashing for my thoughtlessness of others or my blind concentration on my studies, perhaps knocking off some of my more offensive rough edges. I was indeed privileged to share two decades of my life with such a wonderful person.

◄§

The Elisséeffs returned to Paris during the summer of 1933, after visiting the Chinese Christian colleges associated with the Harvard Yenching Institute; on their advice I followed them in early August to St. Jean-de-Luz in the extreme southwestern corner of France, thus joining the usual French trek to the beaches during that month. After returning to Paris in September, I found myself a small pension on the rue de Vaugirard, opposite the Palais du Luxembourg, in the heart of the Latin Quarter. The rue de Vaugirard, known as the longest street in Paris, was at the time almost the narrowest, and my pension was perhaps the cheapest and dirtiest in all Paris. I had a small, dingy, second-floor room that opened onto a sunless courtyard. It was only feebly heated in winter and had a single cold water faucet. The food was tastefully cooked but the ingredients were poor and monotonous. The other boarders were a motley crew, mostly foreigners like myself but fortunately with no other English speakers.

The pension gave me some feel of Parisian life near its lower end, and the university brought me into contact with its intellectual elite, yet there was little chance to become part of the main middle stream. Some society ladies had an association for entertaining American students, arranging teas and occasional trips that were instructive, but I failed to establish any real contacts with Frenchmen. I came to realize that a foreign student could easily build up within himself animosity for the country where he studied. This has been a common response among Japanese in modern times, and I have always tried to avoid the patronizing attitude of most Americans, who assume that the lonely foreign student in their midst appreciates and admires all that he finds around him.

Except for trips by Adrienne and me back and forth between Paris and Vienna, my social life during the school year was minimal. The opera, where I could stand in the peanut gallery for a mere five francs (a movie cost ten), became my chief diversion, and I developed into quite a connoisseur. Although meaningful contacts with the French people were few, my life in Paris was conducted almost exclusively in the French language, and I did absorb something of the French spirit from the environment. I realized this most clearly at the end of my stay when I was making a trip through Italy on my way from Paris to Tokyo. On an Italian train I found myself in an altercation with the ticket inspector. French was our only common language, and we entered into a spirited argument in it that quickly attracted an appreciative audience. To make such a public spectacle of myself went entirely against my whole Japanese and American upbringing, but I found that I did not mind it in the slightest. In fact, when in the middle of the dispute I suddenly realized that I was in the wrong, I simply argued all the louder. I had become more French than I had suspected.

Although my studies in Paris were less important for me than simply living in Europe, they constituted a major portion of my academic training. The centerpiece of my work the first year was a weekly private session at Professor Elisséeff's apartment, in which he expounded on classical Japanese grammar. Burton Fahs joined me for these classes, since he and his wife Jamie were in Paris on a Rockefeller grant, before going on the next spring to study in Japan. There was little of interest that the Sorbonne could offer in Japanese studies. In fact, in all my studies I never had a real seminar or received guidance in my Ph.D. thesis, which are considered the two key elements in graduate training in the United States. In this sense I was essentially self-taught—a hazard one must accept when entering a new field.

Language teaching in Japanese and Chinese was concentrated at the École Nationale des Langues Orientales Vivantes (now renamed the Institut Nationale des Langues et Civilizations Orientales), located some distance from the Sorbonne. Japanese was taught at the "Langues O," as it was called, by Charles Haguenauer and a Japanese assistant. I attended some of Haguenauer's more advanced classes from time to time but did not bother with the Chinese classes. My chief contact with the "Langues O" was through the Russian courses, which Elisséeff insisted I take. I did so with little enthusiasm, but did learn enough Russian to be able to read newspapers and get around in the Soviet Union when I later passed through it on my way to Japan.

French Sinology at the time was dominated by a trinity of scholars: Paul Pelliot, Henri Maspero, and Marcel Granet. I followed the lectures of all three. Pelliot was a dynamic man, who gave a very helpful course at the Sorbonne in the reading of classical Chinese texts. In my second year it fell to me as the most advanced student to do the oral translation in class, which was a strain when translating into a foreign language.

Granet was a flamboyant person who lectured passionately on his interpretation of ancient Chinese society. I did not find his imaginative conclusions at all convincing, and I was appalled by his frequent ill-tempered attacks on Maspero. Maspero by contrast was a quiet, shy, almost mousy man, but he had the most prestigious post, being a professor at the Collège de France. During my two years in Paris, Maspero lectured on the history of the Chinese classics in early medieval times and on the search for physical immortality by medieval Chinese Taoists, which was the subject of his next book. In an almost inaudible voice he would read from his notes, usually with his back to the class, while he scribbled in tiny lettering on the blackboard. Not surprisingly, I was often his only student. I found his scholarship inspiring and his personality appealing, but the lack of contact between teacher and student in the Paris university setting is well illustrated by my relationship with him. We spoke together only once, when I approached him to say farewell before leaving Paris in 1935. He died in a Nazi concentration camp in World War II, imprisoned there because of the participation of his two sons in the *Résistance*.

When Elisséeff moved permanently to Harvard in the summer of 1934 between my first and second years in Paris, there remained even less for me to study there. Probably the most useful instruction I received the second year was outside the university, from Maeda Yoichi, who came to Paris with his wife in 1934 to study French literature. His father, a former vice mayor of Tokyo and for long Japan's delegate at the ILO in Geneva, was an old friend of my father's. Maeda himself became in time a prominent professor at Tokyo University; his son-in-law, Akira Iriye, took his Ph.D. with us at Harvard in the 1960s and is now a distinguished professor at the University of Chicago.

The help I received from Maeda came about because of a project started by Mortimer Graves of the American Council of Learned Societies. Graves had the idea of persuading young American scholars to make abstracts in English of articles appearing in scholarly Japanese journals and to publish these in pamphlet form. I agreed to do this for Japan's two leading historical journals, *Shigaku zasshi* and *Shirin.* I spent a great deal of time on the task, which was by no means easy. Since the articles were written by Japanese scholars for other Japanese specialists in their particular fields, they assumed a general knowledge of the subject and the ability to read classical Chinese or medieval Japanese. I often found myself over my depth and would then enlist Maeda's help. I was apparently the only scholar who made much of a response to Graves's request, and the only place I have ever seen the one thin mimeographed fascicle that appeared is in my own library. Some other abstracts which I completed later I published after my return to Harvard. With my work in Paris becoming something I could better do in Japan, I became increasingly eager to move on to East Asia.

# 9

# Living in Europe

DESPITE its inadequacies for East Asian studies, Europe proved an incomparable classroom for contemporary politics and international relations. I missed five years of the Great Depression in America, but I got a wider view of the disastrous 1930s from Europe and later East Asia. In the winter of 1933–34 a major political scandal, the Stavisky Affair, threw France into political turmoil. There was much rioting by rightists, especially among students in the Latin Quarter where I lived. Conditions became so bad that the police removed the iron gratings from around the trees along the sidewalks in order to prevent students from gathering them up to build barricades. Often, in my trek between the "Langues O" and the Sorbonne, I would run into clashes between the students and the gendarmes. It is a bit disconcerting to see a line of mounted gendarmes riding down the street with drawn sabers and to be forced to scurry up an alleyway to avoid the charge. In February 1934 the political unrest reached a crescendo in an evening of bloodshed in the Place de la Concorde.

When I visited Adrienne in Vienna at Christmas and again in June I saw how tense conditions were there and also in nearby Germany. Vienna was a sad shell of the proud imperial capital it had been a mere two decades earlier. It was full of grandiose architecture but little life, and the worldwide depression had made it all the emptier. On New Year's Eve, Adrienne and I were the only patrons at a small nightclub where a band played forlornly just for the two of us. One evening at the opera some political protestors threw smoke bombs into the pit, forcing the evacuation of the building all the way up to the fifth gallery where we were sitting. Only two months later the dictatorial Austrian chancellor, Engelbert Dollfuss, suppressed a Socialist uprising in the city, bombarding with cannon the Socialist-built apartment buildings encircling the city. There were several days when Adrienne was unable to leave her pension because of the fighting, and the shell holes in the apartment houses were still unrepaired when I returned in June. The next month Dollfuss was assassinated by Austrian Nazis.

My Harvard Yenching fellowship grant stipulated that it would be void if I got married; the only way we could see to get around this was to have Adrienne self-supporting. Bob and Jean were returning to the United States after two years in Tokyo, where Jean had taught at an Episcopalian institution, Rikkyo Girls' School, or St. Margaret's as it was known in English, and this position was open for Adrienne if she hastened out there. The ploy worked, but not without gloomy mutterings by Ware that I was endangering my future.

Before Adrienne left for Japan by way of the United States, we took a wonderful trip to Budapest, still a beautiful and lively city. Then we went to Prague, and on to Dresden in Germany. Hitler had come to power in early 1933, and Germany was seething with uncertainty. The day Adrienne and I arrived in Dresden late in June 1934 was the day Hitler purged his chief rival in the Nazi Party, Ernst Roehm, the head of the S.A. We had not heard the news and were surprised at the noise and bustle in the streets, concluding that Germany was a very lively country.

Adrienne and I said our adieux in Berlin, but I stayed on there for a month. A fellow American student, George Kennedy, who was to become the professor of Chinese at Yale, took me with him on occasion to classes at the University of Berlin, where I was disgusted one day to see most of the class leap to its feet to give the Nazi salute to a band and Nazi flag passing by. While in Berlin I had many long discussions with Germans of all types from clandestine opponents of the Nazis, like my cultured and aristocratic landlady, to groups of young Nazi enthusiasts who frequented a nearby beer garden.

My experiences in France, Austria, and Germany taught me a great deal about the political ills of Europe and prepared me for the conditions I was to discover on my return to Japan; but except for letters from my parents and later from Adrienne, I received no news whatsoever about what was happening in East Asia. For the average European, Japan and China might just as well have been nonexistent.

In Berlin I was joined by Frederick Ficken from the Oberlin Castle group, and the two of us moved to Munich. There, I concentrated on improving my spoken German but had plenty of time to visit cathedrals, museums, and other places of interest. I also took a two-week bicycle trip to Austria, heading for the border near Salzburg, then going east into the mountain and lake country of the beautiful Salzkammergut. Next I rode northeast to the town of Efferding near Wels because my Uncle Ed had told me the Reischauer family had come from that area. The pastor of the Protestant Church at the nearby village of Scharten looked up the church records, and indeed found my Reischauer grandfather's birth and baptismal records. When I returned to Scharten by car with my teenage children after World War II some twenty-two years later, a new pastor at the church obligingly dug up the records again for us.

During my summer in Germany, I paid most of my expenses through a shady financial operation. To encourage tourists, Germany was then selling *Reisemark,* or "travel marks," which one could get abroad at about a 40 percent discount. The amount bought was duly marked in one's passport, and one was limited to a specific sum per day, but this was far beyond my actual expenditures. I would exchange the full amount for regular marks, however, and, concealing the excess in my hat, would smuggle it out across the border to Austria, France, or Belgium, where the German marks could be sold at full value and more *Reisemark* bought at a discount with the proceeds. This was easy enough to do in Strasbourg or Brussels, but I remember an uncomfortable day in pro-Nazi Innsbruck in Austria, where I wandered back and forth along almost deserted streets until I found a banker who did not simply eye me suspiciously and refuse to exchange my proffered marks. It was all highly illegal and possibly somewhat dangerous, but I soothed my conscience by assuring myself that I was striking a small blow against the Nazis.

Before classes started in Paris in November 1934, I spent the month of October at the University of Leiden in the Netherlands, where Hugh Borton was studying. Then I returned to France by way of a sightseeing tour through Belgium. My second year in France was to prove decidedly less stimulating than the first. The bloom was off the rose. Adrienne was far away on the other side of the world—and the cloudy, dark winters of Northern Europe were depressing. Winter in Japan is the sunniest season of the year, but in Paris the daylight hours in winter were incredibly short, and weeks would pass with only a few brief glimpses of a sickly sun through city smog.

When the glorious European spring finally arrived, I started my preparations for departure, eager to push on to the promised land of Japan and to Adrienne. After spending the spring vacation in England, where I visited Fred Ficken at Oxford and Herb Norman at Cambridge and also had some time in London, I headed for Japan, taking a long circuitous route and the better part of two months to travel from Paris to Tokyo.

I started with a swing through Italy, covering it quite thoroughly as far south as Capri. From there I went on to Scandinavia, and entered the Soviet Union from Finland. I divided a week in Russia between stately Leningrad and fascinating Moscow, visiting the universities and professors of Japanese in both cities, seeing the "Elisséeff stores," as they were still unofficially called, and taking in all the sights I could. In both cities I found that I could exchange my foreign currency at black market prices by simply standing on the steps of certain public buildings and waiting to be approached by some seedy-looking youth. All of this must have been perfectly obvious to the police, but the Soviet Union happened to be in a period of relaxation toward foreigners, and the Russians were eager for *valuta*, or foreign currency, being ready to exchange it at black market prices with cheapskates like me who could not afford the unrealistically high official rates.

The trip across Siberia by the Trans-Siberian Railway took a week. I traveled third class, also appropriately known as "hard" class. The Siberian *taiga* had always sounded romantic to me, and I imagined stately forests of fir and other evergreens, but all we saw from the train windows was a miserable growth of straggly poplars and birch. The villages were forlorn places, with many of the homes sunk into the ground and roofed with sod. Patches of snow lay around in hollows in the middle of May. The train crawled slowly along and paused for incredibly long stops every few miles. It is hard to imagine a more boring trip. At Lake Baikal, however, the landscape suddenly changed. We skirted the south shore of this great mountain-encircled body of water, and beyond it the sharper edges to the mountains and the rolling steppe land looked decidedly East Asian.

At Manchouli, the border town between Siberia and Manchuria, we clearly entered a war zone. Two miles of open plain separated the last Soviet outpost and the first of the Japanese Army, and a little train chugged between the two to transfer the passengers. On the Japanese side I was closely interrogated about the double tracks and double tunnels the Russians were constructing on the railway where it ran close to Lake Baikal; the Japanese were also interested in a couple of broken windows on one of the railway carriages, obviously hoping they represented rioting somewhere along the way.

From Manchouli we rode at a more efficient Japanese clip overnight to Harbin, where I was struck by the lingering Russian appearance of the city and the well-patronized Russian Orthodox shrine in a corner of the main waiting room of the station. I then proceeded down the South Manchurian Railway to Mukden, the present Shenyang, which was the first great walled Chinese city I had ever seen. An overnight run took me to Heijo, the present Pyongyang, now the capital of North Korea. My stop there was to see the archeological remains of the area, which had been the capital of Chinese colonies founded in Korea in 108 B.C. While wandering around the countryside looking at the ancient Chinese tombs, I had my first brush with the Japanese police, who picked me up and escorted me to the local government headquarters, where for the first and only time in my life I was treated rudely by a Japanese official. The petty local magistrate subjected me to a surly questioning, keeping me standing while he lounged in his chair sipping tea, which he never offered to me. He actually was a Korean, and I have assumed that his extraordinary rudeness was because of his own self-hate at being a collaborator of the Japanese.

My next stop was Seoul, Korea's capital since 1392. Then a train ride to Pusan, an overnight ferry to Shimonoseki, and a long train ride through the lovely Japanese countryside brought me back at last to Tokyo. Despite my eight years away, everything seemed familiar and homey. But I was soon to become aware of a pervasive though subtle change in the atmosphere that boded no good.


# 10

# Tokyo


THE JAPAN I returned to at the end of May 1935 was very different from the country I had left eight years earlier. As I have mentioned, the Taisho Democracy of that time had faded, to be replaced by militarism and incipient fascism. The 1889 constitution had established a Diet, or parliament, with a wholly elected lower house and a largely unelected House of Peers. The Diet's electorate and powers were strictly limited, but its approval was required for all budget and tax matters and all permanent laws. On the advice of German experts the government authorities had sought to keep control of the purse strings by a constitutional provision that, if the Diet failed to vote the current budget proposed by the cabinet, last year's budget would remain in effect. Unfortunately for the planners, last year's budget was never enough. They were forced into compromises with the elected politicians of the lower house, until finally in 1918 the advisors around the throne found it necessary to give the post of Prime Minister to a party politician as the head of an openly party cabinet. By 1925 the originally restricted electorate was expanded to include all adult Japanese males. This political evolution, which paralleled in a few decades the centuries-long development of the British Parliament, had been accompanied by strong liberal influences of all sorts, heightened by World War I. The democracies had emerged from the war triumphant, and the three great European autocracies had all collapsed. Democracy and liberalism seemed the wave of the future, and most of the Japanese people had gone happily along with the tide.

By 1935, however, a great change had taken place. The 1920s had seen slowed economic growth, which threatened the future of Japan because growing industrialization had made it increasingly dependent on foreign markets and sources of raw materials. Military men and other conservative Japanese compared their country with the great powers of Europe, which possessed huge overseas empires, or with the United States and Soviet Union, and came to the conclusion that Japan needed its own broad empire to be secure from the vagaries of world trade. To such people it seemed utter folly that the country had abandoned its earlier start toward the building of an empire. The constitution of 1889 had given the armed forces operational independence of the civilian government, and the army took advantage of this situation to take direct action on its own authority. It started with the conquest of Manchuria in September 1931 and continued its expansion by biting off smaller chunks of territory in eastern Inner Mongolia and North China proper.

The seizure of Manchuria had been easy and had stirred up Japanese nationalistic euphoria. The influence of the military and their conservative sympathizers increased in Japanese politics, while that of the political parties waned. On several occasions, young self-styled patriots, some of them army and navy officers, assassinated cautious government leaders and conservative businessmen. As a result, others who disapproved of the course Japan was taking were cowed into silence. Most of the liberal trends of the 1920s were reversed and attempts were made to revive traditional Japanese attitudes and ways of life at the expense of what was considered by many to be the corrupting influence of the West. Parliamentary government, capitalism, modern liberal concepts, and "corrupt" Western influences were lumped together as interrelated threats to the true Japanese spirit.

In the summer of 1935 it was still not clear whether all this was merely a temporary detour in Japan's road to modernization. Millions of Japanese, very possibly the majority, were not in sympathy with what was happening. Certainly my family's associates in educational work and the Christian Church, as well as the intellectuals I came into contact with, were for the most part deeply disturbed, though reluctant to talk about the situation. Elections showed a continued strong backing for the political parties, and a rising leftist vote was even more clearly anti-military. In the election for the lower house on February 20, 1936, the two traditional parliamentary parties won close to 78 percent of the vote, and about 6 percent more went to the parties of the left.

Hard on the heels of this election, however, came the so-called "2-2-6 Incident," which tipped the scales definitively in favor of militarism. Early on the morning of February 26 (the source of the term "2-2-6"), under the leadership of captains and lieutenants, elements of the fractious First Division assassinated several of the top government leaders and seized some of the government buildings in the heart of the city, throwing up defense lines and camping out in the snowy streets. I remember the ominous sight they caused the next few days. At first the public had no idea what was happening, and rumors ran rife.

In the end, however, the civilian government, bolstered by the outrage of the Emperor, stood firm, and the bulk of the army failed to back the attempted coup. Faced with overwhelming might, the rebels meekly surrendered; but the whole incident served to strengthen the grip of the military over the government. Though it was not obvious at the time, Japan had started on its now unstoppable slide into total war. I remember being encouraged by the results of the 1936 vote and elated by the 1937 elections, in which the leftist opposition made significant gains and the Minseito, then the stronger of the two traditional parties, ran successfully on the slogan "What shall it be? Parliamentary government or Fascism?" The army, however, closed ranks following the "2-2-6 Incident" and suppressed factionalism and youthful extremism among its own members. All prime ministers since the assassination by military extremists of Inukai Tsuyoshi on May 15, 1932, had been nonparty men, and the number of party members in each cabinet had become smaller with each change. In early February 1937, General Hayashi Senjuro assumed the prime ministership with no party men at all in the cabinet, and on July 7 war with China broke out, marking the start of World War II.

All this was very reminiscent of what I had encountered in Europe. Step by step the Japanese seemed to be turning their backs on all the values my parents had devoted their lives to fostering in Japan. The war in China stretched on, and as Japan became bogged down deeper and deeper in it, the United States, which supported Chinese resistance and possessed the only rival naval power to Japan's in the Pacific, came to be viewed increasingly by the Japanese as the ultimate enemy. Friendly feelings for the United States turned to hostility. A great disaster was obviously starting to unfold before our eyes, but there was nothing people like us could do, except stand by and watch in fear and frustration. Neither side had any understanding of the other's problems and fears nor any will to try to develop such understanding. This was a clear prescription for disaster. I should note, however, that never once did I or the members of my family feel the slightest sense of animosity among Japanese toward us personally, and our relations with our Japanese friends remained as warm as ever.

<sup>≈§</sup>

Although Japan had undergone great physical as well as spiritual changes during my eight years away, I fitted back into life in Tokyo without a ripple.

Adrienne and I were married on July 5 and occupied the same room in my parents' house I had lived in during my last year in high school. The official marriage took place in a downtown ward office, where we were accompanied by a representative of the American Embassy who vouched for us and our supposed residence in that ward—an open deception that both sides found convenient. After fussing with the documents, the Japanese functionary in charge finally looked at us, but instead of smiling and saying "*Omedeto* (Congratulations)," as I had expected, merely muttered "Twenty sen please," the cost of the stamp for the marriage license. That afternoon, we had a somewhat more romantic wedding at home, with Adrienne dressed in her mother's wedding gown. The ceremony was performed by my father and attended only by the family and our two servants. Adrienne was still teaching, so after the ceremony my parents left for Karuizawa while we stayed on in the house. This reversal of honeymoon roles, especially for a person who had been traveling for the past two months, was an excellent arrangement.

During our year in Tokyo, Adrienne and I were so immersed in our Japanese studies that we had virtually no contact with the Western community, except for my family and a few fellow scholars, such as the Fahses and the Bortons, who had preceded us to Tokyo. Adrienne enjoyed her teaching of English at the girls' school, but she was also eager to learn more about Japan. She had studied the language with a private tutor all the previous year yet had learned very little. I took on her instruction myself and was gratified to see the progress she made. Her conversational skills improved rapidly, and with the aid of the Chinese characters she already knew, she was soon reading Japanese reasonably well. To focus her efforts and combine them with her interest in art, she began the translation with my help of a short history of Japanese art entitled *Zusetsu Nihon bijutsu shi (An Illustrated History of Japanese Art),* which had been published in 1933. Unfortunately, by the time we returned to the United States, people were thinking of Japan more in terms of guns than art, and our translation was never published.

Upon reaching Tokyo, I had of course quickly settled into my own studies. On the side, I continued advanced language lessons with the wife of a young professor and spent a lot of time buying books in the Kanda bookstore area, but my main work was in connection with Tokyo Imperial University. I brought with me a letter from Elisséeff to Professor Tsuji Zennosuke, the rather conservative and nationalistic head of the Department of Japanese History in the Faculty of Letters, and he accepted me as a special research student. So far as I know, I was the only Occidental student at the university at the time. In the fall I concentrated on my proposed Ph.D. thesis, a translation of the lengthy diary in Chinese of the Japanese Buddhist monk Ennin. Posthumously known as Jikaku Daishi, he had recorded his years of travel and study in China from 838 to 847.

This work, which had been suggested to me in Paris by Paul Demiéville, a young professor of French-speaking Swiss background and later the leading professor in the Chinese field in France, was a good choice. Both Elisséeff and Ware were insistent that my thesis should consist primarily of a translation of a text, and this one combined my interests in early Japan and China. It was also a historical document of major importance, which had as yet been studied only in a fragmentary manner by Japanese scholars and not at all by Chinese or Westerners. It had been printed four times in Japan, and there was a photographic reproduction of its earliest manuscript dating from 1291. A prominent Sinologist, Okada Masayuki, had drawn from it the materials that bore on the political history of China and the great Buddhist persecution of 845, which was the most severe religious persecution in Chinese history and is best documented in this text, but otherwise it had attracted relatively little attention. It was only after I completed my translation that Japanese scholars began to pay much attention to it and made a careful full translation into Japanese.

Ennin's diary, which goes by the cumbersome title of *The Record of a Pilgrimage to China in Search of the Law (Nitto guho junrei gyoki)*—"the Law" referring to the Buddhist way of life—is a lengthy document filling 409 pages in my translation. It is a remarkable work, being the first outsider's account of China and probably the first genuine day-by-day diary in the world. It is also the most detailed account we have of the great missions the Japanese government sent to China during the seventh to ninth centuries, which played a major role in introducing Chinese civilization into the isolated island country. Its accuracy is attested to by the fact that its accounts of Ennin's wanderings throughout China can be followed virtually mile by mile on modern maps. It contrasts with the much better known account by Marco Polo, who visited China more than four centuries later and recounted his experiences orally in broad outline only several years after returning to Italy. Ennin himself also differed from Marco Polo in seeing China from the inside as a fellow Buddhist writing in Chinese, rather than as a "barbarian" outsider.

Ennin's text is by no means easy to read. It is in standard classical Chinese but is full of documents he exchanged with Chinese bureaucrats written in the officialese of the time, which is as obscure in places as contemporary American bureaucratese. Long descriptions of Buddhist and civil ceremonies no longer known also offered difficulties, as did numerous misprints in the printed texts, occasional miscopyings in the cursively written manuscript text, and a large section of the text which is reproduced in confused sequence in both the manuscript and printed editions. Another problem was that, in the early part of the text, Ennin's Chinese was rather inaccurate and clumsy. I obviously needed assistance in tackling the harder parts of this formidable document. For this, Professor Tsuji provided me with the aid of Katsuno Ryushin, a monk of the same Tendai Sect to which Ennin had belonged. Katsuno was a learned, conscientious scholar, and I owe him a great debt for his help in my early grappling with Ennin's diary.

# 11

# Kyoto

At the beginning of the summer of 1936, Adrienne and I moved to Kyoto, in accordance with Professor Elisséeff's original plan. Kyoto is one of the great historic cities of the world, laid out as a new capital for Japan in 794 in imitation of the checkerboard street plan of Chang-an (the modern Xian), then the capital of China. Innumerable Buddhist monasteries containing gardens of surpassing beauty dating from medieval times have grown up around Kyoto, particularly along the skirts of the hills on its eastern side. The city rightly ranks with Peking, Paris, Rome, Vienna, and Washington as one of the most stately capitals in the world, and I count myself fortunate to have had the chance to live in most of them. Kyoto has been seriously despoiled of much of its beauty since World War II, but when we lived there, it was still a lovely city.

On arriving, we located a small two-story Japanese house on the northern side of the city in an area called Kuramaguchi. We were delighted with our little house, the first home of our own, and we particularly liked the fact that it had open space on two of its four sides. One of these sides was occupied by a graveyard —a quiet neighborhood, as we called it. The other was what appeared to be an unaccountable scrap of agricultural land. In time, we learned that people had avoided building there because it was beside a community of *burakumin*, the traditional outcasts of Japan whose discriminatory treatment, though now illegal, is still very much alive and constitutes a major blot on Japanese society.

Our Japanese friends were obviously a little uncomfortable about the proximity of the *burakumin* community, and they openly disapproved of the unshaded sunny location of our house. Invariably they remarked, "My, it must be hot in summer." We had in mind the winter sunshine. Kyoto is a dank, cold city in winter, and Japanese houses before the advent of heating by electricity or gas were almost unbearably cold for three or four months of the year. A couple of small charcoal *hibachi* to warm one's wrists were little solace, and direct solar heat was the best antidote in the relatively sunny winters. We supplemented this by a wood-burning iron stove, but most of its heat escaped at once through the flimsy construction. More effective was an iron bathtub set over a wood fire. Each evening it would give us a euphoric glow of warmth that lasted until bedtime. It also gave us the feeling of being early Christian martyrs boiled alive for our faith.

In the warmer months, the house was delightfully airy at night, and while at home I usually wore cool Japanese summer clothing—the *yukata* type of kimono. A young Japanese couple lived in one of our two downstairs rooms, and the wife served as our maid, relieving Adrienne of the household chores. Our way of life as well as our diet was almost completely prewar Japanese style. The only exceptions besides the wood stove were two desks and chairs in our study-bedroom. We slept on the *tatami* rush mat floor and ate at a low table while sitting on the floor. Our compromise between Eastern and Western styles of living was probably somewhat on the Japanese side of what would be considered average in urban Japan today.

After an exhausting month-long sightseeing trip by bicycle around the whole Kyoto region in the full heat of summer, we settled down in Kyoto, and I resumed my studies. An elderly lady named Miss Kuroha proved a superb language teacher and stern disciplinarian on the niceties of Japanese grammar. I also studied calligraphy with a venerable bearded teacher called Kato Sensei (*Sensei* means "master" or "teacher"). I doubt that he had ever had a more inept pupil, but by struggling hard with brush and India ink, I achieved a level of penmanship in Japanese that at least was no worse than my hand in English, which through years of frantic note taking had been reduced to a messy scrawl. I even studied a little of the tea ceremony, which Adrienne was pursuing in connection with her flower-arrangement lessons, and perhaps learned more about traditional Japanese culture from its slow, measured pace than I did from reams of books on the subject.

My chief studies in Kyoto were as a special research student in the Japanese History Department of the Faculty of Letters at Kyoto Imperial University (now Kyoto University), Japan's second most prestigious university. My mentor this time was Professor Nishida Naojiro, the head of the department and a specialist in Japanese cultural history. Because he was a particularly jovial man and the university was considerably smaller than Tokyo University, I became a member of the group to a greater degree than I had been in Tokyo, and I habitually wore the regular black university student cap with its mortarboard cut. In the autumn Professor Nishida led the seniors and graduate students of the department on a research trip to western Japan, and I was included as a matter of course. It was a delightful as well as instructive expedition. We started with Nagasaki, where we saw the Catholic cathedral which was to be the epicenter of the second atomic bomb eight years later, and then worked our way back from there. I developed a deep respect for Professor Nishida, with whom I kept in contact until my final call on him at the Kyoto University Hospital in the 1960s when he was dying of cancer.

Not finding a suitable person with whom to continue my Ennin studies, I temporarily dropped them and worked instead on translating various pieces of medieval Japanese literature, several of which I published after returning to Harvard. Among those who helped me in Kyoto was Inaba Keishin. Inaba, who became a close friend, was a very pleasant person and a good scholar. I later learned to my sorrow that he had been lost at sea in the evacuation of the Japanese troops from Burma during the closing days of World War II.

Although my studies throughout had been ill focused and were distinctly amateurish, these handicaps were compensated for by the freedom possible in pioneering a new field. At Harvard and in Europe I had studied whatever I found available. In Tokyo I had concentrated through Ennin's diary on ninth-century Chinese and Japanese history. In Kyoto I worked largely on eleventh- to thirteenth-century Japanese literature. Although Adrienne taught part time in Baika Girls' School in nearby Osaka and had a few private students of English, we found time to work on her art book and visited at leisure the many great art treasures of the Kyoto area. Later in Korea and China I followed still other interests. There was in all this freedom the danger that I would spread myself too thin to gain adequate mastery of any specific subject. But the advantages were far greater than the perils, especially for a person who wished to obtain as broad an understanding of Japan and East Asia as possible. The freedom I enjoyed during my student years is scarcely imaginable in these days of greater specialization and briefer periods of training.

The year Adrienne and I spent in Kyoto was certainly one of the best in our whole lives. We were under no pressures, and Kyoto was a marvelous place to be. We had plenty of good Japanese friends, and we knew most of the small Western community, which was limited to a handful of students like ourselves and a few missionaries. Among the latter were the Shivelys, who were old friends of my parents, having come to Japan at about the same time. He was a tennis star and with his youngest son, Donald, then a senior at the Canadian Academy in Kobe, and some fourth player we had an occasional game of tennis. Don, in time, studied as an undergraduate and graduate student with us at Harvard and became, not only one of the postwar wave of Japanese specialists who now constitute the senior statesmen of the field, but for some time my own successor in some of the posts I held.

One time my mother came down from Tokyo with her sister, my Aunt Myra, who was visiting Japan for the first time. She was a portly lady, who found sitting on the floor a trial. After struggling up the steep, narrow staircase to our bedroom-study, her eyes fixed with relief on the slightly raised floor of the *tokonoma,* the alcove for displaying art objects; pushing aside Adrienne's flower arrangement with some comment about the flowers being in disarray anyway, she gratefully plumped herself down. Her actions well illustrate the level of Western knowledge about Japanese culture in those days.

~§

Our idyllic year in Kyoto ended in tragedy. My brother, Bob, had become an instructor at Princeton, where he quickly established a reputation as a marvelous teacher. In the summer of 1937 he organized a study tour to East Asia, coming to Kyoto after visiting Tokyo. Adrienne and I served as guides for his group of about fifteen young people. The Sino-Japanese War had just broken out on July 7, and the night the whole group gathered in our small house for a party coincided with a blackout practice, rigorously enforced by the Japanese police despite the impossibility of the Chinese attacking a city as far away as Kyoto. All the windows had to be covered with heavy drapes to prevent the emission of any light, and we almost steamed to death in the humid summer heat.

Since the fighting had broken out near Peking and not spread southward yet, Bob decided to reroute his tour, avoiding Peking and going straight from Japan to Shanghai. As we later learned the story, Bob on arriving in Shanghai on August 14 registered his group at the front desk of a hotel while the others went to their rooms. Just at this point, the Chinese Air Force attacked the Japanese warships in the river at Shanghai. Inexperienced in marksmanship, the airmen missed the ships entirely, dropping their bombs on the streets of Shanghai instead. One landed in front of Bob's hotel, blowing in the plate-glass windows, which sheared off one of his heels. An ex-Marine member of his party commandeered a motorcycle with a sidecar and, with Bob lying on a shutter on the sidecar, headed for the nearest hospital. Bob lightly remarked that a scholar could do very well without a leg, but by the time he arrived at the hospital he had lost so much blood that he went into shock and never recovered. I later noted in the dedication of one of my books, Bob was, in a sense, the first American casualty in World War II.

On receiving the news of Bob's death, Adrienne and I hastened to Karuizawa to be with my parents. It was, of course, a terrible shock for them, and they needed all the consolation we could give them, as well as help in handling the constant flow of visitors coming to offer condolences. I remember one well-meaning Japanese pastor who, despite his genuine sympathy, could not conceal

The freshman basketball team at Oberlin (EOR seated second from left).

With friends at "The Castle," 1930.

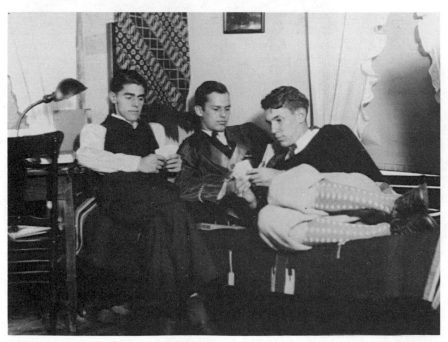

In the Luxembourg Gardens in Paris, 1935, in newly acquired London outfit before departure for Japan.

The house in Kyoto, 1936–37.

In Chinese gown and hat, 1937.

Serge Elisséeff with his wife Vera. A devoted and inspiring teacher who helped shape EOR's future.

With Adrienne, Peking, 1938.

his elation over the Japanese victories in this latest war of aggression. The emotions of war can sweep everything before them.

The Japanese government, apparently feeling some responsibility for Bob's death, sent his ashes back to Japan, hand-carried by a young official. Since my parents felt unable to bear the emotional strain of going to Tokyo to receive the remains, I went to represent the family. I remember some hundred persons or more, virtually all of them Japanese friends of the family, gathered on the platform at Tokyo Station as the official emerged from a first-class compartment with the box of ashes, tied up carefully in a white cloth, and ceremoniously handed the bundle to me. First-class carriages were limited to only a few special expresses, and I suspect that this had been Bob's first ride in one.

Ambassador Joseph Grew had asked to see me, so after thanking the assembled group, I went to the American Embassy. This was my first visit to the Embassy Residence and my only meeting with this truly great diplomat. Thirty years later, however, when I was his successor as Ambassador, I had the satisfaction of insisting that the new Embassy apartment building be named in his honor, even though he was then still living. Bob was buried in Tama Cemetery in the western suburbs of Tokyo, where Japanese friends of the family have taken care of his grave throughout the war and during the several decades since then.

In Bob's death, the United States probably lost the most promising of its younger specialists in modern Japanese affairs. He was only three months beyond his thirtieth birthday, but he had already published a very useful two-volume reference work entitled *Ancient Japanese History (c. 40 B.C.—A.D. 1167)*. He had also all but completed a short book, *Japan: Government—Politics*, which his wife Jean brought out in 1939 with the aid of a young scholar friend. It was for long, I felt, the best brief account of Japan in the 1930s. His untimely death had a profound effect on my own future. Bob was specializing more on modern Japan and I on early Japan and China. If he had still been alive when the war broke out with Japan, it would have been he rather than I who would have been pushed into various positions involving modern affairs.

Bob's death brought home to me the bitter fact that the world was now fully at war and the United States and Japan were becoming likely adversaries. I hoped against hope that peace could somehow be restored between Japan, the land of my birth, and China, for which I had developed a great respect through my studies and through Adrienne's childhood there. I hoped even more fervently that war could be avoided between the two countries that meant the most to me —the United States and Japan. But the prospects were indeed gloomy. The bomb that killed Bob had already swept me and my family into the great catastrophe that was soon to engulf the entire world.

# 12

# Korea

Adrienne and I were not deterred by Bob's death or the war in China from continuing with the plan of study Elisséeff had outlined for me, but we encountered an unexpected obstacle in our attempt to go to China at the end of the summer of 1937. At that time American passports were issued for two years and were renewable for only two more. After four years abroad ours were no longer usable, and new ones were being stamped "Not valid for China," because it was a war zone. Since Korea was part of the Japanese Empire, we decided to go there until we could obtain new passports valid for China.

This apparent setback in our plans proved fortunate in terms of my overall education because my enforced two-month stay in Korea gave me a chance to discover that country. I had been there briefly, but this time I had an opportunity to get to know Koreans and see the country from the inside, learning about the oppression of Japanese colonialism and the high culture and pride of the Korean people. They had formed a united nation ever since 668, vying with the Japanese for second place after China as the world's oldest existing country. Brought up in Japan after Korea had been annexed, I had simply taken Japanese rule over Korea for granted. Now I saw that Korea was a very different country, with its own traditions and long history.

Japanese colonialism was not openly brutal, and there can be no doubt that Japan did much to develop the land economically and in other ways. As it had only a small empire, its investment in Korea was proportionally much larger than the investment of the European nations in their far more extensive colonies. But spiritually Japanese rule was very cruel. The Japanese were attempting to force the Koreans to give up their national identity and become Japanese. Only the Japanese language could be used for official purposes. Eventually the Koreans were forced to give up their own names and adopt Japanese ones. Since less educated and older Koreans could speak no Japanese, the absurdity and inhumanity of these policies were obvious.

At the time the world was oblivious to Korea. Japan had been allowed to annex this ancient, highly cultured nation in 1910 without a word of protest from any other country. Only a few foreign missionaries, mostly Americans, were aware of the situation. Thus when I came to realize what the true conditions were, I felt that I was discovering the country. I have remained ever since a strong supporter of the national aspirations of the Korean people and have sympathized deeply with them in the national division, war, and harsh rule they have been subjected to during the past few decades.

Adrienne and I set out for Korea in September. We planned to travel by a coastal vessel down the most scenic part of the Inland Sea between Onomichi and Hiroshima, but to our surprise we were not allowed to board the ship. The port at Hiroshima was the major staging area for the war in China, and the Japanese wanted no prying Western eyes. No amount of arguing did any good, and we finally were forced to resume our trip by train.

When we reached the Hiroshima railway station, a military policeman in plain clothes immediately joined us at the exit wicket. Our plan was to cross town by streetcar to a private electric railway which would take us to Miyajima, one of Japan's most beautiful and historic shrines. The policeman stuck to us like a burr, attempting to engage us in casual conversation. It was all so obvious as to be ludicrous, and I began to tease him to his embarrassment and the obvious amusement of the other passengers. I discovered that he was from north Japan and had never visited Miyajima himself, so I urged him to take advantage of the situation by accompanying us there; but he said, I believe with genuine regret, that his responsibility for us ended once we were entrained for Miyajima.

On arriving in Korea, we came under the even heavier handed care of the Japanese Army stationed in the peninsula. Each time the train crossed from one province into another, a new plainclothes policeman subjected us to the same set of questions. These clearly revealed that the policeman already had a full dossier on us and was quite aware of what our answers would be. Many of the police were Koreans who spoke Japanese with a pronounced accent, which was at first hard to understand.

We established ourselves in Seoul in a small boardinghouse run by a pathetic but brave American lady, whose Japanese husband was obviously ashamed of her in those days of Japanese hypernationalism and treated her with embarrassing rudeness. In mid-October, at the height of the autumn foliage, we took a marvelous trip up into the incomparably beautiful Diamond Mountains, now off limits to Americans, being in North Korea.

We continued to see a good deal of the Japanese police. One man called on us regularly each week until we became quite good friends. In the end he proved most helpful in arranging our trip from Seoul through Manchuria to Peking. In fact, he saw to it that a policeman camped outside our compartment on the overnight ride from Seoul to Mukden in Manchuria. I was never sure whether the man was supposed to protect us from others or to protect them from us, but he was very helpful when we crossed the frontier into Manchuria in the middle of the night. In Mukden we said goodbye to him, and thereafter we were never conscious of the presence of the Japanese police until we returned to Japan almost a year later. Either the Kwantung Army, under whose jurisdiction we fell when we entered Manchuria, was more subtle in its surveillance techniques or else too busy fighting a war to be bothered with innocuous foreigners.

~§

One thing I had hoped to do while in Korea was to learn the system for transcribing Korean names into the Latin alphabet. I had run into many Korean names in my study of Ennin, because he had stayed in a Korean monastery for a while in China and on his return trip to Japan had traveled with Korean traders, who then dominated the commerce of the East China Sea. The Korean names in my translation I felt should be put into some standard Korean transcription rather than into contemporary Japanese, Chinese, or the mishmash of transcriptions I encountered in Western books on Korea. To my dismay, however, I discovered that there was no standard system and that everyone simply followed his own whim. Theoretically the language was banned, and Japanese pronunciations were officially used, as on all maps. Koreans Romanized their own names as each saw fit. Some books in English used Chinese pronunciations of Korean names and others the author's unique rendition.

Faced with this problem, I approached George McCune with the proposal that together we work out a consistent system, which at least the two of us could use. George and his wife Evelyn were both children of well-known missionaries in Korea, and he was preparing for a life of scholarship. George agreed to my proposal and provided the knowledge, while I supplied the enthusiasm. Through his wide connections, we enlisted the aid of many Korea specialists in Korean phonetics. I was amazed at their number, but I soon realized that the subject attracted so many people because it was one of the few fields in Korea studies that was politically noncontroversial enough to be safe for Korean scholars.

Our task was considerably aided by *hangul,* the excellent phonetic system for writing Korean, which was created by royal decree in the early fifteenth century. We never imagined that an independent Korea would soon be needing a national Romanization system, and therefore thought only in terms of developing a system for use by a handful of Western scholars. As a result, we emphasized phonetic accuracy more than orthographic convenience, making generous use of diacritic marks. If we could have foreseen the future, we probably would have devised a simpler system, since newspapers and popular books invariably pay diacritic marks no attention, just as I have ignored them in this book, not only for Korean, but for Japanese as well.

George and I had not completed our work when I left Korea for China, but we continued it by correspondence between Peking and Seoul and eventually published the results in 1939 in Volume 29 of the *Transactions of the Korea Branch of the Royal Asiatic Society*. George threw himself into propagating the McCune-Reischauer system, as it came to be known. He persuaded the American Army Map Service to adopt it, and through the Korean War it became the foundation for most current Romanizations of Korean place names. The situation, however, remains somewhat confused. Most Koreans continue to transcribe their own names as fits their fancy. But the McCune-Reischauer system is probably the leading Romanization system used for Korean, and I enjoy having my name linked with those of Wade and Giles for Chinese and Hepburn for Japanese as a "father" of one of the standard Romanization systems of East Asia.

# 13
# China

I N LATE November passports good for China finally came through, and Adrienne and I went at once to Peking. If four years earlier I had found Vienna a shell of a former sparkling imperial capital, Peking was an even emptier, dingier reminder of a once far greater empire. It was a half-dead city, its former leaders fled or in inconspicuous retirement, and its economic activities reduced to bare subsistence levels. The only bustle of activity surrounded the occupying Japanese Army, whose large trucks barreled down the streets with no concern for the safety of pedestrians. Otherwise the scanty traffic consisted of a few streetcars and private automobiles, bicycles, an occasional line of two-humped camels padding along under bags of coal to be ground up and mixed with the local dust to form briquettes for fuel, and swarms of rickshas, gathered largely around the spots where Westerners might congregate.

The rickshas were filthy contraptions, pulled by even filthier, decrepit men who looked to be on the point of death, and often were. Many were consumptives, painfully dragging rickshas around in their last efforts at survival. The average remaining lifespan of men once they had taken up this work was said to be two years. It was no kindness to them to refuse them patronage, but I found that I simply could not endure having these pathetic fellow human beings haul me around, and I was constantly revolted at the sight of Chinese and foreigners lolling back in apparent pleasure as other men literally coughed out their life blood serving them as beasts of burden. Instead of renting rickshas, I bought a bicycle and used it exclusively, despite the piercing winds of a Peking winter.

Though no longer China's capital, Peking had remained in a way the intellectual center of the country; but now, with the Japanese occupation, that too had ended. Peking University, China's leading institution, and Qinghua University, where Adrienne had grown up, were both closed, and the professors and students for the most part had fled west to escape the Japanese. When Adrienne and I attempted to visit Qinghua, we found it transformed into an encampment of the Japanese Army. By sentimentally explaining Adrienne's childhood spent on the campus, I persuaded the guards to let us in to look at her old home. The sight through the windows was depressing. The water pipes had been allowed to burst in the unheated house, and the rooms were a solid mass of ice up to the level of the windows. Only Yenching, the Christian university, remained open, protected by the continuing aura of extraterritorial Western privilege.

The grinding poverty and horrible suffering of prerevolutionary China was a revelation to me. Ever since the middle of the nineteenth century, the Chinese Empire had been running down seriously, wracked by vast disorders and revolutions as well as foreign depredations. Famine and pestilence stalked the land. Nightly, people starved or froze to death in the streets. On more than one occasion our servant informed us that a dead body had been found that morning at our own gate. Most Chinese lived in little more than hovels, people were dressed in rags, beggars were everywhere, and the view in midwinter from the city walls revealed a virtual desert beyond.

Compared to this, one cannot but be impressed by the Communist Peking of the People's Republic. Granted that the regime has been terribly repressive and cruel, that personal freedoms are sharply limited, and that the government is given to incredible inefficiency, absurd experiments, and wild reversals of course, which have squandered much of what little wealth the nation has; granted that the people remain pathetically poor and ill housed and that the prospects for rapid economic growth remain gloomy; there is still a world of difference between the Peking I visited again for the first time since the war in 1981 and the city I had known forty-three years earlier. Once more it is a capital city, bustling with life and vigor. Hordes of bicycles clog the streets. Most important, everyone seems to be fed and clothed adequately, even if simply. This alone is a tremendous achievement.

On the other hand, Peking is less beautiful and impressive today than it was then. Though a forlorn, impoverished city in 1937, it had an imperial grandeur about it. It was still essentially the great thirteenth-century capital of the Mongols, given its modern shape by the Ming Dynasty in the early fifteenth century. It was surrounded by massive walls which, together with their towering gates and the great halls of the imperial palace, completely dominated the city. There were no rows of drab and ugly government buildings and apartment houses. In fact, the skyline was marred only by a single multistoried building, the old portion of today's Peking Hotel. Except for the great dust storms which bore down from the Gobi Desert in spring, obscuring the streets and penetrating every house with a thick layer of dust, the air was crystal clear during the colder months, not the smoggy miasma of today.

On arriving in Peking, we first had to find living quarters. This was not difficult because some of the Western residents of the city had left to escape the war. We located a reasonably spacious Chinese home surrounding a courtyard in the eastern part of the Inner City. The next spring we moved into a Chinese-style house with a beautiful garden on the north side of the city. Except for breakfast, we ate an almost completely Chinese diet with great satisfaction. Keeping warm in winter was our chief problem, but we survived thanks to a few coal stoves and long, padded Chinese gowns. Outdoors I wore a workingman's dog-fur hat with large earflaps and a high flared front.

Since non-Chinese names are not recognized by Chinese, acquiring a name was almost as important as finding a house. I settled on the surname of Lai and the given name of Shihe, meaning "world peace." Lai is a standard, even if unusual, surname that had been used by a famous early nineteenth-century Japanese historian, Rai Sanyo. The three characters of my name come close to spelling out Raishawa in Japanese, the form my name takes in Japan, though the phonetic syllabary is always used for foreign names there.

My formal studies in China were not very significant. There was no one I could find in Peking to help me with my research on Ennin, so I spent my time largely on language training, which I sorely needed. Adrienne, with her childhood knowledge of Chinese, was a great help and naturally ran the household and most of our daily affairs. I found that my long years of study of written Chinese had left me completely unable to speak the language or understand it by ear. The pronunciations I had learned at Harvard and in Paris were far from the way the language sounded in Peking.

At first I attended the School of Chinese Culture, operated by a Dr. W. B. Pettus and designed for the training of missionaries. It was good at teaching pronunciation, and perhaps I should have continued there, but its slow pace and its emphasis on phrases that might be useful in spreading the Christian gospel but hardly in scholarship got on my nerves. I therefore shifted to private tutors. Unfortunately the ones I found were not very good, but they helped me to master the materials Ware informed me I would be using as a teaching fellow, responsible for second-year Chinese when I returned to Harvard in the autumn. The text was a book by Hu Shi, the famous scholar and proponent of the use of *baihua,* the spoken language, for the writing of Chinese. Hu Shi's *baihua* style seemed to me much influenced by English and therefore relatively simple to read, but I am afraid I left China in the spring still far less fluent in spoken Chinese than I had hoped to be.

Besides the language, the chief value to me of our seven months in Peking was the feel it gave me for prewar and prerevolutionary China and the life style of the last generation of Western imperialists. The Occidental community of Peking was a curious mixture. There were some missionaries and a very few students like ourselves. On the less conventional side were a great number of stranded White Russians, whose womenfolk often worked in nightclubs or places of less savory repute, and a miscellany of eccentrics, misfits, and adventurers, who found in Peking a congenial no-man's-land between cultures, where the rules of society did not apply. For many of these people, the lure of the Orient was clearly the lack of social restraints and the cheapness of human labor. They could lead off-beat but lordly lives at very little expense. Prices were extremely low, pushed down all the more by chaotic exchange rates caused by the war. Even poor students were rich foreigners in Peking.

The remnants of the foreign legations still occupied an area cut off from the surrounding city by a glacis, cleared of houses to provide a parade ground for foreign troops and a field of fire for their defense. We had a friend in the American legation and knew a cultivated, gentlemanly Japanese naval officer and his wife, but otherwise had no contact with this remnant of the past. When the American Marines held their last parade before withdrawing from Peking for good in the spring of 1938, I self-consciously stayed away, unwilling to give this outdated symbol of imperialism the tacit blessing of my presence.

We did our best to mix into Chinese life, but few Chinese with intellectual interests similar to ours were left in Peking. Yenching University was too far out of the city for much contact, though I do find in my files a copy of a speech I gave there on "The Study of Japanese History from the Chinese Point of View." Our best friend was Shui Tiantong, who had been a classmate of mine at Oberlin and a long-time admirer of Adrienne.

Adrienne and I saw all that we could of Peking and its environs. We spent long hours at the antique markets. We visited the central palace through the kind offices of Dr. John C. Ferguson, a distinguished long-time American resident of Peking. The whole area was normally closed to everyone and was slowly decaying in empty splendor. We patronized the Peking opera, a raucous experience. The plays were full of noisy battles, represented by banner waving and gymnastic feats; the patrons ate and talked noisily while a play was in progress, then suddenly quieted down as some famous scene was about to commence. Travel outside of Peking was more of a problem. As we approached the city from Korea, we had noticed that every bridge and culvert was protected by soldiers, and one did not dare travel beyond the range of their rifles for fear of bandits or Chinese guerrilla forces. We were able to visit the summer palace at the edge of the Western Hills beyond Yenching. It was also possible to go to the Great Wall at the place where visitors now stream to see it, because the train line into Inner Mongolia crossed the mountains at this point, which was therefore well garrisoned by Japanese troops. Unlike today, there were no tourists—only the military garrison and ourselves. The valley that contains the great tombs of the Ming Emperors, which lies only a few miles to the east of the rail line, was bandit territory and definitely off limits.

In the spring of 1938 Arthur Billings, a friend from Paris days, visited us for a few weeks. He had followed in my footsteps in learning Russian at the "Langues O," though with much more enthusiasm and success than I, and had then become a member of a goodwill mission of French youths dispatched to the Soviet Union. A bureaucratic upheaval in Moscow, however, had eliminated their prospective hosts, leaving the group stranded there. The French Embassy got the French citizens back home but would do nothing for Billings, who was the one foreigner in the group. He had therefore gone to the American Embassy, where he had so impressed its members with his knowledge of Russian that the Ambassador, William Bullitt, took him on as an interpreter. After two years in Moscow, he emerged from the Soviet Union by way of the Trans-Siberian Railway and came to stay with us.

Billings appeared wearing a Russian tunic and a Soviet Central Asian skullcap, a costume that I would have thought would arouse the suspicions of trigger-happy Japanese soldiers. Within the next year, the Japanese Army was to engage in two limited but bloody wars with Soviet forces along the Manchurian boundary. Billings was a confirmed Socialist, a staunch pacifist, and a man of unbounded kindness. Because of his doctrinaire leftism, I found his gloomy report on the Soviet Union all the more convincing. He had lived there for more than two years, deeply immersed in Russian society and speaking the language fluently. His constantly repeated summation of his experiences was that the Soviet Union made a "mockery" of all he believed in. It was probably in large part because of what I learned from Billings that I never fell into the trap that engulfed so many liberally minded Americans in the 1930s of converting their disapproval of fascism, Nazism, and militarism into admiration for the Soviet Union.

In June 1938, Adrienne and I started back to Harvard. Not only had I completed my five-year program of study abroad, but we had been noticing that whenever we went to a film—a rare occurrence—we found views of life in America the most exotic thing we saw. The United States was beginning to seem far away and wondrously unreal. It was obviously time for us to go back to our own country and sink our roots again in its soil.

By the time of our departure, we had increased our impedimenta greatly by the purchase of rugs and other useful items and still more through the addition of copies of the *Kanjur* and *Tanjur,* which the Harvard Yenching Institute had requested that I bring back with me as part of my baggage. The *Kanjur* and *Tanjur* are two extremely bulky compendiums of the Buddhist scriptures in Tibetan, and they alone filled several crates. We also had traveling under our care an American girl, Janet Smith, who had lived in China her whole life but was coming to the United States to attend college at Radcliffe.

Going by ship, we passed through Japanese customs at Shimonoseki, which was noted for a very tough customs officer who gave Westerners a hard time. When the man came on board, he did indeed prove surly and unpleasant, but after I engaged him in conversation in Japanese, he changed completely. Apparently he had hoped to become a professor of English literature; having failed in this, he had been taking out his disappointment on his helpless victims. He could not have been nicer to us, and I felt truly sorry for him. The dragon of Shimonoseki turned out to be nothing more than a pathetic old man.

After a brief stop in Tokyo, we sailed by a fast Japanese silk freighter bound for New York by way of the Panama Canal. It was exciting to be returning to the United States, so rich and peaceful compared to the rest of the world, and I was enthused to be embarking at last on my career after so many years of preparation. The long ocean voyage was idyllic for everyone except Adrienne, who suffered a great deal from what we took to be seasickness. The ship stopped briefly at San Pedro, the port of Los Angeles, where Burton and Jamie Fahs came to meet us from Claremont College. Jamie suspected Adrienne's indisposition was something beside *mal de mer,* and a checkup at a clinic revealed that she was pregnant. We obviously were entering a new phase in our lives in more ways than one.

# PART THREE
# THE WAR YEARS
# 1938-1946

Teaching new wartime Japanese language class at Harvard in 1942. Translation: "Japanese wasn't as simple as I had thought."

# 14
# Getting Started at Harvard

THE AMERICA Adrienne and I returned to in the late summer of 1938 was outwardly little changed, but beneath the surface deep new currents were running. The recession of 1937 had revived the economic anxieties of the early years of the depression, but there was also a new concern over the storm clouds in Europe and the war in East Asia. A debate was beginning to smolder over American involvement and burst into full flame with the outbreak of war in Europe a year later.

No one was more concerned than I over the dangerous situation abroad, but I viewed it more as an onlooker than a participant. I did not think anything I could do would help to overcome the disastrous lack of international understanding in the United States as well as in Asia and Europe, and so I stuck resolutely to my long-range goal of getting East Asian studies established at Harvard as a first step toward increasing knowledge between the West and Asia. Elisséeff and Ware saw no reason to modify their plans of five years earlier, and the general spirit at Harvard continued unruffled by world events, though under the presidency of James B. Conant the school was beginning to become somewhat less a parochial New England college and more of a nationally and even internationally oriented university. The field of East Asian studies had become a little more accepted, but it continued to be regarded as a peripheral and exotic adjunct to the university's real work. Other professors saw it as an amusing illustration of the universality of the title "university." The occasional undergraduates who wandered that far afield from the more accepted programs of study tended to justify this eccentricity by claiming they were taking a course on East Asia "just for kicks."

Adrienne and I had planned to spend some time in Schenectady, where her father was then teaching at Union College, but we did not stay long. Even though the starting of a family had been a deliberate decision on our part, her parents viewed her pregnancy as an unmitigated disaster. They felt that we were financially much too insecure to have a child. The mood around the house was so gloomy that we hastened on to Cambridge, where we found a cozy home in an apartment house on Hawthorn Street.

I was assigned a dingy, dusty office in Boylston Hall, then the headquarters of the Harvard Yenching Institute. It was an old building with massive black stone walls opposite the west side of Widener Library. I was there when the great New England hurricane struck on September 21, 1938, the first hurricane in a century to hit the Boston area but all too reminiscent of the much more frequent typhoons of Tokyo. The walk home through the storm was exciting. Hawthorn Street, though only a block long, was closed for almost a week until workers could cut a way through the many trees that lay across it.

My first academic year back at Harvard was devoted primarily to the completion of my Ph.D. thesis and the teaching of the second-year Chinese course in Ware's place. For the thesis I limited myself to an introduction of Ennin's diary and a translation of the first of the four scrolls into which it is divided. I finished the undertaking in plenty of time, and the oral examination on the thesis offered no problem because no one around Harvard knew enough about the subject to give me anything but a very perfunctory questioning.

I was awarded the Ph.D. degree in June 1939 and was made an instructor for the 1939–40 academic year. This was the lowest rank and only an annual appointment. In those days, it was followed on the academic ladder by a three-year appointment as a university instructor, an indefinite number of three-year appointments as an assistant professor, then an associate professorship of unstated length, which was a tenured position, and finally a full professorship. The achievement of a full professorship thus required decades, and few ever made it to the top. Academic hopefuls at Harvard tended to bunch up at the nontenured level of assistant professor, because there were many scholars who were convenient to have around but were not deemed quite worthy of permanency. It was this problem that brought about a revision of the system after the war to a quicker one of "up or out"; the professorial shortage of the 1960s subsequently speeded up the process so that candidates moved directly from a teaching fellowship as a graduate student to an assistant professorship and then within a few years a tenured professorship. In 1939, however, a long row lay ahead for the lowly annual instructor.

I did not find the teaching of my Chinese course very arduous because I had only three students. Unfortunately, they had to be taught in two different classes, since one of the students was Janet Smith, and it was against the regulations for Harvard and Radcliffe students to be in the same class. This seemed a complete absurdity to a person like me from a coeducational college, and the compensatory extra pay, figured on a per capita basis, was not much consolation when only one student was involved. Fortunately all this nonsense was to be swept away after World War II.

Janet, of course, knew a great deal more spoken Chinese than I, but since it was a reading course, I had something to offer her. My two Harvard students were undergraduates who had both been in China for their junior years. One became a physician in upstate New York. The other was Kenneth T. Young, who went on to a career connected with Southeast Asia, was appointed by President Kennedy to be the American Ambassador to Thailand at the same time Kennedy sent me to Japan, was subsequently the president of the Asia Society of New York, and had the chair for Vietnamese studies at Harvard named for him after his untimely death.

The high point of the year for Adrienne and me was the birth on February 23, 1939, of Ann—to be followed two years later, on January 18, 1941, by Robert Danton. We were delighted to be parents and, in our youthful vigor, took the great change in our lives in stride. Adrienne made a marvelous mother, and I found my work schedule little affected, though the doubling of the family forced us to move to somewhat larger quarters on Longfellow Road.

Life in Cambridge was pleasant, and we fitted into it with ease. The group interested in East Asian studies had grown but was still small enough to have a clubby atmosphere. In addition to Elisséeff and Ware, Langdon Warner and Benjamin Rowland taught in the Department of Fine Arts, and two new instructors in Chinese history had turned up during my absence. Charles Sidney Gardner did not remain at Harvard very long, but John K. Fairbank was to become my closest colleague and a lifelong friend. Three and a half years my senior, he had gone from Harvard to Oxford as a Rhodes Scholar in 1928 and while there had become interested in studying nineteenth-century British trade with China. After several years of further study in Peking with his wife Wilma, he had returned to Harvard in 1936, assuming a position in the History Department.

The group of East Asian graduate students at Harvard was also slightly larger than in my student days, including such persons as Arthur Wright, James Robert Hightower, and John Pelzel. Arthur and his wife Mary became in time the backbone of Chinese historical studies at Yale. Bob Hightower became the first professor of Chinese literature at Harvard, and John Pelzel became an anthropologist at Harvard and my successor as the director of the Harvard Yenching Institute.

Our circle of friends included others outside our own East Asian group. For reasons I do not remember, I was included in occasional evenings at the apartment of Alfred North Whitehead, the venerable English philosopher, whose wisdom we all would eagerly drink in. The Japanese collection at the Museum of Fine Arts in Boston was at that time certainly the finest outside of Japan and the Chinese collection one of the best in the world. We came to know well the ageless Japanese scholar Kojiro Tomita, genial doyen of the museum group, and his gracious American wife. The Boston Symphony Orchestra played each season a series of concerts in Sanders Theater, the apse portion of the huge brick Gothic edifice at Harvard called Memorial Hall. In this relatively intimate setting we felt like members of a small community. Actually most of the faculty lived at that time in Cambridge near the university, not all over the Boston area as they do today in the great impersonal institution Harvard has now become.

◄§

After finishing my Ph.D. thesis, I settled down to a quiet academic career, continuing work on the remaining three fourths of Ennin's diary and taking on a heavier teaching load. I remained responsible for the second-year course in Chinese until the return of Cleaves in 1940 relieved me of that duty, and I started in 1939 to share the teaching of the Japanese-language courses with Elisséeff. That same year I also undertook a course labeled "Chinese 10." It was to replace one Ware had been teaching ever since 1932, usually under the title of "The Intellectual Background of Chinese Literature," which had become notorious as a so-called gut course, patronized largely by members of the football team looking for easy reading and generous grading. One of the problems in developing a new field of study is the combined paucity of candidates for positions and the difficulty of those not in the field to make choices among these few. Mistakes can easily be made, as Ware all too clearly demonstrated.

Elisséeff and Paul Buck, the dean of the Faculty of Arts and Sciences, wished to have Ware's course stopped and replaced by a more respectable one. In the first year John Fairbank's name was added to mine as an instructor, perhaps to afford a backup in case I proved unequal to the task. I do not remember him taking much part, but from this time on we began to exchange guest lectures in each other's courses. Chinese 10 that first year was called a "Survey of the History of Eastern Asia from Early Times to 1500," and John's course to match it was made a "Survey of the History of Eastern Asia from 1500 to the Present." The use of "Eastern Asia" in these two course names marked the first step toward the eventual adoption of East Asia in place of Far East, which John and I managed to engineer after the war. "Far East," we thought, implied a Euro-centric concept of the world, which we were determined to get away from.

I prepared for Chinese 10 (later renumbered Chinese 11) by giving a summer school course in 1939 entitled "The Historical Background of Chinese Civilization." I based my approach on the Naito school of Sinology at Kyoto University, which stresses the great economic, social, and institutional evolution that took place in Chinese civilization between the eighth and eleventh centuries and serves to divide ancient Chinese history from what might be called early modern times. I have adhered to this interpretation of Chinese history ever since. I had six students in the summer school course and an amazing thirty-five the next spring, sans football players. One of my students in the early years was Lien-sheng Yang, later to be one of the outstanding Chinese historians of his generation and a professor at Harvard until his recent retirement. He always professed to have enjoyed the course, though I suspect it was of more interest to him for learning the English language than for its historical content.

At about this time, W. L. Langer, the distinguished and most likable professor of modern European history, asked me to undertake the sections on Japan and Korea in *An Encyclopedia of World History,* a modern substitute for Ploetz's classic *Epitome,* first published in German in 1883. In 1940, I also joined Elisséeff and Borton, by then ensconced at Columbia, in bringing out a slim volume entitled *A Selected List of Books and Articles on Japan in English, French, and German* for the American Council of Learned Societies. It was a useful work for its time, but I so dislike any sort of bibliographic chore that I managed to beg off when later an expanded version of the book was produced.

During the summer of 1940, an institute on East Asia was held at Harvard. There were courses on Chinese and Japanese Art and on the Histories of Chinese and Japanese Civilization. Burton Fahs joined me for the one on Japanese History. The institute seemed little influenced by the threat of war hanging over the United States and was in spirit much like the one held in 1932.

During these years Elisséeff and I put a great deal of effort into improving the teaching materials for the Japanese-language courses. He had been employing the elementary reading texts used in Japan, but I felt that such children's books had the wrong vocabulary for university students eager to learn to read scholarly materials, and failed to present the structure of the language in a coherent way. I therefore persuaded Elisséeff to undertake jointly the preparation of a more appropriate set of textbooks. I devised the general plan, selected the characters to be presented in each lesson, and organized and wrote the grammar notes, while Elisséeff devoted his fertile imagination and literary talents to preparing the Japanese texts within this overall framework. It was a happy collaboration we both enjoyed.

Elisséeff and I, of course, were not trained language teachers, and our work now seems hopelessly antiquated. It was still the time when scholars who happened to know so-called exotic languages were expected to teach them on the side in addition to their basic scholarly studies. We had no thought of teaching speaking or aural comprehension but merely reading, since the reading of scholarly texts was the main objective of most of our students, and we felt that an adequate speaking knowledge for scholarly purposes could best be picked up by spending a little time in Japan. Such ideas are now entirely out of date, but the materials Elisséeff and I prepared were a considerable improvement over what had preceded them and proved useful for about two decades.

Our texts first appeared in printed form in 1941 in two volumes entitled

*Elementary Japanese for University Students.* The outbreak of war with Japan the following year induced us to publish an enlarged revised edition together with two volumes of photographically reproduced advanced reading materials. (A third volume of literary and historical texts published in 1947 showed a return to scholarly interests after the war.) The original textbook proved to have too steep a gradient, and many of Elisséeff's texts, though amusing, were impractical. I remember the proverb "An ogress at eighteen—second grade tea in its first infusion," which means "Even an ugly woman isn't too bad at a tender age." We therefore brought out a third revised textbook in 1944, renamed *Elementary Japanese for College Students.* Takehiko Yoshihashi, a *nisei,* or second-generation Japanese, who was to become one of my closest friends, helped us with this.

Teachers of language are generally considered second-class citizens on a university faculty. Those of us who were involved in language teaching in the Asian field were pitied by our colleagues, but I found language teaching to have a special appeal of its own. One has a chance to get to know one's students personally and to have the satisfaction of watching them make visible progress. In contrast, lecturing in a large hall full of students may be more stimulating and make one's adrenalin flow, but it is all very impersonal. Graduate students serving as examination graders and tutors for group discussions cut the professor still further off from his class, until one's students become merely long lists of unknown names on grading sheets to which one automatically affixes one's name. I always enjoyed my language teaching and happily participated in the Japanese courses until I left Harvard in 1961.

# 15
# The Coming of War

M Y PARENTS returned to the United States on a regular furlough in the summer of 1939, and we had a family reunion at the "camp" in Michigan at the end of that summer. When the European war broke out on September 1, 1939, I was surprised to see how calmly my cousins took it. As with most other Americans, Europe seemed far away. I saw the war clearly, however, as the start of a world disaster that would alter all our lives and probably bring the United States into conflict with Japan as well as Germany.

Not much changed in our own lives for quite a while. The national debate over American involvement heated up, but even at Harvard and in the field of East Asian studies we went about our normal work as if nothing unusual were occurring. The first whiff of what was going to happen came to me when I was approached by the Marine Corps in the spring of 1941. They suggested that I enter the Corps—as a major, I believe—to help organize a body of Japanese combat translators. Nothing could have been further from my career objectives, and I promptly declined.

A different sort of sign of the approaching crisis was the increased efforts in public relations on the part of the Japanese government. It had created an International Society for the Advancement of Culture (Kokusai Bunka Shin-kokai), under which it had set up in New York a Japanese Cultural Center, headed by Maeda Tamon, the father of my friend of Paris days. Maeda invited me to New York in February 1941 to speak on the Japanese language. It was my first paid public speaking engagement, bringing me a princely fee of $100 plus expenses. I was intensely nervous but prepared notes in such detail that simply reading them aloud would have virtually constituted a lecture. I remember that the example I cited for the inflected nature of Japanese was *uchikorosaseraretakunakattaraba*—"if (he) had not wished to have (him) caused to be struck dead." It was not a phrase one would find much use for, but my audience of about a hundred people seemed to find my talk both interesting and entertaining. To discover oneself a successful speaker is an insidious virus. As its symptoms grew, I gradually turned from the once tongue-tied avoider of speaking in public into an inveterate and practically indefatigable lecturer.

By the summer of 1941, war was obviously close. A summer seminar on Japan was organized at Cornell by the American Council of Learned Societies, this time with the crisis needs of the nation in mind, and I agreed to teach at it. But before it started, the Department of State requested my services for the summer in the Division of Far Eastern Affairs. This was much more appealing because it had to do with diplomatic efforts to avert war. Elisséeff graciously agreed to take my place at Cornell after the first two weeks, and I then proceeded to Washington. That I, a fledgling scholar of early Chinese and Japanese history, should be asked for by the State Department showed how scarce American experts on Japan were at the time.

I had never expected to be in government service, and my first experience was not particularly enjoyable. I spent much of the summer in an intolerably hot little room in a private home in the northern part of the city, where sweat dropping from my brow made my nightly letters to Adrienne almost illegible. I had no social life. The only person who took the slightest social notice of my presence in Washington was a colleague, Alger Hiss, later to become the central figure of the famous spy trial.

The Department of State was then located in the old State War Navy Building, the present Presidential Executive Offices, next door to the White House. I took delight in its old-fashioned, fussy architecture, its marble floors with their fossilized shells, and its swinging doors, like those pictured in films of bars in the Old West. But I did not have much work to do. Being summoned to Washington sounds very exciting; yet, as I was to learn from repeated experiences, government offices are quicker at requesting one's aid than in finding useful work to occupy one's time. I spent a lot of time reading newspapers and eventually was asked to draft a weekly survey of American press opinions on Japan for Ambassador Grew in Tokyo, who sent back word of the value of the material to him. It seems incredible that the Tokyo Embassy should have been so ill informed at such a crucial time in Japanese-American relations as to find my weekly reports of use.

Maxwell M. Hamilton was the gentlemanly chief of FE, as the Division of Far Eastern Affairs was called, but his health was too poor for him to exercise strong leadership. Far above him, Stanley K. Hornbeck, who had taught the precursor of Fairbank's course on the modern Far East at Harvard in the 1920s, exercised the real power as a special assistant to the Secretary of State. Beside him was his assistant, Alger Hiss, who always seemed pleasant and efficient. Hornbeck by contrast was a prickly personality, apparently quite sure that he alone could steer American relations with China and Japan, despite his unconcealed bias against Japan.

There were about fifteen officers in FE at the time, of whom I was not just the newest and youngest but by far the lowliest. Still, most papers circulated through my hands, and I was included in the occasional councils Hamilton called to discuss important decisions. The most memorable concerned the cutting off of oil for Japan. As I remember it, we were about evenly divided in our opinions. I voted in the negative on the grounds, which proved correct, that this would inevitably force Japan into war with us before we could get ready for it. Others felt that it would induce Japan to back down instead. Hornbeck and the men above him, I am sure, made their decision to cut off oil with no concern for any recommendations from FE. As history was to show, Japan, with its two-year supply of oil starting to dwindle away, elected for a lose-all-win-all gamble on war.

At the end of the summer the State Department asked me to stay on in a more permanent capacity, but I felt committed to returning to Harvard. I had my normal teaching load, and Elisséeff and I had also agreed to set up a special program for the navy. The navy was creating two Japanese-language programs, one at Harvard, the other at the University of California in Berkeley, to train reserve naval officers for intelligence work.

In retrospect, I see that my summer in Washington was a turning point as my interests shifted to include contemporary affairs. Before returning to Cambridge, I wrote on my own initiative an eighteen-page memorandum entitled "The Adoption of Positive and Comprehensive American Peace Aims for the Pacific Area." Since it has never been published and probably has not been preserved in the State Department archives, I give the gist of its argument as an indication of my thoughts at the time.

After vigorously supporting American aims to block Japanese aggression in East Asia, I noted: "We have demanded that Japan abandon steps already made towards the fulfillment of its programs . . . but in return what have we offered? Certainly nothing definite and constructive . . . in fact, nothing more than implications that Japan's legitimate claims and aspirations may be considered if and when Japan abandons her present program. Can we hope for any peaceful solution of the present Far Eastern situation until we have a comprehensive, concrete and fair alternative program?" I then pointed out that we seemed to be "committed to a restoration of the *status quo ante bellum*," but in East Asia, in contrast to Europe, this implied the maintenance of vast colonial empires and a system of unequal treaties. "Are we prepared," I asked, "to oppose and even to fight Twentieth Century imperialism while tolerating and actually maintaining the injustices of Nineteenth Century imperialism?" I went on to say that the "Eight Principles" recently enunciated by President Roosevelt and Prime Minister Churchill, if clarified for the Far East, would constitute a "concrete and comprehensive program for the reorganization and future peace of that area," pointing out that the dependence of the European colonial powers on the United States put us in "a peculiarly favorable position for winning the adherence of those nations to any just program this Government wishes to put forward."

The main body of the document was a proposed statement of "American Peace Aims in the Pacific Area," calling for "the creation of a Pacific sphere of international cooperation and mutual prosperity" based on four main principles. The first was that "all the peoples and nations of the Pacific Area are by nature equal as nations, peoples and individuals." I made clear that this included the colonies of the European powers in Asia and was also aimed at ending "all discrimination based upon differences of race," as exemplified by the 1924 American Exclusion Act. The second principle was that all the nations of the area should "enjoy complete sovereignty and Territorial Integrity"; it was specifically aimed at the withdrawal of all Japanese armed forces beyond Manchuria and the relinquishment by all the powers of concessions, extraterritoriality, and the right to maintain foreign garrisons in China. The third principle called for the equal rights of all nations to access to the products of the area, subject only to the interests of the local people but not to the interests of distant colonial rulers. And the fourth stated that "the administration of the present colonial territories of the Pacific Area shall be primarily in the interests of the permanent inhabitants of these territories and shall be directed toward preparing those territories and their inhabitants for self-government and independence." I am embarrassed to admit that, among the colonial lands to achieve independence, I omitted "for reasons of practical politics" Korea and Taiwan, and I regarded Manchuria as a territory that would become an independent nation separate from China. This probably showed a lingering Japanese bias in my thinking and a keen realization of the limits to which the Japanese, still in the flush of victory in China, might be persuaded to go.

Looking back with the hindsight of more than forty years, my proposals, except for the obvious blind spots on Korea, Taiwan, and Manchuria, now seem rather self-evident. The dissolution of the empires and most of the other proposals I made actually did take place within the next two decades. But in terms of the thinking of the time, I was light-years ahead of most other people. Who could envisage the disappearance of the British, French, and Dutch empires? My State Department colleagues, regarding what I had written with condescension, quickly pigeonholed it; I doubt that it ever went beyond the desk of Hamilton to anyone with real power. In any case, at that late date the slide toward war was probably too far advanced for any new concepts to halt it.

The autumn of 1941 was a busy time for me. I had my regular teaching, and I began to receive outside requests for talks on the East Asian situation. In addition, there was the special navy program. Elisséeff and I had three excellent teachers to help us and some twenty students, all with some previous acquaintance with the Japanese language but of greatly differing ability, age, and knowledge. The best in the group was John W. ("Jack") Hall, the Japan-born son of a missionary, who was to become a close personal friend and the core of Japanese historical studies, first at Michigan and later at Yale.

While our teachers were good and some of our students excellent, we had troubles with the navy authorities, who insisted that we meticulously follow all their directions. At the end of the academic year, we were relieved to have the navy close down both its Harvard and Berkeley programs and consolidate its Japanese-language training work under its own direct control at the University of Colorado.

The signs of impending war were all around us, but still it was a shock when it came on December 7. Adrienne and I were listening as was usual on a Sunday afternoon to the radio broadcast of the New York Philharmonic Orchestra when the program was interrupted by the announcement of the attack on Pearl Harbor. I telephoned a friend with whom I had had an argument about the situation at dinner the night before and was flabbergasted by his response, "Oh good! Now we can help the Chinese." Many other Americans, little aware of Japan's strength, probably reacted similarly. I, however, had a much clearer concept of what we were in for. The popular belief that Japanese were mere imitators who might be able to defeat other Orientals like the Chinese but could not stand up to Western armies I realized was merely racial prejudice. I find an article that appeared on December 9 in the Boston *Globe* under my name and that of a newsman named John C. Goodbody, which warns against underestimating the ability of the Japanese and predicts a tremendous struggle lying ahead of us in the Pacific. I might also mention a later *Globe* article of March 30, 1942, quoting me as condemning the unfairness of the treatment accorded Japanese-Americans in rounding them up on the west coast and placing them in the equivalent of concentration camps. I was quoted as asserting my belief in the complete loyalty of these people to the United States.

The war might have raised questions for me as to where my true loyalties lay. I had been born and raised in Japan, which had been my home for more than half of my life. I respected and liked the Japanese as individuals as well as much about their culture and country. But I had always felt myself to be one hundred percent American and had no doubt in my mind that Japan was basically in the wrong in the war. Within Japan I deplored the military rule that had blotted out the promising start made toward democracy and led to ruthless aggression abroad. Despite the validity of Japan's condemnation of Western imperialism in Asia and the unjustified racist treatment of Japanese in America, Japan's acts of aggression in China and now Hawaii could in no way be justified. The Japanese war machine, I felt, had to be stopped for the sake of world peace and in the long run for the Japanese themselves. I took all this so much for granted that I do not remember ever needing to ponder over it.

At first the outbreak of war brought surprisingly little change in our lives. A year earlier my father had developed a serious ulcer, no doubt brought on by the apparent collapse of his life work. He had returned to the United States in February 1941 for an emergency operation, and he, my mother and sister were now living in the Los Angeles area. Only slowly did the rationing of gasoline, meat, and some other foods begin to bring a change in our life styles. Even Japanese citizens living in the university community went on much as before. Tsuru Shigeto, who had fled military dictatorship to study at Harvard and had become an economics instructor there, continued to sit with his wife in the front row at the concerts of the Boston Symphony Orchestra in Sanders Theater. Later he was to become the president of prestigious Hitotsubashi University and received an honorary degree from Harvard in 1985. Tsurumi Shunsuke, the son of a famous intellectual, Tsurumi Yusuke, virtually forced the authorities to imprison him when he replied to their inquiries that he was a "theoretical anarchist." A strange boy, whom I had had for a reading course, Shunsuke thrived on the regular sleeping and eating habits forced on him in jail and, provided by his friends with books, graduated from Harvard while still incarcerated. Both Tsurumi and Tsuru were repatriated to Japan in the summer of 1942, and Tsurumi in time became a well-known commentator, though he always retained a strong anti-American bias.

The war made our colleagues aware of the presence of those of us teaching in the Japanese field, and we became virtual celebrities. I found myself invited to be a nonresident tutor (though I did no tutoring) at Adams House, one of the undergraduate residential units, with which I have maintained an association ever since. This enabled me to get in on the last few months of the time of prewar elegance at the Houses when students and faculty, dressed in coats and ties, sat down for meals at tables covered with white tablecloths and ordered their choice of dishes from a printed menu. It is hard even to imagine today, and I sometimes wonder if my memory is playing tricks on me.

With the war in progress, requests for speeches increased. I remember talking at Smith College in Northampton on an evening which happened to coincide with an air raid practice. I was becoming accustomed to lecturing with much flailing of my arms and eye contact with the audience. Eye contact was of course impossible in the darkened hall and waving my hands seemed pointless. It was like lecturing in an unlighted closet with the door closed, and I found it next to impossible to keep my mind on what I was saying. To maintain my concentration, I started walking back and forth until I realized that I might inadvertently fall off the platform. In desperation I crawled up on the broad lectern and sat there cross-legged, which somehow helped focus my thoughts.

Elisséeff and I were asked by the army to come to New York to help in the preparation of a Japanese-English dictionary of scientific terms. We devoted a week or so to this task, attempting to find translations for thousands of Japanese terms. Since neither of us was in any way a scientist, our results were hopelessly amateurish, but this again illustrates the thinness of American knowledge of Japanese when we entered the war.

A more important lexicographic project in which I became involved was the pirating of Japanese-English dictionaries published in Japan, which suddenly were in great demand. Since it was wartime and all commercial treaties had been abrogated, the term "privateering" might be more appropriate than "pirating." With a small fund obtained from the Rockefeller Foundation—I believe it was $10,000—Elisséeff and I had the Harvard Yenching Institute republish photographically a series of standard dictionaries, which we innocuously labeled the "American Edition." These sold like hotcakes, producing big profits, which became a revolving fund for the publication of books that is still in use by the

Institute. Had we been businessmen, we would have invested our own money and become war profiteers.

The magnitude of the change that was taking place in our lives did not strike either Elisséeff or me until the start of the second semester at the beginning of February 1942. We realized that in view of the situation we should start an elementary intensive Japanese class that semester, instead of waiting until September, which was our normal practice. We expected a group somewhat larger than the usual five or ten but were stunned when we found close to a hundred students cramming the small classroom in Boylston Hall. Many undergraduates, graduate students, and even former students, expecting to be drafted, realized that they probably had more to offer their country in terms of language skills than brawn. Classes were exploding in size in the few places where they existed across the country and many more universities were preparing to inaugurate Japanese instruction. We cut our class back to a more manageable sixty or so by making the work too difficult for any but the truly gifted, but obviously the war was carrying the study of Japanese to undreamed-of new heights.

# 16

# The Army School at Arlington Hall

DURING the summer of 1942 I became even more fully involved in the war effort when the Army Signal Corps asked me to come to Washington to set up a school for the training of translators and cryptanalysts for work on Japanese coded messages. To ensure that the university would put up no objections, John McCloy, the second man in control of the army as the Assistant Secretary of War, approached President Conant of Harvard University directly. I agreed because the code work appeared to be of vital importance. It was also extremely secret; everything about it, down to scraps of paper in wastebaskets, was automatically given the rating of Top Secret. Because of the highly secret nature of the work, I was subjected to a most rigorous security clearance, which required considerable time but apparently went smoothly.

Our family of four moved to the Washington area at the end of the summer, finding a little brick box of a house for rent in Arlington, Virginia. It was new but simple, virtually devoid of trees and shrubs, and terribly hot in summer. My place of work was Arlington Hall, a former girls' school, where the Signal Corps had concentrated its decoding activities. It was fortunate that at this time of gas rationing Arlington Hall was only a two- or three-mile bicycle ride down Glebe Road from our house, but it was a cold and dangerous trip in winter. Wartime year-round daylight saving and the eight o'clock starting time meant that I rode both ways in the dark at that time of year. Later, when I sometimes worked in a windowless part of the Pentagon Building, I found it quite disorienting to pass days on end without seeing daylight.

It was a gloomy time in the war. The first American attempt to stop the Japanese on land had started in August with the landings on Guadalcanal in the Solomon Islands northeast of Australia, and our men were just hanging on desperately by their fingernails in September and October. I remember a regular army colonel saying pessimistically to me that he was afraid we had made our move too early. On the intelligence side, however, the picture was brighter, since the United States had broken several of Japan's most important codes.

After World War I, the United States had penetrated the Japanese codes to some extent, but in 1929 Secretary of State Henry L. Stimson had terminated these activities on the grounds that "gentlemen do not read each other's mail." Frantic efforts, however, under the leadership of William F. Friedman, a genius in such matters, succeeded in September 1940 in breaking the chief Japanese diplomatic code known as "Purple" *(Murasaki)*. Before the war the United States Army and Navy had shared the work on Purple, but with the outbreak of hostilities, the navy handed this task over to the army in order to concentrate on breaking the Japanese naval code. Its partial success in this was greatly rewarded at the Battle of Midway in early June 1942, which was the first major victory the United States had in the war.

The army continued to translate the diplomatic code, which yielded a wealth of material, especially about the war in Europe. The most accurate reports on the results of Allied bombings in Germany, for example, came from the messages to Tokyo of the Japanese Ambassador in Berlin. The army also made progress in breaking the relatively simple Japanese Army transport code, which was important for identifying the routes and times of sailing and arrival of army transports and cargo vessels. Obscure names like Biak, Wewak, and Kavieng were constantly on our lips. This information contributed immeasurably to the destruction of the Japanese merchant marine, which was a key factor in winning the war. As shipping declined, the Japanese became progressively less able to move men and supplies around for defense or import raw materials needed to feed war industries at home. Progress on the main army code, however, went slowly.

To do all this work, the army needed many more Japanese-language experts than it had, which is where the school I set up came in. I had three assistants, all my seniors in age. Two were missionaries and the third a son of a missionary. We used as our basic teaching materials the texts Elisséeff and I had prepared at Harvard. These fitted the needs ideally, because they gave grammatical analysis well suited to the sophisticated linguistic background of most of our students and wasted no time on unnecessary oral or aural skills or the chit-chat of normal conversation. In addition, we prepared a lot of new materials based on actual intercepted Japanese messages.

The school started with about twenty students, half of whom I had selected from our February class at Harvard and the rest drawn from Japanese classes at Columbia. Among the Harvard students were Howard Hibbett, who eventually became Elisséeff's successor as professor of Japanese literature at Harvard, and Benjamin Schwartz, who shifted his focus to Chinese intellectual history during his subsequent graduate studies at Harvard and became a noted specialist on Chinese thought on the Harvard faculty.

I helped to recruit a second and larger batch of students early in 1943, for the most part from the newly started classes at Yale. George Kennedy, whom I had met in Berlin, was in charge of instruction there. Realizing that I could not tell much about the innate abilities of the students in a brief interview, I suggested that he place his foot on one side or the other of a crack in the floor to indicate which candidates I should select or reject. The results on the whole were satisfactory. It was only later that I discovered that George had a drinking problem and did not have the faintest idea who any of the students were.

It was not all work and no play at Arlington Hall. The graduates of the school organized a softball team, on which I played second base. Being on average a decade their senior, I was the old man of the team. My closeness to the Arlington Hall group, with whom I was to be associated for three years, built up a strong spirit of camaraderie. Ever since those days I have been constantly approached by people who happily told me that their fathers, uncles, cousins, and the like had been with me at Arlington Hall.

While at the school I indulged my penchant for writing memoranda on policy matters. Among my papers I find two dated December 12 and 22, 1942, on psychological warfare and surrender propaganda. This was a time when people were proposing all sorts of wild schemes on these subjects. Surrender leaflets were being printed on pieces of paper shaped like leaves and rained down on Japanese soldiers in the jungles of Guadalcanal, who probably never noticed them in the leafy darkness and would not have been influenced by their blatant appeals in any case. One fanciful scheme, which was apparently attempted, was based on the magical qualities of foxes in Japanese folklore. A batch of foxes painted a fluorescent white was released at night from a submarine near the Japanese coast and was expected to swim ashore and panic the superstitious Japanese. I doubt very much that this would have happened, but we shall never know. The foxes, when released, all headed resolutely out to sea.

My memoranda struck a more sober note. I urged that surrender propaganda be limited to situations in which the Japanese soldiers faced certain destruction; that it should be aimed solely at the commanding officers; and that, instead of emphasizing self-preservation, it should stress the saving of the lives of the soldiers under their command for postwar service to their country. I also argued that all short-wave radio propaganda should be aimed at a few hundred intelligent and well-informed leaders in Japan, whose attention to the propaganda broadcasts could be won through reliable war news, full texts of official documents, and serious cultural features, and who would be influenced by rational arguments about the impossibility of Japanese victory and reasonable proposals for a postwar world order. I find too an undated document, obviously from the early years of the war, in which I argued that care should be taken not to denigrate the Emperor because he might prove of vital aid in winning the cooperation and democratization of the Japanese people after the war. I also pointed out that if Americans of Japanese ancestry were allowed to prove their loyalty to the United States by forming units in the American military, this would help play down the racial overtones of the war and prove that we were not intent on fighting the Japanese people but only their military masters. Actually such a force was later created and, through fighting in Italy and Belgium, distinguished itself as the most decorated unit in the whole American Army. I still remember my thrill when I saw it march up Pennsylvania Avenue at the end of the war to receive a special presidential unit citation. Senators Daniel Inouye and Spark Masayuki Matsunaga are among the veterans of this unit.

The school I set up at Arlington Hall continued throughout the war, drawing students from diverse sources. Many became distinguished scholars, several were to serve under me later at the American Embassy in Tokyo, and others had prominent careers in a wide variety of fields. In all, the school trained several hundred future officers. I am proud to say that, so far as I know, none of them ever showed any special animosity toward Japan and most became more sympathetic and understanding because of their extensive study of the country. I myself left the school at the beginning of the summer of 1943. I had agreed to come only for one academic year to get it started, after which I was scheduled to help Elisséeff and others set up an Army Special Training Program (known as ASTP) at Harvard to train Japanese specialists for other more general uses by the army. The authorities at Arlington Hall were indignant at my leaving, but being a civilian, I could do as I wished.

Lt. General Hoyt S. Vandenberg awards the Legion of Merit in 1946.

# 17

# In Uniform

JUST BEFORE I left Washington, G2, the intelligence section of the general staff, asked me to accept a commission as a major and join the section in charge of all intelligence derived from intercepted messages. This section was so secret that it was known only as Special Branch. Its processed product, called *Magic,* was hand-carried from the Pentagon Building to the President and a few other top officials for immediate reading, and then carried back again. Even the President was not allowed to see the raw messages for fear that he might inadvertently give away the secret by quoting directly from them. Special Branch was staffed almost exclusively by bright young lawyers in uniform. As the people in Special Branch used to say, the work was too important to leave to military men.

As a thirty-two-year-old father of two, I was in no danger of being drafted, but the work sounded so interesting and important that I was willing to give up my freedom as a civilian to do it. I still had my promise to Elisséeff to fulfill, however. Luckily, the invitation to join Special Branch came early enough for Adrienne and me to hold onto our home in Arlington, and she and the two children spent the summer there and at the beach at Ventnor, New Jersey, where my parents were temporarily living. I went back to Cambridge, staying in the old Gold Coast section of Adams House, where President Franklin D. Roosevelt had once lived, and spent the summer working with Elisséeff on setting up the ASTP program. Harvard had changed greatly in the year I had been away. There were very few regular students left except for freshmen too young for the draft. Soldiers in various special training courses for the military, from accounting to the Japanese language, made a sight disturbingly reminiscent of the Nazis I had seen in Germany, as they marched singing through the streets from their quarters to their classrooms.

My commission as a major in the army came through on August 31, 1943, and I purchased an officer's uniform at the Harvard Coop together with the gold leaf emblems of a major and the crossed guns of an infantryman, which I fixed on the uniform with great uncertainty. Intelligence had its own insignia, but they were not used in wartime, so I had my choice, deciding upon the infantry as the least conspicuous. Then, feeling like a complete fraud, I boarded a train for

Washington, terrified lest some soldier salute me, forcing me to attempt to salute him back. In time, my former students at Arlington Hall taught me how to make as snappy a salute as any in the whole army, but that was the full extent of my military training. I never once even held a revolver or a gun in my hands. Elisséeff is reported to have said in class after my departure, "Reischauer is no more a major than I'm a bishop." He was quite right, but my slimness at least made me look the part. I also enjoyed being in uniform because it was a pleasure to be free for more than two years of any thought about my clothes and to know that I would be suitably attired no matter where I went.

Starting work at Special Branch proved slow, though I took my regular turn as night duty officer, sleeping on a cot behind its locked doors deep within the confines of the Pentagon Building. In time I discovered that my best function was as a liaison officer between Special Branch and Arlington Hall, a few miles away, and I moved my main area of activity back there. I believe that the officers in charge at Arlington Hall resented my presence somewhat, since my former students tended to look to me as their real leader, but I had the powerful backing of Special Branch, and Captain (later Major) Douglas W. Overton was cooperative. After the war he was to serve for several years as the extremely effective executive director of the Japan Society in New York. In December 1944, I was promoted from major to lieutenant colonel, and in later years, when asked by rank-conscious people whether I would prefer to be addressed as Ambassador, Professor, or Dr., I always found I could quash the question by replying that if Mr. was not adequate, they could call me Colonel.

The authorities at Special Branch regarded my liaison work to be of such importance in facilitating the selection and rapid processing of the most important intelligence that they urged me to build up a staff of assistants, giving me priority over all other requests. I selected some personal friends, such as Bob Hightower, recently repatriated from captivity in China. Others I took from the list of graduates at the army's general school for training Japanese intelligence personnel at Fort Snelling, later called Camp Savage, near Minneapolis. One person I chose from this source was Richard McKinnon, the son of a Japanese mother and an American teacher of English in Japan. He and one of our Arlington Hall products I used as my alter egos, who in my absence from my desk would decide which intercepted messages were important enough to transmit at once by secret phone to Special Branch. After taking his Ph.D. with us after the war, McKinnon became a professor of Japanese literature at the University of Washington in Seattle.

We were just beginning to solve the main army code and produce a few useful messages when suddenly we struck a bonanza. In early January of 1944, during the campaign westward along the north shore of New Guinea, a complete Japanese Army code system was found intact, and suddenly we could read everything. Our machines, which did the deciphering and decoding, spewed forth a vast waterfall of messages, and we were inundated with riches. How to locate and translate the materials of greatest interest became a pressing problem. A scanning unit to glance through messages to be sure they were sufficiently free from garbles to warrant translation had earlier been created, so I connived with the young officer in charge, Zeph Stewart, now a professor of classics at Harvard, to shift his unit's attention to looking for certain key bits of information that I knew would be important. I was searching particularly for order of battle information, that is, the military units and weaponry of the Japanese at places where we were planning future operations. Zeph's unit, aided by my own group, performed this task quite successfully, ignoring the command of their direct military superiors to continue their work as before. By the time this breach of orders was discovered, it had proved so successful that nothing was said about my meddling or Zeph's failure to follow orders.

I cannot imagine a wartime job more fascinating than the one I had during the last year and a half of the conflict. All the most crucial intelligence about the Japanese Army and its whereabouts went through my hands, and I also saw the vast flow of Japanese diplomatic messages. Thus, I had a birdseye view of the war, though primarily from the Japanese side. My chief pleasure was in locating new Japanese units, and one of my bitterest failures was missing a message which showed that the crack Japanese Second Armored Division had recently been transferred from Manchuria to Lingayen Gulf in Luzon in the Philippines. The message ironically turned up two days after American forces had stormed ashore there.

The Japanese seem to have assumed that their language itself would act as a barrier to American intelligence work, and they never dreamed that we would be so successful in breaking and reading their codes. They also put a great deal of faith in code names and numbers for military units. Code names, such as *Tora* ("Tiger") or *Akatsuki* ("Dawn"), were chosen at random, but the numbers were assigned by blocs, and we became able to guess the nature of a unit simply from the number of code numbers assigned it. By reading the Japanese messages we also could tell what progress they had made in solving our codes. They never got beyond what is known as traffic analysis—the identification of the nature of units and their activities from the number and length of messages being sent from some particular point—but they were very good at that. I remember Japanese messages which would estimate the number of American carriers, battleships, cruisers, and lesser craft assembled at Ulithi, a very large atoll that figured little in the news but was a key point of rendezvous for the American Navy. When

I checked these Japanese estimates against our position maps, I would be surprised to see how close they came to the actual figures.

~§

While I, as a member of the "Army Chair Corps," was fighting the "Battle of the Potomac," Adrienne had the harder task of caring for two small children and running a household under wartime conditions. Services of all sorts were difficult to obtain. Between the children and my long hours at work, we had very little social life, even though we had a great number of old friends in the Washington area. Shortly after our third and final child, Joan, was born on June 9, 1944, we suffered a blow when we were ousted from our home by its returning owner. In the early summer of 1944 housing of any type was almost impossible to find around Washington and we ended up in a miserable, rat-infested, one-story home, heated by a single large vent from a cellar furnace. It was in a semi-rural area named Chesterbrook, which we called the "rural slums," though today it is a posh residential suburb. We lived there until June 1945, when, after a long wait, we got a very pleasant apartment in a new development called Fairlington.

As the war in the Pacific neared the main Japanese islands in 1945, the disposition of the armed forces within Japan became of increasing concern to intelligence, but because messages were sent by land lines there, they could not be intercepted. Since the United States had no spy system operating within Japan, we were delighted when we discovered that the Japanese telegraph offices were beginning to send uncoded messages by wireless within Japan itself. Probably the telegraph lines had become overburdened or damaged by bombing. Relying on the supposed secrecy of the code names and numbers of their military units, the Japanese saw no harm in sending by wireless low-level messages informing a private in a "Kuma 7112 unit" in southern Kyushu, for example, of the death of a relative, or requesting a corporal in some similarly designated unit to return from Kyushu to Hokkaido in the north for the funeral of his father. It was not difficult to piece messages of this sort together into a fairly clear picture of the massing of a great number of newly created divisions on the coast of Miyazaki Prefecture in southeastern Kyushu, just where the American forces were in fact planning to land after the completion of the Okinawa campaign. The number of new divisions was so great that the top officers in G2 called me in to question the reliability of the information. I assured them that it was quite accurate, though I had no idea how young, ill-armed, or poorly trained these divisions might be. The picture was grim enough to make the high command start thinking of skipping the invasion of Kyushu and taking one giant stride to the beaches of Chiba and Ibaraki east of Tokyo, which were to be their ultimate point of invasion in any case. Before this new concept could be given much thought, however, the war suddenly came to an end in the middle of August 1945, and the invasion of Kyushu remained on the books as the next step planned for the march on Tokyo.

The atomic bombs, which were the main factor in bringing the war to an abrupt close, had originally been planned for use against Germany but were completed too late for the war in Europe. On the morning of August 8, I was called into the central office of Special Branch together with about five other officers and told about the dropping of the bomb on Hiroshima. It was necessary that we know so we could be on watch for the reaction of the Japanese. We were even given a list of the other potential target cities, which to my horror included Kyoto, though it was fortunately placed near the bottom. The United States had made a special effort to avoid the destruction of cultural monuments, but Kyoto was the largest of the few cities not yet burned out by fire-bomb raids and was a key railway crossroads.

All of us at Special Branch were stunned and dismayed at the news. Through the military and diplomatic messages, we knew how near to defeat Japan already was and how eager some elements in the government were to bring an end to the fighting. We were aware that the economy was grinding to a halt because the merchant marine had been virtually eliminated by early 1945, and we knew of the many discussions and diplomatic efforts aimed at terminating hostilities then going on. We looked dazedly at one another, and someone muttered something about hitting below the belt when the opponent was already on the ropes. I felt that I would burst with the awful secret bottled up inside me. It was therefore a great relief when President Truman made a public announcement about the bomb a few hours later.

At the time I believed the dropping of the atom bomb was a terrible mistake. My own estimate was that Japan would surrender some time before November. The Japanese would figure that we would not wish to attempt an invasion during the typhoon season and thus court a repetition of the *kamikaze* that had destroyed the Mongol invaders of 1281. Following this reasoning, I thought they would count on almost three more months in which to bring the war to an end, and I felt certain they would do so during that time. However, the results of historical research since then have made me much less certain about this conclusion. The various alternative proposals for demonstrating the capacities of the bomb without using it on a populated target would probably have been ineffective. Even with the two atom bombs dropped on Hiroshima and Nagasaki and the invasion of Manchuria by the Soviet Union, which was launched between the two bombings, it was touch and go whether the Japanese military would permit the civilian government to surrender.

Without the dropping of the bomb, the military would probably have insisted on fighting on, leading to hundreds of thousands of American casualties, the death by starvation if not in the fighting of many millions of Japanese civilians, and the virtual destruction of the Japanese nation. Living up to the agreement made at Yalta in February that it would enter the war against Japan within ninety days after the German surrender, the Soviet Union would probably have occupied the whole of Korea and possibly part or all of Japan, creating an entirely communized Korea and a Japan resembling either a Soviet-dominated Poland or a divided Germany. I also wonder whether people generally would have come to realize the horrible potentialities of nuclear weapons if one had never been used in war. We might not then have the present worldwide horror of nuclear warfare, which is mankind's best hope that such an end to civilization and the human race can be avoided.

If there were some possible justification for the first atomic bomb, however, there was none for the second, dropped on Nagasaki on August 9. The top American authorities did agonize over the decision to use the first bomb but seem to have given the second little if any thought, snuffing out some seventy thousand lives almost inadvertently.

After the war the Japanese popularly attributed the sparing of Kyoto from atomic attack and serious conventional bombing to my respected colleague, Langdon Warner of the Art Department at Harvard. In his typical modesty, Warner always denied all credit for this and refused permission for the erection of a bronze statue of him, claiming that he did not wish to go through eternity bearing the burden of pigeon droppings on his head and shoulders. Actually, a tasteful stone lantern was erected in his memory outside the gates of the beautiful seventh-century Horyuji Monastery in Nara. Some Japanese shifted the credit for the sparing of Kyoto from Warner to me, and a German book, entitled in English translation *Brighter Than a Thousand Suns,* has a moving story of me appearing in tears before the high command and begging for the sparing of Kyoto. I probably would have done this if I had ever had the opportunity, but there is not a word of truth to it. As has been amply proved by my friend Otis Cary of Doshisha University in Kyoto, the only person deserving credit for saving Kyoto from destruction is Henry L. Stimson, the Secretary of War at the time, who had known and admired Kyoto ever since his honeymoon there several decades earlier.

# 18

# Planning for the Future of Japan

THE SUDDEN end of the war made the intelligence work I had been doing quite pointless, and I became eager to transfer to more meaningful work. Hugh Borton, being a Quaker, had not entered direct military service but had spent most of the war in the State Department, laying plans for the future of Japan, and this sort of activity appealed to me greatly. A high-level Advisory Committee on Postwar Foreign Policy had been set up as early as February 1942, and it sponsored various subcommittees, of which Hugh served as secretary for the Interdivisional Area Committee for the Far East, under the chairmanship of George H. Blakeslee, the venerable international relations expert from Clark University in Worcester, Massachusetts. On a few occasions during the war, I had been invited over to the State Department to join the deliberations of this committee, and the group at the State Department was now eager to get my services on a full-time basis. But this was not easy to arrange. Being in uniform, I was under army control, and the army had a point system whereby military men were made eligible for demobilization depending on their length of service and the period of time spent overseas. According to this system, it would be a long time before I would qualify.

Unable to switch to the State Department, I considered some other possibilities. A request from General MacArthur's headquarters in Tokyo that I be sent out to join the CIC (Counter Intelligence Corps) held no appeal. The CIC was in essence a high-level police force; since I was expecting to spend the rest of my life as a student of Japan, I did not wish to be branded a police spy. Through my old Oberlin friend, Jack Service, the State Department asked me to join the group going out to Japan under George Atcheson, who had been appointed Political Advisor to General MacArthur, the Supreme Commander of the Allied Powers (or SCAP, as both he and his headquarters came to be known). This sounded more interesting, but actually the Political Advisor was given almost no authority by MacArthur. I declined, thereby possibly escaping the fate of Atcheson, who subsequently disappeared in a plane that ran out of fuel returning to the United States. Somewhat later General MacArthur's headquarters asked for me to come to Tokyo to serve as the chief historian of the Occupation, but by then I was a civilian again and the master of my own fate. I was not tempted because I had no desire to serve as historian to a man who I knew was too egotistic to tolerate a reasonably balanced account. Someone else took the job, but the ponderous work produced was never published, probably for the reasons I had foreseen.

Although I was stuck in the army, I refused to waste my time on the useless task of reading outdated messages from an army and government that had already surrendered. During my remaining period in the army, the only military function I performed was to write recommendations for decorations for men who had served under me. Subsequently I received the Legion of Merit myself from the hands of Lieutenant General Hoyt S. Vandenberg after he had become the head of intelligence at the Pentagon in February 1946.

Instead of twiddling my thumbs, I decided to write a short book. During the war, I had on occasion been asked to give three- or four-hour courses on Japanese history to the intelligence officers who passed through the Pentagon in large batches in preparation for work on the battlefield. I enjoyed these lectures and hoped they would be some compensation for the fact that these earnest young men were being forced to memorize Japanese order of battle I knew from my code work to be incorrect. (They were denied the full truth so that if they were ever captured they would not inadvertently reveal the source of their information.) My lectures had always been well received, and it occurred to me that I might be able to do the same sort of thing in written form. Since the United States was now responsible for the Occupation of Japan and the shaping of its future, there was all the more reason for Americans to know more about that country. I had no reference works but figured that the three years away from history books had allowed inessential details to drop out of my mind, leaving the basic outline of Japanese history all the clearer.

I wrote the book in September and October, bringing it up to the end of the war, and later adding a bit about the postwar situation. My chief emphasis was on the sad decline of Japan into militarism and dictatorship in the 1930s. Entitled *Japan Past and Present,* and dedicated to my brother, this became my first published book. Sir George Sansom, who at the time was at the British Embassy in Washington working on postsurrender plans for Japan, graciously consented to write a Foreword. I felt it was a great honor to have this acknowledged dean of Japanese historians give me his blessing.

The prestigious firm of Alfred A. Knopf accepted my manuscript, and its editor, Roger Shugg, gave it a thorough going over, which irritated me at the time —I thought some of my careful nuances were being overlooked—but no doubt improved its readability a great deal. A second revised edition of *Japan Past and Present,* which took the story through the American Occupation of Japan, was published in 1953, and a third revised and expanded edition in 1964. As in the case of various of my later books, these editions were published in Japan by the

Charles E. Tuttle Company, incongruously of Tokyo and Rutland, Vermont; they were also translated into Japanese and some of the editions into several other languages.

↵

On November 12, 1945, I received an early release from the army. Since I had been persuaded to join the army through a direct appeal to President Conant of Harvard by John McCloy, the Assistant Secretary of War, I persuaded Harvard to use the same channel in reverse. The ploy worked, and I joined the State Department at once.

The Interdivisional Area Committee on which Blakeslee and Borton had worked during the war had been limited in its power by various other persons, who had sharply opposing points of view. At first Hornbeck, whom I had known earlier in the State Department, was a clearly anti-Japanese force. A more friendly attitude was taken by former Ambassador Grew, who, after serving as the director of the Office of Far Eastern Affairs, became the Assistant Secretary of State. Because of his support, the members of the Area Committee were able to suggest liberal policies that looked toward the reconstruction of a democratic Japan based on the parliamentary progress made during the period of Taisho Democracy prior to the 1930s. Some of the committee's more liberal proposals, however, were turned down by Grew, who was essentially quite conservative. One such measure was a sweeping land reform to transfer land ownership from the hands of non-farming landowners to their tenants. This was quashed in Washington; but after the Occupation had started, General MacArthur chanced to learn of it from Robert A. Fearey, one of the former members of the Area Committee. He took up the proposal with enthusiasm, and it became one of his most popular and successful reforms.

A State–War–Navy Coordinating Committee, known as SWNCC and made up of the assistant secretaries from the three departments, was given charge of the coordination of postwar planning in December 1944, and in January 1945 it created a Subcommittee for the Far East, chaired like SWNCC itself by the representative of the State Department as the senior department. Blakeslee and Borton were members of the subcommittee; much of the work they and their colleagues had done in the earlier Area Committee was continued through this new body and then adopted without change by the main SWNCC committee. In this way a basically more liberal approach to postsurrender Japan was adopted than that forced on Germany. It was summed up in a policy statement called the "United States Initial Post-Surrender Policy for Japan," which was dispatched to General MacArthur on August 29, 1945. This became the single most significant policy statement on postwar Japan, because MacArthur, backed by the army, did his best to resist all later instructions, claiming that the "initial" statement covered all that he needed.

The work of the Area Committee and SWNCC Subcommittee also lay behind the hasty drafting of the Potsdam Proclamation, issued on July 26, 1945, which defined Allied "conditions" for Japan's "unconditional surrender." It allowed the United States to wriggle out of Roosevelt's unwise demand for an "unconditional surrender" by permitting the phrase to shrink to "the unconditional surrender of all Japanese armed forces" and agreeing to the continuation of the Japanese imperial institution in suitably modified form, if that was what the Japanese people wished.

After Japan's surrender, a change in leadership at the State Department had made my presence there all the more desirable. Grew and his whole group of senior Japanese officers were retired, and the younger Japan specialists in the Foreign Service remained scattered all over the world. Policy for postwar Japan had been largely shaped while the war was in progress by men who knew Japan personally, but now a group of China-oriented officers took over under the firm but gentlemanly leadership of John Carter Vincent as the director of the Office of Far Eastern Affairs. These men quite understandably were very anti-Japanese, but Vincent at least realized that he needed more knowledge about Japan. While I was still in uniform, he asked me over to discuss policy regarding the institution and person of the Emperor, which was still under bitter dispute in Washington and around the world. I managed to convince him that the United States should not try to do away with the Japanese throne or punish the Emperor, and he lamented that I was not yet on his staff to help draw up such a policy statement. When I finally joined the State Department as a special assistant to Vincent, Borton and I were the only two senior Japanese specialists in the Department; this situation continued until John Allison, the later Ambassador to Japan, returned to Washington in 1946 to join us.

The first job I was given in the State Department was to revise the agenda of the SWNCC Subcommittee for the Far East. Being entirely unfamiliar with what had already transpired, I was the least capable member of the subcommittee for the task, and I struggled unhappily with it. Another of my early assignments was to draw up plans for the division with the Soviet Union and the other Allies of the remaining destroyers of the Japanese Navy. I had no idea how one went about this. It did not seem quite right to start out: "Dear Uncle Joe: We happen to have some Japanese destroyers on hand." Gradually, however, I became familiar with the way the SWNCC Subcommittee worked and how one handled international negotiations.

In December at a conference in Moscow of the Allied foreign ministers, it was agreed that an eleven-nation Far Eastern Commission should be the supreme international body in control of the Occupation and that there should be a four-power advisory Allied Council for Japan in Tokyo, made up of representatives of the United States, the Soviet Union, Great Britain, and China, to advise MacArthur. Neither organ proved effective. The United States held a veto power in the Commission and the right to proceed with interim policies pending agreement there. Thus the Commission could do little more than approve what the United States was already doing. And MacArthur chose to ignore the Allied Council almost completely. It became merely a forum for the exchange of harsh words between the Soviet and American delegates.

The ineffectiveness of these institutions was not at first realized, and both Blakeslee and Borton transferred their main field of activity to the Commission, leaving me to run the SWNCC Subcommittee. Vincent was the titular chairman, but he found himself too involved in other work to attend meetings, so I normally served as the acting chairman, helping to guide the few decisions which MacArthur allowed it to make. Since the subcommittee worked on the principle of unanimity, each participating department in effect had a veto, which the War Department exercised freely on MacArthur's behalf. But I discovered that in matters left open for debate, I could count on a more liberal response from the army than from the navy. On a disputed point, the best I could hope for was a statement of lack of interest by the navy, whereas the War Department usually took the same relatively liberal stand on Occupation problems as the State Department. At first this puzzled me, because the Japanese Navy had always been more liberal than the army. Then I realized that the explanation was that massive popular participation in an army made it more responsive to national trends than was an elite force like a navy. In Japan, where there had been a popular shift toward militarism, the army had become more reactionary than the elitist navy, which had a high proportion of technically competent and internationally oriented officers, whereas in the United States mass participation in the army made it more democratically conscious.

My most interesting job while in the State Department was the drafting of a policy regarding the Emperor and the future of the imperial institution. Actually a working policy had already been established through the implicit assurances of the Potsdam Proclamation and MacArthur's insistence that, if the Emperor were to be forcibly deposed or the imperial institution ended, his forces would have to be increased several fold. However, no formal policy had been adopted. I wrote a draft policy on this matter on December 11, 1945, which I amended only slightly in a second draft on December 18. Subsequently it was officially adopted as the basis for American policy, and after considerable delay but essentially unchanged, it became the policy of the Far Eastern Commission.

In this document, I argued that, through the Potsdam Proclamation and the subsequent exchange of communications with the Japanese government concerning its meaning, we had tacitly accepted the continuation of the Japanese monarchy and should permit this, provided a monarchy proved to be the wish of the

Japanese people and did not interfere with the establishment of a peacefully inclined and responsible government. After all, our ally Great Britain itself was a constitutional monarchy. To ensure that the throne did not stand in the way of the development of a democratic government, however, certain parts of the constitution would have to be changed to limit the Emperor clearly to a symbolic role. The bulk of the personal fortune of the imperial family should also be made public property, the Emperor should mix more freely and on terms of greater equality with his people, public schools should not be permitted to teach the divinity of the imperial line or a sense of blind devotion to the Emperor, and the Emperor himself should be encouraged to demonstrate that he was a human being not different from other Japanese and that there was no such thing as an "imperial will" distinct from government policy. Actually all these things did happen, but more as a result of natural evolution in Japan than of any policy formulated by outsiders like me.

The main difference between the two drafts I drew up was the omission in the second one of any reference to the person of the Emperor himself. In the first, I had argued that he should not be treated as a war criminal, since he had done no more than act as a constitutional monarch in unwillingly sanctioning the war decisions of his government, and most Japanese would feel his punishment to be an act of revenge rather than justice. I also urged the retention of Hirohito on the throne at least as long as his heir was a minor, because an active adult Emperor was needed to help demonstrate the changes taking place in the position of the throne and attitudes toward it. The subject of the Emperor, however, was still a hot issue, since many Americans and most of our Allies demanded that he be punished as a war criminal. I do not remember the details now, but probably others decided that it would be politic not to mix this violently debated problem with the general policy statement.

Another issue of some interest concerned the definition of which outlying, minor islands were to be retained by Japan. I have the initial policy draft I drew up on this on March 6, 1946. The only points on which it differed from the lines defined in presurrender statements and generally accepted immediately after the surrender concerned the Kuril and Ryukyu chains. For the Kurils I argued that the Soviet Union should be induced to allow Japan to retain Shikotan and the Habomai group of islands and whatever other islands the Soviet Union could be persuaded to give up. For the Ryukyus—better known for their main island as Okinawa—I argued that the whole chain should if possible be returned to Japan, but that if American bases were felt to be absolutely necessary, all the islands north of Amami Oshima should be returned to Japan and the central and southern Ryukyus should be made a nonstrategic trust area, with as small an area as possible set aside for an American strategic-area trust territory. My own memory is that I included Amami Oshima among the islands which should be returned, but possibly I was talked out of this before I wrote the March 6 draft.

It is interesting to note that Shikotan and the Habomai Islands form part of the "northern territories" still in dispute between Japan and the Soviet Union and that the United States returned all the northern islands of the Ryukyus, including Amami Oshima, in 1953, and the rest of the Ryukyu chain in 1972.

◄§

Although I was in the State Department because of my knowledge about Japan, I actually spent much of my time on Korean problems. In an effort to coordinate American Occupation policy in Europe and East Asia, Major General John H. Hilldring was made Assistant Secretary of State for Occupied Areas in February 1946, and under him secretariats were created for Germany-Austria and Japan-Korea. I was made the chief of the latter and at once had thrown into my lap the problem of implementing the Soviet-American decision made at the December meeting in Moscow to set up a four-power, five-year trusteeship for Korea, with a view to the subsequent unification of the country and its restoration as a fully independent nation.

One of the great lasting tragedies to emerge from World War II has been the division of Korea, which had been a unified nation ever since the seventh century. At the time of Japan's sudden surrender two American colonels, one of them the later Secretary of State Dean Rusk, hastily drew lines to demarcate the areas in which the various Allied nations should receive the surrender of the Japanese armed forces. Since Soviet troops were already across the border in northern Korea and it would be several weeks before the United States could start landing its forces in Korea, Rusk and his colleague decided to use the 38th parallel in the middle of the peninsula as the dividing line between the Soviet and American zones of surrender. It never occurred to them that this would become a permanent frontier; but when the Americans finally landed, they found Soviet defense posts along the parallel and the country already in effect divided. The Russians proceeded to create a Communist government in the North, under the leadership of Koreans trained in the Soviet Union, while on the American side Lieutenant General John R. Hodge, who had been in Okinawa preparing to lead invasion forces against Japan, floundered around in an unfamiliar political situation without effective guidance from Washington or Korean experts on his staff. It is ironic that the United States, though it expended great efforts in preparing for the future of its enemy, Japan, made virtually no preparations for the future of a friendly Korea it was liberating from thirty-five years of Japanese rule.

The agreement made in Moscow in December 1945 for a five-year, multi-power trusteeship, created in consultation with Korean democratic elements, was the first effort to recoup this oversight, but it failed completely. We needed a detailed plan of negotiations with the Soviet Union to guide us in our talks with them, and since the only State Department officer dealing exclusively with Korea was simply incapable of writing clear prose, I was given the assignment of drafting such a plan. I worked hard on it, designing a procedure which, as I remember, led through six major steps. The negotiations, however, never got past the first, which was consultation with democratic Korean groups. When the plans for a five-year trusteeship were first announced, almost all Koreans raised their voices in protest against the delay in independence. The only groups who did not object or quickly shifted to acquiescence were those under direct Communist control, for these were ordered by Moscow to give the plan their support. The Soviet Union then argued that all those who had opposed the trusteeship proposal had by this act demonstrated that they were not "democratic" and should not be included in the consultations. This, of course, would have limited the Koreans consulted only to those under Communist control.

After months of unsuccessful haggling over this point, the negotiations were abandoned in the summer of 1946, and therefore the rest of my plan was never put to the test. The Soviet Union went on consolidating a Communist regime in the North, and the United States fumbled around trying to create a government in the South, allowing the political situation to become polarized. As a result, the more centrist elements were eliminated and power gravitated into the hands of the extreme right under the aged Syngman Rhee. From this unhappy situation grew the terrible Korean War of 1950–53 and the succession of military dictatorships in South Korea in more recent years.

I was happy in my work in the State Department. With attention beginning to swing toward plans for a peace treaty with Japan, I might well have continued on indefinitely had not Harvard cracked the whip and demanded my return if I wished to retain my post there. Paul Buck, who during Conant's absence had been serving as provost of the university as well as dean of the Faculty of Arts and Sciences, quite rightly felt that the loaning of his faculty for government service could not go on forever and started to recall those who had not already returned on their own. I had held the second rank of faculty lecturer when I left in 1942, but he had promoted me over the grade of assistant professor to the tenured position of associate professor. He stipulated, however, that if I wished to retain my position at Harvard, I should be back in harness by the fall semester of 1946. Facing a clear decision between a career in academia or the government, I unhesitatingly chose the former. There was no doubt in my mind that I had more to offer as a scholar and teacher than as a government bureaucrat restricted by my superiors and government policy. But I did not regard my years in Washington as lost time. They had expanded my area of interest and experience from ancient history to include modern international affairs, and had taught me much about the working of government and the realities of the world situation which would be of great help to me in the future.

# PART FOUR
# THE GOLDEN YEARS
# AT HARVARD
# 1946-1960

Holding forth at the Japan-America Society in Tokyo, 1960.

# 19

# A Second Start in Academia

T HE FIRST decade and a half after the war proved to be a sort of golden age for East Asian Studies at Harvard and the high point in my own scholarly career. I published extensively and had the satisfaction of witnessing the achievement of my original goal, which was the secure establishment of East Asian studies at Harvard. I was made a full member of the History Department as well as my own Department of Far Eastern Languages and was promoted in 1950 to full Professor of Far Eastern Languages (a title I subsequently had changed to Professor of Japanese History).

During 1945 and 1946 those of us who had been teaching in the field before the war returned to our jobs from a variety of enriching experiences full of new ideas and enthusiasm for our work. We resumed our teaching more or less where we had left it when we scattered in 1942, though now everything was on a much larger scale. I took up my ancient Chinese history course again, and Elisséeff and I shared the various courses on Japanese language, adding in 1947 an advanced seminar in the reading of literary and historical texts. But he apparently had forgotten the plan we had in 1941 to share the advanced course in Japanese history and held onto it himself until he finally retired. I was frustrated at being kept out of my main field of specialization, but our relationship had too much of the Japanese and European master-disciple tone about it for me ever to mention the matter. By the time I took on the course in 1958, my interests and activities had spread so widely into other fields that I lacked the interest and expertise to teach the course well.

During my second year back at Harvard a new plan for General Education went into effect, under which Fairbank and I finally put our two history courses together as the "History of Far Eastern Civilization." I lectured on the pre-1200 history of China and all of Japanese history and John on the rest. Listed as Social Sciences 11 (later renumbered Social Sciences 111), it served as the basic introduction for all graduates as well as undergraduates in the field and became a permanent feature of the curriculum. Today, as Historical Studies 13 and 14 and divided by countries rather than periods, it is part of Harvard's Core Curriculum.

Because of interest engendered by the war, our introductory course was popular right from the start, usually drawing two hundred students or more and swelling to several hundred when crises like the Korean War arose. As a sign of its popularity, it won its own nickname of "Rice Paddies." Our graduate students, who after starting with Rice Paddies eventually became assistants and graders in the course, often set up similar ones in the various universities to which they went after winning their Ph.D.'s; Rice Paddies came to be used throughout the country as a generic term for an introductory course in East Asian history.

In time others joined John and me in teaching the course, principally Benjamin Schwartz from Arlington Hall days in 1951 and later Albert Craig, who was added to the History Department to handle the field of modern Japanese history; but John and I remained the main lecturers until our respective retirements. The students seemed to like our contrasting lecture styles. He spoke somewhat slowly, with a great deal of dry humor and a somewhat ambiguous, cynical tone, whereas I talked with machine-gun rapidity and much verve and earnestness. At occasional discussion sessions we would consciously emphasize any points of disagreement between us, to the delight of the students, who circulated rumors of a deep animosity existing between us. In actuality, our collaboration could not have been more harmonious.

Although "Rice Paddies" was jointly created by Fairbank and me, he was the chief architect of most of the other postwar innovations in East Asian studies at Harvard. In 1946, his first year back, he started a full-time seminar, leading to an M.A., which he called "Regional Studies: China," though it spilled over to include Japan and other parts of East Asia. I joined him in the project, and in 1952–53, when he was away on leave, took over the program for the year. Subsequently it became merely the introductory M.A. program in the field.

There were many routes by which a scholar could achieve a Ph.D. degree in East Asian studies, but the one that became the most popular was another of John's innovations—the Joint Degree in History and Far Eastern Languages. John also assembled a research group, which formally became the East Asian Research Center in 1955 and when he retired in 1977 was appropriately named the John K. Fairbank Center for East Asian Research.

In his memoirs, *Chinabound: A Fifty-Year Memoir* (1982), John refers to our relationship as a sort of sibling rivalry, but I never felt it as such. We were intellectual siblings, to be sure, cooperating closely in our work at Harvard and both filled with missionary zeal for our field—a characteristic which we shared with many of our contemporaries and students, who, like us, had the fervor of a minority sect, confident in its vision and struggling for recognition by the established academic community. But I never saw us as rivals. I was delighted to have John as a staunch ally, because he was a master of the entrepreneurial skills that I myself lacked. He was an indefatigable writer, or rather dictator, of memoranda and letters, a skilled raiser of funds, and a wily academic politician, who was deeply entrenched in the Harvard community and knowledgeable about the levers of power. I, by contrast, was more of an intellectual loner, preferring to work by myself. One of the chief appeals of academic life to me was that each person was judged on his own merits as a scholar and teacher and not on the size of the scholarly empire he controlled. All stood equally on the ground, not on the shoulders of academic subordinates. I enjoyed my teaching and loved my research work and writing, but I hated the busy work of letter writing, phone calls, committee meetings, and the like. Too much of such activities would make me feel that my day had been wasted. I shuddered to think that that was the way most administrators and office workers spent their whole time. John's efficiency in handling such matters thus was a godsend, and I relied heavily on his entrepreneurial talents to help develop the field for all of us.

There were only two points of friction. One was that Elisséeff clearly disapproved of John's lack of classical Sinological training and at the same time was jealous of his popularity with the students and prominent role in the university. John never showed any irritation with Elisséeff, but he envied him his control of the sizable Harvard Yenching Institute funds. There was, as a result, a definite strain between Elisséeff's classicism and John's modernism, which I felt it my duty to try to patch over as best I could.

The other point of friction concerned John's forceful leadership, or domineering ways as some saw them. He always tried to co-opt me by having me as the associate director of his various projects, and I usually went along with him as the course of least resistance. But some of his less politically agile colleagues were irritated by the way he would let his own enthusiasms overwhelm the interests of others. He unconsciously allowed East Asian projects to narrow down to specifically Chinese undertakings and these in turn to concentrate mostly on the nineteenth century, which was his own chief area of research. There was considerable carping about John's "guided democracy," but it did provide strong leadership for Chinese studies that was sorely missed when he retired.

During these years East Asian Studies blossomed with new faculty, courses, and programs, but the chief reason this was a golden age was the quality of the students. Among the thousands of young men trained during the war by the army or navy in Japanese or some other East Asian language, only a small fraction decided to go on academically in the field; but those who did included many of the most talented, and for several years we had more than our share of the best students in the university. A list of the more prominent of the Ph.D.'s we produced at this time would read like a *Who's Who* of East Asian studies for the next few decades. Several have already been named, but others merit mention. There was, for example, Marius Jansen, who had been in the wartime ASTP program at Harvard and became the mainstay of Japanese historical studies at

Princeton. Henry Rosovsky, who decided to concentrate on Japan during a stint of service during the Korean War, became an economist of note, though he was later lost to the Japanese field for a decade because of service as dean of the Faculty of Arts and Sciences.

Besides the scores of brilliant future scholars who studied with us during the early postwar years, Fairbank's Regional Program drew many men who distinguished themselves in government service and in some cases served later with me in Japan. The Nieman Foundation brought a stimulating group of former war correspondents interested in East Asia back from the Pacific or Korean wars for a year of reflection and intellectual retooling at Harvard. Another unusual group of graduate students was supplied by the Jesuit order, several from French Canada, who took Ph.D.'s with us before going on to prominent academic positions in Japan. Even Elisséeff's younger son, Vadim—today the director of the Musée Czernuschi in Paris—and some other European students came to study, showing that the tide had reversed since my student days, and now Harvard rather than Paris was looked on as the Mecca of East Asian studies. The State Department also sent small groups of men to be trained under my direction for the Japanese service, until the Department built up its own training facilities. This was how Edward Seidensticker came to Harvard, though he did not stay long with the State Department. He and Donald Keene, who also spent a year at Harvard, are generally regarded as the best of a number of extraordinarily talented translators and critics of Japanese literature who emerged from the war and its aftermath.

East Asian studies expanded during the postwar years, not only at Harvard but also at universities throughout the country. As the field grew, it became evident that it should have its own scholarly association rather than continuing as a half-unwanted stepchild of the venerable American Oriental Society, which was devoted largely to ancient Middle Eastern studies. As early as 1941, Hugh Borton and others had founded a journal called *The Far Eastern Quarterly* and a Far Eastern Association to support it. But this was almost exclusively a Columbia undertaking. After World War II the journal was in dire need of broader financial support, and there was also a growing feeling that there should be a national organization in the field. An informal meeting was held on January 3, 1948, to discuss the needs, and I and two others were chosen as a committee to make arrangements for a meeting to found a national society. There were two distinct groups: those who were primarily interested in the finances of *The Far Eastern Quarterly,* and those who were afraid that the desires for a national association would be subverted to this narrow objective. I was selected as a neutral chairman and had the privilege of calling to order the founding meeting of the new Far Eastern Association.

The early presidents of the association were all very senior persons, but I was elected as vice-president in 1954 and automatically became president in 1955, being by far the youngest president to date. This made me realize that I was already becoming one of the *genro,* or "elder statesmen," of the field. The war had drawn a sharp line between those of us who already had positions before its outbreak and the large wave of able scholars who started their studies either during or shortly after the end of the war. The postwar group soon became the backbone of the field, but it has itself since then come to be regarded as the old guard by new waves of younger scholars, while we survivors from prewar days, now all retired, have become "elder statesmen," curiosities, or dinosaurs, depending on one's point of view.

At the meeting of the directors of the Far Eastern Association in the spring of 1955, when I took over the presidency, an important decision was made to expand the association to include South and Southeast Asia, that is, all of Asia east of Pakistan. I happened to be abroad during most of my period as president, but the crucial decisions were made before I left. The Southeast Asian group wished to have an association of its own, and it was expected that the South Asian group would soon follow suit, but it was feared that both groups would be too weak to stand on their own feet. At the risk of diluting the East Asian contingent, we decided that the association should lend the other two groups a hand by forming an overall Asian society, exclusive of the Middle East. The name of *The Far Eastern Quarterly* was changed to *The Journal of Asian Studies* in the November 1956 issue and the name of the society to the Association for Asian Studies the following May.

꙰

Despite the rapid development of East Asian Studies at Harvard after the war, the teaching staff was still small enough to have a strong esprit de corps, and it was a pleasure to be surrounded by enthusiastic students of high caliber. Since growth in our field seemed almost unlimited, there were none of the petty rivalries that have plagued academic life more recently. Our Ph.D.'s were snapped up by prominent institutions as quickly as we could produce them.

All of us were excited by the subject matter of our studies. Although Japan and China had become areas of major interest in the United States, they had been little studied by persons trained in modern scholarship, except in the case of Japan, where the strong Marxist bent of the social sciences in Japan tended to distort the results. When it was time to write their Ph.D. theses, our students could pick among any number of fresh topics and end up with significant new discoveries and interpretations. I spent endless hours, usually in the evenings, working with some of the foreign students, mostly Chinese, who needed help with their English writing. For the others it was largely a matter of reading their drafts and making suggestions. I had the habit of doing this work while listening on the radio to Red Sox baseball games, and my students would claim that they could not fully understand my comments unless they read them to the accompaniment of a baseball broadcast. In any case, I learned from the research work of my students far more than they learned from me, and my thinking about modern Japanese history was basically changed as a result.

I also revised my concept about the role of the Western student in East Asian scholarship. Before the war I had seen him (or her) primarily as a transmitter of knowledge: his own research work, it seemed to me, was most valuable as training to make him better able to judge the value of the work of Japanese and Chinese scholars. Now I realized that there were sufficient Western scholars who were well enough trained to make major original contributions of their own. American studies of modern China, and especially those done at Harvard, became the center of modern scholarship on China. Similarly, American studies of the more developed field of Japanese studies came to be looked upon in Japan as the one rival school of scholarship in this field. I myself do not hold to schools of scholarship, feeling that each scholar must be his own individual master; the more diverse my students' work, the more stimulating I found it. But Japanese scholars began to speak of an American school or even a Harvard school of Japanese studies, usually with disapprobation because our students often challenged the Marxist stereotypes that had become virtually sacrosanct in postwar Japan.

Another factor that revised my scholarly thinking about East Asia was my experience in teaching the Rice Paddies course with Fairbank. He would describe the Chinese inability to respond effectively to the impact of the West in the nineteenth century as being quite natural and virtually inevitable, whereas I would describe Japan's very different and far more effective response to the same stimuli as being equally natural. Obviously there were some very basic differences between nineteenth-century China and Japan which had previously escaped our attention. Japan's vigorous and successful response to the Western menace and its subsequent success in developing a workable constitution and parliamentary form of government clearly required some explanation. Scholars had tended to compare Japan with institutionally more advanced countries in Europe and to interpret Japan's problems in modernization and its imperfect democracy in Marxist terms as an example of a failed or aborted revolution. But using nineteenth-century China instead of the West as the yardstick, Japan's social and economic modernization and remarkable progress toward democracy appeared to be an amazing success story that required more explaining than its less surprising failures.

When I had written *Japan Past and Present* just after the end of World War II, I had been much under the influence of the dominant Marxist interpretation of the day. With my new insights, I began to emphasize the intellectual diversity and entrepreneurial vigor of the late Tokugawa period rather than its social stratification and political decline, the positive aspects rather than the repressive measures of the new government created by the Meiji Restoration, and the successes rather than the failures of parliamentary development and party government in Japan. This interpretation I injected bit by bit in the later editions of *Japan Past and Present* and *Japan: The Story of a Nation,* which took the place of the earlier book in 1970 and came out in revised editions in 1976 and 1981. The 1981 edition of *Japan: The Story of a Nation* contains the clearest statement of my interpretation of modern Japanese history, which had moved by that time a long way from my first formulation of it in 1945.

In emphasizing the late Tokugawa background for Japan's successful modernization and the spontaneous development of elements of parliamentary democracy, I became intrigued by the fact that the chief areas where democracy has proved a successful form of government—namely, Western Europe (including its geographic offshoots like the United States) and Japan—have the only societies in the world that have undergone a full feudal experience. I concluded that there must be some relationship between the social diversity and regional and functional autonomies of a feudal system and the pluralistic societies that are found in democratic countries. This concept I first suggested in a chapter on Japan in a volume entitled *Feudalism in History,* which was edited and published by the late Rushton Coulborn in 1956 on the basis of a fascinating conference he organized at Princeton in the autumn of 1950. In this chapter I also speculated on the development of feudalism in Western Europe and Japan from analogous mixtures of tribal, aristocratic societies with the legal concepts of more advanced civilizations. German and native Japanese tribal institutions, I suggested, supplied the one ingredient and Roman and Chinese administrative law the other. I have never had the chance to develop these ideas myself thoroughly; though they have been frequently referred to, they have never been fully studied by anyone else either.

For several years after the war I edited with Cleaves the extremely scholarly *Harvard Journal of Asiatic Studies.* This job entitled me to a secretary, and I have never lacked one since, gradually losing as a result my ability to type. They all quite spoiled me with their loyalty and hard work, and several still remain fondly remembered friends. Despite the heavy administrative and teaching schedule I handled during those years, I found time to work a great deal on my own research and writing. But I remember the shock I felt on my fortieth birthday in 1950 when I suddenly realized that my life was probably more than half over and I had not yet gotten around to any of the major scholarly projects I had planned.

My most substantial work in the early postwar years was *The United States and Japan,* published in 1950. It was part of a series called the American Foreign Policy Library, started after the war by the Harvard University Press and edited at first by the former Assistant Secretary of State, Sumner Welles, with the assistance of Professor Donald C. McKay of the History Department. Considerable emphasis was placed by the Press on this series at the time, and I considered it quite an honor when I was approached to do the volume on Japan. After a discussion of Japanese-American relations in general and a description of the physical setting and economy of Japan, the book concentrated on an analysis of the Japanese character and an account of the course of the American Occupation to date. It was well received and the press subsequently brought out second and third revised editions in 1957 and 1965. In these books I was much more optimistic about Japan's political future than were almost all the other contemporary scholars and popular writers. I based my optimism on Japan's spontaneous growth toward democracy in the years before 1931, and, while I viewed Japan's economic future with deep concern, I was less pessimistic than most. Almost all of the criticism of my writing singled out what was considered my excessive optimism, but each time I came to revise one of my books, I found that I had to make my predictions much more optimistic than before. One can guess how wrong my critics were, but I have discovered that pessimism somehow is regarded as being more scholarly than optimism.

By far the largest of my scholarly undertakings during these years was the completion of my work on Ennin. Because of the war, I had not gotten much past the first of its four scrolls, so the bulk of the work still lay ahead of me. It was difficult and painstaking labor, requiring endless hours for checking out small points. Lien-shen Yang and Achilles Fang, who was a Chinese research scholar at Harvard, were both extremely helpful on many obscure passages. When I finally completed the translation, I had written more than 1,550 footnotes. Then followed endless work to standardize translations throughout the long text and to see it through repeated word-by-word proof readings as it was transformed into print.

Ennin's diary contained such rich materials that I decided to use it and related historical materials to write a more general book on the main subjects it touches on. In other words, I produced what is known in French by the delightful term of a *vulgarisation.* In it I discussed not only Ennin and his diary but the Japanese embassies to China of that period, popular life in China at the time, the great persecution of Buddhism in 845, and the domination of the East China Sea by Koreans and their important role as traders in coastal China. The difference in the two books is epitomized by the mere 346 footnotes in the second. Quite naturally it has been the more widely read. The two volumes, beautifully styled without charge by W. A. Wiggins and Dorothy Abbe, were published together in January 1955 by the Ronald Press under the titles of *Ennin's Diary: The Record of a Pilgrimage to China in Search of the Law* and *Ennin's Travels in T'ang China,* the T'ang having been the ruling dynasty at the time of Ennin's visit.

The work on Ennin stretched out for twenty years from its inception in the autumn of 1935 until its publication in 1955, but I enjoyed every minute of it. I realized, however, that I would never again have the time for a lengthy and leisurely study of this sort. I put away my Ennin studies with regret, feeling that I was bringing to an end a whole phase of my life and also was saying farewell to an old friend.

# 20

# Government Contacts

W<small>HEN</small> I returned to Harvard, I did not break off all my relations with the government and crawl back into my academic hole. Nor did I lose interest in current problems. Although I had avoided going out to Japan at the end of the war because of the uncongenial nature of the positions offered me, I was eager to see for myself what conditions were like in postwar Japan. I was therefore delighted to receive an invitation in the summer of 1948 to be a member of a mission to Japan to give advice on research in the humanities and social sciences. Called the Cultural Science Mission (*Jimbun Kagaku Komon Dan* in Japanese), our group consisted of five university professors from different fields of study and different institutions.

We were in Japan about four months and had ample opportunity to see the miserable conditions of life still prevailing three years after the end of the war. But I was encouraged to note the great changes for the good that had already taken place in the social and political system, and the hard work and bravery with which the Japanese were tackling their problems. Japan was recovering much more slowly from the devastations of war than the other major war-ravaged lands, but already a thin scum of shacks covered most of the huge burned-out sections of Tokyo and other cities. There was, however, almost no heating, and food and clothing were in very short supply. The American Occupation had commandeered most of the good housing and many of the remaining buildings. Most cars were being operated in behalf of Americans, and the best rolling stock on the railways was reserved for them. Japanese scrambled through windows to get into dangerously overcrowded and dilapidated train carriages and hung precariously like flies on the outside of streetcars. All scraps of land, even parts of little used roadways or the sites of unrestored homes, were devoted to pathetic efforts to grow more food. City people made regular trips to the countryside to trade their remaining clothes and family treasures for extra food. They wryly called this an onion existence, as, in tears, they peeled off successive layers of their remaining possessions.

The ease and luxury in which Americans lived and traveled in Japan made me feel ill at ease when there was so much poverty and suffering all around us. Most Americans seemed to accept this without thought, looking on the Japanese as a deservedly punished people, but to me the Japanese were old friends, and I could not feel easy seeing us Americans living in plenty to the point of waste in the midst of millions of Japanese on the borderline of starvation. I discovered one small way to be of help. Through my father, I arranged for shipments of old clothes and stockings from the United States to his old school, Tokyo Women's University, which sold the rewoven stockings and held extremely successful bazaars featuring the castoff clothing.

The plight of the Japanese tugged at my heart, yet at the same time my overall impression was one of hope. There was excitement and enthusiasm over the creation of a better, more just and peaceful Japan. I have noticed that Americans who first came to know Japan at this time think of it as the "good old days," when the countryside and the few undestroyed cities, like Kyoto, still preserved some of the charm of prewar Japan. But to me these were only fragments that had survived from an earlier Japan I had once known much more fully. I saw the postwar years primarily as the "good new days," when earlier efforts at building a peaceful, democratic Japan were being renewed with astounding vigor and were producing promising results. It was on the basis of this trip that I wrote the positive assessment of Japan's future that appeared in the first edition of *The United States and Japan* in 1950.

Our mission held many meetings with scholars in Tokyo. The leadership on the Japanese side was taken by President Nambara Shigeru of Tokyo University, Japan's most prestigious educational institution. President Nambara was a Christian and a pacifist. The helplessness of such persons before the war seemed epitomized by his personal account to me of how he had been reduced by police and public pressure to expressing his opposition to Japan's aggressive policies in *haiku* written in the secrecy of his home. In Tokyo our group also held a private off-the-record meeting with some leaders of the leftist student movement but found their extremist patterns of thought and unrealistic ideas beyond our comprehension.

From Tokyo we made trips to other university centers throughout the country, and we visited Hiroshima, where I was impressed once again by the enormity of the bombing but struck by the fact that few Japanese talked about it at that time. Hiroshima had not yet become a symbol of anti-Americanism or of the worldwide fight against the nuclear threat to mankind. Most Japanese were more conscious of their own experiences with American bombs in Tokyo and other cities. Probably more lives were lost to bombing in Tokyo alone than in Hiroshima, and death through the less bizarre effects of fire bombs was, if anything, more harrowing.

The trip to Japan came to its double crowning climax for our group with a pair of audiences—the word is suitable for both occasions—with the Emperor and MacArthur. The letter I wrote home describing the first of these could have served as well for the dozens of times I was to have audiences with the Emperor later as the Ambassador to Japan. He seemed nervous and fidgety, but dutifully asked each of us appropriate questions, while punctuating the conversation with "Ah, so?" ("Oh, is that so?"), spoken in a high, squeaky voice. At the same time, he exuded a warm sense of frankness and friendliness. He had been well briefed on me, knowing of my birth in Japan and my father's part in founding Tokyo Women's University, for which he expressed his appreciation. The five of us run-of-the-mill professors seemed very much at ease compared with his Imperial Majesty, but what could one expect of a man raised in the formality and seclusion that had always been his lot. After an unusually long audience of an hour, we were given the privilege of a tour of the palace grounds, including the Emperor's superb collection of *bonsai* trees, a treat that had been dropped from audiences when I returned as Ambassador twelve years later.

The meeting with MacArthur was in the form of a luncheon at the American Embassy Residence, where he lived. His protocol officer, a full colonel, took us there by limousine, timing our arrival carefully so that we would drive up to the entrance precisely at a minute before twelve. The conversation was lively, and I was surprised at MacArthur's quick wit. Most of the time, however, was taken up with long monologues on his part. If one of us tried to make a comment during one of these, Mrs. MacArthur would skillfully intercept the conversational ball and toss it back to her husband with the query, "What do you think, General?"

MacArthur was a grandiloquent, spell-binding speaker, given to grandiose overstatements. The Chinese Communists had just bypassed Mukden in Manchuria in their drive on Peking, and he was ready to write Chiang Kai-shek off completely. Fixing us with piercing eyes and holding his hands dramatically in front of him, he declaimed, "If I were in command of the Communist armies in China, my aim would be"—here came a long, dramatic pause—"the Indian Ocean." He certainly thought big, but he had overestimated the strength of the Communists and their immediate objectives. He was even further off in another prediction: his conviction that Christianity would sweep Japan. In my letters I quote him as saying to us, "A thousand years from now, when only a line in history books is devoted to this recent war, a whole paragraph will say that at this time the ideals of democracy and Christianity came to Japan from America to become the foundation of all future Japanese civilization." The success of democracy was indeed to be spectacular, but the number of Japanese Christians has remained around the 1 percent mark.

At three-thirty our allotted time was up. MacArthur majestically ascended the beautiful curving marble staircase to take his siesta, while we were quickly bundled off. Having reached the acme of any visit to Japan at that time, there was nothing left for our mission to do but write its report and return home. I got back to Cambridge by the end of January 1949, just in time for the second semester.

&

After I had returned to Harvard from Washington in 1946, the State Department continued its contacts with me, still regarding me as part of its team. It not only sent me young Foreign Officers to train, but called on me for consultations from time to time. It was also assumed that Borton and I would be delegates to the peace conference with Japan when that stage was reached.

I went down to the State Department periodically to suggest revisions in the drafts of the proposed peace treaty with Japan as it slowly took shape. I would go to and from Washington by sleeping car, the common mode of travel in those days, and would spend two or three days looking over the treaty drafts and furiously composing comments. The chief feature of those early postwar peace drafts, as I remember them, was their restrictive nature. Because they envisioned an early treaty and American military withdrawal from Japan, they included strict limitations on Japanese rearmament for a number of years. By the time the treaty was finally signed in 1951, this no longer seemed necessary, and world conditions had so changed that a continuing American military presence was required. Thus all of the earlier restrictions were missing from the final document.

While the American Occupation of Japan went very well, the situation around Japan changed for the worse. The Chinese Communists won out over the Nationalists in 1949; the North Koreans launched a sudden attack on the South in June 1950, involving the United States in a major war in Korea with the new Chinese regime; and the deepening cold war with the Soviet Union, which was largely over Europe, chilled all international relations. MacArthur had himself visualized a three-year Occupation of Japan, and I believe that this would have been about right, but it gradually became evident that Moscow and the new Communist rulers in Peking would not agree to terms for a Japanese peace treaty which the United States could accept. American attention was also swinging away from Japan to the bitter war with North Korea and China. Peace plans for Japan were put on the shelf.

In the course of these developments, I received in the early spring of 1950 a call from John Allison, then in charge of Japanese and all Far Eastern matters at the State Department, urging me to come down to Washington the next day, a Sunday, for an important meeting with the Secretary, Dean Acheson. On arrival, Allison informed me that there was a plan to give up on a peace treaty with Japan and to settle instead for some interim arrangement that would give full autonomy back to Japan but leave its sovereignty still subject to the Allied Powers, represented by the United States. I felt this would be psychologically quite unacceptable to the Japanese people and I made my opposition to this scheme perfectly clear. The only alternative was a peace treaty without Soviet and Chinese participation. Though fraught with problems, I thought that this would be far better than an ambiguous situation which would leave the United States as the occupying power and the object of increasing Japanese resentment.

I convinced Allison of my viewpoint, and the two of us then went in to see Acheson, stating our strong objections to the plan. Acheson was noncommittal but said that the matter would be reconsidered. The story ends here for me; I never learned exactly what happened, though there was never any public talk of a settlement less than a full peace treaty. I received no further phone calls from the State Department nor even a postcard. Instead, it was announced on April 6, 1950, that John Foster Dulles, the chief candidate for the position of Secretary of State in the Republican administration expected after the 1952 election, would take charge of preparing a peace treaty. This was only two months after Senator Joseph McCarthy had given a speech which started him on his irresponsible campaign against alleged Communists in government and anyone suspected of leftist leanings. Professors from Harvard had become an embarrassment to the State Department. In fact, I was the last member of the faculty among my acquaintances to maintain a close relationship with the Department, and I was therefore not surprised to be suddenly dropped and ignored for the next decade.

Dulles, with Allison as his chief assistant, went about negotiating on a bilateral basis the terms of a peace treaty with the various countries concerned. He got off to a quick start, visiting Japan and Korea a few days before the outbreak of the Korean War on June 25, just in time to be accused by the Communists of triggering the war. On September 8, 1951, the peace treaty was signed at San Francisco with neither Borton nor me present, and it went into effect on April 28, 1952, bringing the American Occupation to an end but not the American military bases. The Japanese at the time called it a one-sided peace treaty because of the failure of the Soviets and Chinese to sign it. For this reason there was great dissatisfaction with it in Japan, but I believe it was vastly preferable to the settlement short of a peace treaty which I had helped squelch two years earlier.

ঙ৹

Meanwhile Senator McCarthy was running rampant with his absurd accusations against supposed Communist sympathizers in the government who had "lost" China. Despite heroic efforts by General George C. Marshall as Secretary of State, great historic forces within China and the corruption and ineptness of Chiang Kai-shek's Nationalist government caused the "Mandate of Heaven" to pass from the Nationalists to Mao Zedong's Communists. Nothing the United States could have done would have changed this outcome, but Senator McCarthy and other unprincipled or uninformed men made the most of the Communist victory in China to attack the Democratic regime and seek out scapegoats.

Lightning struck all around me, but I was never myself a victim of McCarthyism, probably because I was associated primarily with American policy in Japan, and MacArthur, as the hero of conservative Republicans and the appointee of a Democratic regime, insulated Japan from heated political debate in the United States. As a result, few persons in Japanese studies were affected by these attacks, but those in the Chinese field were more exposed, and many of my close friends were severely hurt. My college classmate Jack Service, as I have mentioned, was among several Chinese specialists in the Foreign Service who had their careers ruined for having reported correctly on the collapsing fortunes of the Nationalists and the rising strength of the Communists. John Carter Vincent, who had been my boss at the State Department in 1945–46, was removed to innocuous posts in Switzerland and Tangier before being shunted off into early retirement.

A special case was my childhood tennis partner, E. Herbert Norman, then the Canadian Ambassador to Egypt, who was hounded into committing suicide. When I had seen Herb at Cambridge in 1935, I had envied the way he, as a British subject, could involve himself in English politics. At the time I understood that he was working for the Labour Party, but actually his affiliations were further to the left. At a conference on his life and accomplishments held in Halifax in Canada in October 1979, one of his friends from Cambridge days revealed quite casually that Herb had had the task of organizing the Asian students at Cambridge University for the Communist Party. While I was in Asia, he studied modern Japanese history at Columbia and Harvard, winning his Ph.D. degree at Harvard in 1940, the year after I did. His thesis, based on the work of Japanese Marxists, became a very influential book in the United States, and he had several other important publications. I admired Herb greatly, and for a while was strongly influenced by his interpretation of modern Japanese history. I saw him only once after our student days, however, when he was the chief Canadian representative in Japan and had me for lunch in the autumn of 1948 at the palatial Canadian Embassy in Tokyo. He had entered the Canadian Foreign Service, having been cleared several times by the Canadian authorities for his political activities at

Cambridge, but zealots in the American Senate would not leave him alone. His death was not only a great personal tragedy but a serious loss to Japanese studies, for he played an invaluable role as a link between Western scholarship and the heavily Marxist scholarship of postwar Japan—a point I brought out in my keynote speech at the Halifax Conference in 1979.

The stories of Norman, Service, and Vincent are all well known; Americans know less of the case of my old Harvard friend, Tsuru Shigeto. After playing a prominent role in the Socialist Party in Japan during the early postwar years, Tsuru was invited back to Harvard by the Department of Economics for a year as a visiting lecturer. During this time he was summoned to Washington for questioning by McCarthy's committee. He went down full of confidence that he would set straight various false charges about his activities during his student days in the 1930s, yet he fell instead into a typical McCarthy trap. The senator asked him if he knew a long list of alleged Communists. Tsuru did not know most of them and the rest only slightly. But McCarthy emerged from the hearings and, waving the list, announced to the eager but naïve Japanese press that, "in connection with the hearings of Professor Tsuru," his committee had a list of about a hundred Communists. The Japanese press swallowed the announcement hook, line, and sinker, and over the next several months virtually crucified Tsuru as a turncoat who had welched on his former leftist associates.

John Fairbank, who had spoken out boldly on political realities in China and had early seen the hopelessness of the Nationalist cause, was much harassed at this time. Eventually he insisted on a special hearing before Senator Pat McCarran's International Security Subcommittee, at which he cleared himself of all charges, but the wounds lingered on. The whole field of Chinese studies in the United States became deeply divided by the controversy over China policy, with a small group vigorously attacking most of the others for being what they felt had been "soft" or naive about the Chinese Communists. It took decades for the split to mend.

Despite my deep involvement in Japanese and Korean affairs, the only troubles I got into during the McCarthy period were over my much more restricted contacts with China policy. In October 1949, after the Communist triumph in China but before the outbreak of the Korean War, the State Department called a special meeting to consider what policy should be taken toward the new regime in Peking. I was invited to attend and was also asked to make a special presentation on the bearing of Japan on our Chinese relations. I was the only person outside government service asked to make such a presentation, since I was still regarded as part of the State Department team. I took the whole thing rather lightly, catching the usual night train down to Washington and turning up for the first meeting a few minutes late, only to find such notables as General Marshall already assembled around the table. I felt very small indeed, but performed my role and in the discussions suggested the coordination of our actions toward Peking with other large countries, such as India. My idea was that we could thereby kill two birds with one stone by strengthening our ties to India as well as making a decision on China. There were few professors in the group, but one, Kenneth W. Colegrove of Northwestern, saw fit later to denounce me as being pro-Communist because of my statements at this meeting.

My attitude during these years toward the People's Republic of China is probably best expressed in an article I find among my papers written some time after the Communist triumph but at a date and for a journal I have not been able to identify. It was called, probably at the publisher's request, "How Can the United States and Mainland China Coexist?" I started with the statement, "The most significant thing about this question perhaps is that anyone should ask it." Then I predicted an inevitable Sino-Soviet split, stating, "Perhaps a more meaningful question than the one we started with would be: 'How Can the Soviet Union and Mainland China Coexist?' " From the early 1950s on I would frequently point out in lectures that a sure source of trouble would be when the proud Chinese felt able to stand on their own feet and challenged the Soviet Union's claim to determine as it saw fit the verities of Communist dogma. As I put it, the Communist "religion" has no room for two popes, and the Chinese will not go on forever accepting the dictates of the Communist pope in the Kremlin. I favored moving toward American recognition of Peking in part to help bring about this inevitable Sino-Soviet split. At the same time, I sympathized strongly with the 85 percent of the people in Taiwan who were of native Taiwanese origin and longed for an independent nation of their own, free of both Communist and Nationalist domination. Taiwanese frequently sought my counsel, and I urged them then, as I still do, to go slowly in pressing their hopes, because time essentially was on their side and they eventually would fall heir to their own homeland. These ideas seemed radical at the time yet subsequently became widely accepted.

ᵉᔕ

Ostracism by the State Department after 1950 did not mean the end of my contacts with the government or other public activities. There was an increasing demand for my presence at conferences and as a public speaker. It was around this time that the National War College began to ask me down to Washington for an annual lecture on Japan. The College has a distinguished student body, mostly colonels and navy captains on their way to becoming generals and admirals, and the group always provided an intelligent and appreciative audience. I would present my views quite freely, even when they differed markedly from accepted American policy. I continued these annual lectures almost without interruption until 1975, by which time I had established the record of having lectured annually at the College longer than any other person.

During my 1948–49 trip to Japan I had discovered that I was becoming quite well known there, and after my return to the United States many requests for articles came from Japan. The most important articles I wrote in response were for the *Mainichi*, all of which were featured on the front page. Among other themes, I argued the need for Japan to overcome its mood of pessimism; suggested that Japan could be a leader in the development of Asia; and pointed out that Japanese democracy was uniquely its own and was the source of Japan's progress. At the time the Japanese were in need of encouragement; my articles were appreciated as offering them hope and a chance to regain some of their pride.

After John Foster Dulles was appointed Secretary of State early in 1953, I became increasingly disenchanted with American policy in Asia. I vented my disapproval through my speeches, but this did not seem enough, so I wrote a book in the summer of 1954, which was published by Knopf in January 1955. I gave it the dramatic title *Wanted: An Asian Policy*, since I felt that we did not have an overall policy consistent with basic American ideals and interests. The book has a strong cold war flavor, taking for granted the basic confrontation between the Soviet Union and the United States, but my chief point was that we were going about this confrontation in the wrong way, at least in Asia.

I shared the general feeling of the time that the United States was justified in the Korean War in repelling the blatant invasion by the North, and I still feel that way today. But I believed that Dulles was making a great mistake in trying to extend the stand we had taken in Korea to the whole of Asia. He seemed to see the world as split between Communist and non-Communist countries and the dividing line between the two as being like a dike which, if breached anywhere, would allow the flood waters of communism to inundate the whole free world. I argued in my book that the great bulk of Asians did not wish to be part of either the Soviet or American camps but desired only to be allowed to stay neutral and attend to their own problems. Dulles's assumption that all those who were not specifically on our side were against us, I felt, was a reversal of the true situation in which all those who were not specifically against us were really on our side as supporters of national freedom and self-determination.

I also pointed out that, in seeking to meet the Soviet menace, we had our priorities upside down. We placed the bulk of our effort on military defense, which in most of Asia was inevitably very feeble. SEATO (the Southeast Asian Treaty Organization) was a fraud fooling only the American people, because its only reality was the American commitment to the defense of a curious assortment of weak Southeast Asian states. CENTO (the Central Treaty Organization) was little better. Fortunately both organizations have long since been allowed to fade away. I specifically pointed out that we could not repeat what we had done in Korea to stem Communist aggression by military means in an area like Vietnam, or French Indo-China, as we still called it in those days. Ironically, it was exactly while I was writing this book that the United States started its unwise involvement in Vietnam by taking over the place of the withdrawing French and thus launching us on our road to catastrophe.

My chief argument in the book was that economic support for the countries of Asia and the championing of our own ideals of self-determination and national independence were far more important than alliances or military defense. Nationalism was a much greater force than communism or socialism or any other set of ideas from the West. We could rely on it to keep the countries of Asia free of control by either Moscow or Peking. We were selling nationalism short, I felt, and also the appeal of democracy. Back of all these problems, I maintained, was our dangerous ignorance of Asia. We desperately needed to know more about this half of the world so that we could pursue a wiser course in our relations with its diverse lands.

McCarthyism proved a temporary setback for American foreign policy, but our continuing ignorance of Asia and Dulles's concept of a worldwide division between Communist and "democratic" countries set the stage for disaster. Ten years later our appalling misinformation about the realities of Vietnam and Dulles's legacy of trying to maintain clear-cut defense lines in places where these were neither necessary nor possible had launched us on our unstoppable slide into the traumatic Vietnam War.

*Wanted: An Asian Policy,* despite favorable reviews, dropped into the pool of public opinion without raising a ripple. The nation, under Dulles's unwise leadership, was headed determinedly in the opposite direction. Of course, I have had the satisfaction of seeing us slowly change course since then, until three decades later American policy in Asia is much closer to what I advocated back in 1955. But this is small comfort in the face of the national tragedies and appalling waste mistaken policies have caused in the meantime. And there are signs today that we may follow the same mistaken course that led us to catastrophe in Vietnam in our policies toward Latin America and other less developed areas. We still need to put less faith in military defense and more in economic aid and the support of self-determination and democracy.

With Adrienne and family in 1947: Ann (left), Bobby and Joan.

Welcomed with a bowl of soba, well known in Japan as one of his favorites, during the Cultural Science Mission, 1948.

With a Korean monk, 1955, holding thirteenth-century woodblocks used for printing Buddhist scriptures. *(U.S. Army Photo)*

At two-way discussion for publication with Prince Mikasa (second from right), 1956.

With Haru, Ann and Joan at wedding reception given by Tokyo Women's University, February 1956. Maeda Yoichi in left rear.

With Haru Matsukata, Bobby, Ann and Joan on a ski trip to Mt. Akakura, Christmas 1955.

Where it all began: writing "The Broken Dialogue" for *Foreign Affairs* at Misaki, 1960.

John King Fairbank, 1959.

# 21
# Family Matters

Iɴ 1946, when our family of five moved back to Cambridge from Washington, I found a large old house for us, which we shared with another family. It stood at the northern end of Divinity Avenue, named for the former site of the School of Theology. Ample lawns, big trees, and an informal, little used parking lot made this an island of tranquility, lying between the university and the crowded streets of Cambridge. Our house was a mid-nineteenth-century Gothic wonder, with gingerbread decorations and impressive folding indoor shutters. It had a vaguely cathedral-like layout, with the entrance way forming the apse. Once the residence of the university president, it had stood in the Harvard Yard but since then had been moved repeatedly. In the process its joints had loosened considerably, and it leaked heat like a sieve. It was connected to the university heating system, and even in those days of cheap fuel we paid more for our heat than our rent.

We shared the house first with the William G. Perrys and then with Bob Hightower and his family. The dividing line ran rather vaguely down the front and back hallways. This sharing of a not clearly divided house with another family might seem a formula for internecine strife, but nothing like that ever occurred. The children were almost like siblings, and our contacts with both families remained warm even after we had moved miles apart.

A house next door was occupied by Myron Gilmore, a professor of Renaissance history, his gregarious wife Sheila, and four children. Arthur Schlesinger, Jr., of the History Department, who was married to Wilma Fairbank's younger sister, lived nearby. Their children and those of the two houses on Divinity Avenue were mostly of similar age and tended to form a sort of gang. I spent a good deal of my spare time playing with them. My son Bobby, with a liberal touch of imagination and the hyperbole that makes him an amusing conversationalist today, captured something of the spirit of those days in a schoolboy essay which he called " 'Mr. Reischauer' and 'the Gang.' " Since it is, as far as I know, the only contemporary biographic piece on me, I hope I will be forgiven for quoting it in part:

"Mr. Reischauer" has been considered as "one of the gang" for as long, as I can remember. . . .

Probably the most famous of his accomplishments was the parking-lot baseball league. . . . "Mr. Reischauer," exercising his incredible judgment, would divide the odd assortment of athletes, who had gathered under the shady elms of Divinity Avenue, into two equal teams. . . . On the mound serving as umpire and pitcher for both teams was "Mr. Reischauer." The whirling sphere, a tennis ball, crossed the plate according to the batter's ability and temperament. . . . Miraculously enough almost all the games ended in a dead tie or a one run victory.

Another escapade which only "Mr. Reischauer" among the adults dared to undertake was the trips to the beach. Many times during the hot New England summer the aging "Reischauer-mobile" was crammed with throngs of tanned, swim-suit clad children, heaps of beach equipment, and picnic lunches. The hour trip to the beach always passed quickly as "Mr. Reischauer" had a bagful of games and songs which could be played and sung in the car. After an exhausting day of hikes, games, and swims, all led by our chauffeur, we were herded back to the car and then home, to be deposited happy but weary on our thankful parents' thresholds.

When I look back on my youth . . . I . . . find it hard to tell whether "Mr. Reischauer" or we enjoyed our childhood more; but one thing's for certain —we shared it.

From 1950 to 1953 we spent a month each summer at Truro on Cape Cod. Truro, which is near the end of the Cape, is by far the least crowded and most unspoiled part of that lovely area, and the house we rented from a friend was comfortable and secluded. The town consisted of a post office and a store or two, with two churches some distance away. We would attend the Saturday night town square dance, where I would usually dance with our eldest daughter, Ann. (Adrienne, who was a superb dancer, was too ill by then to participate.) Sunday mornings the town softball team would play a game: as the newest member, I was given the least desirable position of catcher.

The Divinity Avenue period of our lives ended in April 1952. The university had decided to tear down our house, and in any case we faced a problem of schooling as Ann and Bobby moved from grade school to junior high. The local Agassiz School had been all right for the early years, but at the higher levels the Cambridge school system left much to be desired. The solution to the problem was to move to Belmont, the next town to the west from Cambridge and reputed at the time to have a fine public school system. Being the closest suburban area to Cambridge, it was also full of professors from Harvard and MIT. As a result, it boasted the highest per capita ratio of Nobel Laureates and people listed in *Who's Who.* I have often wondered how many other towns make this claim. But I do recall playing a game of doubles at our local tennis club a few years ago and realizing that I was the only one of the four who was not a Nobel Laureate.

The move to Belmont was complicated by the fact that my father was retiring that summer, just short of the age of seventy-three, after several years of teaching a course on world religions at Union Theological Seminary in New York, and he and my mother and sister wished to live somewhere near us. Since none of them drove, I found a nice two-family house for them near public transportation and within a five-minute walk of a simple single-family house I bought for us at 3 Long Avenue.

⋖⋗

By this time clouds were looming on the family horizon. My own health had not been robust for some time, so that I had almost annual bouts with influenza, viral pneumonia, and the like. Worse, I was knocked out about once a month by terrible migraine headaches. These had started when I was studying in Japan and had become progressively more frequent, reaching a crescendo around 1950. I would be laid low in complete misery for a couple of days, unable to eat or tolerate any light. The doctors prescribed abstinence from chocolate and various other foods and steady doses of thyroid pills for a supposed hypo-thyroid condition. None of these treatments had the slightest effect. Mr. Elisséeff had the comforting advice that he too had suffered similar migraine headaches at about the same age but that they had simply gone away in time. He proved to be right. They gradually tapered off around 1960, with one final brief attack in the spring of 1966. Since then I have not had a headache of any sort.

Adrienne's physical condition was much more serious. She had contracted a severe case of diphtheria as a teenager in China, which had affected her heart. She was never very strong physically and had had a very hard time with Joan's birth. But a much more critical blow struck suddenly in January 1951. While at the luncheon table one day, Adrienne suddenly keeled over, to the terror of the children. Her heart had stopped beating and, though it soon started up again, she was miserable for several days. She had developed a heart block, which meant that her heart was cut off at times from the rest of her nervous system, not responding to exertion and leaving her out of breath even when she simply walked upstairs.

Her condition remained poor. A second complete stoppage of the heart occurred about six months later; thereafter they became gradually more frequent. I accidentally discovered that I could get her heart going again by giving it a good thump. Over the next few years I revived her in this way probably close to a hundred times. Each attack left her semi-dazed for several hours and in great distress for two or three days. The doctors hospitalized her repeatedly but could do nothing for her. A pacemaker, which had already been developed in the laboratories at that time but had not yet come into general use, could have cleared up her problem easily, but neither we nor the doctors knew of this possibility.

As her attacks grew more frequent, it became increasingly hazardous to leave her alone. We canceled our 1954 stay at Truro because it was too dangerous to be that far away from doctors and hospitals. Gradually my life became focused almost completely on trying to keep Adrienne alive. I went to Harvard as briefly as possible to teach my classes and attend to other necessary business but spent most of my time working on my books at the dining room table at home. The children had to look out for themselves, because I could not drive them around or pay much attention to their activities. A series of helpers cleaned the house. Toward the end a Mrs. Leonard gave us more time, doing most of the cooking and watching over Adrienne when I had to be out of the house. I did the rest of the cooking in a slapdash manner—largely rice and a nondescript mixture of vegetables and meat in a vaguely Chinese style—and I became a whirlwind shopper.

These were grim years, as I kept one ear cocked all day long for some unusual sound from Adrienne and even at night was always conscious of the sound of her breathing. But they were also wonderful years that brought the two of us very close together. She remained marvelously cheerful to the end. In every hospital where she was placed, she almost immediately became the center of life on the whole floor. At home our children and their friends would gather almost nightly to play cards with the two of us on our bed.

But the inevitable finally happened. On January 17, 1955, while I was at Harvard, her heart stopped permanently. Her attacks had increased greatly, and her suffering was such that even she admitted that life seemed hardly worthwhile. Her death therefore was not unexpected, but the shock was nonetheless numbing. The children and I carried on as best we could. The next day we held a forlorn party with a cake and candles for Bobby's fourteenth birthday. I continued my work at Harvard, and Mrs. Leonard looked after the house. I have often heard of people at times like this throwing themselves into their work with renewed vigor, but I felt as though my whole internal wiring system had been burned out That is the only way I can describe it. I continued doing my routine work, but had no drive to do anything new. Adrienne's death had ironically come in the very month that saw the simultaneous appearance of three of my books—the two Ennin volumes and *Wanted: An Asian Policy*—yet I had no heart for research or writing and stopped work on a new book I had just begun.

❧

Shortly after Adrienne's death another major change came in my life. Donham, the chairman of the board of trustees of the Harvard Yenching Institute, died, and his successor, a conscientious and high-minded Boston businessman named Gregg Bemis, decided that the time had come for a change of leadership at the Institute, particularly since Elisséeff was nearing retirement. I was chosen to be the new director. This is the only job I remember ever having aspired to in my whole life—not because of the power it brought with it, though that was considerable at the time since the Institute was then the chief funding source for East Asian studies at Harvard, but simply because I did not wish to be placed under the control of any of the other people who might have been considered for the position. I explained to Bemis, however, that I was not ready to take the position just then. I was too drained of energy, and I felt the need to revisit East Asia again, having been virtually immobilized by Adrienne's illness since shortly after my trip to Japan in 1948–49. It was agreed that I should take a leave of absence to go out to East Asia and on my return should then assume the directorship.

The three children and I got off in June, starting with a grand tour of the United States in Adrienne's father's car. It was the sort of trip that every American should take at least once in his life, and we all thoroughly enjoyed it, though the fact that I was the only driver and only adult made the control of three bickering teenagers quite a problem.

It was a great pleasure when we reached Japan to find that the country was incomparably more prosperous than it had been when I last saw it in 1948–49. Knowing that I would have to be away for long periods on Harvard Yenching business, I had arranged to rent our old home on the campus of Tokyo Women's University so that the children would be in a safe environment. The outside bronze ornamentations of the house, confiscated during the war, were still missing, and the garden my mother had devoted much attention to had gone to ruin. The house, which was being used as a guest house by the school, was austerely furnished, and its reinforced concrete construction made it bleak and chilly, since the school heating was only on from December through February. But all in all, it was a good place for the children to be, and I felt reassured to have them surrounded by old family friends.

On arriving in Tokyo at the beginning of August, I started in at once teaching a three-week special seminar that was held at the International Christian University. For the fall, I got the three children into The American School, then located at Kami-Meguro, about an hour away by bus and two commuting railways. The children adjusted with enthusiasm to their new life and the strange surroundings, taking in stride the long daily commuting and the problems of a foreign language. They all picked up some Japanese, although Joan, as the youngest, learned the most.

I managed much less well than they, though I did have a lot of friends in Tokyo, both Japanese and American, who were very kind to me. My old colleague from the State Department, John Allison, was then the American Ambassador to Japan, and he invited me to the Embassy Residence for a small dinner with Eleanor Roosevelt, thus giving me a chance to meet and talk at length with that wonderful person. I bought a lot of scholarly Japanese books and read them, but still felt completely burned out inside and unable to do any constructive scholarship. I had offered my services to Tokyo Women's University to hold a weekly seminar for faculty members. I used the foreign policy ideas of my *Wanted: An Asian Policy,* but the subject was not very suitable, and I suspect that the few who attended did so mostly out of loyalty to the family.

I was both emotionally and physically run down and would have been completely lost without the support and counsel of Kuwabara Motoko, our housekeeper. Motoko had joined our family as the second maid just before Adrienne and I passed through Japan on our way back to the United States from China in 1937, and she had stayed on at the house ever since. A wing had been added in which she lived with her two sons and husband, a worker in a small factory. My children tutored the two boys in English, but Motoko counseled me on life, being a fount of common sense. We would talk together by the hour, and I do not know what I would have done without her those first few months. When we left Japan the next summer I gave her a small amount of money, which she wisely put into land rather than the stocks I suggested. With the rapid increase in real estate prices, this nest egg grew into a sum with which Motoko and her husband in time built their own home; they eventually saw their boys through college and into suitable marriages. Their story is that of most Japanese who, during these years of rapid economic growth, passed into the middle class in which 90 percent now claim membership.

During the autumn I went to Korea and then to Hong Kong and Taiwan to familiarize myself with the universities with which the Harvard Yenching Institute was connected. The rumor of my impending directorship had leaked out, and I was accordingly wined and dined to the point of gustatory exhaustion. In Korea I gave speeches at most of the leading universities in the Seoul area and developed a close friendship with Yu Chin-o, the prestigious president of Korea University and a prominent liberal figure in Korean politics, as well as with Kim Che-won, the director of the Seoul National Museum, who during the Korean War managed through subterfuge to keep its treasures in Seoul despite the efforts of the Communists to remove them to the North.

In Hong Kong I stayed at the sober but beautifully placed "lodge" of the vice chancellor of the University of Hong Kong. He was a former British brigadier and, according to the British system, the actual head of the university. I spent most of my time, however, visiting the various Chinese-language universities— New Asia College and the two Christian institutions, United College and

Chongji (Chung-chi) College—seeing the latter's proposed new campus on the mainland north of the built-up parts of the city, where these three institutions subsequently merged in 1963 as the Chinese University of Hong Kong.

During my trip to Taiwan I visited and spoke at some of the leading universities. In talking to student bodies I could estimate the number of native Taiwanese, as opposed to recently arrived continental Chinese, by slipping in occasional phrases in Japanese, to which about half of the audience would respond with titters because Japanese was then still well remembered by the native Taiwanese. In riding taxis, I would always try out some Japanese on the driver. If he responded, I knew he was a Taiwanese, and was usually treated to a diatribe against the Nationalist government and sometimes even some nostalgic references to Japanese rule, which in retrospect did not seem so bad when compared to current Nationalist oppression.

I returned from Taiwan to find that Bobby had been kicked out of The American School because he had refused to welch on a friend who had stolen a watch. I got him reinstated, but he was having a hard year. For one thing, he had difficulty in keeping up his favorite sport—ice hockey—of which there was little in Tokyo at the time; the best he could do was work out occasionally in the middle of the night with the Keio University team. At times I felt that the whole family was just hanging on by its fingernails.

# 22

# A Fresh Beginning

M Y YEAR in East Asia was not proving very restful, and my internal batteries were not recharging the way I had hoped. But just when things looked blackest, my life took a sudden turn for the better. I began to go out seriously with Haru Matsukata, my present wife. I knew something of her family and had often wondered how the descendants of Prince Matsukata Masayoshi, one of the *genro*, or founding fathers of modern Japan, had become Christian Scientists, but I was unaware of Haru herself until I met her in August 1955 at the Foreign Correspondents Club in Tokyo. I was lunching with a newspaperman friend, who, upon seeing James Michener at a nearby table, asked me if I knew him. Since I did not, he took me over to introduce me, and the lady Jim Michener was dining with stood up and said, "I'm Haru Matsukata, and I remember you from The American School." She had been a sixth grader when I was a senior in high school and therefore knew me as the captain of the basketball team, though I had no remembrance of small fry like her.

I had hoped all along to get married again. Having had a happy marriage, I found being alone quite intolerable. During her fading years Adrienne expected me to remarry and would frequently question me as to what type of person I would choose, though neither of us happened to think of a Japanese as a possibility for the second Mrs. Reischauer. But Haru and I shared a mixed Japanese and American heritage and a devotion to friendship between our two countries. Except for her far wealthier and more aristocratic background, she was for me much like the girl next door.

Haru's paternal grandfather, as the Finance Minister for fifteen years, had been the creator of Japan's financial stability, and he had served twice as Prime Minister in the 1890s. Her maternal grandfather had gone to the United States at the age of twenty in 1876 and had become the leading figure in developing the silk trade with the United States, which was for long Japan's chief source of foreign exchange. She has told their fascinating stories in her own book, *Samurai and Silk* (1986). Her mother was raised in New York and Connecticut as an American and had brought up her six children to be more American in spirit and education than Japanese. Haru had graduated from The American School in Japan and Principia College, a Christian Science school in Illinois near St. Louis. She returned to Japan in 1937, full of hopes to further Japanese-American understanding, just in time to see her dreams shattered by the outbreak of the Sino-Japanese War and the swift descent of Japan into an all-out conflict with the United States. Since the war's end, she had worked as an assistant to correspondents for the *Christian Science Monitor* and *The Saturday Evening Post.* As a result she became the first Japanese member of the Foreign Correspondents Club and then, as its secretary, its first woman officer.

Haru had always felt that she could never marry a Japanese man because of the prevalent male chauvinism in Japan, but she also found American men distressingly ignorant about Japanese matters. In me she seemed to find someone who escaped both drawbacks. Neither of us had the slightest sense of being of different nationality or race. My father would often ask me confidentially if we did not encounter embarrassing situations, but I could honestly assure him that none had ever arisen. Our racial difference, which must have been all too obvious to anyone else, never entered our minds, except when we jokingly reminded each other of it.

Haru and I did not start seeing each other seriously until after I returned from my trip to Hong Kong and Taiwan. One evening I remarked tentatively, "I hope you haven't ruled out completely the possibility of marriage," and she replied rather fiercely, "I wouldn't want to see you again if we weren't going to get married." She had had her fill of American friends, both men and women, who came to Tokyo for two or three years and then moved on.

On returning from a Christmas ski trip with the children to Mt. Akakura, we were married as soon as the Japanese marriage license bureau opened after the New Year's Holiday. This was on January 6, 1956. I wished to keep the matter secret until after the first anniversary of Adrienne's death, because I feared that some of Adrienne's friends and relatives might feel I had acted with unseemly haste. John Allison, as the American Ambassador, helped make this secrecy possible, but we did tell the missionary ladies living next door so that we would not shock them by seeming to be living in sin. The marriage, like my first one with Adrienne, was an unromantic official transaction conducted in a downtown ward office, and again the clerk offered no congratulations but simply asked for the official fee. Then, on February 4, we had a small wedding ceremony attended only by our two families and a few close friends, including our housekeeper Motoko-san, who had been enthusiastic for the match from the start.

Marriages between Japanese and Americans were still rather rare in those days and frowned upon by many in both societies. Mixed couples were commonly scorned because they frequently consisted of an ill-educated American soldier and a Japanese girl of humble background and dubious profession. Since I was somewhat in the public eye and Haru of distinguished descent, we both felt that we owed it to all the other mixed couples to ensure that our marriage be a success. The Japanese papers did make quite a bit of it. I remember one account sentimentally describing us as sitting side by side at our desks in school, even though I had been identified a few lines above as five years older than Haru. It made me sound like a very retarded student indeed.

At the time of our marriage, I was an exhausted widower of forty-five with three teenage children, long neglected because of Adrienne's illness and getting progressively more out of hand. Haru was a forty-year-old spinster, as they would have called her in an earlier day. It might sound like a marriage of convenience, but it most certainly was not. We were deeply in love with each other, and Haru proved to be a wonderful wife, much like Adrienne in some ways, but very different in others. She has Adrienne's great thoughtfulness for others and good sense, but none of her effervescence and demonstrativeness. In a typically Japanese way, she is not given to any outward show of affection, and even today she has not learned to call me to my face anything but "you." She did, however, give me tremendous support, especially during the early months of our marriage when I continued to be below par both physically and psychologically and was in desperate need of help.

Haru also proved to be a wonderful mother, deeply loved by all three children, and in time by their children as well. It is she rather than I who is the center of our family. The children took to her at once. Ann, who has always had a taste for the unusual, was simply delighted to have a Japanese mother, and Joan was happy to have a mother of any sort. Bobby was more of a problem. Because he had been closest to Adrienne, he at first seemed to resent my marrying again, but he took out his feelings on me and always treated Haru herself with respect and kindness. And eventually his animosity toward me faded away completely.

All of us wished Haru to be the real mother of the children, not just their stepmother, so after we returned to the United States, we corrected the situation in a way that is unique as far as I know. I put the three children up for adoption, and then Haru and I adopted them. It was all done in a brief court hearing. The five of us put on our best clothes and sat on the front bench in the courtroom, while our lawyer conferred in whispers with the judge. He signed the necessary documents but to our disappointment never even glanced up to see the family going through this strange procedure. But the law was satisfied and all three children now have two birth certificates, one listing Adrienne as their mother by birth and the other Haru. Some future historian could become very confused over this conflicting documentation.

❦

Haru had a little house, part Western and part Japanese in style, located near the center of the city in the Azabu area right beside her childhood home. It was a pretty, snug little place and served as a convenient office for us in town. She also had a tiny Fiat, but it was much too small to accommodate the five of us, so she traded it in one day for a Toyopet, the current popular Toyota model. Since I had to provide the money, I had to explain to her that married couples did not enter into such financial transactions without consulting with each other first. But her purchase proved a wise decision. Though I must have been one of the first Americans even in Japan to buy a Japanese car, it proved serviceable and made possible a family trip to Kyoto by way of the miserable roads of the time.

While I did not accomplish much in the field of scholarship during my year in Japan, I did keep myself relatively busy. I gave innumerable lectures and also did a lot of conferring with Haru's older, very distinguished cousin, Matsumoto Shigeharu, on preparatory work for the founding of an English Language Educational Council (ELEC) and the further development of the newly established International House of Japan, of which he was director. Both were undertakings of particular interest to John D. Rockefeller, III, and it was largely in his behalf that I was acting. He had long been interested in Japan and had served as Dulles's assistant on cultural matters in negotiating the peace treaty. Subsequently he had become the president of the Japan Society in New York. Since both our names started with R, we often found ourselves seated beside each other at conferences and became in time quite close friends. He frequently consulted with me about the Japan Society and had me join its board of directors in March 1952. In return I later persuaded him to become a trustee of the Harvard Yenching Institute for a while. Although Rockefeller did not come out to Japan the year I was there, I met often on ELEC and International House matters with Matsumoto and also with Dr. Takagi Yasaka, the refined and gentlemanly scholar who had served as the first professor of American constitutional law at Tokyo University.

Prince Mikasa, the Emperor's youngest brother, happened to be an instructor in ancient Hebrew history at Tokyo Women's University, where he was extremely popular because of his unpretentious ways, eating noodles at lunchtime in the cafeteria with the other professors. We became good friends, and the university arranged a published discussion between us on scholarly matters. The Prince also invited Haru and me to his home for a family supper. We were surprised at the modesty of the middle-class Japanese-style home near Meguro where he lived and were charmed to hear the children racketing around in the next room and to have them ushered in to meet us. They were like any other family in Japan or America.

One sad incident during the spring was the death of my mother. She had started to fail mentally just when she moved up to Belmont in 1952, probably suffering from a series of small strokes. She had become able to do little more than smile, but I had taken her as well as my father and sister each week for a drive out into the country, which she seemed to enjoy. She died on March 22, just short of her seventy-seventh birthday. The Tokyo Women's University held a big memorial service, which the five of us attended in the frigid but beautiful chapel of which my father was so proud.

Our year in Japan came to an end on June 1. We sailed from Kobe on board the *Sado Maru*, a spotless new 10,000-ton freighter on its maiden voyage. Haru was coming to America as an immigrant, which permitted her to take a great deal of baggage, of which she had plenty, and also, according to the regulations, a yoke of oxen, apparently to meet the frontier conditions that had faced my paternal great-grandfather more than a century earlier.

The *Sado Maru* was bound on a fifty-three-day trip to Rotterdam. We feared that it might prove tedious, but it turned out to be a delightful delayed honeymoon *à cinque*. We all reveled in having the run of what might as well have been our own 10,000-ton private yacht. A freighter is limited by law to twelve passengers; sometimes we were the only ones on board. Haru and I both had much writing and reading to do, and we all felt some regret when our peaceful days at sea were broken by occasional stops along the way at ports in Asia, North Africa, and Europe. In Rotterdam we rented a car for a crowded sightseeing tour through Belgium, France, Italy, Austria, and West Germany. Then we sailed by a one-class liner for home. This was to prove my last trip by ship—that best and most civilized of ways to travel—and I was glad the children got a taste of it before it disappeared for good. We landed in New York, happy to be safely back, but a new life lay ahead of us—for Haru as a mother and housekeeper, for me as the director of the Harvard Yenching Institute.

# 23

# Director of the Harvard Yenching Institute

Haru was greeted with open arms by my father and sister and warmly welcomed by my colleagues and friends. Adrienne's father drove east from the west coast to spend some time with us, apparently finding his daughter's successor entirely satisfactory. She herself made a surprisingly quick and smooth adjustment to her new life in the United States, and the children too fitted back easily into life in Belmont. On May 5, the Boys' Festival day in Japan, they raised a tall pole in our yard and flew three large paper carp from it, representing both sexes, not just boys as is the custom in Japan. This was probably the first time the *koi-nobori* ("ascending carp") had ever been seen in Belmont.

My own adjustment was more difficult because I still was physically below par and faced some unpleasant problems in taking charge of the Institute. I suffered from what was called a wandering pace maker. This meant that my heart beat irregularly, producing extra beats that would break up my flow of words—a very disconcerting experience when presiding at an important meeting. The problems at the Institute were serious though not new. The original focus of its work had been on China, but since the war this emphasis had become impossible because of the rupture of relations between China and the United States. Meanwhile the bulk of the Institute's income was being diverted to Harvard. Since this was not the intention of Mr. Hall, whose will had provided the money, the Institute was getting on thin legal ice, as had been pointed out repeatedly by its lawyer and even more vigorously by Eric North, the vice-chairman of the board of trustees, who represented the interests of the original mission schools in China with which the Institute had been connected. Although a good deal of the money was being spent for fellowships, the bulk of which went to East Asians, this did not contribute much direct aid to education in Asia, since most of the students did not return home.

The problem had become clear in the early 1950s, and I had started measures to meet it. By that time Elisséeff, who disliked administrative work even more than I, had gotten into the habit of relying on me in such matters and would sometimes bring me with him to the meetings of the Institute's trustees. I had proposed the creation of Research Councils in Japan, Korea, and jointly in Taiwan and Hong Kong for the stimulation and support of research activities in those areas, and these Councils were operating successfully by the time I went to East Asia in 1955. I had also proposed the creation of a Visiting Scholars Program at Harvard, which would provide sabbatical years of study there for a few young but already established scholars in the humanities and social sciences from certain specified universities in East Asia. As the professors had jobs and usually families awaiting them back home, there was no problem about their returning to Asia. This program had been put into operation under the direction of John Pelzel, half of whose tenured salary in the Department of Anthropology was assumed by the Institute. The Research Councils were later phased out as the countries of East Asia became economically strong enough to bear the costs themselves, but the Visiting Scholars Program is still a flourishing part of the Institute's activities, with scholars from the People's Republic now forming a large part of the total. It has been interesting to see over the years how the Japanese were the first to bring their families with them, then the Koreans, and finally the Taiwanese; but the mainland Chinese still come alone.

These two programs had restored the balance somewhat between funds being spent in Asia or for Asians returning to Asia and those funneling into Harvard's coffers. But they were not enough, and a clear line had to be drawn between the Institute and Harvard. A limit had to be placed on the Institute's funding of new teaching positions at Harvard and its support for the Chinese-Japanese Library, which mainly benefited Harvard and like all libraries had an insatiable financial appetite. Drastic cuts in some of the Institute's other activities at Harvard also had to be made.

The chief of these cuts involved the Chinese dictionary project. Ware and Elisséeff had dreamed up the idea of having a large number of standard Chinese classical dictionaries and reference works cut up in China and each slip pasted on a separate large card so that all known lexicographical references to a Chinese character could be assembled together. These were to be worked on, character by character, by individual scholars, who would make translations into English, and the results were to be made into a huge multivolume dictionary. During the disturbed times following the war, the project had become a sort of relief program for refugee Chinese scholars; but despite the expenditure of sizable funds, the results were pitifully meagre. A fascicle on a single character, *zi,* which among other meanings is the word for "child," was brought out as an example, but from its size and cost it was clear that more than the whole income of the Institute would be swallowed up by the project and it would take centuries to complete at the current rate of progress. I had to be the hatchet man to put an end to the whole undertaking.

This and other budget reductions naturally brought howls of pain. The whole experience was almost as distressing for me as for those directly affected. When I went for counsel to McGeorge ("Mac") Bundy, the brilliant young dean of the Faculty of Arts and Sciences and one of the Institute's trustees, he offered me little solace. As hard as he was brilliant—a sort of diamond of a man—Mac simply quoted President Truman's famous statement, "If you can't stand the heat, get out of the kitchen."

I slowly got control of the Institute's problems, working out a loose understanding on what proportion of its revenues would go to Harvard in return for the use of Harvard's facilities and name. I also made it quite clear that the Department of Far Eastern Languages, despite its funding by the Institute, was a regular department of the university and not just an extension of the Institute, though I remained head of both. Pelzel, my successor as director, later made the relationship between Harvard and the Institute a clear legal and financial agreement.

Despite my program of restricting the Institute's financial role at Harvard, there were some areas in which I expanded it. I had a particular interest in developing East Asian studies in other parts of Asia, because I felt that the countries of South and Southeast Asia had much to learn from Japan and China. But these countries showed scant interest in either. The only significant exception was in Indonesia, where Lie Tek Tjeng, an Indonesian of Chinese ancestry specializing in modern Japanese studies at Harvard, became an influential person in Indonesian scholarly and diplomatic life.

My most important innovation was establishing Korean studies at Harvard. Since Korea lay between China and Japan and had historically strong ties with both, I had felt for some time that it should be included in our field of activity. Korea represented the closest variant to the classical Chinese pattern of government and society, and had close cultural ties with Japan in early times. Like Japan, it had a national history dating back to the seventh century, and its population was almost equal to one of the traditional great powers of Western Europe. Although the recent Korean War, as well as the earlier Sino-Japanese and Russo-Japanese wars over Korea, showed its strategic importance, it was unfortunately not big enough to attract study in the West the way China, Japan, or India had. America, because of its lack of national universities and research institutes such as are to be found in most advanced modern nations, is poorly equipped to study the less prominent parts of the world. Individual state or private universities do not feel that they have the funds or responsibility for such academic "frills."

I had agitated for several years for the inclusion of Korean studies in our work at Harvard, arguing that we were the perfect place for such studies because of our strength in the Chinese and Japanese fields. It is not easy to convince scholars to specialize in an area like Korea, which requires complete mastery of three very difficult languages—Chinese and Japanese in addition to Korean—and offers job prospects that are extremely dubious. However, I helped persuade Edward Wagner to enter the field, and finally in January 1958 got the Rockefeller Foundation to divide the funding of a chair of Korean studies at Harvard with the Institute. The cost then was $400,000 per chair, not the current $1 million. Ed Wagner, who had completed his Ph.D., took up his teaching duties that autumn. Language assistants were later added, and the Koreans themselves eventually funded a second professorship.

The later effort to add Vietnamese studies at Harvard had a more difficult course. Since Vietnam is also an offshoot of the Chinese political and cultural system, the reasons for having Vietnamese studies at Harvard are much the same as for Korea. John Fairbank took the lead in assembling funds for a chair from outside sources, but when this had been done, no suitable person could be found to fill the post on a permanent basis.

On my return to Harvard, I had also found myself facing the need to find a new home for the Harvard Yenching Institute. Boylston Hall, though housing a priceless Chinese library, including scores of printed works antedating the Gutenberg Bible by centuries, was at that time a virtual fire trap. Eventually we were able to exchange our space there for the first floor and basements at 2 Divinity Avenue, the handsome former home of the Department of Geography. By renovating the basements and first floor and adding a four-floor wing, of which three floors were occupied by additional library stacks, we acquired a convenient, clean, and fireproof home for the Institute, its library, and the Department of Far Eastern Languages. We moved into our new quarters in September 1958, and took over the remainder of the space in the building in 1973.

During my directorship of the Institute, my chief focus of interest remained my teaching and writing. I was quite sure where my priorities lay. When Erwin Griswold, the dean of the Harvard Law School and chairman of the board of trustees at Oberlin, who was an old friend, called up one evening to ask me if I would be willing to be a candidate for the presidency at Oberlin, I gave him an unambiguously negative answer without a moment's hesitation. A college presidency was the sort of diffuse administrative job that did not interest me in the slightest. Oberlin, however, did give me my first honorary degree at this time. The college customarily awarded an honorary degree each year to a member of the twenty-fifth reunion class, but since I was on the opposite side of the globe at the time of my reunion in 1956, it postponed the honor until June 1957.

My chief writing during these years was on the textbook Fairbank and I had long planned for the Rice Paddies course. I threw myself into this work with great enthusiasm in the autumn of 1956, and it finally appeared as two large, well-illustrated volumes published by Houghton Mifflin that totaled more than 1,800 pages: *East Asia: The Great Tradition* in 1960, and *East Asia: The Modern Transformation* in 1965. The volumes were divided around the end of the eighteenth century, corresponding to the two halves of the course. I covered China up until 1279, Korea through the eighteenth century, and Japan through the nineteenth. John handled Vietnam, Central Asia, modern Korea, and all of China after 1279. Twentieth-century Japan I had to leave to Albert Craig to do in my place because of my sudden departure for the ambassadorship in Tokyo. The work was closely collaborative throughout. John and I made liberal comments and corrections on the sections the other had written, even redrafting whole paragraphs and making fundamental suggestions for reorganization, and I did the same on the period of Japanese history Craig covered.

Writing a textbook may sound like a very pedestrian thing to do, but it was an exciting undertaking. Although the history of Japan was reasonably well analyzed by modern historians, and I had started making my own interpretation of it in *Japan: Past and Present* more than a decade earlier, there were no well-rounded histories in Western languages for China, Korea, and Vietnam, and no attempts at all to knit the historical experiences of the four countries together. The Japanese sections were actually the least interesting for me, because they could be based on a broad literature of modern historical writing and only required an expansion of writing I had already done. China and Korea, however, were virtually *terra incognita*.

For Korea, there were traditional histories in Western languages concerning dynasties, kings, and court politics, but no account of a developing nation. I relied heavily for my general interpretations on a small book on Korean history in Japanese written by a modern Japanese historian, Hatada Takashi. For China, the standard work in English then was a massive tome by Kenneth Scott Latourette, yet it too was a traditional account, which made the history of each dynasty sound like a repetition of the preceding one and told little about institutional, social, economic, philosophic, or cultural developments. Other works usually stressed one aspect of Chinese history or one period, giving a very partial or distorted view of the whole. None of these works, it seemed to me, presented a comprehensive account of the flow of Chinese history, which would make it clear how China developed and changed over time while holding on to certain strong cultural traits. It was a great challenge to try to put the mass of detail we knew about China's past into trends and patterns that made sense.

The writing of the *East Asia* books proved a most satisfying undertaking and marked the high point in my studies of China and Korea. It also helped establish the use of the term "East Asia" in place of "Far East." Even the old Far Eastern section of the State Department is now known as the Bureau of East Asian and Pacific Affairs. Still more important, our textbooks served as a starting point for some generations of students of East Asian history. It is gratifying to see the tentative theses and concepts I put forward in the books with the enthusiasm of discovery referred to now as the "conventional wisdom." Usually the references are derogatory, and the authors or speakers then proceed to refute in part what I wrote or to elaborate on it with new, more detailed information. Their uncomplimentary tone might seem distressing to some, but to me it shows that my work has at least been used as a stepping stone to further progress in the field.

◄§

Apart from my writing, teaching, and work for the Harvard Yenching Institute, these were busy years for me. Some of my activities involved my students, as in the case of the son of John D. Rockefeller, III, normally known as Jay, who enlisted my help in arranging for his temporary transfer from Harvard to study in Japan. He was immensely popular in Japan and perhaps derived from his study of Japan and Japanese some of the breadth of talents that have characterized his political career as the governor of West Virginia and more recently the junior senator from that state.

Other activities were more institutional. Boston had had a Japan Society since 1904, making it the oldest in the country, and some of us now revived it, though it did not become very active until the late 1960s. The biggest cultural event concerning Japan at this time was a visit to Boston by the imperial troupe of *Gagaku* performers in the summer of 1959 under the sponsorship of the Boston summer festival. *Gagaku* is the ceremonial court orchestral music and dance which has been maintained virtually unchanged since the eighth and ninth centuries and probably represents the oldest authentic musical tradition in the world. *Gagaku* was performed on two successive evenings on the Boston Commons. I served as master of ceremonies, giving a short explanation of *Gagaku* in general and then briefer introductions to the individual pieces. Despite inclement weather, the Commons was estimated to have been thronged by more than ten thousand people the first night and even more the second. I suspect that these were the largest *Gagaku* performances ever seen anywhere in the world.

My most time-consuming activities outside my regular job were attending meetings and giving public speeches all over the country. I developed through experience into a fairly effective public speaker, casually drafting my notes as I traveled by air to an appointment and getting to know the pleasure of holding an audience in my hand. My most common fault was to continue in my enthusiasm well past my allotted time. This was particularly unwise for me because it would cut into the time for questions and answers at which I was usually more effective than in the speech itself. I always avoided reading a speech if possible, feeling that writing and speaking are essentially two different arts. But this meant that if I were required to provide a text for publication, I usually had to redo it from scratch. During summers I frequently lectured for a week or so at some summer school or conference. One year I did this at Lake Couchiching north of Toronto and another summer at Chautauqua in upstate New York, which I had thought had faded into history a half century earlier.

My life had become a very full and rewarding one, both at Harvard and elsewhere. I found full scope to work on the lifetime objectives I had set myself to help develop interest in and knowledge about East Asia and greater understanding between East and West. At fifty, I was happily settled in my course, little suspecting that external events were soon to push me in a new direction.

# 24
# The Broken Dialogue

I N THE summer of 1960 I went out to East Asia in my capacity as the director of the Harvard Yenching Institute. Although I received no time off from teaching for my work—now it is considered to count for half one's time—periodic trips to East Asia were accepted as a necessary part of the job. I was given a leave of absence for the autumn semester, and Haru and I took off in late June for six months abroad.

Our children by then were all old enough to no longer need our presence. After a lackluster year in college, Ann had gone out to California in 1959 to be with her boyfriend, Stephen Heinemann, at the California Institute of Technology. When they both turned twenty-one early in 1960, they were married with our blessing in a simple ceremony in California performed by an Episcopalian minister. This was a fine arrangement for the parents of the bride, since it involved no financial pain. Bobby had entered Harvard in 1959 and was quartered there. Only Joan, then a high school senior, needed some care, which we provided by lending our home to a young couple who kept an eye on her.

Unencumbered by children for the first time in two decades, I happily hastened out to Japan with Haru. It had made stunning economic progress since we had been there in 1956, and one no longer felt any of the physical effects of the war and postwar poverty. Japan was well launched on what was later to be called the Japanese miracle. In contrast to my earlier postwar evaluations, I could see that it was the political aspects of society that now merited concern, rather than the economic. The country was still reeling from the blowup in May and June over the revision of the Treaty of Mutual Security and Cooperation with the United States. Usually called simply the Security Treaty, its revision in 1960 caused a ruckus that was to prove the greatest crisis in Japanese politics and Japanese-American relations experienced after World War II.

Underlying this crisis was a deep and widening chasm within Japanese politics. On the right was the remainder of the prewar establishment, consisting of the bureaucracy, big business, and the major prewar parliamentary parties, and supported by the bulk of rural and small-town Japan, where the roots of the old parties ran deep. Although the parties and much of big business had been considered the liberals in prewar days, the elimination of the military and the purging from politics of most of the wartime leadership now made this remainder of the prewar establishment the conservatives. Their place on the left had been taken by the Marxist movements, which had made their appearance in the 1920s and 1930s under the leadership of intellectuals and organized labor, appealing primarily to city dwellers and university students. This new left, which had been harshly suppressed in the years of military domination, was deeply suspicious of the old liberals, who had allowed themselves to be compromised into impotence by the militarists, and it feared that these remnants of the old establishment were bent on returning Japan to the prewar system.

In the early postwar years the political situation was confused and attitudes toward the United States were ambiguous. Although the conservatives were keenly aware of Japan's dependence on the United States both economically and for defense and accepted most American reforms as being unavoidable if not always desirable, they were the chief critics of American policies in Japan, chafing against American controls and deploring what they considered to be serious American blunders damaging to Japanese society. In contrast, the progressives, as the leftists called themselves, were enthusiastic about the American reforms and clamored for more. In the later years of the American Occupation, however, the two groups changed sides in their attitudes toward the United States. The left was dismayed to see the Americans complete their reform program far short of socialism and shift their emphasis to economic recovery. They became sharply hostile to the United States as the cold war gradually spread from Europe to Japan and the United States in 1950 became embroiled in war in Korea with the Communist nations the left tended to admire. When the Peace Treaty of 1952 left extensive American military bases in Japan, the leftists saw the United States as being a militaristic warmonger attempting to force Japan to follow in its train, while the Soviet Union and the People's Republic of China became for them the "peace camp."

The division between left and right was made all the sharper in 1955 by the reunification of the Socialist Party (it had divided over the issue of support for the Peace Treaty) and the amalgamation of the two historic parties as the Liberal Democratic Party (LDP), which has been in power ever since. The left demanded a socialist system and an end to military involvement with the United States. The right favored rapid economic growth over further social and economic reform and felt that the defense relationship was essential, even though it necessitated the retention of American military bases. Since the economy was growing spectacularly, there was little that the left could criticize on this score, but American military bases and the involvement of Japan in the cold war through its defense relations with the United States were vulnerable aspects of LDP policy on which the left could effectively concentrate its attack.

Under these circumstances, Prime Minister Kishi Nobusuke agreed with the Americans to revise the most objectional aspects of the Security Treaty. The revision, signed in January 1960, eliminated the broad rights of the United States to utilize its bases in Japan at its own discretion for "the maintenance of international peace and security in the Far East," as it had done in the Korean War, and the right to employ American forces at the request of the Japanese government "to put down large-scale internal riots and disturbances in Japan." It also provided for the termination of the treaty after ten years at the request of either government. These were all improvements even from the point of view of the Japanese left; but all the opposition groups, except for a moderate faction among the Socialists which became the Democratic Socialist Party, decided to oppose the revision on the grounds that, unlike the treaty it replaced, which had been dictated by the United States, the Japanese government shared responsibility for the new treaty.

Since the LDP held 61 percent of the seats in the lower house of the Diet, there was no doubt about the eventual ratification of the treaty, but the dispute over it grew into a major crisis because of extraneous factors. The main one was President Eisenhower's scheduled visit to Japan on June 19. Kishi, probably in order to have the treaty go into effect by that date even without action by the upper house of the Diet, "rammed through" its ratification by the lower house on the night of May 19, using dubious parliamentary tactics to do so. The opposition exploded in fury over what they considered to be Kishi's "undemocratic" actions and American "intervention" in Japanese politics. Mass demonstrations and rioting broke out, especially in Tokyo, and hundreds of thousands of people took to the streets in protests against Kishi, Eisenhower's visit, and the Security Treaty. The Japanese government was forced to request the cancellation of the presidential visit, although once the treaty went into effect on June 19 the disturbances quickly subsided. Despite the fact that Kishi was forced to resign in July, the LDP in a general election held in November won virtually the same popular vote as in the previous election and actually increased its seats slightly. The political chaos of May and June, however, had badly shaken the nation as well as the confidence of Americans in Japan.

Just before we left for Japan, the distinguished quarterly magazine *Foreign Affairs* asked me to write an article about the disturbances, and I promised to do so after I had had a chance to study the situation for myself. I therefore spent most of July interviewing people of all types and then wrote a brief article entitled "The Broken Dialogue," though in actuality the dialogue I was referring to had never existed. I devoted the bulk of the argument to the different perceptions of the situation by the Japanese conservatives, the various opposition parties, and the American government. The leftists had wildly inaccurate concepts of American foreign policy and the world situation and feared that the right was striving with American connivance to return Japan to prewar militarism and limited democracy. The right saw the left as being made up of unrealistic and sometimes traitorous fools. The Americans saw the Japanese ruling groups as timid but faithful allies whose support could simply be taken for granted, and they ignored the views of the left as not being worthy of notice. My chief conclusion was that the whole Security Treaty incident had revealed "a weakness of communication between the United States and opposition elements in Japan." I saw a gap in understanding that was "a truly frightening phenomenon," and pointed out that this gap required Americans to establish a dialogue with all sections of Japanese society.

The article appeared in the October issue of *Foreign Affairs* and drew considerable attention. In the meantime, the Japanese had become aware of it, and the radical monthly magazine *Sekai,* which was then at its height of popularity, asked to publish it in translation. The American Embassy was also acutely conscious of its critical tone, and the Ambassador, Douglas MacArthur, II, a nephew of the great proconsul, took umbrage at my writing that "The shocking misestimate of the situation in May and June on the part of the American Government and Embassy in Tokyo reveals how small is our contact with the Japanese opposition." MacArthur summoned me to the Embassy and dragged out volumes of Embassy telegrams to prove that their evaluation of the situation had not been a "shocking misestimate." He had some justification for his objections, and I agreed to tone down my wording a little in the Japanese translation. *Sekai* was somewhat put out by my changes, probably attributing them to the "fascistic" interference of the American government in the free expression of American intellectuals.

While the writing of the article for *Foreign Affairs* was to prove the most significant activity for me during the summer, another high point was a conference of American and Japanese scholars of modern Japanese history, held at the Miyanoshita hot springs near Hakone, a resort area close to Mt. Fuji. The conference was organized by Jack Hall, Marius Jansen, Don Shively, and a few others of their generation, and was the start of an ambitious multi-year program of conferences and publications on the process by which Japan had modernized itself during the past century. The results eventually came out in a substantial six-volume set published by the Princeton University Press. The Hakone Conference, as it came to be known, was notable for being the first (and perhaps still the only) conference between Westerners and Japanese in which Japanese was used as the primary language without translation, while English was relegated to a backup position. It became even more famous for marking the start of what was to be known in Japanese intellectual history as the "modernization controversy."

The work of the postwar generation of students at Harvard and elsewhere in the United States had proved to be a sort of revisionism of the prevailing Marxist interpretations of modern Japanese history. Because of the Hakone Conference this revisionism came to be known pejoratively in Japan as the "modernization theory" and usually was attributed to the "Harvard school" of Japanese history. But there never was any Harvard school on any specific modernization theory in the field of Japanese studies. "Modernization" may have been used by some American social scientists to denote certain rather rigid concepts, but in the Japanese field it was simply a vague term covering all the tremendous changes that had been occurring in Japan since the mid-nineteenth century.

A profound difference in the interpretation of modern Japanese history showed up at once between the young American scholars and the established Japanese academicians attending the conference, and as a result considerable intellectual heat developed on the Japanese side. The Japanese participants perceived the basically positive view of the Americans regarding the changes that had been sweeping Japan for the past century as a direct challenge to their own deeply entrenched Marxist concepts. To them, "modernization" implied a specific process leading to specific ends—socialism and democracy. They assumed that it had an equally precise meaning for the American participants, which must be anti-socialist and even anti-democratic, since it differed from their views.

I played only a minor role as an ordinary participant at the Hakone Conference, but since the organizers were largely my former students and since I have at times been accused in Japan of being the father or at least the grandfather of the nefarious "modernization theory," I should perhaps make clear my views on the subject. "Modernization" to me is a completely neutral term, merely designating the multitudinous great changes that have come to the world with the acceptance of the concept of progress, the scientific method, and the widespread use of inanimate sources of energy, known as the industrial revolution, and all the attendant side effects of speeded-up communications, the centralization of power, and the urbanization of society, as well as the manifold institutional changes in economics, society, and government that have resulted. I see totalitarianism and the ills of contemporary urban life as being as much the products of modernization as are contemporary mass democracy and affluence. My own firm belief in democracy, human rights, and social and economic equality are value judgments quite separate from any theories about how and why modernization has been taking place in the world. Thus I have always found it difficult to comprehend what the Japanese scholars were attacking as the "modernization theory" and the vehemence of their condemnation of it. The same applies to the new wave of revisionism which emerged among young American scholars in the late 1960s. It seemed to me that what they advocated was not anything new but simply a return to the rather rigid Marxist interpretations of an earlier day, which had been rejected once already and, as I see it, are being rejected once again, this time not just in the United States but in Japan as well.

While in Japan I devoted the early autumn to my Harvard Yenching Institute duties, getting in touch with the Research Council we had founded, visiting the universities we had contacts with and others as well, meeting with many of our former Visiting Scholars, and conferring with various colleagues and friends. In October, Haru and I went to Korea for two weeks in order to visit the universities and scholars there. As in Japan, it was a pleasure to see the country so much restored since my last visit in 1955 and a particular delight to see it at last in the hands of democratic leaders. I had no idea that their tenure was to last less than a year.

In planning for our visit to Korea, we had worried about the possibility of hostility toward Haru because of the bitter Korean resentment of Japan's harsh rule in the past. In part to offset this, Haru had taken the beginning course in the Korean language at Harvard during the preceding academic year, struggling to keep up with the other students whose young minds were better prepared to absorb a new language. This impressed our Korean friends favorably, and they could not have been nicer to her. Haru in turn was much impressed by Korea. Like most Japanese, she had grown up to think of Koreans as troublesome neighbors and an uneducated minority at the bottom of society in Japan. She was surprised to find many Koreans to be people of high education and their country proud of a cultural heritage comparable in all respects to that of Japan. To see what a revelation this was to her underscored once again for me the unhappy state of affairs in which Koreans and Japanese, two peoples more closely related to each other in culture than to any other people in the world, continued to view each other with contempt and hatred. Haru thereafter joined me in doing what we could as outsiders to help change these attitudes into respect and friendship.

At the end of October we went to Taiwan to visit the universities and research institutes there. As the American presidential elections were approaching, I questioned my Chinese friends about their preferences. The Chinese from the mainland were uniformly for the Republicans, believing that they would be more steadfast than the Democrats in defending Taiwan from the Communists, while the native Taiwanese were equally uniform in their preference for the Democrats, who they felt would be more sympathetic than the Republicans to native Taiwanese aspirations for self-rule.

From Taiwan we went to Hong Kong on November 8, again visiting various universities and scholars. We had planned to fly to Saigon and from there to visit the earlier Vietnamese capital of Hue, which was said to be a small replica of Peking, and then Angkor Wat in Cambodia. Unfortunately our proposed trip coincided with the first military coup in Saigon, and all planes were canceled. After waiting around a day or so, we were forced by our schedule to skip Vietnam entirely and fly on to Thailand and Burma. Hue subsequently was destroyed in the Vietnam War, and Angkor Wat is likely to remain off limits to visitors for the rest of our traveling days. In Thailand and Burma I scouted out interest in East Asian studies in the universities but found very little. Burma seemed to be drifting off into the long slumber that has characterized it ever since.

From Rangoon we flew to Calcutta, where we were immediately overwhelmed by the terrible poverty of India. We were also struck by the difference in mien between the Indo-Europeans in India and the Mongoloid peoples of the lands further east. Whether it is a superficial matter of the shape of the eyes and jaws or something of greater cultural significance, the contrast between the smiling faces of East and Southeast Asia and the sad-eyed, doleful looks of most Indians is startling. The swarms of beggars and the constantly outstretched hands of pathetic children demanding baksheesh added to the cultural shock.

In India my chief objective was to try to stir up interest in the study of China and Japan in universities and to build ties between them and the Harvard Yenching Institute; but again, except for the scholars at the Delhi School of International Affairs, I found very little interest in either China or Japan in those days before the Sino-Indian War and before the Japanese economic "miracle" had begun to attract worldwide attention. There was so little interest, in fact, that I was at times received with a boredom bordering on rudeness.

Although our trip to India was a failure in terms of producing institutional bonds in East Asian studies, it was a great success as simple tourism—from the Taj Mahal at full moon to the remarkable Buddhist rock caves of Ajanta. It was also very instructive to me in a deeper way. I had long been a student of Indian Buddhism, yet I soon saw that I understood nothing about the country. I had many good Indian friends and found the historical sites and art of India absolutely fascinating, but I realized that I had already stretched my capacities as far as they would go intellectually and emotionally in trying to understand East Asia, North America, and Western Europe, and could stretch them no further to include India. Philosophically, India had always represented for me the opposite end of the human spectrum from East Asia, and now I found that even close up it was quite beyond my powers of comprehension. It seemed to me that almost to the extent that I understood East Asia, I was incapable of understanding India. I am afraid the same applies for me with regard to the Middle East and some other parts of the world. It was a depressing thought that I, who had spent my life trying to understand diverse cultures, should be so limited in what I could comprehend.

Accepting my limitations, however, I was content to continue to do what I could to spread knowledge about East Asia in the United States and strengthen the intellectual ties between these two areas. My life seemed to stretch out placidly before me, and retirement now loomed only fifteen years down the road. I had not the slightest forewarning of, nor any desire for, any such change.

# PART FIVE
# AMBASSADOR
# TO JAPAN
# 1961-1966

Departing to present credentials to the Emperor accompanied by DCM William Leonhart (on EOR's right), Economic Minister Philip Trezise (back row, left), three Counsellors and chief of the military attachés, April 27, 1961.

## 25

# Lightning Strikes

WHEN HARU and I returned home from India by way of Europe late in December 1960, we found things both at Harvard and in our family calm and entirely normal. I had some chores to perform before the start of the spring semester in February, such as buying a new car, and I had several new projects on my mind. Before leaving Japan in October, I had laid plans with Professor Inoue Mitsusada of Tokyo University and Professor Toyoda Takeshi of Tohoku University to join them in writing in both Japanese and English a "History of Japan Until the Sixteenth Century." We had drawn up a list of chapters and had agreed on our respective assignments, the length of the chapters, and their date of completion, which was to be in 1964. This project could have diverted my life down other channels than it took, but in fact all that ever came of it was that Inoue substituted for me at Harvard in 1961–62.

In Korea I had promised Chang Myun, the Prime Minister, to go to Washington on my return and speak to people of influence about the perilous condition of the new Korean regime. Chang was all too right in his fears, for his democratic government was to be overthrown by a military coup only a few months later. To fulfill my promise, I got in touch with James C. Thomson, Jr., who had been the head tutor in our Rice Paddies course for several years and had just become the personal assistant to Chester Bowles, the new Under Secretary of State in President John F. Kennedy's administration. Jim, who later was to be the curator of the Nieman Fellowships at Harvard, seemed the best contact I had with the new regime in Washington, and Bowles an appropriate person to speak to about Korea, because he was a warm-hearted internationalist and we had received honorary degrees together from Oberlin in 1957 (though I later discovered he did not have the slightest remembrance of this fact). Jim scheduled an appointment with Bowles on January 26; I also made a date to lunch on that day with John Newhouse, a staff member of the Senate Foreign Relations Committee, who had asked to discuss my *Foreign Affairs* article with me if I happened to come to Washington.

Before January 26 arrived, however, the situation took a surprising turn.

While in Japan I had been amused by occasional speculation in the press that, if Kennedy were elected, he might appoint me his Ambassador to Tokyo. In Japanese minds my assumed connection with Kennedy through Harvard made this seem reasonable, but I had never laid eyes on any of the Kennedys and was in no way involved in politics. Becoming Ambassador to Japan could not have been further from my thoughts. As January progressed, however, I began to receive phone calls from American newsmen in Washington informing me that my name was being bandied about as a possible Ambassador. A flattering misconception on the part of the Japanese suddenly was turning into a frightening possibility. To go down to Washington under these circumstances would make me look like a job seeker, but to self-consciously cancel my visit would be even more embarrassing.

On the fateful day, when I was ushered into Bowles's office I realized at once that something was up. He asked me to wait in the room with him while he transacted some fairly confidential business. After all these years, I was obviously being treated as a member of the team again. Then he turned to me and, after saying that Korean matters could wait, requested me to be the new Ambassador to Japan and beyond that to act as a sort of supervisory Ambassador at Large for all of East Asia. Bowles, who was an ebullient person, was quite impractical in this second suggestion. No animal has a stronger sense of territorial prerogatives than an Ambassador, and I would have been torn to bits by my colleagues if I had tried to act in a supervisory capacity outside of Japan. Even for Japan the thought of serving as Ambassador filled me with terror. I presented Bowles with a long list of reasons why I was not suited to the job, but he brushed them all aside, only accepting my plea for a few days to think it over and consult with Haru.

My appointment with John Newhouse turned out to be instead with his boss, Senator William Fulbright, chairman of the Senate Foreign Relations Committee, whom I had long admired but had never met. After some talk about Korea, Fulbright inquired about the possibility of my going to Japan as Ambassador and was delighted to learn that Bowles had just made me the offer. Then I returned to the State Department, where I saw Dean Rusk, the newly appointed Secretary of State. As I recorded at the time, he was "calm, non-committal and cagey"— a description that I found would fit all my dealings with him. He seemed much less enthusiastic about my appointment than Bowles, listened carefully to what I had to say about Korea, and even suggested that I might rather go to Seoul than Tokyo. I suspect he had other preferences for the Tokyo post, but Bowles had been specifically given the job of finding new ambassadors.

Since a heavy snow storm blanked out my return flight, I spent the night in Washington, dining with Jim Thomson in a small hash joint near the State Department. I discovered that Jim was largely responsible for arousing Bowles's interest in me. At first Bowles did not even remember my name, but Jim kept putting it at the top of the list until it finally sank in. His persistence came second only to the stir my *Foreign Affairs* article had caused in explaining my choice. My Harvard connections, contrary to Japanese concepts, played no part. Kennedy had already selected a lot of people from Harvard, and I am sure he was dismayed at the thought of having another Cantabrigian on his team.

When, on my return to Belmont, I told Haru what had happened in Washington, she went into instant shock. Despite her aristocratic background, her experience as a newspaperwoman had given her a contempt for the type of social life that surrounds embassies and an image of herself as a rebel against the establishment. During the American Occupation her contacts with leftist American newsmen and Japanese politicians had even put her on MacArthur's black list for a while. In addition, she had resolved never to marry a professor, because they were too dull, or a diplomat, since they were too stuffy. She had given way on the one resolve but was determined to hold firm on the second. But what stood foremost in her thinking was that she was sure the Americans in Japan at the Embassy, in the business community, and especially in the military, which still loomed very large, would never accept her as the American Ambassador's wife, and that prominent Japanese would look on her with contempt and possibly as a traitor.

Despite Haru's violent opposition, I realized from the start that I had no choice but to accept. For years I had criticized America's Asian policy in my books, articles, and speeches, and I could scarcely turn my back now on an opportunity to try to improve it. It was for me a case of "put up or shut up." This was a once in a lifetime chance to work in a key position on what meant most in my life—Japanese-American relations. I simply could not turn tail and retreat in cowardice into my academic lair, though I regretted the thought of leaving my congenial Harvard job and especially having to give up finishing the *East Asia* volumes with Fairbank.

While I realized I had no option but to accept, I was extremely apprehensive about the prospects. Two possible objections were quickly dispelled from my mind. My recent trip to Asia had demonstrated that my physical strength had been sufficiently restored for me to fulfill an Ambassador's taxing role. Another more basic concern was that my deep affection for Japan might make me an unsuitable representative of the United States in Tokyo. After some thought, however, I came to the conclusion that this should offer no problem, since the fundamental interests and goals of the two countries were now so similar that my love for Japan need not clash with my loyalty to America. It seemed to me that I could serve America best by working for the well-being of both countries and especially for greater understanding between them.

At the same time the job was one of great importance and difficulty, and I wondered if I could master it well enough to achieve anything worthwhile, or whether I might simply be setting myself up for a humiliating failure. The position of American Ambassador in those days still occupied the high pedestal on which until recently the towering figure of MacArthur had stood and it was surrounded by his aura. I was no heroic figure of that type. Nor did I have any acquaintance with diplomatic life or any hankering for it. My previous State Department experience had been of a quite different nature, and I had always avoided any contact with politics, feeling that it and scholarship did not mix.

Even granting that I might be able to do the job, there was the question of whether I would be able to get beyond the routine chores of the position and be allowed by Washington to do what I thought was needed. In this age of instantaneous communications, ambassadors are usually kept on a short leash, and as a result many serve as little more than errand boys. I had no desire to abandon my useful work at Harvard for a meaningless even if glamorous post. Would Washington permit me the freedom and would I have the ability to do the things I thought necessary? The only way to find out was to take the plunge and give it a try. I had reason to believe I might be given the necessary leeway. My selection had grown largely out of my criticism of the "broken dialogue" with Japan, and it was clear that President Kennedy and my backers in Washington expected me to do something about this. Perhaps I would be able to avoid being swamped by the superficialities of diplomatic life and would be given a chance to carry out some of my ideas regarding Japanese-American relations.

I realized, however, that I would face a tremendous task, as the recent Security Treaty disturbances had shown only too clearly. The chief problems did not lie between the two governments but in misunderstandings between the peoples of the two countries. Both had a residue of racial prejudice, wartime hatreds, and cultural unfamiliarity. There was an even greater feeling of inequality. Many Japanese, remembering the lost war, the country's postwar poverty, and the American Occupation which did so much to restructure Japan against the will of some of its people, felt helpless and resentful in their dependence on the United States. They feared that America's adventuristic foreign policy, as they perceived it, combined with American nuclear power would involve Japan in a new tragedy. They saw themselves as being at the mercy of American callousness and political folly. Although they believed that they had no choice but to remain economically dependent on trade with America, they wished to distance themselves politically as much as they could from United States foreign policy.

Americans for their part tended to be oblivious to the feelings of Japanese and took the country for granted as an ally which had no other choice. Finding no immediately critical problems in Japan, they concentrated their attention instead on remote trouble spots like Laos. For example, in Arthur Schlesinger's *A Thousand Days,* which recounts the Kennedy presidency, Japan does not even appear in the index and is mentioned only twice, both times in connection with my appointment, whereas Laos, which does not have a hundredth of Japan's importance to the United States, occupies twenty-five lines in the index and is spread over no less than fifty pages of the text. Even McGeorge Bundy in his crucial post as security advisor to the President saw no necessity of learning more about Japan. I constantly urged him to come for a visit to educate himself, but he never got around to it until the spring of 1966, by which time he had resigned from his White House position. Insofar as Americans were aware of Japan at all, they resented the lack of appreciation Japanese showed for the benefits of their relationship with the United States and the open hostility of many Japanese to the military alliance between the two countries. Japanese seemed to Americans to be content to take a "free ride" at America's expense in matters of defense and unwilling to pull their share of the load in world affairs.

It was necessary for Japanese to realize that the United States was not an inherently aggressive, militaristic country, but that it had to maintain some military strength in the Western Pacific to help stabilize a disturbed part of the world and give an undefended country like Japan some security. They would have to comprehend that for a virtually unarmed and isolated Japan an American military presence was by far the cheapest form of defense and also the best guarantee against Japan remilitarizing to an excessive degree. They also needed to see that when Japan was prosperous and strong enough, it would have to contribute to world stability at least through economic means. Such ideas at this time were still far away from the thinking of most Japanese, who basked in the comforting thought that, if they did not bother anyone else, other countries would leave them alone to enjoy their new-found affluence.

I saw my task as being basically to help correct all these distorted concepts and encourage Japanese and Americans to look on each other as equal partners. Japanese saw the United States as more powerful and domineering than it actually was, and Americans saw Japan as less cooperative and far less important than it was. As was frequently pointed out, the two countries seemed to be viewing each other across the Pacific through the same set of binoculars but looking through them from opposite ends. It would be my duty, I felt, to encourage Japanese to comprehend that the United States was less large and all-powerful than they thought and to help Americans understand that Japan was more important to them than they realized. This would be a curious role for an American Ambassador to play and it would be one that I would have to undertake on my own initiative, because Washington was obviously not aware of the needs. It was a huge task, since the entire populations of the two countries were involved. The Japanese reached the hundred million mark the same year in the late sixties that Americans achieved the two hundred million mark. Their relations were vast and diverse. A constant image that would float into my mind was of Japan and the United States as two giant icebergs grinding against each other, while I, armed with a frail bamboo pole, tried to steer them away from this abrasive contact.

~§

Haru continued her resistance to going to Japan for three days, stating flatly that I could go but it would be without her. Then she gave in, though harboring the same misgivings that I did. What influenced her most in changing her mind was the memory of Kennedy's stirring statement in his inaugural address: "Ask not what your country can do for you; ask what you can do for your country." This may sound corny now, but it was fresh and challenging then. Bob and Joan also delivered touching speeches about our patriotic duty to accept, and Ann wrote from California in the same vein.

Haru and I consoled each other with the thought that, if we fell flat on our faces, the worst that could happen would be that we would return to Harvard, which was what we intended to do anyway. And in any case my appointment as American Ambassador despite my Japanese wife would have demonstrated to Japanese and the whole world the openmindedness of Americans and their willingness to accept other races as equals. Actually Bowles had asked me casually if Haru were an American citizen, adding, "Not that it makes any difference." This was in sharp contrast to the long-established diplomatic custom that an Ambassador never be sent to a country of which his wife was a native. As it happened, Haru's citizenship had come through in December 1959.

Both Haru and I felt better once our minds were made up. I arranged a two-year leave of absence with President Nathan Pusey of Harvard and Gregg Bemis, the chairman of the board of trustees of the Harvard Yenching Institute. Haru and I suspected that we would be slinking back home in disgrace long before the two years were up, but I was resolved to resign my Harvard post if all were going well and my continuation in Tokyo seemed worthwhile at the end of two years. Our mental turmoil during the past few days had made it seem an eternity, but I was actually able to phone Bowles on January 31, five days after the original invitation, to inform him that I would accept.

Haru and I felt that our worst worries were now over, but we were sadly mistaken. There ensued a long gestation period, which proved the most disagreeable time in our whole ambassadorial experience. A security check had to be carried out on us by the FBI, and because many other persons were being checked out at the start of a new presidency, it took much longer than I had expected. A flat statement, however, had been printed in *The New York Times* before the end of January that I would be the new Ambassador, and this had become headline news in Japan. We were soon deluged with letters, phone calls, and newspapermen, though we had to feign ignorance until the appointment was officially announced. Several Japanese television crews came to Cambridge to take pictures of me teaching my Japanese classes and of our house, which they described as being lower middle class. Eisenstadt, the famous *Life* photographer, came to take pictures of us. All sorts of silly things were printed, but there was little I could do to correct them. *Time* suggested that I would be useful in furthering American policy to bring Korea back into the Japanese orbit. No policy could have been stupider, but I managed to calm Korean fears through an interview with a Korean reporter. Meanwhile weekly phone calls from the State Department would promise that a definite announcement would be made the next Monday. But no announcement would be made and we would be left in limbo, forced to avoid answering all questions, which is a most distasteful situation for a professor accustomed to speaking his mind freely on all subjects.

The long delay gave ample opportunity for all sorts of rumors to spring up. The former Japanese Prime Minister, Yoshida Shigeru, was pictured as opposing the appointment. Conservative politicians, businessmen, and bureaucrats were also said to be distressed at the prospects of a nonprofessional academic Ambassador; there was probably considerable truth in this, because professors were regarded in Japan as impractical, leftist-leaning dreamers. There certainly was some truth to the rumor that elements in the State Department were opposed. The Tokyo ambassadorship was probably the most important and prestigious one that had normally been reserved for members of the Foreign Service, and there naturally was resentment that this plum was going to an outsider. Some writers built up these rumors into a tremendous battle being waged in Tokyo and Washington over my appointment. Well-meaning friends kept us fully informed, and one made the prediction that, in my academic innocence, I would be cut up into mincemeat by Washington politics. Newspapers and magazines commented frequently on the rumored appointment, and I found myself deeply hurt to be referred to as a "controversial" figure. I realized that academic life had left me very thin-skinned for public life. Still, our friends at Harvard and elsewhere were very supportive. I especially appreciated a letter from my old friend Yu Chin-o, the former president of Korea University, who, himself in a difficult position in his new job as the chief Korean representative in Japan, wrote: "Your coming is to me like 'the sounding of human footsteps in an empty valley.' "

John Kenneth Galbraith, who was being proposed for Ambassador to India, was in somewhat the same position as I. Haru and I would confer with him and his wife Kitty from time to time, starting a close friendship which has left us deeply in their debt for many kindnesses. Galbraith was ecstatic about the prospects of his own appointment, being in no way troubled by the self-doubts that plagued Haru and me. I have always found him delightfully amusing in his well-phrased arrogance. He had played a very active role in Democratic politics for some time, and, when I asked him if he had sought the Indian post or it had sought him, he smiled and said, "A little of both." Kitty on the other hand was as terrified as we were, though she eventually came to enjoy her Indian sojourn even more than he.

Haru and I tried to lead as normal lives as possible. I started teaching my second semester classes at the beginning of February, though my heart was not really in the work and I found myself unable to get back to my other scholarly activities. I even stopped writing the twentieth-century section of *East Asia: The Modern Transformation*. In my frustration over the situation, I kept a journal briefly. From it I see that Haru and I had already thought of many of the plans we later carried out in Japan.

In Japan, meanwhile, interest in our expected appointment engendered great popular enthusiasm and support. The idea of a Japanese-speaking American Ambassador with a Japanese wife appealed to the public, and such strong sentiment built up in our favor that it would have been difficult for Washington to change its mind or Tokyo to register opposition. Favorable editorials appeared in the Japanese papers and a spate of political cartoons. My favorite one was of Prime Minister Ikeda Hayato boning up on classical Japanese with the caption: "Reischauer-san Is Coming." When the FBI clearance finally came through— my first word of it was from Arthur Schlesinger in the White House—and the American government asked Tokyo for the *agrément* to my appointment, the Japanese government acted with unprecedented speed, taking the extraordinary step of releasing the news in Tokyo before it had been formally announced in Washington. Phone calls and letters poured in, one reading "Omedeto [Congratulations] stop We thought you'd never drop the other *geta.*"

The degree of public interest shown in my appointment as Ambassador may now seem surprising, but at that time the aura of General MacArthur still surrounded the position. Even in the United States a great deal was made of ambassadorial appointments that year. It was part of Kennedy's policy that his administration would make special efforts to build better relations with the various peoples of the world. In addition to Galbraith and me, many unusual ambassadors were chosen, including George Kennan, the former very successful Ambassador to the Soviet Union, who was asked to go to Yugoslavia, and Kenneth T. Young, my first student at Harvard, who went to Thailand. In a way 1961 might be called the Year of the Ambassadors. *Time* devoted the cover story of its January 12, 1962, issue to "The New Ambassadors," featuring pictures on the cover of Galbraith, me, and Kennan in descending order of size.

᠊ᢈ

The official announcement of my nomination was made in Washington on March 14. After a delightful informal farewell party given by my colleagues in East Asian studies, we moved with all our baggage to the beautiful Georgetown home of Haru's college roommate, Eleanor Jordan, and her husband, François, a retired navy captain. The Jordan home was a peaceful pied-à-terre for us as we were now caught up in a veritable maelstrom of activities. Under the efficient guidance of Richard L. Sneider, who was in charge of the "Japan desk" at the State Department and much later became the Ambassador to Korea, I was briefed on numerous aspects of the job in Tokyo and was taken to meet various important personages, including the Joint Chiefs of Staff. Certain of my books which had been "black-listed" for American libraries around the globe were hastily removed from the list. Haru was given some logistic information about the Embassy Residence. When she asked for instruction about how to conduct herself as the Ambassador's wife, she was told that there was a course for Embassy wives on their duties and on how an Ambassador's wife should be treated, but nothing for the Ambassador's wife herself.

My hearing before the Senate Foreign Relations Committee took place on March 23. I was one of four nominees questioned that morning but was clearly the star of the occasion, being scheduled first and having the bulk of the time devoted to me. The only sticky point was when a senator asked if I favored the recognition of Communist China. Fulbright hastily interrupted to say that my advocacy of that policy had been before the outbreak of the Korean War; although I did in fact favor moving toward recognition, I thought silence on my part would be the better part of wisdom. At the end of the proceedings, Mike Mansfield, the vice-chairman of the committee, who is normally an extraordinarily taciturn man, made a gracious statement about the United States being lucky to have Haru as the Ambassador's wife and the country getting two ambassadors for the price of one, and he and Fulbright made a point of meeting Haru afterwards. We have both been very grateful ever since for this kind gesture, which greatly boosted Haru's morale.

On March 25 I had my first meeting with the President, along with a couple of other new ambassadors. It was an entirely pro forma occasion at which he gave each of us a signed photograph of himself, which was to be placed prominently on our ambassadorial desks to impress visitors with how close we were to him. Then on the 29th my official appointment came through, and it was followed by several social events before we could depart for Japan. The Japan Societies in both New York and Washington held big receptions in our honor, at which we got our first taste of one of the major ambassadorial tasks—the shaking of hundreds of hands.

The most interesting social event was a farewell dinner party given in our honor by the Japanese Ambassador, Asakai Koichiro, who had been rumored to have been one of our leading opponents but showed no signs of any ill will. This was our first diplomatic dinner, but since no one saw fit to give us any instructions, we had to play it by ear. I soon learned that the setting of the table with three wineglasses—one for white wine with the fish course, a second for red wine with the meat course, and the third for champagne for toasts—was a sure sign that toasts would be exchanged. At the end of the dinner, when Asakai rose to give a generous toast, I guessed that it was up to me to reply in kind. Since we were tired, we excused ourselves early in the evening, learning only later that until the guests of honor depart, the others, be they senators, cabinet members, or ambassadors, cannot leave. Pleased with the early ending of the evening, my tablemate, an experienced Washington dowager, leaned over to me and whispered, "Young man, you will do well in diplomatic life."

As the Japanese press corps was the largest foreign group in Washington and was avid for news about us, the State Department broke precedent in allowing them to have a press interview with me before our departure, disguised as a guest appearance by me at a regular press briefing by the Department's press officer.

After a couple of days in Los Angeles where we were guests of honor at a reception of the Japan-America Society, we stopped for a few days of rest in Honolulu. Joan had joined us, since Belmont High School was allowing her to complete her senior year by correspondence from Japan. While in Hawaii I was thoroughly briefed at CINCPAC (Commander-in-Chief, Pacific), the military headquarters for the whole Pacific area, and we were given a large formal dinner by CINCPAC himself, Admiral Harry Felt.

When we flew on from Hawaii, Haru and I were itching to get started on our new work, though we also had the uncomfortable feeling of being lambs led to slaughter. After a virtually sleepless night, we landed at the old Haneda Airport in Tokyo at 6:40 a.m. on April 19. I was riding up in the cockpit with the pilot —this was permitted in those days—when he remarked that all the airways had been cleared and the plane was being brought straight in to Haneda, an experience he had never had before. I rushed back to my seat and had barely gotten my shoes on and tied my tie before we were being ushered off the plane to shake hands with a long line of Embassy officials and their wives and appropriate Japanese officials. There were at least a hundred scrambling newspapermen and photographers and, despite the early hour, a crowd of old friends and well-wishers, including a small group led by a former Indian student of mine with a banner reading "Harvard Students Welcome Ambassador Reischauer."

We were herded into the waiting room where, in front of an impressive battery of cameramen, I delivered my arrival statement. It included a reference to the "fruitful partnership" through which our two countries could help build "a peaceful and prosperous world." This was to remain my theme song for my five and a half years in Japan—and ever since for that matter. When I completed reading the English text, I read it in Japanese. The Japanese text had taken a lot of effort, but this paid off. Our arrival in Tokyo was being played live on the seven o'clock national television news—the reason for the plane's rapid landing at Haneda—and the public was much impressed to be addressed in Japanese by a foreign envoy.

Once the arrival statements were over, we were whisked from the airport to the seclusion of the palatial Embassy Residence in the big ambassadorial Cadillac, with the American flag fluttering from one fender and my personal ambassadorial flag from the other. The six-mile route had been cleared of traffic, and policemen were stationed at every crossroad. The whole arrival procedure was said to have been unprecedented for any Ambassador, being more comparable to the arrival of a chief of state. We had obviously taken a giant step away from the comfortable obscurity of academic life.

# 26
# The Tokyo Embassy

F ROM THE moment I stepped onto Japanese soil, I became fully responsible for the American Embassy. All telegrams and messages sent out from it bore my name, although the bulk of them, which were on routine matters, I never saw, and I took part in drafting, or more frequently correcting, only the most important ones. Naturally it took considerable time before I could really take charge of what was going on at the Embassy or make the necessary contacts with the Japanese officials. We could not even start on the second task until I had a chance to present my credentials to the Emperor. Until then we were in a state of diplomatic purdah, denied official contact with the Japanese government and the diplomatic corps.

This, however, gave us a breathing space in which to get our bearings. It was a pleasure to have Haru's sweet and gentle mother and father and one of her younger sisters, Tane, living nearby in a small but comfortable home. Our Japanese staff always called it the *honke,* or "main house," though it wasn't a tenth the size of our veritable palace. Tane had founded and ran an excellent little school, called the Nishimachi International School.

We also started at once to familiarize ourselves with the Embassy we were to lead. While some of the Embassy staff consisted of former students of mine who were enthusiastic about our appointment, and the Japanese employees were generally happy about it, we realized that some of the Foreign Service old-timers might resent our selection and were possibly still influenced by my predecessor's pique over the *Foreign Affairs* article. We were particularly nervous about William Leonhart, our chief Minister and Deputy Chief of Mission (DCM), and his wife, "Pidge," on whom we depended heavily to teach us the ropes. Our fears, however, were entirely unfounded. Whatever the Leonharts may have felt originally, they gave us all the support and loyalty we could have hoped for. In fact, during the five and a half years we were at the Embassy, we never felt that any of its members, either American or Japanese, gave us anything less than their full support, and we were constantly impressed by the hard work of the Foreign Service officers and their wives.

The Embassy proper consisted of four major divisions. First came the Political Section under the DCM and a Political Counsellor, who conducted most of our relations with the Japanese government and also with the large American military establishment quartered in Japan. The DCM acted as my deputy in all matters and as the chargé d'affaires, that is, my substitute, when I was absent from Japan. Next came an Economic Section under an Economic Minister and Economic Counsellor—with a subordinate Commercial Section under a Commercial Counsellor which was concerned with helping to foster American business activities in Japan. One of the chief weaknesses of the Embassy was its almost complete lack of competent economists who were also well trained in the Japanese language. A third major branch was the Consular Section, which issued passports to Americans, provided foreigners with visas, and helped Americans who had gotten into trouble. It had two consul generals and several consuls scattered in consular posts around Japan. Associated with the Consular Section was a Japanese-language school located in Yokohama to train more Japanese-language experts for the Foreign Service. On graduating, they usually went to consulates as their first posts because these provided them with the best opportunity to further strengthen their Japanese. Finally there was the Administrative Section under the Administrative Counsellor, who ranked at the bottom of the pecking order of counsellors.

Affiliated with the Embassy proper were a variety of attached representatives of other parts of the American government. The largest of these was the United States Information Service (USIS), the usual term in the field at that time for the USIA of Washington. Under the direction of a Public Affairs Officer, it had one of the major tasks of the Embassy, which was to spread information about the United States and try to create a favorable image of it. USIS maintained a series of American Cultural Centers around the country.

I felt that USIS should be regarded as a fully integral part of the Embassy, and I encouraged its members not to see themselves simply as public relations officers, dispensing news and measuring their success by the number of lines printed, but more as the developers of significant intellectual and cultural contacts which would help engender mutual appreciation and understanding with Japan. But our USIS, even though it included many exceptionally competent Japanese, was one of the weakest parts of the Embassy. It was also too large for me to get hold of easily. Eventually I decided that I should find someone I could trust to run it for me. It occurred to me that the whole work of USIS could be upgraded and pointed in the right direction by having it placed under a good Cultural Minister of equal rank with the Political and Economic Ministers. There had been a Cultural Attaché all along, and that position continued, but a Cultural Minister was an entirely new concept. I began to think of Burton Fahs for the post, since he was concluding his term as director of the humanities at the Rockefeller Foundation. After several months of indecision Burton did join the Embassy at the end of March 1962, making it at that time the only American Embassy in the world with a troika of ministers. He did a fine job, establishing close contacts with a wide range of Japanese intellectual leaders, though, after a period of experiment, it was decided to place the administrative control of USIS back under the Public Affairs Officer.

The position of Cultural Minister unfortunately did not long outlive my stay at the Embassy. The allocation of resources in our foreign relations leaves me constantly dismayed. Money spent on diplomatic and cultural activities is proportionately far more productive than that spent on military programs but is always the first to be cut, even though the sums are absolutely inconsequential compared to military budgets. In our later years in Tokyo, Washington decreed the closing of several consulates and American Cultural Centers. The post of Cultural Minister was also considered an unnecessary frill; after I left it was first downgraded, then finally dropped altogether.

Next in size to USIS among the attached offices was the Military Aid Assistance Group (MAAG), consisting of sixty to seventy officers under a major general and concerned with providing military hardware for Japan; but the connection between it and the Embassy was rather tenuous. Somewhat closer to the Embassy were the three military attaché offices of the army, navy, and air force, which were well staffed by specially trained officers who generally handled their own housekeeping matters. I was never clear about the division of work between them and the much larger MAAG and resident American military establishment, but my own contacts and those of the military affairs subsection of the Political Section of the Embassy were largely with the resident American military.

The military attaché offices illustrated the differences in support our government provides its military and diplomatic representatives. Whereas the Embassy was always tight on personnel and many of its officers had received little or no preparation for their assignments in Japan, the military attaché offices were manned by officers who had spent two or three years of language and Washington office training in preparation for their jobs in Tokyo, which certainly were not as important as those performed by the Foreign Service officers. But I should not complain, because I was the beneficiary of the military's more generous set-up. The air force attaché had a plane at his disposal, which I used on occasion to visit various parts of Japan.

Among the many other attached groups was the CIA, which by this time was limited in Japan for the most part to intelligence efforts directed toward China and the semi-clandestine support of the Asia Foundation, an organization that supported worthy causes such as the exchange of labor leaders between the two countries. Normally one would expect this to be a function of USIS; but the State Department and especially USIS were so much the low men on the totem pole with Congress that such activities, which though valuable might not be appreciated by the average congressman, required a CIA cloak to obtain funding. Revelations in recent years of CIA skulduggery elsewhere in the world have made me wonder if I was given the full story of its activities, yet the station chief during much of my stay in Tokyo was a former student of mine, whom I was inclined to believe. In any case, the Agency played a very modest role in Japan at the time and was only connected with the Embassy in theory.

More integral parts of the Embassy were the two labor attachés from the Department of Labor, who acted more or less as members of the Political Section. A Treasury attaché worked closely with the Economic Section. In addition to him but quite separate was a larger office representing the Treasury Department, which was staffed by long-term members of the Embassy engaged in working with the Japanese officials in staunching the flow to the United States of drugs from the so-called golden triangle, where Laos, Burma, and Thailand meet. Japan itself has virtually no drug problem. There were various other attaché offices besides these. Indeed, the ramifications of the Embassy were multitudinous, and the paperwork involved in the management of all these different groups must have been tremendous, but I did my best to stay away from such housekeeping and personnel matters. Thanks to efficient officers as DCM and Administrative Counsellor, I usually was able to do so.

 ⚬ð

Our Embassy Residence was a beautiful building standing on a hill above the Chancery but now dwarfed by the Okura Hotel which looms above it. One entered the Residence through a large entrance hall flanked by an impressive broad curving stairway and a handsome foyer, all with stately marble floors. The entrance way and foyer led to a "small" dining room that could accommodate twenty with the greatest of ease, a large dining room suitable for fifty or more guests, and a reception room, which was easily a hundred feet long. This room is best known for a famous picture of a tieless General MacArthur and the formally clad Emperor standing in front of the pillars at its far end. In addition, on the first floor there was a "cozy" study which would have been a respectably sized living room in any normal house. Except for this last room, all the ceilings were incredibly high. In fact, before we left the Embassy, Haru and I gave a party for some of our ambassadorial colleagues at which we played badminton in the reception room with no fear that the birds would hit the ceiling. The whole of the first floor was scarcely homey. It gave us the feeling of living in the National Art Gallery, and it took us several years before we really felt at home eating by ourselves in the smaller dining room or sitting alone in front of a fire in the large reception room.

Upstairs was a little less overpowering. For one thing, the ceilings were of reasonable height. At one end was a suite where the Eisenhowers were to have stayed in June 1960. Ambassador MacArthur and his wife had converted the decor of these rooms and much of the rest of the Embassy into the pink that Mamie Eisenhower was said to like. The results were ghastly. At the other end was another suite which General MacArthur had occupied. We slept there happily for our full stay at the Embassy, untroubled by dreams of the great man. Eventually Haru had the hallway leading to our suite closed off with a partition and door, making the area somewhat more our own private preserve where we spent most of our free time.

The whole building was decorated in a stuffy, old-fashioned way, and it took a great deal of hard work on the part of Haru to refurbish the rooms. One of her first acts was to get rid of the Mamie pink voile curtains which were on most of the windows. We were helped tremendously by a generous loan of works from the Museum of Modern Art in New York. I selected them on my first trip back to the United States in June, and they made a stunning display of modern American art. I was particularly proud of a handsome Kline, strongly reminiscent of Japanese calligraphy, and a beautiful abstract by Kenzo Okada, which we hung at opposite ends of the large dining room. Both pictures belonged to John Rockefeller's gracious and charming wife, Blanchette. On entering our dining room for the first time, she exclaimed, "Oh, I'm so glad you have my Kline." Then she turned to the Okada and said nothing. I was amused to see that she had forgotten that she owned such a magnificent work of art.

Off the downstairs foyer was a broad terrace and in front of it a large fountain and extensive lawn, ideal for croquet. It was a great place for recreation until the Okura Hotel, on which construction had just started when we arrived, rose high above it; later an even taller annex was added, permitting hundreds of pairs of eyes to look down on what the Ambassador and his wife might be doing in their garden.

A pathway led down the hill from the Embassy Residence to the Chancery compound below. It is one of the most beautiful hillsides in all Tokyo, with a fine stand of old trees. No one ever had a pleasanter trip between home and office than I during those years. At the base of the hill was a small swimming pool which Haru and I opened to all Americans who resided or worked in the Chancery compound.

The Chancery and two satellite buildings were graceful structures, done in the same pseudo-Spanish style as the Residence. But they were built on an entirely inadequate scale for current Embassy needs. The bulk of the Embassy offices had to be located a few blocks away in a separate six-story structure. Only a few of the key officers were in the Chancery. My own office was a spacious, dignified room. Behind its big desk a large American flag stood on one side and on the other an equally large ambassadorial flag, which closely resembled that of the President. The walls were decorated with large relief maps of the Japanese Islands. The higher officials of the Embassy all had beautiful homes scattered around Tokyo, while the lesser staff members were concentrated for purposes of economy in two large apartment buildings on the so-called Mitsui property not far from the Embassy.

The total Embassy staff, including some of the attaché offices, the outlying consulates and Cultural Centers, the Marine Corps guards, and the many Japanese staff members, motor pool drivers, and servants, amounted to about three hundred Americans and more than twice as many Japanese. One of the first things I did was to meet and shake hands with all of those who were in Tokyo, delivering short "inspirational" speeches whenever there was a large enough group to make this seem appropriate. I addressed myself particularly to the Japanese employees, who unlike the Americans—generally in Japan for two or four years—were permanently with the Embassy. I emphasized their role in giving our work continuity and in helping to make the contacts with the Japanese public which contributed to the development of the equal partnership I felt should exist between the two countries. Over a longer period of time, Haru took on a more ambitious program of getting to know the Embassy women. She had all the women officers, secretaries, wives of American officers, and Japanese female office workers come in small groups to the Embassy Residence for morning coffee. There were some six hundred fifty of them in all. One Japanese woman remarked that she had never seen an Ambassador's wife before, much less been invited to the Residence. Later we added a monthly coffee for new American members of the Embassy and their spouses, whom otherwise we might never meet. Including the attached agencies, the newcomers averaged about thirty a month.

From the start Haru took over the supervision of the thirteen servants at the Embassy Residence, headed by our very efficient and loyal housekeeper, Mrs. Yamagata Nobu. There were also several gardeners, a boiler man, and three chauffeurs, two for me so that my Cadillac would be available at all times, and a third for Haru, who, contrary to precedent, was assigned her own car and chauffeur to help her out in her many official activities. These were so heavy that, unlike previous ambassadors' wives, she was assigned a full-time Japanese secretary and later an American one as well.

More than twenty people just helping us in the problems of everyday life, together with a large office staff to prepare and back up our activities, greatly increased our efficiency, and we found that we could do surprising amounts of work. Our strength seemed like "the strength of ten," not because of any special purity of heart, but simply because we had so many people propping us up. But the big household establishment was also costly. A complicated formula divided salaries for the servants and the other running expenses of the Residence between the Embassy and us personally, but the stream of American dignitaries who stayed at the Residence and occasional dinners for large American government delegations were considered our financial responsibility. Since we personally did not have the money for life on this scale, official "representational" funds were increased somewhat, and an additional confidential fund was provided to help with our entertainment expenses. As things worked out, we just about broke even, ending our five and a half years at almost exactly the same financial level at which we had started out.

For the whole time we were in Japan, Haru took charge of all our personal financial matters, and I did not give them a thought. Since I never went anywhere except in my car or with aides who looked after my tickets and expenses, I never carried any money with me. To be completely free of all financial concerns I found to be one of the pleasantest aspects of my years in Japan. The only money that ever passed through my hands was 500 yen Haru gave me every two weeks to pay the barber, who came to my office to cut my hair while I read nonconfidential documents. I suspect that this fee had become a gross underpayment by the time we left Tokyo, but the barber was happy to give me the service for the prestige it brought him. Incidentally, he had also cut General MacArthur's hair, and was one of the very few Japanese I ever met who had actually exchanged a word with him.

Each Ambassador is expected to set the tone of his Embassy and we naturally opted for informality and friendliness. This didn't, of course, prevent the Embassy staff from always addressing me as "Mr. Ambassador" or "Your Excellency"; it was quite disconcerting to find that I had in a sense lost my name. Even at a mixer for new arrivals at the Embassy, my card read simply "The Ambassador." On the other hand, I found it a great convenience to be able to address all my ambassadorial colleagues as "Your Excellency." I have never been good at remembering names, especially on the spur of the moment, and it was a relief to know that I could get by with this on any occasion.

Our informal style was appreciated by the members of the Embassy, and Haru was a welcome relief after some of her predecessors, who had been either sickly and offish or tyrannical. Foreign Service wives have now established their independence, but then they were expected to work for the Embassy without pay and serve the Ambassador's wife like so many slaves. A request by the Ambassador's wife could not be refused, nor could an invitation to the Residence, even if one already had a pressing engagement. Embassy members were expected to arrive at functions in the Residence before any of the other invited guests and to stay until the last had left, but we found this custom impractical for big receptions. Some guests, seeing so many Embassy personnel around, would think the party was still in full swing and would linger on interminably. We devised a system whereby the Embassy staff would begin slipping away after the bar had closed, making it clear to everyone that the party was over. The members of the Embassy, however, could never leave other functions until the Ambassador and his wife had departed, and they would never precede us through doorways. Despite such continuing diplomatic formalities, we were able to make a more friendly, informal style prevail at the Embassy. In fact, a certain Ambassador Flake, who at the time of our arrival happened to be at the Embassy for a two-month tour of inspection and evaluation, told us upon leaving that never in his thirty-five years in the Foreign Service had he seen the morale and spirit of an Embassy rise so sharply as ours did after we came.

# 27

# Getting Acquainted

I PRESENTED my credentials to the Emperor on April 27, 1961, and thus became diplomatically sanitized. I was permitted to take with me to the palace the six top officers of the Embassy, who were Leonhart, the Economic Minister Philip Trezise, who later occupied several ambassadorial posts, three men of Counsellor rank, and the chief of the military attachés, who at the time was a two-star air force major general. All except the military man were dressed in top hats, morning coats, and striped trousers, the official court costume. In commemorative photographs we look like the cats who just swallowed the canaries.

I entered the audience chamber alone, while the others concealed themselves behind a screen. After walking down a red carpet and bowing low before the Emperor, I went through a formalized exchange in which I announced my predecessor's departure and presented my own credentials from the President. The Emperor was flanked by his grand chamberlain, Mitani Takanobu, the brother of the Miss Mitani I had called "Aunty" in my childhood, and by an interpreter. The latter translated what I said, but after the Emperor spoke I replied immediately. This was a serious *faux pas*. When I had finished, the translator, with a pained expression, translated carefully into English the Emperor's remarks to which I had already replied and followed this with a Japanese translation of my answer. I dutifully waited thereafter for his two-way translation. The Emperor appeared to me younger and stronger than when I had first met him almost thirteen years earlier. Our whole conversation seemed incredibly stiff, but Mr. Mitani later informed me that the Emperor had been unusually relaxed and friendly. It was always a great convenience to receive readings on the Emperor's and the court's reactions to our appearances there, either through Mr. Mitani, or still more often through Haru's various contacts among the people at court.

At the proper moment I presented the six members of my retinue, one at a time. Each in turn emerged from behind the screen and bowed deeply where the red carpet made a right-angle turn and again on arriving in front of the Emperor. I then presented him, and he withdrew, walking backwards and bowing again at the turn in the carpet. After watching how awkward they all were walking in reverse, I came to a quick decision that the time was past for such antiquated foolishness. When it came the point for me to withdraw, I bowed, turned around and walked to the turn in the carpet, bowed deeply again, and walked out. We never heard any comment on my action so I presume my disregarding of court etiquette was not taken amiss.

The presentation of my credentials did not complete the preliminary formalities for getting started on our work in Japan but simply opened the door for a whole flood of lesser but similar activities. For one thing, we were now cleared for functions at court and attended two days later the big reception held to celebrate the Emperor's birthday. On such occasions the Emperor and Empress normally walked around each room shaking hands with the ambassadors and their wives, who would form a circle. They never shook hands with any Japanese regardless of the occasion. This had raised the question in our minds as to whether Haru, as a native-born Japanese, should bow or shake hands. We had even wondered about her curtseying on the proper occasions, as the wives of American diplomats did in many places, but we came to the conclusion that she, as the American Ambassador's wife, should act in a purely American way and should always shake hands with all Japanese. This proved the right decision and never occasioned any embarrassment or uncertainty.

At court functions, the Emperor could not conceal his boredom as he gravely murmured to each person in turn, "*Yo koso* (You are welcome)." However, on more than one occasion early in our stay, he suddenly broke his usual solemn round when he looked up and saw that he was shaking my hand and, bursting into a broad smile, would say with enthusiasm, "*Honto ni yo koso* (You really are very welcome)." The Emperor is indeed a very straightforward, genuine person, without an iota of guile in him. But I was thankful that my ambassadorial neighbors could not understand the variation in his greeting. After the hand shaking was completed, the court chamberlains would usually insist that I join the Emperor in conversation and Haru the Empress, since we were virtually the only persons able to speak with them in Japanese. This gave us a chance to get to know them far better than any of our colleagues did. I also took many persons for audiences with the Emperor, helping to introduce them and keep the conversational ball rolling. The Emperor was by no means a skilled conversationalist, but I never took a person for an audience who did not come away remarking on his sincerity and goodwill.

Haru and I were expected to make formal calls on the Crown Prince and Princess and the brothers and widowed sister-in-law of the Emperor, and to entertain each of them at a formal diplomatic dinner. Over time we developed quite a warm relationship with the Crown Prince and Princess. She is a most charming, cultivated person, and it was a pleasure to watch him develop the skills and image his ceremoniously heavy burdens demanded of him. Less busy ambassadors interpreted the duty of entertaining the members of the imperial family to mean a dinner for each every year, but we chose to take it to mean a dinner once during our stay in Tokyo. I am sure that the members of the imperial family, who were heavily engaged in ceremonial functions of this sort, were grateful for our looser interpretation. Official calls on the members of the cabinet and many of the other higher officials in the government were also part of the preliminary formalities; Haru and I also were expected to make short formal calls on each of the other ambassadorial couples in Tokyo, who at the time numbered about sixty.

◆§

My contacts in Japan had hitherto been largely with scholars, intellectuals, and family friends, most of whom were engaged in educational work. These I kept up, but it was important now for me to get to know leading politicians, bureaucrats, and businessmen as well. Whatever their reservations may have been about a professor Ambassador, they appeared eager to see for themselves what I was like, and they received me quite warmly. Through them I came to see Japan from a new angle and gained a more rounded view of how Japanese society actually operated.

The day after I presented my credentials to the Emperor, I called on the Prime Minister, Ikeda Hayato. He was a very impressive man, for whom I developed immense respect, and over time we built up a strong friendship. The next day I called on the Foreign Minister, Kosaka Zentaro, whom I already knew, and followed this by calls on various other ministers. Since the cabinet was usually shifted around each year, I eventually established close relations with many of the top figures in the ruling Liberal Democratic Party (LDP), including all of those who have since become prime ministers, except for Suzuki Zenko, who was a fisheries expert with whom I had few contacts.

Sato Eisaku, who succeeded Ikeda in 1964 and was in office for an unprecedented term of seven and a half years, was a very jovial, friendly person, but I felt he lacked the backbone of Ikeda. His successor in 1972, Tanaka Kakuei, was a wealthy, self-made man of modest education, entirely unlike any of the others. He was a hard-driving leader, who won himself the nickname of the "computerized bulldozer." Although indictments over financial scandals forced him in 1974 to resign from the prime ministership and also the party, and he was subsequently convicted (though he is still appealing the case), he has remained a major power in the LDP. I always found him very friendly, but there was too great a gap in our backgrounds to establish any real sense of intimacy. Miki Takeo, as an old liberal, being the only member of the group of future prime ministers who had been a member of the Diet before the war, was naturally a sympathetic figure, but I did not get to know him as well as I would have wished. Fukuda Takeo was friendly enough, but he was 100 percent bureaucrat by background and nature, and this seemed to put a limit on our closeness.

Ohira Masayoshi, who followed Kosaka as Foreign Minister in 1962 and was Prime Minister from 1978 until his untimely death in 1980, was the member of the group I felt closest to. We often joked about both having been born in 1910. He was seen as an enigmatic figure by the Japanese public, yet I found him always to be straightforward and reliable. The fact that he was a Christian—a member of the group of intellectuals known as the "No Church" Movement—may have contributed to these traits. His experience as a teacher of English in his early years had left scarcely a trace, though he sharpened up his English considerably before becoming Prime Minister. Ohira seemed to me the most effective of the politicians, having the daring to steer the public toward necessary though unpopular goals and the wisdom to do this slowly and with tact. I felt that he and Ikeda had a clear vision of the international role that Japan was compelled by its economic strength to play.

My contacts with Nakasone Yasuhiro, who is now Prime Minister, went back the furthest. In the 1950s Henry Kissinger ran a summer seminar at Harvard for younger public figures from around the world, and I regularly went through the applications from Japan to help him in his selections. Nakasone, then a junior member of the Diet, was in the first group of Japanese to come in 1953, and he and the other Japanese spent an evening of discussion with me at my house. In 1961 he was one of the faction leaders of the LDP, and today as Prime Minister he is playing a world role more in keeping with the times than have most of his predecessors.

I also came to know some of the still active political leaders who had preceded Ikeda; but curiously enough they were all persons with whom it was difficult for me to establish meaningful contacts. I had many talks with Kishi, Ikeda's immediate predecessor as Prime Minister, yet I never felt close to him. As a member of the Tojo cabinet which led Japan into war against the United States, he seemed to me a man of another age. I felt the same way about Ono Bamboku and Kono Ichiro, who, although never prime ministers, had already been prominent parliamentarians before the war and remained contenders for the position.

Naturally many of the politicians whom I came to know through their official posts did not achieve the position of Prime Minister, though some are still in the running. Miyazawa Kiichi is a good example. He stands out as an exceptionally bright and likable person and the only senior member of the Diet who speaks English well enough to conduct a serious conversation in it. Even more remarkable, he is familiar enough with Western ways of thinking and is himself enough of an intellectual to be a good participant in international conferences. I got to know him best through such conferences after I left the ambassadorship.

In addition to the leading LDP politicians and the top bureaucrats, I came to know well many of the prominent businessmen as well as leaders of the opposition parties. On the business side, I particularly valued the close relations I established with Ishizaka Taizo, who as the president of Keidanren, the powerful Federation of Economic Organizations, was the undisputed grand old man of the Japanese economic world.

Among the opposition political groups, I avoided the small ultra-conservative party, the Aikokuto (Patriotic Party), like the plague. Its members plastered the cities with wildly anti-Communist propaganda and rushed around in noisy sound trucks, waving big Japanese and American flags. It was my nightmare that some day their leader, Akao Bin, would manage to slip up to me for a handshake and picture. I also did not meet with the Communist leaders, who were so anti-American and doctrinaire that a useful exchange of ideas would have been impossible; but I did get together often with the successive leaders of the chief opposition party, the Socialists, even though they were not much less anti-American or doctrinaire. A discussion held in my office with some of them in the summer of 1961 was the first formal contact between the American Embassy and the Socialists for over a year. There was one prominent Socialist, Eda Saburo, I never met, even though I would have liked to very much. He was definitely a moderate in his views and less antagonistic to the United States than the others, but I feared that my talking with him might harm his status within his party.

The leaders of the Democratic Socialist Party were close enough to me in their thinking to make discussions easy, and I talked frequently with Nishio Suehiro and Sone Eki, their two chief leaders. I also talked often with Ikeda Daisaku, the head of the vastly popular new religious movement, the Soka Gakkai, which in the course of the early 1960s spawned the opposition Komeito Party. I had even more frequent talks with the heads of the two largest labor federations. Meetings with the leaders of Zenro (later called Domei), the more moderate group, were always congenial, but my discussions with Iwai Akira and Ota Kaoru, the two top men of the far-left Sohyo federation, were invariably vehement, though a lot of fun. Both men were very outspoken in their anti-American feelings but personally genial, and arguing with them was always stimulating.

Many parties of welcome were organized for Haru and me. Most were decorous and cordial, as in the case of the reception given by the United Protestant Church of Japan. Others were quite formal, as when I officially visited the Self Defense Forces, reviewed an honor guard, and met all the top officers. I called such an affair a "hat occasion," because I had to take along a hat to be held over my heart during the ceremonial playing of the two national anthems. I always found it spine-tingling to realize that it was I who was the national representative for whom the Star Spangled Banner was being played and American flags were flying. A particularly boisterous welcoming reception was held by Tsutsumi Yasujiro, a Japanese business tycoon. He made a point of including all the members of the Japanese cabinet and the full diplomatic corps. The Foreign Minister spoke, but the Soviet Ambassador quite properly declined on the grounds that I had not yet made my courtesy call on him and it was, in any case, the prerogative of the dean of the diplomatic corps, then the Ambassador of Ceylon (now Sri Lanka), to speak on such occasions. But the Soviet Ambassador was prominently in attendance, and Tsutsumi referred to the whole affair as a Far Eastern Summit Meeting, having in mind the Kennedy-Khrushchev summit that had just taken place in Vienna. Normal protocol procedures were disregarded, with the result that the whole occasion was completely unpredictable, a little chaotic, but very amusing.

One particularly formal event in our honor was a big luncheon held by the America-Japan Society. The purpose was to install me as honorary president, and I, of course, delivered the main speech. Japan's grand old man of politics, Yoshida Shigeru, came up from his beautiful home in Oiso on the coast some miles west of Tokyo to preside over the occasion. Yoshida had been the Prime Minister during most of the period between May 1946 and December 1954 but was nearing his dotage by this time, and I was never able to have a very satisfactory conversation with him. When he gave short introductory speeches at dinners or on other public occasions, he would often make embarrassingly frank or even outrageous statements, with mischievous disregard for current political sensitivities in Japan. Fortunately both the politicians and the press, perhaps in deference to his age, always chose to ignore them.

~§

Making contacts with my ambassadorial colleagues was a less pressing task than getting to know the Japanese leaders and could be spread over a longer period of time. Haru and I were expected to make a courtesy call of fifteen to twenty minutes on each of the other sixty-odd ambassadors and their wives. Since there are roughly twice that number today, I hope some relaxation of the custom has been made. I found that most ambassadors were eager to talk about their countries, and later, when the calling was being done on us by more recently arrived ambassadorial couples, the time often stretched well past the twenty-minute limit. For example, the Greek, Yugoslavian, and Bulgarian ambassadors all became so excited in their replies to my queries about their respective national definitions of Macedonia that they quite lost track of time. The young Czechoslovakian couple named Hrdlicka who arrived in the summer of 1964 turned out to be two former scholars in the Chinese field who had studied with us at Harvard shortly after World War II and had met and married in Cambridge. I was always treated as the venerable master of the Ambassador whenever I went to the Czechoslovakian Embassy.

Each Embassy held a national day reception, and we dutifully attended all of those we could. Haru and I were very conscientious on this score because the American Ambassador loomed so large in Tokyo at the time that there were sure to be hurt feelings if we failed to turn up. Ken Galbraith in New Delhi ignored such affairs on the valid grounds that the American Ambassador was too busy, but we felt that as outsiders both to the Foreign Service and to American politics, we had best be as punctilious as we could about diplomatic rites and ceremonies. The chore was very time-consuming, particularly the hours spent driving to and from receptions through crowded Tokyo traffic. Including other official receptions and those of large business enterprises, we often found ourselves attending as many as three in a single afternoon, sometimes followed by a formal dinner. Since we both hate cocktail parties and receptions and found those in Tokyo completely unproductive for developing meaningful contacts, we devised a way to make our stay at any reception as brief as possible. The main point in going was simply to be seen by the press and one's colleagues. Therefore we would move rapidly around each room shaking hands and when the tour was complete would beat a hasty retreat. We found we could "do" most receptions quite thoroughly in fifteen minutes or less.

While we were very dutiful about attending large receptions, which offered high visibility to a large number of people, we did draw the line on diplomatic dinner parties and tête-à-têtes with diplomatic colleagues. Since none of the other embassies had a staff comparable to ours and none of my colleagues had as much experience in Japan as I, a one-to-one conversation with another Ambassador would amount to a sort of tutorial in which I was the giver and he the receiver. I felt my time could be better spent in talking with Japanese or in briefing influential Americans who were passing through town. As for diplomatic banquets, they never got around to substantive conversations, lasted late, and left us tired for our duties the next day. We let it be known that we normally were not available either for personal conferences with diplomatic colleagues or for dinner parties.

Nonetheless, we made some good friends among the diplomatic corps. In our later years at the Embassy, a square dancing group was formed by some of the ambassadors and their wives. The Emperor's youngest brother, Prince Mikasa, whom we had known ever since our mutual connection with Tokyo Women's University in 1955–56, was an enthusiastic participant. On another level, the Dutch Ambassador was an acquaintance since my student days. He was Robert van Gulik, a Leiden graduate, who was famous for his series of fast-moving short murder mysteries featuring Judge Dee, done in the style of Chinese writers of the Ming Dynasty of the fourteenth to seventeenth centuries but ostensibly dealing with episodes in the T'ang Dynasty of the seventh to tenth centuries. In one of his mysteries he stated that he had drawn material for it from my own books on Ennin.

Our relations with the Soviet Ambassador usually drew public attention because of the strains between our two countries, even though our personal contacts were always quite pleasant. On both sides we were careful to attend each other's receptions, and a mass of pictures were taken of us with Gagarin, the first man in space, at a reception at the Soviet Embassy. When we arrived in Japan, the Soviet Ambassador was Dr. Nikolai T. Federenko, known as a student of early Chinese poetry. His interest and scholarship in this field was genuine, and our conversations were limited largely to this subject. Curiously enough, most of the Iron Curtain ambassadors were of a scholarly bent. One wonders if this was just happenstance or the product of some sort of policy. Federenko was followed by a man called Vinogradov, whose young daughter attended Tane's Nishimachi International School. Because of this connection, we invited the Vinogradovs to lunch alone with us. When we asked Mrs. Vinogradov what she liked about the school, she replied, "Its freedom." I wanted to ask her what she meant by "freedom" but felt it best to let the subject drop there. We left Japan just before Oleg Troyanofsky, who had been two years behind Haru at The American School in Japan, arrived to take up the Tokyo post.

The elderly, patrician Ecuadorian Ambassador and his wife insisted that Haru and I be included in the informal club of "American Ambassadors." Since all the others were Latin Americans and spoke little English, while I knew no Spanish and Haru very little, we felt somewhat out of place, but were touched by the gesture and hoped our response contributed something to United States–Latin American solidarity. This was still in the days before oil had fattened the Ecuadorian economy, and I remember the Ecuadorian Ambassador sidling up to me at a sumptuous reception put on by an oil-rich Middle Eastern country to whisper, "You can't do this on bananas."

Ambassadors ranked strictly according to the date on which they had presented their credentials. I thus started at the bottom and slowly worked my way up, as older ambassadors departed and newer ones arrived. At many court functions we would all line up in accordance with this pecking order, so that we got to know well those directly ahead and behind us in date of arrival. The Ambassador who had been in Tokyo longest served as dean of the diplomatic corps, a position which required various little ceremonial duties such as giving the farewell speech at the reception for a departing Ambassador. Only two ambassadors outranked me when we finally left Tokyo in 1966, showing how perilously close I had come to being saddled with these chores.

Haru and I also needed to establish friendly relations with the local Americans, particularly the business community and still more the military, which numbered around forty-five thousand in uniform together with a large number of dependent wives and children. To our surprise, we discovered that the hearty welcome the Japanese gave us helped greatly in our contacts with the American armed forces, because they were eager for better relations with the Japanese and they saw us as helping them in this. In fact, in contrast to Haru's fears about the attitude of the American military, they proved to be among our strongest supporters and her greatest admirers. She was invited to address the women's clubs of practically all the major American military bases, and the officers and their wives delighted in introducing her as "America's first lady in Japan."

One of the first things I did after arriving in Japan was to fly by helicopter to the headquarters of United States Forces, Japan, at Fuchu in the western part of Tokyo to inspect the facilities, be briefed, and meet all the American generals and admirals stationed in Japan. This trip included several firsts for me. It was the first time I inspected an honor guard; I had no idea what I was supposed to do, but I believe I carried off the occasion about as well as most civilian dignitaries seem to, as shown on television. The helicopter ride too was something new for me. I was initially startled at the unfamiliar angle of takeoff, as the contraption lurched off the landing pad at a steep angle, and the occasional clatter of the rotors was alarming, giving the impression they were about to fall off. But such thoughts were more than compensated for by the intimate, close-up views one gets of the geography and life below a low-flying helicopter. A week later Haru and I drove out to Fuchu for a big reception and dinner in our honor, attended by all the ranking American and Japanese military officers and their wives.

During our first few months in Japan, we visited almost all of the American bases in the Tokyo area. As there was an American helicopter landing pad conveniently near the Embassy and traveling in this way to the Tokyo suburbs could save up to an hour, we commonly went by helicopter. The military had strict regulations against women and other so-called dependents riding in helicopters—they are considered a relatively dangerous mode of transportation—but this rule was waived for Haru on my authority, so she became the only civilian woman allowed to ride an American helicopter in Japan.

United States Forces, Japan, was under the command of a three-star air force lieutenant general, who also commanded the Fifth Air Force in Japan, Korea, and Okinawa. At the time, this was Lieutenant General Robert W. ("Bobby") Burns, who was extremely helpful to Haru in her work of getting the Embassy Residence into better shape. For example, she discovered that by calling General Burns directly on the phone, without going through all the endless Embassy red tape, she could get many things done, such as acquiring new vacuum cleaners, in a fraction of the time it otherwise would take.

The bulk of the American bases in Japan were clustered in or near the western side of Tokyo, but there were some outlying posts, such as the air base at Misawa in northern Honshu, the Itazuke air base at Fukuoka in Kyushu, the marine base in Iwakuni, in western Honshu, and the naval base at Sasebo in Kyushu. In the Tokyo area, the Fifth Air Force had airfields at Tachikawa and Yokota as well as a few large residential enclaves. The chief army post was at Zama, and the main navy installation was the great base shared with the Japanese Maritime Self

Defense Force at Yokosuka, a short distance down Tokyo Bay past Yokohama, which had a supporting air base a little inland at Atsugi. The Seventh Fleet, which included all American naval vessels in the Western Pacific, was based at Yokosuka under the command of a three-star vice admiral.

One curious thing I noticed in dealing with the American military, and with Americans in general for that matter, was that they would often address me as Admiral, but never General. This happened to me even in the formal speech of farewell at the official dinner given me in 1966 by the military. I doubt that there was any deep significance in this blunder and assume that it was the initial letter "A" that steered nervous or confused persons to "Admiral" rather than "General," whenever "Ambassador" eluded their tongues.

Establishing contacts with the American business community in Japan presented no particular difficulties. I usually held a monthly session with the board of governors of the American Chamber of Commerce, and in later years we instituted a "Know Your Embassy Day" for all the members of the Chamber and their wives to help offset their feeling that the Embassy was not working as hard as it should on their behalf. I am not sure it helped overcome this attitude, but the day was always a great success, with lectures, seminars, and a concluding reception.

Another of my services to the American business community was to attend trade fairs, visiting the booths of American participants and thereby creating media publicity for them. The Embassy also had a nearby trade center where monthly shows of new American products were displayed. I usually cut the ribbon at these affairs, thereby drawing a few newsmen and making a minor news event of what was in reality a no-news occasion. The local American business community and its various clubs also held numerous black-tie balls, at which we were normally the guests of honor; I was often expected to offer the proverbial "few well chosen words" and start the dancing with Haru. We had scarcely danced at all since our courtship, but our life at the Embassy produced a last fling before we withdrew into more sedate middle age.

♫

Meeting with ordinary Japanese and getting to know them offered more problems than meeting with Americans, diplomats, and high Japanese dignitaries. This was because we were celebrities by the time we arrived in Japan. The problem was brought home to us very early in our stay. We planned a quiet trip out to Tokyo Women's University to see our old friends and former home. Word of this leaked out, and the simple expedition turned into a sort of television extravaganza. Later, when we took an official trip to Nagasaki in October, we happened to have an open evening, which was a rare treat. We and our Embassy escorts decided to try a simple but good one-room restaurant specializing in seafood. We were immediately recognized, and the now crowded restaurant was soon rocking with merriment. It was all great fun, but when we emerged to return to the hotel, we were engulfed in the narrow streets by several hundred people who had thronged there to get a glimpse of us. This made us realize that we simply could not go around casually but would have to be the prisoners of the police, bodyguards, and officials during our whole stay in Japan.

At first everything we did seemed to be newsworthy; our pictures appeared constantly in the newspapers and magazines, and we were frequently shown on television. For some nationwide TV programs, I would carefully prepare in Japanese my answers to serious questions submitted in advance, but on other occasions Haru and I would ad-lib the interviews in Japanese on lighter matters. Through the media, our faces became familiar to almost everyone in Japan. If we tried to walk the streets in a spare moment, we would invariably be spotted and surrounded by autograph seekers and picture takers. This was particularly true when Haru and I were together, and even today, over twenty years later, we are more likely to be identified when we are together than when either of us is alone. Haru, being less conspicuous than I, did go out of the Embassy on her own from time to time, but I found myself limited to a brisk walk early Sunday mornings from the Embassy around the perimeter of the extensive palace grounds and back, before many people were stirring. We discovered that the best way to handle photographers and cameramen was to be completely oblivious to their presence, but hand shakers and autograph seekers always required a cheerful response.

Joan too was much in the news, and she handled herself in interviews and on television like an old pro. She agreed to serve as an assistant teacher in English-language lessons on one TV and two radio programs. I was amused to see that on the very same day my first formal press interview was featured on the front page of an English-language newspaper under the headline "Reischauer Charms Press Corps," another article appeared on page 5 under the headline "Joan Charms as TV Star."

The tremendous interest the Japanese public showed in us caused problems, but it was also an asset. It meant that what we said attracted attention, and this was helpful in getting our message across. Most American ambassadors dread public attention and press interviews, fearing that they may stumble between local sensitivities and Washington policy, but I welcomed them as a way to reach the public. My first formal press interview was the lead story in every paper the next day. Usually the Japanese reporters designated one of their members to ask some well-selected questions they had agreed on. These were always straightforward, and they were usually reported in a straightforward way, emphasizing the main points I wished to get across, no matter how much my answers might have rambled. I cannot say the same for all the American correspondents. Some of them seemed to want to trick me into unwise statements which would make good copy, however disastrous they might be for me or Japanese-American relations. At my first interview I was appalled to find an old and good American friend throw a question at me that was definitely a curve ball. If your friends would do this to you, I wondered, what could you expect from your enemies? But my contacts with both the Japanese and American press were on the whole very friendly. A group of the leading American correspondents, including Abe Rosenthal, now the editor of *The New York Times,* would periodically invite me to a Chinese dinner for a good off-the-record session.

Haru and I were treated by the mass media and the Japanese public as if we were screen celebrities, pop stars, or at least visiting royalty. She came to be generally called *Haru Fujin,* "Madame Haru." This public use of a first name was most unusual in Japan, being limited for the most part to Haru and Princess Michiko, the Crown Princess. It was all a bit overwhelming. Positions of prominence are not often thrust on persons with little or no previous training or any thought of occupying them. Admirals do not walk off the street onto the bridge of a battleship, nor generals to high command posts. Politicians, though often unprepared, must have striven hard for any high office they win. Even young athletes have devoted years of concentrated effort before they become champions. Only the proverbial waitress spotted in a restaurant by a film executive and elevated to sudden stardom—if such persons actually exist—would be comparable to Haru and me, who had been unexpectedly summoned from the college classroom and suburban motherhood to the top circles of diplomacy. We found the situation both amusing and frightening. A cartoon—I believe it was in *The New Yorker*—expressed our feelings very well, and we framed and hung it in our private upstairs living room. It shows two gorillas cowering in a cage in front of a gawking crowd, while one laments to the other, "They expect so much and we have so little to give."

The publicity surrounding our every move, our palatial living quarters, and our contacts with a particularly punctilious court, the oldest by far in the world, all gave us a sense of unreality. Since many of the rules and customs of diplomatic life had hardened into their present form in the eighteenth century, I often felt that I had slipped a century or two back in time. I could not get away from the feeling that we were somehow engaged in a huge theatrical performance. It seemed as if I had been dragged off the street, equipped with a helmet and sword, and pushed out onstage in the middle of a performance of a Wagnerian opera. I was told to sing, and lo, when I opened my mouth my voice bellowed forth, apparently to the satisfaction of the audience. For a long time I half expected our gilded coach to turn into a pumpkin and to wake up in my bed in Belmont.

# 28

# An Ambassador's Job

Haru and i adapted easily to diplomatic life and quickly learned the ropes, but none of this had much to do with what we had come to Tokyo to accomplish. I have often been asked, "What does an Ambassador do?" Perhaps I should digress here to attempt to answer this question and explain how we went about trying to perform our job as we saw it.

Ideally, an Ambassador fulfills the following functions: he is the visible representative of the United States in the land to which he has been assigned; he performs certain services for individual Americans there, especially if some crisis arises, and oversees contacts with nationals of the other country wanting relations with the United States; he keeps Washington informed on conditions and attitudes in the country; he acts as an official channel of communication and participates in negotiations between Washington and the other government; he takes part in developing American policy toward the other country; and, to perform these various duties, he naturally must maintain a reasonably efficient Embassy. I would add another duty, even though it is all but ignored by many ambassadors: the building of attitudes of friendship and goodwill toward the United States on the part of the government and people of the other country and the deepening of understanding between the two lands.

Needless to say, the ambassadorial ideal is not often achieved. It requires an unusual combination of qualities, particularly a deep knowledge and understanding of the other country, a broad enough comprehension of American policies and world conditions to see the other nation in proper perspective, acceptance there as an authentic representative of American views, and sufficient respect in Washington to have some influence in the United States. Often ambassadors are woefully ignorant of the country to which they have been sent, lacking even knowledge of its language, and not many have these other qualities either. As a result, most of them remain confined to the lower levels of the functions they are meant to perform. They naturally must keep their embassies operating. They carry out their representational duties with gusto, often because there is little else for them to do. They perform the necessary services for individuals. They act as mailmen in keeping communications open between the two governments. They report to Washington on conditions and attitudes in their assigned countries, though the value of this information differs radically depending on the knowledge of those reporting and the other sources of information available. But few ambassadors play much of a role in building understanding or in conducting important negotiations, and most may do nothing in the way of establishing policy, either because of ignorance or timidity.

Washington regrettably makes scant effort to train its ambassadors to perform these potentially more valuable roles. One major problem is the spoils system of American politics, which has inappropriately pervaded our diplomatic establishment. About half of the ambassadors, including most of those in the more desirable posts as well as the bulk of the top officials in the State Department, are diplomatic amateurs, many of whom are being rewarded with these positions for campaign contributions or are being consoled for having lost their own election campaigns. The resulting appointments are sometimes ludicrous, as when a newly appointed Ambassador proves ignorant of the name of the Prime Minister of the country to which he is being sent.

The professional Foreign Service officers in ambassadorial posts are normally better informed, but they labor under some serious handicaps. Usually they are not well known to the political leaders in Washington and are overshadowed by a thick layer of less knowledgeable political appointees in the State Department. They are also not encouraged to become heavily involved in any one country or region. Nothing is considered more damning than to be accused of "localitis." A long war has raged in the State Department between the generalists and the local experts, with the generalists emerging almost invariably the victors. The lesson has not been lost on the young Foreign Service Officer, who must have an unusual devotion to some particular area to persist in developing his expertise in it. He is also unlikely to show much initiative or daring. Control by uninformed political appointees above him has shown him the danger of displaying fully his own expert knowledge or any unorthodox judgments derived from it.

Both amateur and professional ambassadors suffer from another sharp limitation to their effectiveness. Representatives of other Washington departments and agencies, such as the Defense, Commerce, and Treasury departments, AID, and CIA, who may have narrower points of view and less knowledge, often preempt parts of the Ambassador's field of activity. In many countries it is the major representative of the American military, the administrator of economic aid, or the head of the CIA station who is regarded by the local government and people as the chief representative of the United States.

Under these circumstances it is not surprising that American ambassadors as a whole do not win much respect. Half of them are amateurs, and many of the others are emasculated by the system. Some of both groups have proved themselves invaluable public servants, but in no other advanced country in the world is the choice of ambassadors so haphazard or the role of the Foreign Service so humble and insecure. It is a wonder so many members of the Foreign Service stick it out.

Clearly a better system is needed to bring true expert knowledge and responsible leadership together in the task of formulating and executing American foreign policy. This is an area that is steadily becoming more important for the United States and the whole world. I myself believe that almost all ambassadorships and top State Department posts, except for the Secretary of State himself, should be occupied by professional Foreign Service officers, as is the situation in almost all other advanced countries, and that amateur ambassadors like myself and other nonprofessionals in the embassies and State Department should be limited to a few special cases in which persons of exceptional expert knowledge or special political influence in Washington are needed to handle some very unusual situation.

The specific role an Ambassador actually plays of course depends to a large degree on his personal qualities and his contacts with the White House and his other Washington superiors. It also depends on the nature of the country to which he is assigned. In the advanced Western democracies, such as Canada and the countries of Western Europe, policy problems and diplomatic negotiations are mountainous, involving a tremendous flow of non-Embassy officials back and forth. A free press also quite overshadows embassies in the collection of information. Since there are no serious language or culture barriers and cabinet officers and other high officials usually can talk directly with each other, the Ambassador and his staff are frequently bypassed and end up by becoming mere facilitators in arranging meetings which others will attend. As a result, the post of Ambassador as it is now constituted does not necessarily require much specialized knowledge or experience and can safely be given to an amateur. If such a person is to make a mark in diplomacy, it is likely to be in the social field through lavish representational activities. Of course, not all of our ambassadors to our Western allies have been people of this type, but these countries have come to expect amateur diplomats from the United States. Some, such as Australia, have grumbled at times over the unsuitable choices Washington has made; but the United States remains unruffled, assuming that nothing could possibly go wrong in our relations with Australia, no matter who our Ambassador is.

The Communist countries stand at the opposite extreme. Since social life is minimal and contacts with the local people are almost nonexistent, ambassadorial life there has little appeal to the glamour seeker. Severe control of the mass media and personal contacts may make clandestine intelligence operations more important than the open information gathering of the Embassy. Diplomatic negotiations may be sparse, but they are likely to be so delicate that they must be kept under strict control by Washington. This may leave the local Ambassador with little more than the letter carrier's role.

In much of the rest of the world, where countries are likely to be both small and underdeveloped, there may not be much intelligence of significance to be collected, diplomatic negotiations are likely to be over minor matters from the American point of view, and policy cannot be made country by country but must be made in Washington on a regional basis. As a result, an Ambassador's job is likely to be neither glamorous nor important. In many developing countries, policies also may be so heavily slanted toward economic or military aid or, as sometimes has happened, toward clandestine efforts to control the local political situation, that it is the head of the economic or military aid mission or the CIA station chief, rather than the Ambassador, who is in fact the major local American representative. Or again in some countries, such as South Korea, a military alliance with the United States may be regarded as being of such overwhelming importance as to make the commander of the local American military forces the dominant representative of the United States.

◄§

These are, of course, only broad generalizations, and many countries do not fit into them at all. Certainly Japan did not when I was the Ambassador in Tokyo or even today. Relations of all types with Japan were immense and diplomatic negotiations diverse, as in the case of the major countries of Europe. However, barriers of language and differing cultural backgrounds stood between the leaders of the United States and Japan, and Americans knew relatively little about the Japanese and their country. Washington needed the services of a well-informed Ambassador and Embassy staff, and it tended to make full use of them. When I was in Tokyo, moreover, the Ambassador no longer had any serious contenders for the role of chief American representative in Japan. Economic aid had dwindled to a small pipeline operation channeling aid to other countries. CIA activities were minimal. Only the American military stood out prominently. Military matters, however, were the area of chief delicacy in Japanese-American relations and therefore had to be subordinated as much as possible to political control. Thus, despite the memory of General MacArthur's recent military proconsulship, the American Ambassador clearly took precedence over the local American military commander.

My position was greatly strengthened by the fact that in addition to having a strong staff, I myself was the focus of much favorable attention on the part of the Japanese public and government, and I was early able to win the confidence of Washington. As a result, I was in a position to play a substantial role in policy formulation and the shaping of attitudes between Japan and the United States. If I had not been able to do this, I would not have gone on with the job. I was distressed by the tendency of many of the Embassy officials to fuzz up their own conclusions in telegrams to Washington by balancing almost every judgment by a contrary one, introduced by "On the other hand," and I was irritated by their almost routine conclusion of important telegrams with the phrase "Await instructions." No doubt, these were the natural precautions of professional bureaucrats not wishing to stick out their necks. But, as I pointed out, no one was in a better position than we at the Embassy to evaluate the situation in Japan and make clear recommendations. I would refuse to sign out important telegrams requiring action which, instead of including our own forthright recommendations for action, would meekly end with a noncommittal "Await instructions."

I realized that I must not neglect any of my other ambassadorial duties and should be sure that I had an efficient, smoothly running Embassy, but I was determined not to be swallowed up by the petty minutiae of administration and diplomatic life so that I could instead devote my chief energies to helping guide the overall relationship between the United States and Japan. Deepening the understanding between the two countries had been the core of my life work, and the ambassadorship to Japan appeared to me the most strategic possible position for contributing to this work.

In a way, Japanese-American relations are a model for relations across cultural and racial lines for the whole world. They constitute the relationship between the world's two leading industrialized, trading democracies and the closest relations that have ever been developed between a Western country and a major nation of non-Western cultural background. As a sort of model for the world's future, they illustrated the need for mutual understanding and trust and the ability to cooperate successfully in all fields, despite differences of language and culture. Helping to meet these needs I saw as the core of my whole effort in Tokyo.

The problem of understanding between Japan and the United States in the early 1960s, as it is today, was not so much between the two governments as between the people on both sides. I found contacts between the two governments very efficient and even smooth. Negotiations between them were for the most part routine, involving hard bargaining but not serious animosities. The most persistent areas of negotiations during my early years at the Tokyo Embassy concerned textile imports from Japan to the United States, Japanese catches of fish in the Gulf of Alaska and of salmon from American rivers on the high seas, and problems arising from the presence of American military forces in Japan. These were handled largely by various members of the Embassy staff or teams sent from Washington. I usually would participate only when it was felt that my presence would serve to emphasize a point or at symbolic sessions when agreements were finalized.

Relations between the two peoples, however, were far different. There were serious misapprehensions, suspicions, and lingering popular prejudices. Trying to correct these seemed to me much more important than reaching agreements on technical points of difference between the two governments. Thus I saw my job as being essentially educational, as it had been at Harvard. Japanese had a deep feeling of inequality in their relations with the United States and a fear that America was a fundamentally aggressive nation bent on a policy of military adventurism. I did my best to try to show that America's postwar policies were governed by a desire to maintain peace and restore world prosperity, that the American people were every bit as peaceloving as the Japanese had become since the war, and that the only reason the United States continued to maintain a strong position of military defense in East Asia was to guarantee its own security and reduce the danger of war for other countries, including Japan.

I was particularly anxious to have the Japanese stop thinking of the American military as being the real United States and the relationship between the two countries as being primarily military rather than a matter of shared ideals and economic interests. To many Japanese, an American general or admiral seemed much more of a genuine American than a Harvard professor. To correct this attitude and show that even an off-beat scholar Ambassador was the unchallenged representative of Washington in Japan, I made a point from the start of asserting my precedence over the American military in Japan. There was an annual defense conference between the two countries, which was jointly chaired by the Foreign Minister and me, and, though it was an empty pro forma exercise, it was symbolically important. At it I would emphasize my leadership of the American side, making sure that the Commander of United States Forces, Japan, and even Admiral Felt, who as CINCPAC was said to have the largest military command in the world, were at the meeting simply as my aides. I even carried the matter to trivial though visible details, such as insisting on walking first through doorways whenever I was with high American military officers in the presence of Japanese.

I was convinced that the misunderstandings between Japanese and Americans were based on insufficient knowledge of each other. I was aware that Japanese and Americans had sharply different views of their relations and of world problems, but I knew that the two nations shared common basic ideals of democracy, human rights, and egalitarianism, and yearned alike for a peaceful world order made up of truly independent nations bound together by as free and open world trade as possible. I saw Japan rapidly catching up with the United States in most matters and felt that a relationship of full equality was an absolute necessity for the future. I expressed this concept by the term "equal partnership," which I made the key phrase of my efforts. In view of Japanese sensitivities to military matters, "partnership" had a more acceptable ring than "alliance," with its heavy military overtones, while equality was the essence of my whole approach.

"Equal partnership" had been casually used a few times before, but I tried to make it a central concept that both sides would accept completely. At the time, however, feelings of inequality and of differences in goals remained too strong for the idea to win easy acceptance. Japanese often felt the term to be mere flattery, and Americans, if they noticed it at all, probably thought of it as clever diplomacy on my part. But I was absolutely sincere in using the term; although it was in a way somewhat premature for describing the reality of the situation, I am delighted to see that it is used by both sides today as being merely a succinct definition of the present Japanese-American relationship.

The approach I took in Japan was called by some Japanese "the Kennedy-Reischauer line," or simply the "Reischauer line," usually used in a pejorative sense by those who opposed close Japanese-American relations. At first I was shocked to see my ideas described as being a "line" like some underhanded plot, but in time I became both amused and flattered by the term. In view of the close control kept by Washington over its ambassadors, it may seem strange that I was in a position to have my own "Reischauer line," but this illustrates the rather unusual position I had as Ambassador. Naturally I stayed within the bounds of American policy as established in Washington and faithfully followed instruc tions on specific matters, but I felt free to try to create my own mood in Japanese-American relations and develop my own approach in dealings with the Japanese authorities and public. When Washington saw that I was taking effective control of the Tokyo Embassy and our relations with Japan, it seems to have simply turned its attention elsewhere. As I saw the situation, Washington had assigned me to try to build a better understanding with Japan following the blowup over the revision of the Security Treaty; there was little profit in my checking back with it as to how this should be done. I simply decided on my own to make "equal partnership" and other such terms key concepts, and no one in Washington ever questioned me about my doing so.

This, of course, is not the way most ambassadors could or should act. It was the exception rather than the rule, having been a case of an unusual Ambassador in an unusual situation. Normally Washington should keep closer control over an Ambassador's activities, and most ambassadors are either too nervous about their own careers in government or too ignorant of the country where they are stationed to act with the freedom I did. But I had confidence in my knowledge of Japan and was free of career ambitions. The worst Washington could do to me was fire me, thus allowing me to return to Harvard, which was what I was planning to do in any case.

Haru and I naturally had no way to measure how much we accomplished, if anything. At best we could have moved the two great icebergs of public opinion only a very little. But we did our best, even though burdened down with the other onerous responsibilities of diplomatic life. As the years passed and we came to feel at ease in our work, we would often marvel that fate had given us the opportunity to occupy positions where we could best contribute to the cause we both felt was the most important thing in our lives. It seemed a chance not granted to one person in a thousand, and we were very grateful for it.

꿍

Whatever our goals, they could be achieved only a day at a time. In keeping with worldwide American practice, the Embassy started work at 8:00 a.m. each morning, despite the fact that comparable offices in Tokyo did not open until 9:00 or even 10:00 a.m. After a hearty Japanese breakfast centering around fermented bean soup *(miso shiru)*—a good antidote for the disastrously rich fare of diplomatic luncheons and banquets—I ran briefly through the newspapers. These consisted of one of the leading English-language papers and the three largest Japanese papers, the *Asahi, Mainichi,* and *Yomiuri,* which between them had a nationwide morning circulation of between 15 and 20 million. Together they gave me a good idea of what most Japanese had on their minds that particular morning. Then I had a half hour or more of practice in speaking Japanese. I initially assumed that a few weeks in Japan would wear off the rustiness that had developed in my speech since I had last been in Japan, but I soon discovered that, ensconced in the heart of the American Embassy and forced to speak with precision on a much wider range of topics than had ever concerned me before, I needed more practice in expressing my ideas exactly. Under a tutor's guidance, I would translate into Japanese editorials from the English-language newspaper. After this a quick run through the important messages that had passed overnight between Washington and Tokyo prepared me for the main work of the day.

When other activities did not intervene, I held a brief staff meeting each morning with my chief officers. I did not confine this, as had been the custom, to factual reports on current developments, but encouraged the group to discuss broad and long-range issues. Foreign Service officers like to say that they handle problems as they arise, but I pointed out that in a crisis they in fact acted on the basis of long-held concepts which it was best to consider in advance before a crisis struck. These discussions also gave me a chance to try to indoctrinate my chief lieutenants in my own thinking. Occasionally the staff meeting was expanded to include more of the Embassy's senior officers, some of the attachés, and also representatives of the resident American military. The first of these expanded meetings, which I called my "inaugural address," was attended by forty-six persons, the full capacity of the conference room, and I used it to outline my concepts of Japanese-American relations and what we should be trying to achieve.

The rest of the morning I devoted to talks or negotiations with top Japanese leaders, or more frequently to a series of calls on me by Japanese leaders of all types and prominent visiting Americans. My very efficient and loyal secretary,

Alice Seckel, prepared a card each morning on the day's activities and other cards on each of my callers so that I would be well briefed on them, usually to their surprise and pleasure.

On most days, luncheons were devoted to meetings and sometimes speeches elsewhere with various Japanese groups or to small luncheons for Japanese leaders or sometimes Americans at the Residence. The luncheons I gave were usually limited to twelve persons or less, because I discovered that a meaningful general conversation became difficult if the group were any larger. If my schedule permitted me to return to my office after lunch, I would devote the time largely to receiving callers and having long discussions with some of them. More often, though, I would be out visiting some Japanese leaders, giving speeches, or attending special events.

Late afternoons were the most hectic time of the day. It was then that the various diplomatic and business receptions were held. Even we were forced to give quite a few—sometimes as many as three in a single week—for visiting American dignitaries, international conferences, and various Japanese groups. A small reception at the Residence would be for less than 100 persons, a large one for 250 to 350. Haru and I and any guests of honor would stand in the foyer leading from the entrance hall to the large reception room, shaking hands with all the guests as they entered and then again as they left. This double chore excused us from the strain of making small talk in between, and whenever a break would open up in the receiving line I would have a chance to read, modify, and sign sometimes very lengthy drafts of telegrams to Washington. Because of the time difference, a message sent back to Washington in the early evening would arrive in time for the start of work there that same calendar morning, and a reply could then be expected by the time we started work in Tokyo the next morning.

Haru and I had imagined that all the hand shaking would be a severe physical strain, but this did not prove to be the case except for an occasional burly American man who would seize one's hand in a grip like a judo hold. The real wear and tear was on one's feet, particularly one's heels. I used to say that diplomatic life was proving easy on the head but hell on the feet. We mitigated this problem by placing two thick carpets on the marble floor where we stood.

Most evenings were devoted to banquets, balls, or to the small dinners we ourselves gave at the Residence for Japanese or American leaders. We estimated that, except for breakfasts and weekends, we averaged only one meal a week by ourselves. But the pleasantest time of the day also came in the evening when we were often expected to attend concerts and other cultural events, commonly seated beside members of the imperial family. These occasions gave us a chance to hear a great deal of good music and to meet many of the outstanding artistic figures and public personalities of the day.

One of the first to come was Leonard Bernstein with the New York Philharmonic, and we became good friends. Arthur Rubinstein and Van Cliburn were pleased to play for our guests when we invited them to dinner. Duke Ellington embraced us at once among his throng of kissing cousins. Danny Kaye was aglow with his sincere efforts to help the less fortunate. Helen Hayes proved as charming as one would expect. There were dozens of others of comparable fame and ability. The chance to meet such delightful and talented people was an unexpected bonus in our ambassadorial work.

While our chief efforts were directed toward more meaningful endeavors, our position inevitably placed us in the social limelight. I discovered that on almost any occasion I might be called on to say a few words and developed the habit of never entering a room without first giving some thought to what I might say if asked. What was most visible in our lives to the public was all the protocol of diplomacy, which had grown out of the niceties of diplomatic life as practiced in the eighteenth and nineteenth centuries. This is what has earned American diplomats the contempt of most of their compatriots. But it is merely the dazzling icing which hides from view the solid hard work and devoted efforts of everyday diplomatic life.

Haru and I at first found this icing of diplomatic life very amusing, because it was ironic that we of all people should have been plunged into this sort of existence. We both have always avoided ceremonies and "society" as much as possible, finding even the mild pomp of Harvard and restrained social life of Cambridge beyond our tastes. But now that we found ourselves immersed in diplomacy, we decided to make the most of the situation and enjoy it as best we could. Our obvious amusement with the glitter of this new life made others respond in a friendly way and helped us to establish smooth and often warm relationships with them.

In a sense it was one of my duties to make myself as visible socially as possible. I was in theory the President's alter ego in Japan, outranking any other American who might come there. Naturally there was a considerable gap between theory and reality. When the Secretary of State came to Japan, I of course yielded precedence to him, and when I was back in the United States I found that my status plummeted. Haru, because of her usefulness with the wives of visiting Japanese prime ministers or cabinet ministers, might be seated high at the head table at a White House function, while I would be barely squeezed into the last table in front of the passageway leading to the kitchen. But in Tokyo we both ranked somewhere between the imperial family and the cabinet.

The triple life of social butterfly, responsible government official, and self-appointed shaper of attitudes between Japanese and Americans added up to a heavy schedule. It absorbed every hour of each day every day in the week and stretched out uninterruptedly month after month. For both of us it was indeed hard labor, but it was labor we undertook with pleasure and enthusiasm.

## 29

# Setting to Work

I T SEEMED to take an inordinate amount of time to get embarked on our real work in Japan, yet in retrospect I see that we slipped into it with remarkable speed. One interesting diplomatic problem I faced when we arrived in Japan was the negotiation of the return by Japan of funds for subsistence lent the Japanese government during the Occupation. These were known as Government and Relief in Occupied Areas (GARIOA). I had many formal meetings about this problem with Kosaka, the Foreign Minister, and after each session, as was the custom with important negotiations, we held a joint press conference. Usually we chose to inform the press of the items discussed and decisions reached at the meeting before the current one. This always proved satisfactory, giving the press a sense of forward motion and us some leeway in our continuing negotiations. At times the Foreign Minister and I would meet in complete secrecy in order to avoid all press attention.

The GARIOA discussions came to a climax on June 10, 1961. As I wrote home at the time, "Financially I made out well for the U.S. this week." On the 8th I gave the Foreign Minister a check for $8 million as recompense for the displaced residents of the Bonin Islands, which at the time were still in the hands of the American Navy, and on the 10th the Foreign Minister and I agreed to the repayment of $490 million by Japan on the GARIOA account. To my surprise, all that was required for the agreement was our initials. I had always supposed that references in history books to the initialing of agreements were merely a matter of elegant variation in terminology. The final formal agreement concluded in 1962, however, did require our full signatures. The payment of $490 million approximated the earlier settlement with West Germany of roughly one dollar for three actually spent. I felt that we were wise in not having tried to squeeze more out of the Japanese, because a great deal of goodwill was engendered by our generosity. I was particularly pleased that $25 million was earmarked for cultural relations with Japan, and the Japanese public liked this too, but subsequently I was outraged when Washington went back on this understanding and devoted the money instead to defraying the regular cultural budget of the Embassy. It was not until several years later that, thanks to the hard work of Senator Jacob Javits of New York, the residue of the original $25 million was lumped with $25 million more received from Japan in connection with the return of Okinawa in 1972 in order to provide the funding of the United States–Japan Friendship Commission, which undertook new cultural activities outside of the regular budget.

On the night of June 11, less than eight weeks after arriving in Japan, I left for Washington to be on hand when Ikeda paid a visit there for the first time in his capacity as Prime Minister. I had been doing a lot of negotiating about this with the Foreign Minister, because such visits are always carefully choreographed in advance. I had asked that Haru accompany me, since Mrs. Ikeda was going, but Washington, in its ignorance, had refused. It never made that mistake again, once it learned how valuable Haru could be with visiting Japanese wives.

I came to look on trips back and forth to Washington as a chance for a rest. For a few hours there would be no telephone calls, no aides with important documents, and no crises. This first time I discovered something else, too. I was routed by way of Seattle, and walking around the Seattle airport between planes, I suddenly realized that no one recognized me. The cheerful smile which had practically frozen on my face during the past eight weeks melted away. It was a positive pleasure to wander around the airport looking glum and surly.

Shortly after my arrival back in Washington, President Kennedy asked to see me to discuss plans for Ikeda's visit. Later, whenever I returned to Washington on routine leave or for any other reason, he would find out about it and send for me for a long private talk. Obviously he could not have had the time to see many American ambassadors in this way, but he was intensely interested in our relations with Japan. Each time, we talked about his making a visit to Japan himself, which he was determined to do as soon as possible. Whenever I went back to Washington I would also confer with many of the top civilian and military leaders. I usually saw several of the cabinet officers, members of the Joint Chiefs of Staff, and CINCPAC in Hawaii either on my way there or on my way back.

The three days of conversations between Kennedy and Ikeda went very well, with Rusk and me flanking the President at all the talks. The final communiqué, which had been long in preparation, was issued without any hitches. The two leaders were impressed with each other and established a good rapport. The Japanese were very pleased, and Ikeda attributed much of the success of his trip to my influence in Washington. In fact, if I made any contribution, it was in giving Ikeda confidence in his dealings with Kennedy. But I was happy to see that both men had picked up my term of "equal partnership" and used it constantly.

The chief substantive decision to emerge from the meetings was the establishment of three binational committees to strengthen and broaden our relations. The chief of these was the Joint United States–Japan Committee on Trade and Economic Affairs, made up of appropriate members of the two cabinets, headed by the two foreign ministers. The idea for this had come from Washington before my appointment, but I was enthusiastically for it, believing it would ensure that a large part of the American cabinet would concentrate on relations with Japan at least for a few days each year.

Leonhart had suggested to me that our Tokyo Embassy should also contribute some input to the Ikeda-Kennedy talks and, in view of my position as a scholar Ambassador, this might be in the intellectual field. From this came our suggestion that there should be a permanent United States–Japan Conference on Cultural and Educational Exchange and a similar body for the natural sciences. All three groups were to meet alternately in the two countries. The Economic Committee met for several years; the science committee got off to a quick, enthusiastic start and almost at once began spawning all sorts of working subcommittees; the cultural group started more slowly, but it still has an important role today under the acronym of CULCON.

During Ikeda's visit, I had an interesting experience at a White House luncheon. Angier Biddle Duke, the Chief of Protocol, tapped me on the shoulder at my relatively lowly spot in the room and said that I should move up to the center of the main table where the tardiness of Douglas Dillon, the Secretary of the Treasury, had left an embarrassing gap. I complied and found myself seated beside Mamie Eisenhower. She proved a much more interesting conversationalist than I had imagined, making all sorts of snide comments on how things had changed at the White House. This was her first visit back since she and Ike had left, and she remarked scathingly that an episode such as this one with an empty seat at the head table had never happened even once when they had lived there. Unfortunately, after the fish course, Dillon turned up, and Duke sent me slinking back to my original place.

Arriving back in Tokyo on June 28, I found that Haru and I were both in something of a slump. As I wrote to my family, "This job simply can't be done right unless we have bounce but we have bounced so much the past two months that for the moment there is no bounce left." But things had to go on. The Fourth of July, our official "national day," was only a few days off, and since this was our first one, it had to be on a big scale. We invited some fourteen hundred people—top government officials and politicians, the governors of the forty-six prefectures, prominent businessmen, intellectual leaders, cultural figures, the other ambassadors, and representatives of the American military and civilian communities. Ikeda and his wife attended despite their rule never to go to national days. The approach to the entrance to the Residence is on the same narrow road on which the Okura Hotel stands, and the crush of traffic held cars up literally for hours. Some seven hundred people managed to get to the Residence, straining it to the bursting point, and two hundred more were said to have given up and turned back. The muggy heat was almost unbearable, since the downstairs of the Residence had no air conditioning. The occasion could have been a fiasco, but the Harvard Glee Club, which happened to be touring Japan sixty strong, helped save the day. When they serenaded Haru on bended knee before departing, the crowd was delighted. I remember seeing Ikeda over the heads of the Glee Club hardly able to contain his amusement.

The occasion ended up a triumph, but it put three strong resolves in our minds. One was to get the air conditioning, which was limited to the bedrooms, extended to the rest of the house; this grew increasingly necessary as almost every other important building in Tokyo became air-conditioned. Haru carried the ball, buttonholing every State Department official, senator, or congressman who passed through Tokyo and pleading her case until she finally won her point.

The other resolves were never to hold so large a reception again and not to hold our "national day" on July 4 in the middle of the summer heat. The Foreign Ministry was startled when we informed them that the American national day henceforth would be February 22, Washington's Birthday, but it grudgingly complied, and after initial surprise the diplomatic corps made the adjustment.

⋅∮

The high point of the summer for me was a trip early in August to Okinawa, which the American military always referred to as the Ryukyu Islands. Except for the Consulate there, which came under my jurisdiction, Okinawa was under the control of an American High Commissioner, Lieutenant General Paul Caraway, whose parents had both been senators from Arkansas. He was a rigid, bull-headed man and demonstrated his autocratic ways by keeping the brigadier general who was the Civil Administrator of the Ryukyus cooling his heels for a couple of hours in an adjoining room while Caraway and I discussed conditions in Okinawa and its future. At the same time, he was a very amusing man, and the two of us got along personally very well.

The relationship between Caraway and the American Embassy in Tokyo, however, was a delicate one. The American military looked on the retention of Okinawa as essential to America's future military position in the Western Pacific, because it feared the loss some time of its bases in Japan. It saw the Japanese government as its chief challenger for control of Okinawa and suspected our Embassy of conspiring with the Japanese in this. Caraway had to work through the Embassy in his relations with the Japanese government, which at the time was trying to give more economic aid to Okinawa to raise its living standards a little closer to the Japanese average. As a result, I would find myself in the absurd position at the annual conference on Okinawa held in Tokyo of insisting on keeping Japanese aid down so that it would not exceed aid from America and thus supposedly cause the United States to lose face. Fortunately we were able in time to get rid of this ridiculous strategy. Another bone of contention was the Okinawan desire to elect their own chief executive and not have him selected by Caraway. I was in a difficult position during my visit to Okinawa, because Caraway viewed me as especially suspect as a professor Ambassador, and the Okinawans for the same reason expected me to take their side in their struggle for greater autonomy and eventual reversion to Japan. If I pleased one side, I would surely tread on the toes of the other. Somehow I managed to thread my way between the two without causing ill will on either side.

Since this was my first visit to Okinawa, I knew little about the islands and had half accepted the American contention that, though there were some troublemakers demanding more autonomy, the Okinawans were a docile people, quite different from the Japanese and on the whole desirous of remaining under American rule rather than being returned to Japan, which had callously exploited them before and during the war. Immediately after the end of the war there might have been some truth to these views, but as soon as I met with some Okinawans I saw that such concepts were now quite mistaken. The Okinawans were slightly different from the mainland Japanese in dialect and culture but felt themselves to be fully Japanese. Virtually all of them wished ultimate reversion to Japan, and I saw that the die had already been cast when the Okinawans had been allowed to adopt the Japanese school textbooks, in which "our country" *(waga kuni)* clearly meant Japan. Perhaps the American military could keep the Okinawans under control, but it was clear to me that sooner or later the other Japanese would get excited over Okinawa as a *terra irredenta,* and this might ruin the whole Japanese-American relationship. Oddly enough there was relatively little popular concern over Okinawa in Japan as yet; it was sure to rise, however, as the Japanese got back on their feet economically and began to feel a sense of national pride. I quickly came to the conclusion that Okinawa would have to be returned to Japan some day and that in the meantime the Okinawans should be given more autonomy.

It seemed to me that the American military had their reasoning about Okinawa backward. They argued that Okinawa must be held at all cost because we might lose our bases in Japan, which was an uncertain ally. When I had the opportunity, I pointed out to CINCPAC in Hawaii and the Joint Chiefs of Staff in Washington that if we lost our bases in Japan, it would be because we had held on to Okinawa, forcing the Japanese to turn against us, and making our Okinawan bases quite useless because of the hostility of both the Okinawans and Japanese. It was a case of having bases both in Japan and Okinawa or in neither, and the key to this situation was the reversion of Okinawa.

This argument between me and the American military developed only over the years. In the summer of 1961 I faced the more immediate problem of not transgressing beyond established American policy, winning Caraway's confidence, and yet not discouraging legitimate Okinawan hopes. One gesture I made to the Okinawans, which seemed very significant to me, was not to refer to them in public speeches as Ryukyuans or Okinawans but as "you Japanese who live in Okinawa." Dulles had earlier admitted that Japan had "residual sovereignty" in Okinawa, which was an ill-defined concept, but I believe that my statements were the first admission by a responsible American official that we accepted the Okinawans as being Japanese. Caraway did not seem to notice the significance of what I was saying, and he and I worked out a number of small concessions on Okinawan autonomy with an apparently complete meeting of the minds. Possibly the coordinated messages we sent back to Washington had some influence in inducing President Kennedy to send out a commission to Okinawa in October, under the leadership of a former Harvard acquaintance of mine, Carl Kaysen, who was on McGeorge Bundy's staff in the White House. Kaysen's recommendations were eventually to lead to a number of liberalizing reforms announced the next spring.

Aside from the subtle political footwork required, I found my first visit to Okinawa a fascinating experience. I saw most of the things of interest in the southern two thirds of the island, where the bulk of the fighting had taken place during the war, and visited the main American military installations by helicopter. At the headquarters of the Marine division I was not only welcomed by the playing of the Star Spangled Banner but practically jumped out of my skin when a battery of field guns began a nineteen-gun salute right beside me. A quieter surprise was my discovery of two burly Americans constantly shadowing me, even following me in a second helicopter. This was my first conscious experience with bodyguards. In time, as I traveled around more in public places in Japan, I became accustomed to Japanese bodyguards and learned to pick them out among the crowd of officials that surrounded me everywhere I went. A small inconspicuous pin above their buttonholes was a common symbol and a surreptitious peek around a sharp corner in a hotel hallway was a sure giveaway.

Next to the Okinawan problem, one of the most important and long lasting was the normalization of relations between Japan and South Korea. On this I had numerous talks with Japanese all the way from Ikeda on down and also with many Koreans, especially Ei Whang Pae, who had replaced Yu Chin-o as the chief Korean representative. Ed Pae, as he called himself, happened to be an American as well as Korean citizen, having acquired his citizenship through his American-born wife, and he became a close friend. The normalization of relations was essential for the recovery of the Korean economy and valuable to Japan to give it a broader trading area and more sense of security. But an agreement was difficult to reach because of Korean demands for unrealistically high indemnities and exclusive fishing areas in international waters.

From the American point of view, the normalization of relations was highly desirable for both sides. The problem lay between Japan and South Korea, however, and it would have been most unwise for the United States to take the lead in settling it, receiving the blame from both sides for dissatisfaction with the results. I, in particular, had to be careful to stay out of sight in the negotiations, since I was relatively well known in Korea and would be expected to take a prominent role. It was for that reason that I stayed away from Korea during the whole time I was the Ambassador in Japan. I talked often with both sides, though I was careful to do so in secret and to say the same thing to both. I pointed out that the stimulus to trade would be of far greater value to the Koreans in the long run than a higher indemnity and also that they need not be so demanding on exclusive fishing zones, since the modernization of the Korean fishing fleet through Japanese financial aid would soon mean that the Koreans, with their lower wages, would be catching most of the fish anyway.

Sam Berger, the new Ambassador to Korea, and his wife Margie were old friends of Haru's. They often stopped off with us on their way to and from Washington, and we discussed the problem at length, but Sam felt that we should apply strong pressure on Japan to get Tokyo to give in to Korean demands, which I knew the Japanese would never do. I suggested that in the long run a small American contribution to sweeten the pot for both sides and thus hasten a solution would be a worthwhile investment; this met with flat rejection in Washington. As a result, the problem dragged on for years, and the normalization was not finally concluded until June 1965. Only then did South Korea begin to take off economically in emulation of Japan.

# 30
# Getting into Stride

WE FOUND that summer brought no appreciable letup in our work, yet we needed some break from our rigorous schedule of sixteen-hour days six or seven days a week. We also needed to escape from the muggy heat and polluted air of Tokyo. Air pollution was at its worst during our years at the Embassy; at night, when out of habit I would fling open the windows, I was often tempted to shut them right up again when I smelt the foul fumes rolling in.

The American Embassy, unlike the British and some others, had no summer residence, but Haru's family had a little house near the small fishing port of

Misaki at the end of the Miura Peninsula at the tip of the west side of Tokyo Bay, where we had spent some time in the summer of 1960. It was a purely Japanese house, formerly the home of a famous Japanese poetess, perched on the hundred-foot cliffs that protrude between two inlets, one facing directly out to sea and the other well protected by a double dog leg leading to a beautiful sheltered cove called Aburatsubo, meaning "oil vat." It was an idyllic spot, heavily forested, surrounded on three sides by water, and looking out across Sagami Bay to Mt. Fuji. Unhappily, everything has changed since then. The area has been incorporated into the town of Misaki, now known as Miura City, and has become a far commuting suburb of Tokyo rather than the simple fishing and farming town it once was. Houses have sprung up everywhere. Aburatsubo itself is the site of a crowded yacht club, with a noisy amusement park standing above it. The once clear waters along the coast, which teemed with fish of semi-tropical splendor, have become fouled by the outflow of flotsam from Tokyo Bay. But in the summer of 1961 this process of environmental degradation had only just begun, and our Misaki hideaway was still pristinely beautiful.

At Misaki we saw almost no one and were no longer celebrities, being among fishermen and farmers who had known Haru for decades. The Misaki house, of course, needed some alterations. Glass sliding doors were added to the sliding wooden and paper doors to make it warmer in winter and allow light to come in on a stormy day. A wing was added to house a caretaker cook, who was a widow with two cute children. Electric lights were installed for the first time and, of course, a phone to keep us in touch with the Embassy. A nearby helicopter pad made it possible for an American Navy helicopter to get me back to Tokyo in a hurry. The police surveillance was inconspicuous. In fact, we were completely unaware of their presence except occasionally when I returned from rowing my rowboat and a man would emerge from the bushes to help me haul it in above high tide.

We lived in completely Japanese style while at Misaki. This meant the winters were quite cold, with only a kerosene stove to heat the flimsily built house. We had no motorboat, only the small rowboat in which I rowed for hours up and down the rugged coast. Although we often took a lot of work with us, we both found that our weekends at Misaki refreshed us greatly. We got away down there on an average of one weekend in six, and I honestly doubt that we could have stuck it out in Tokyo for five and a half years without these periodic flights to our seaside Shangri-la.

The summer was enlivened for us by the presence of Bobby, who had come from Harvard in June to take advantage of the government's payment for one trip a year by each underage child. He walked into the Residence one day without warning and, with the arrogance of a college sophomore, proceeded to criticize almost everything about our diplomatic life, displaying his disapproval by emerging from the Embassy compound in torn-off blue jeans and rubber Japanese slippers *(zori)*. When we pointed out the inappropriateness of this costume in downtown Tokyo, he claimed it made him less conspicuous, a dubious assertion at his six feet, five inches. One morning Haru found a sign he had placed on the silver platter for calling cards left by the more punctilious, informing them that this relic of the days of the Congress of Vienna need no longer be observed. He calmed down during the summer, however, eventually becoming somewhat "Embassy broken," as I wrote at the time, adding that he came to see that we "were being extremely revolutionary in the Jacksonian Age we had introduced to the embassy and were not just being the spit and polish slaves of diplomatic life that he at first accused us of being." On the whole Bobby had a fine time, touring Japan at first with the Harvard Glee Club and then with Joan, who had wisely sought more anonymity by quitting her TV and radio jobs.

In Kyoto, Joan and Bobby had a curious incident. They had been given permission from the Imperial Household Agency to visit the famous gardens of the Katsura Rikyu (Katsura Detached Palace), but when the guards found that Joan was not yet twenty, they denied her admission in accordance with the regulations. She had quietly settled down to read a book until Bobby was through, but the press seized on the incident, making it seem at first that she had indignantly demanded admission. Soon the true story was revealed and everything cleared up, though apparently not forgotten. Twenty-one years later, in the autumn of 1982, when Haru and I visited the Katsura Palace in order to see the thorough repair work our architect scholar friend, Mr. Yasui Yasushi, had just completed, our taxi driver regaled us with the whole story, claiming that every taxi driver in Kyoto knew it and felt Joan to have been quite a heroine in accepting the situation so meekly even though she was "Ambassador Reischauer's daughter." Joan, I find, only vaguely remembers the incident.

Joan returned to the United States with Bobby in late August to enter Oberlin College, and in late September my father arrived for a two-month stay. He had a fine time, being lionized by his old friends and entertained by our new colleagues. He was made the twenty-ninth honorary citizen in the history of Tokyo and had a heavy schedule of festivities that would have proved tiring to a man twenty years younger. We, of course, gave a reception for him, and all his old friends held receptions and dinners. He had never been much of a public speaker, but he proved a "star of after-dinner humor," as I wrote at the time, and a real "82 year old socialite." He made emotion-filled visits to Tokyo Women's University, the Japan Deaf Oral School, and the other schools he had been connected with, always with much newspaper coverage. This was his first trip back to Japan since 1941, and he was both amazed and delighted by the progress the country had made and the contrasts to the Japan he had left two decades earlier. We greatly enjoyed his visit, and I am sure that he was equally pleased, but we were never able to persuade him to visit us again. His vigor began to fade shortly after this trip, and he just didn't have the strength for another.

٭

The coming of autumn brought a speeding up of activities of all sorts. Textile negotiations were running in high gear, calling for many meetings on my part with the Foreign Minister and other top politicians. Some of our best officers at the Embassy, including Trezise, the Economic Minister, were assigned to new posts. Haru was asked to help start the Community Chest Campaign by selling red feathers beside the famous dog statue at Shibuya Station, stealing the limelight somewhat from the cabinet ministers and being outshone only by Taiho, the current sumo wrestling champion. She was also the only woman speaker at the founding session of the women's support organization for the United Nations. One evening I returned home to find her on the phone with the Prime Minister, who was telling her about his talks with Park Chung Hee, the South Korean military dictator, who had just passed through Tokyo on his way to Washington. I took over, but it was amusing to find Haru being treated as if she were a high official of our government.

Ikeda often communicated directly with me instead of going through the Foreign Ministry. For example, he told me in detail of his recent trip to India, saying that he had found Nehru arrogant *(ibatte)*. There is a marvelous group picture of this visit that tells the whole story. Ikeda and Nehru are seated side by side in the center of the picture, but they are looking stonily into space in opposite directions.

We had an endless flow of guests, including many old friends. Among the latter was Miss Matsuoka Yoko, a graduate of Swarthmore. She was at the time a popular writer of strongly anti-American articles, and she did not seem to see the incongruity of the situation when she complained to us that she was finding it harder to get her work accepted.

One problem that was constantly arising was the great number of gifts brought us by Japanese. Some were of more sentimental than practical value, such as a Buddhist text of ten thousand microscopically drawn Chinese characters or ropes of one thousand folded paper cranes *(semba-zuru)*, given as a talisman for good health or a sign of goodwill; but others were of considerable monetary worth. A few of the gifts could be used as decorations around the Embassy, where I notice some are still on display. Others were personal and far exceeded the ten dollar value of gifts that the regulations allowed an American official to accept. Returning them, however, was impossible in gift-giving Japan, and reciprocating was quite beyond our pocketbook. We did return a string of pearls to a lady in

Yokohama as being too flagrant an infraction of the regulations, but the uproar and ill will this act engendered showed that this was certainly not the way to better Japanese-American relations. In time, we simply accepted the gifts, deciding that it was wiser to break American regulations than to stir up international resentments. The presents of value we passed on to charity.

A gift of a different sort was a dachshund, given us by General Genda Minoru, the head of the Japanese Air Self Defense Force, and his wife, who were dachshund fanciers and had learned that we had had one in Belmont. Unfortunately he proved definitely neurotic, reacting fiercely to all Westerners except me, so he had to be confined usually to our private upstairs quarters. I mention him primarily to tell of General Genda. In 1941 Genda had been the navy commander who worked out the tactics for the air attack on Pearl Harbor. A few years after the war, when he visited London, he was asked by the press if he had any second thoughts about the attack. Honest military man that he was, he replied after some thought, "Yes, we should have been prepared to follow up our success with an invasion of Hawaii." The British press hit the ceiling, and the Japanese Embassy had to hustle Genda back to Japan.

As we were pursuing our usual busy lives, Christmas sneaked up on us and then suddenly devoured most of our time. Even though less than 1 percent of the Japanese are Christians, they always make a great spectacle of Christmas. We raised a large tree, at least twenty feet tall, in the foyer within the curve of the marble stairway, and Haru appointed David Osborn's wife, Helenka, who had a flair for spectacular decor, to head a committee of volunteer wives from the Embassy to decorate the downstairs rooms. David had been one of the men the State Department had sent me for training after World War II. Helenka's group used only cast-off materials like tin cans and old paper wrappings but produced beautiful, imaginative results, which were viewed, according to Haru's estimate, by about three thousand people who came to the Residence especially for that purpose. The next year there were even more.

On the days surrounding Christmas, we attended the parties of each of the Embassy sections and gave one party ourselves at the Residence for the forty or so people involved in running the house, another for the Embassy children of appropriate age, attended by 190 out of a total of 230 children, and a big dance for all Embassy Americans. (The marble floors I felt were crying out to be danced on.) Our main undertaking, however, was the revival from my youth of the party for the children and teachers of the Japan Deaf Oral School my mother had founded. Half the school—a hundred children and twenty teachers—came, with the other half scheduled for the following year. The older Embassy children helped us out as hosts. Inevitably the press and television got wind of the affair and made something of a shambles of it, though they missed the one point I would like to have had some publicity on, which was that we were presenting the school with a sizable check in place of sending out personal Christmas cards in response to the many hundreds we received.

❧

An almost uninterrupted stream of distinguished Americans passed briefly through Tokyo or stayed for longer visits. A few stayed with us at the Residence, which served as a sort of high-level hotel for American officials, and we entertained many more at meals or receptions. Most wished to be briefed by me or at least to make courtesy calls, and some were so important that they made calls on the Prime Minister or other high functionaries, or even in a few cases had audiences with the Emperor, always accompanied by me.

Among our first house guests in July 1961 were George W. Ball and his wife Ruth. George was Under Secretary of State for Economic Affairs and later was to step up to Bowles's position as the second man in the Department. He was in Japan for a meeting of the DAG (Development Assistance Group), which consisted of the rich industrialized nations which gave aid to the less developed lands. He himself was strongly oriented toward Europe, but he was not insensitive to Japan and could clearly see that it should become a full member of the group of industrialized nations by joining the OECD (the Organization for Economic Cooperation and Development), which it finally did in April 1964, with strong American backing but against considerable European opposition. As early as November 1961, George and I were corresponding about the possibility of creating a Pacific Community centering on Japan, the United States, Canada, and possibly Australia. I was all for the idea, so long as it did not become a substitute for Japan's joining the OECD. The proposal never materialized, but the idea is still alive and surfaces from time to time in one form or another. All in all we found the Balls delightful people, and I feel that he would have made an excellent Secretary of State.

Senators and congressmen visited Tokyo in great numbers in the autumn when Congress was not in session, especially in electoral off years like 1961. The most fearsome of our congressional visitors that autumn was Congressman John Rooney, who, as the chairman of the Appropriations Subcommittee in charge of State Department funding, held the Department in terror of his fiscal powers. The Department treated him with kid gloves, sending us ample warnings about him and having William Crockett, the Assistant Secretary of State for Administrative Affairs, chaperone him on the trip.

It was the Rooneys' first trip to Japan, which they found fascinating, and the whole visit went off swimmingly. Rooney we were told was a meat and potatoes man, so we had an appropriate menu for our big dinner for him and his wife, at which he requested there be no "natives." Haru obviously did not count. He had a marvelous time and was very garrulous. At one point, quivering with remembered rage, he thundered, "At some embassies they serve me little birds standing up in jelly." In his enthusiasm, but to our horror, he talked of canceling his visits to Hong Kong and Manila in order to stay longer in Japan, but fortunately he held to his original schedule. We gained much kudos in Washington for what was regarded as our lion-taming act.

Our biggest visitation from the United States during the autumn of 1961 was the American delegation for the first meeting on November 1 to 4 of the United States–Japan Committee on Trade and Economic Affairs, agreed upon between Kennedy and Ikeda at their June meeting in Washington. It was taken very seriously by the Japanese government and public as representing a new stage in Japanese-American relations, and the American side too looked on it as important. Rusk was accompanied by four other members of the American cabinet, constituting what was said to have been the largest number of cabinet members on a single trip in American history. Under secretaries and other high-ranking officials, including Walter Heller, the chairman of the Council of Economic Advisors and a fellow Oberlinian, represented other parts of the government. In all, thirty-nine American officials and a few wives came by presidential jet, and we in Japan provided ten Marines and a large number of aides from the Embassy, for a total of about one hundred eighty Americans. The Japanese were much more numerous, and about three hundred members of the press corps milled eagerly about.

Upon arrival, the American group drove in a long cavalcade up to the mountain resort of Hakone near Fuji, where the meetings were held. Rusk and I were in the lead car; all along the way people stood on the side of the road waving little flags, which, as Rusk remarked, was an unprecedented display for mere cabinet ministers. The meetings went off smoothly both in the discussions and the entertainment. Nothing important was decided, to the disappointment of the press, but that was as expected. The Japanese had put their strongest politicians in the cabinet for the occasion, and the Americans were duly impressed, saying that nowhere could you meet a more impressive group of cabinet members. In addition to the plenary sessions, each cabinet member had long talks with his counterpart, and both sides thus got to know each other intimately. I was well satisfied for several reasons: the public spotlight was swung for once away from military matters to economic affairs in Japanese-American relations; the spirit of an equal partnership was definitely strengthened; and a large group of top American officials became much more conscious of Japan and knowledgeable about it.

My own role was not prominent among all the stars who had come from Washington. I was simply in a supporting position, but the work in preparation and during the meetings was extremely heavy. I was tabbed for the least desirable assignment. Except for the final press interview, which was handled by Rusk and Kosaka, I and the Vice Minister of Foreign Affairs had to meet the press daily and try to satisfy its appetite with the few crumbs we could dispense. Haru was busy the whole time keeping the cabinet wives occupied and happy in Tokyo. We also had lingering duties after the main body had returned to Washington. Arthur Goldberg, the Secretary of Labor, stayed on at the Residence with his wife Dorothy for a few days to talk with labor leaders, and Stewart Udall, the Secretary of the Interior, remained to climb Fuji, which he did with Haru's youngest uncle, Matsukata Saburo, the president of the Japanese Alpine Association. A North Pacific Fisheries meeting also followed the Economic Conference immediately to keep things rolling.

The joint United States–Japan science meeting, which had also been agreed upon in June, was held in mid-December. Not being a scientist, I did not have much to do with it except for making statements at opening and closing sessions and giving a reception at the Residence for its members. At first the Japanese public harbored some suspicions that the meeting was being held for clandestine military purposes, but these doubts were soon dispelled, and the meeting proved a great success, producing a wide variety of on-going specialized study groups.

The third joint meeting agreed upon in June on cultural matters followed in the last week of January 1962, attended by such notables as Robert Penn Warren, the writer, and Aaron Copland, the composer. Arthur Schlesinger was to have been our chairman, but came late, so I had my old friend Hugh Borton, then president of Haverford, take over as the head of our delegation. He and another old friend, Burton Fahs, stayed at the Residence. The meetings were held in Tokyo, but the whole group took a weekend trip to Hakone, where Hugh and I got into a snowball fight to the open amazement of our sedate Japanese colleagues and the delight of the press. Nothing very notable in the intellectual or cultural fields emerged from the meetings, but the conference did lay the foundation for its later flourishing as CULCON.

The summer and autumn of 1961 witnessed a subtle transformation of Haru and me from neophytes to self-confident old-timers. The Leonharts had been away on home leave most of the summer, and we discovered that we could run the Embassy pretty well without their assistance. The overtones of anxiety and uncertainty that are sprinkled through my letters home in the spring are entirely missing in the letters and memoranda of late fall. By then I could write, "Negotiating with the Foreign Minister is like talking with Fairbank and a reception of 340 like doing the week's shopping." All I had to complain about was our lack of time and energy. I clearly had established full mastery over the Embassy, with the exception of USIS, which in its detailed operations was still not under my complete control or functioning smoothly. Both Haru and I also felt that we had gotten past the mere formalities of diplomatic life and were becoming fully

The Embassy Residence with the hillside, Chancery and affiliated buildings behind.

The Embassy
Residence

The entrance hall
and foyer.

The large dining room. A Kline hangs at one end on loan from the Museum of Modern Art.

The reception room (once used for an ambassadorial badminton match).

At work. *(From the Mainichi Shimbun)*

Meeting the people, Shimoda Black Ship Festival.

The meeting between President Kennedy and Prime Minister Ikeda in Washington, June 1961, with (from left) Ambassador Asakai, Secretary of State Dean Rusk, Foreign Minister Kosaka Zentaro, EOR and translator.

With Ikeda Hayato, 1961.

Foreign Minister and Ambassador lead Foreign Ministry and Embassy softball teams in contest highlighted more by good spirit than skill.

Intrafamily contest. *(Bungei Shunju Ltd)*

With the caretaker's children at Misaki, 1962. *(Leonard Nadel)*

Bobby and Ethel Kennedy
after award of honorary degree
at Nihon University,
February 1962.

Washington's "two ambassadors
for the price of one" dressed for
a court function, 1962.

With Haru visiting former castle headquarters of the feudal lord at a modern prefectural capital.

Formal negotiations, September 1962, with Leonhart and his successor as DCM, Emmerson. Economic Minister Gardiner is on extreme left.

EOR typically communicating with hands as well as mouth.

At a Japanese inn with Air Force Lt. General Jacob ("Jake") Smart, Commander of the Fifth Air Force and United States Forces, Japan, during a visit to a Japanese Air Self Defense Force base on Sado Island, June 1963.

Visiting great Buddhist temple (Enryakuji) on Mt. Hiei above Kyoto on 1100th anniversary of the death of Ennin, EOR's first subject of scholarly study. Behind, from left to right, are Burton and Jamie Fahs and Nishiyama Sen, EOR's superb translator of extemporaneous speeches.

involved in the work we had come to do. Having overcome all the problems we had met so far, we felt able to handle whatever new ones might arise. In short, within seven months we had banished all our original fears and built up considerable self-confidence.

# 31
# Renewing the Dialogue

FROM THE start, Haru and I had considered the establishment of a dialogue with the Japanese people and the deepening of understanding between Japanese and Americans to be our chief work, but at first it was difficult to get much into this with all our other activities. Of course, our contacts with the Japanese leadership and the mass media were a start. I talked with endless Japanese leaders of all types in office calls as well as at luncheons and dinners; I had countless interviews for publication and wrote numerous articles. We both appeared constantly on television. Our educational endeavors we considered to be a two-way process directed as much toward Americans as Japanese. Many ambassadors bemoan the time they must spend briefing visiting Americans, but I welcomed the opportunity to talk to senators, congressmen, high-ranking bureaucrats and military officers, and business and intellectual leaders. Their presence in Japan seemed to me a great opportunity, for it opened their eyes to the importance of the country, thus making them a receptive audience.

We had the support of the whole Embassy in our educational efforts, but I felt the need for more Japanese-speaking officers. The language school in Yokohama was pouring out a stream of young officers with a good command of Japanese, but I thought it a pity that many higher ranking officers with similar language skills should be left scattered around the world in posts where their special knowledge of Japan was of no particular value. I early brought back to Japan David Osborn and Owen Zurhellen (who had also studied with me at Harvard) from Taiwan and the position of Consul General in Munich, respectively. David was later to serve as Ambassador to Burma and Owen as Ambassador to Surinam. John Stegmeier, with his "born in Japan" wife, I brought back from Trinidad to be the Consul General in the Osaka-Kobe area. John K. Emmerson, whom I had first known in Kyoto in 1937, when he was a young Foreign Service

Officer studying Japanese and I an apprentice scholar, came from Africa in the summer of 1962 to be my DCM. With such a crew aboard, Japanese invited to an Embassy reception would be astounded to discover that the thirty or so American Embassy officials and their wives who were in attendance were all able to converse with them in fluent Japanese. One guest at a luncheon given by Haru for women leaders—I believe she was a Socialist Diet member—happily remarked that the year before she had been demonstrating against the United States at the gates of the Embassy and now she was lunching and speaking in Japanese in the Embassy Residence itself.

Many old-line ambassadors tended to look on the work of USIS and all other cultural and intellectual activities as merely a nuisance, dealing only with unimportant "soft" areas. "Intellectual" in fact was virtually a taboo word in the American government. But I felt that intellectual understanding was necessary for any sound cooperation in the "hard" areas of economics, politics, and defense. I was therefore determined to have USIS and the whole Embassy join Haru and me in making a maximum effort in the cultural and intellectual fields. My recruitment of Burton Fahs as Cultural Minister was, of course, a major part of this strategy.

In the autumn of 1961 I also started on official visits to all forty-six of the Japanese prefectures. (Later the number was increased to forty-seven by the return of Okinawa.) In July when I had made my first official trip outside of Tokyo to a conference in Kyoto, Haru had not accompanied me, but I immediately realized that I had made a big mistake. The Japanese were more eager to see her than me and openly expressed their disappointment when she did not appear. We never made that error again.

An official prefectural visit usually involved calling on the governor and the mayors of the principal cities and having them and a crowd of lesser officials and policemen, well equipped with patrol cars, show us around some of the famous historical and beauty spots of the prefecture; seeing the local American Consulate, Cultural Center, or any other American government installations, if there were any; speaking at luncheons and dinners given by local America-Japan Societies or other suitable groups such as Chambers of Commerce; as well as speaking at the major local universities, meeting with the editorial boards of local newspapers, and appearing informally on television shows. The local publicity was always tremendous, and the people of the prefecture were usually surprised and delighted by my historical and geographic knowledge of their area. Commonly prefectures would make elaborate picture albums of our visit, which have given us a mountainous pictorial record of our stay in Japan. I would cringe, however, when the large entourage of police and other officials around us tramped down a station platform or some other public place, brushing aside unsuspecting old men and little old ladies to make way for our "regal" progress.

That September in Hakodate in Hokkaido we ran into the first organized political demonstration against us. It was probably occasioned by the announcement earlier that week that the United States was resuming nuclear testing, which was a very sore point in Japan. At Kokura (now part of the city of Kita-Kyushu in northern Kyushu), leftist students, perhaps in pique because a Chinese Communist delegation had been denied the right to speak at the local university, plastered anti-Reischauer posters all over, but the handful of chanting protestors they mustered looked rather pathetic outside the hall where I spoke to several hundred vociferously enthusiastic students. At nearby Fukuoka the mood was less pleasant, because of resentment over the flight pattern of American military planes, which, as a result of prevailing winds, led from our Itazuke air base just outside the city directly over Kyushu University, drowning out all activities by their roar. The problem had been brought to the attention of our mission in 1948, and now in 1961 I experienced it during my own lecture at the university. During my call on the governor, about a hundred shouting leftists massed outside holding up signs, one of which quaintly demanded in English, "Ambassador Reischauer go to the deuce."

On my first visit to Osaka I gave a major economic speech, prepared by my aides. Unlike most ambassadors, I gave speeches drafted by others only very rarely, but a few were necessary to emphasize some point at Washington's request. Instead of these "boiler plate" presentations, as we called them, I much preferred to draft my own speeches or else give them extemporaneously. On this Osaka trip we introduced significant innovations in my having luncheons and meetings with labor leaders and Haru's meeting with women labor leaders.

In Hiroshima my Embassy companions wished me to follow the precedent of other recent ambassadors in presenting a wreath at the memorial for the victims of the atom bomb early in the morning to avoid any publicity or press photographers. This seemed absurd to me. Of all events, I wished to have this one symbolizing American sorrow and sympathy well recorded, and so I made a visit to the memorial with the same publicity as any other event, and I did the same at the atom bomb memorial in Nagasaki.

✒

While I spoke extensively on our prefectural visits, the bulk of my speeches were delivered in Tokyo, most frequently to student audiences and usually in English, unless I had a written speech in Japanese for some special occasion. After one or two disastrous experiences, I decided that I should be sure to have a competent interpreter always on hand, so I looked around the Embassy and found Nishiyama Sen. A man of almost exactly my age, he is one of the three or four persons I have ever known who is truly bilingual in English and Japanese. He is also one of the finest persons, and we became close and lasting friends. Born in Utah, English was his first language, but he had developed a complete mastery of Japanese by coming to Japan in the depression years, getting a job in the Japanese government, becoming a Japanese citizen in the process, and spending the rest of his life as a Japanese. Later Sen was to become famous in Japan as "Mr. Apollo" for doing the simultaneous translation for Japanese television of the Apollo space mission.

Sen and I collaborated over the years on dozens if not hundreds of speeches. He could remember great chunks of materials simply with the aid of a few cabalistic scratches in a notebook and would produce translations which gave the true meaning and nuance of the English, not just literal translations of the words, which often result in gross misinterpretations. Sen made mistakes at times, but these were usually because of his lesser knowledge of Japanese history and his resulting misinterpretation of my meaning. I would listen carefully to everything he said and would pick up even the slightest slip or a modest omission of a laudatory remark about him. To hear me correct his statements in Japanese, we discovered, delighted the audience, no matter what its composition, so we always made the most of these corrections. A few times with college-age groups we even pulled a switch to amuse them. I would start off for a few sentences speaking in Japanese, and then Sen would solemnly translate what I had said into English. The audience looked stunned for a moment, then broke down in merriment. The Reischauer-Nishiyama act became well known, and all other translators became terrified of working with me.

Although college students on the whole supported the opposition parties and therefore were opposed to the government's close relationship with the United States, I was rarely shown even the slightest hostility, except for anti-American or, more specifically, anti-Reischauer signs that might be posted around by the Communists. Most of my student audiences and some other private groups as well would make a point of calling me Dr. or Professor Reischauer, claiming that these were more honorable titles than Ambassador.

At my speeches, particularly those before student audiences, I usually accepted questions. Most American ambassadors I have known avoided questions at public speeches as best they could. But how could I renew a dialogue with the Japanese without answering questions, or by taking refuge in the common reply of "No comment"? There were, of course, many things I could not say, but I believe I never told a lie or resorted to the "No comment" escape. On ticklish questions about current negotiations or other sensitive matters I did sometimes use diplomatic vagueness, and on specific questions about nuclear weapons I would rely on the standard American reply that we never confirmed or denied the presence of such weapons. In fact, I did not have precise knowledge about the location of nuclear weapons, except for the general proposition that we had agreed not to maintain them in Japan or introduce them into our bases there.

The commonest questions concerned American relations with China, which was a difficult problem for me because basically I approved of Japan's desire to develop relations with the People's Republic and disagreed with Washington's hard line against recognizing it, though I was a strong supporter of the maintenance of a Taiwan that was free to decide its own future. I usually handled questions on China by describing both the Japanese and American positions and the thinking behind them, but would avoid saying which I personally subscribed to. I also found the same general approach effective for the Vietnam War when it became a subject of controversy.

Frequently there were questions, particularly from student audiences, about Japan and its history. I would be asked to comment on Japanese traits and still more on what Japanese policies should be. Of course, it would have been entirely inappropriate for me, as a foreign Ambassador, to lecture the Japanese on their politics and the foreign policies they should adopt. This I would explain. Then I would add that if they would let me slip out of my ambassadorial role and speak as a scholar, my reply would be the following. Naturally there is no such thing as an Ambassador temporarily divesting himself of his ambassadorial status, but the stratagem always worked. I would express myself quite freely, and never once was there any criticism by the government or press on my public comments on Japanese history, society, or politics, or my discussions of Japanese foreign policy. I was, of course, living dangerously in speaking so frankly in public; one reason I got away with it, I believe, was that I did so quite lightheartedly and without fear of the consequences to me.

Often the questions were quite personal, because the Japanese were curious about Haru and me personally. A favorite question, especially from young people, was why I had married my wife, or "a Japanese woman," as they often phrased it. I think they were expecting a reply about the virtues of Japanese womanhood, but I would always answer quite simply, "Because I love her." This invariably brought resounding applause, though many of the young Japanese themselves were not going to be able to marry simply for love.

One ever-recurring topic, raised either by me or in the question period, concerned the sad state of English-language teaching in Japan. This and the Japanese universities were two of the few areas in which Japan had not improved markedly since the war, and yet a good command of English is absolutely necessary for Japan to develop adequate relations with the outside world. I advocated starting English in the first grade, when children learn foreign languages with ease and pleasure. I also advised the teaching of English for the purpose of speaking as well as reading. Specifically, I proposed a greater use of native speakers of the language as teachers and suggested that many young Americans and other native speakers would be eager for the chance to teach in Japan, even at very low pay.

The Japanese students were interested in these ideas, but their elders definitely were not. At the time most of Japan's fifty thousand-odd teachers of English could not really speak the language, and they felt threatened by my suggestions. The most dismal speech I ever gave in Japan was to a convention of English-language teachers, who refused out of pride to have an interpreter but for the most part were clearly unable to understand what I was saying. Japanese bureaucrats did not wish to have their routine disturbed and felt my ideas smacked too much of the "Peace Corps," which was designed for backward countries, not advanced ones like Japan. American senators and congressmen to whom I mentioned the subject were often enraged at what they were afraid would become an American aid program. My concepts fell on deaf ears. Nevertheless they are all still sound ideas, even though the conditions have improved greatly in the meantime.

Nishiyama Sen saved the situation for extemporary speeches, but preparing speeches to be read in Japanese or texts to be published in magazines or as pamphlets was another matter. I would write the text in English, and this would be rendered into Japanese by the translation section of the Embassy. The resulting manuscript I would then work over for hours with the original translator, pointing out where errors in meaning had been made or the nuance of a statement had been lost or distorted. A subtle compliment could easily be changed into a virtual insult.

Many of my speeches and articles were put out as bilingual pamphlets by USIS. Most of them dealt with topics one would expect, but two had somewhat more original subjects. One was called *New Maps of the World* and was built around two maps showing the countries of the world, the first in proportion to their population and the second in proportion to their Gross National Product (GNP) as of that time, which was 1964. The two display a vast discrepancy. The population map shows China and India as two monster nations and makes areas like Southeast Asia, Africa, and Latin America seem quite large. The GNP map in contrast is dominated by the United States, the USSR, Japan, and the countries of Europe, while Latin America, Africa, Southeast Asia, and even India and China shrivel into small appendages to the industrialized nations. The contrast today would be even greater, especially for Japan. The maps revealed a great deal about the problems of the world, and they demonstrated to Japanese the important place their nation held, which was my chief reason for making them. They caught the public attention and were widely reprinted in various reference works.

The other unusual publication was called *A New Look at Modern History.* I based it on a chart in which the vertical line represented the difference between democracy and dictatorship, with democracy at the top, and the horizontal line the difference between a free economy and a controlled economy, with the free economy on the right. Then I placed on this chart the various countries of the

world, discovering that less developed, premodern countries occupied a broad
scattered area centering around the middle but modernized countries fell into
two distinct areas. One group was in the upper right quadrant of democracy and
a free economy, being high on the democracy scale and generally on the free
economy side in the economic scale. The other group was deep in the lower
left-hand quadrant of dictatorship and a controlled economy. I then speculated
on how this sharp division had occurred among modernized countries and also
what future developments there might be.

Haru and I devoted our greatest efforts in these various ways to developing
a dialogue with Japanese, especially younger ones. It was certainly the work I
enjoyed most. Undoubtedly the great charismatic appeal President Kennedy held
for many Japanese, as for people all around the world, helped immeasurably in
producing a mood in which understanding and friendship could be developed.
But I believe that our efforts, too, made some contribution.


# 32
# Bobby Kennedy in Japan


THE VISIT by Robert and Ethel Kennedy to Japan early in February
1962 was a high point and also in some ways a turning point in our stay at the
Embassy. The President's younger brother, closest confidant, and Attorney General was a powerful figure in Washington; and his visit, made on the way to some
negotiations in Indonesia, occasioned great interest in Japan and no little anxiety
at the Embassy. He had a stern side, and heads were said to have rolled when
he had not been pleased with some of the embassies he had visited in Africa.

When I was in Washington in June, the Attorney General had consulted
with me about coming to Japan. (Bobby Kennedy always referred in public to
his brother as the President, and one took care to follow suit by calling him Mr.
Attorney General.) I had, of course, encouraged the idea, and negotiations about
the trip proceeded at a desultory pace for the next six months. Then the Japanese
government decided that decisions must be made. There was a split in plans
among the Japanese. Nakasone, together with Goto Noboru, the young head of
the economic empire called Tokyu, the Tokyo Express Railway Co. (he is now
the president of the Japanese Chamber of Commerce and one of Prime Minister

Nakasone's brain trust), called on me on December 1, informing me that they and some others wished to put the emphasis in the visit on youth in leadership roles. Their idea was to have Robert Kennedy come as the guest of a private group of younger leaders. The government, however, insisted that he be regarded a "national guest" *(koku hin)*. I believe that in the end he was considered to be both.

December and January were full of conferences and confusion over Bobby's visit. On January 5, John Seigenthaler and another of Bobby's right-hand men turned up to scout out the situation, and on the 18th we gave a reception for one hundred members of the "young men's committee" sponsoring the visit. They had dubbed themselves the "R.K. Committee," and the leadership had changed from Nakasone to the Foreign Minister's younger brother and Haru's relative, Kosaka Tokusaburo, in order to make it a purely nongovernmental group.

The visit was set for early February. Bobby and Ethel, of course, were to stay with us at the Residence. Since Ethel had been raised in wealth, she proved quite unconsciously demanding and we had to set up her personal hairdresser in the Residence itself. Bobby could not have cared less about his appearance, having only four well-worn suits, all badly pressed, according to our servants. But he was demanding in his own way. We laid on at his insistence an extremely heavy, "meaningful" schedule, running from eight in the morning to about eleven or twelve each night. When we sent in this schedule to Washington, a telegram came back saying in essence, "Fine, but what do I do from six to eight in the morning?" So we added two more hours of activities that could be carried out at that time of the day, such as a session of ice skating with a workingmen's club.

Bobby and Ethel along with a huge retinue arrived on the evening of February 4. After a tumultuous greeting at the airport and a few press interviews, they slept off the weariness of their long trip in order to start their back-breaking schedule the next morning. As many of their party as possible squeezed into our guest rooms upstairs; Kitty Galbraith turned up just then on her way back to India and joined the throng. Things became very informal. Suzie Wilson, the wife of the Deputy Director of USIA, who was traveling with Ethel, said it was like being back in college. Bobby appeared one morning in the upstairs breakfast room with no pants on, looking for his shoes, which the maids had polished. Since Ethel paid no attention to the schedule, Haru learned to crack the whip by pretending that things were scheduled a half hour earlier than they were. Ethel retaliated by calling her Mother Superior and took the joke to the point of asking for her dispensation to eat meat on Friday. The downstairs of the Residence meanwhile was overrun by newsmen, plainclothes operatives, and Embassy officers waiting to fulfill their assignments. The net result was chaos and a tremendous burden of work for our Residence staff, which rose to the occasion magnificently.

Bobby's first day was largely filled with long discussions with Ikeda and other leaders. A personal message from the President had failed to arrive, so Bobby and I together faked one, which proved quite satisfactory. There were also some rather empty protocol functions, over which Bobby chafed. He had a short fuse for such matters. At the end of the visit, when the R.K. Committee, which had been his host, held a convivial farewell party, I had great difficulty in persuading him to stay around for a suitable period before he walked out on it.

I had been a little dubious about Bobby's past record and reputation, but I was completely won over by his sincerity. He talked and listened well, always remaining calm, cool, and reasonable. As I recorded at the time, he was "a clear-headed, practical idealist with loads of energy and ability," who showed "a real belief in our democratic ideals" and concern for the common man. His low, quiet voice impressed the Japanese very favorably, in contrast to the loud, aggressive tones used by so many Americans, and what he said always made sense. I felt that he could not have handled himself better; in everything he did he strengthened the approach I had been trying to make to the Japanese. His youth and vigor unquestionably had a great appeal for them. He for his part seems to have been well impressed by me. Although I absented myself at first from some of the less important events in order to attend to my other work, he insisted after the first day that I should be at his side on all occasions, except for such things as the early morning skating and a late evening meeting with labor leaders at a bar, where he is said to have distinguished himself by his rendition of "When Irish Eyes Are Smiling." Haru similarly accompanied Ethel all the time.

Bobby's trip had gotten off to a fine start, but it turned into a smashing success on the 6th. In the early afternoon he gave a major address and received an honorary degree, all in decorous fashion, at Nihon University, Japan's largest. Then we headed for a speech at Waseda University, one of Japan's two most prestigious private universities. Reports had been coming in that the various Communist student factions had consolidated for a major effort to break up the affair. Ethel and Haru were with us, and we held a council of war with him and me sitting on the jump seats in the car. An unfortunate incident could be a disaster for Japanese-American relations, but backing out seemed inappropriate for Bobby as an exemplar of the "New Frontier." Ernest Young, a Harvard graduate student and expert in Japanese, whom I had brought to the Embassy as my personal aide and special contact man with Japanese youth—both jobs that he performed admirably—informed us that Japanese police reports and his own observations made him feel sure there was no real danger. The upshot of our discussion was to go ahead with our plans.

On arrival at the square in front of the lecture hall, we immediately saw that the situation was more serious than we had supposed. The square was crammed with more than three thousand unruly though friendly students, and we pushed our way on foot through the crowd with great difficulty. The lecture hall was not much better. A yelling crowd filled it quite literally to the rafters. The stage was overrun by stampeding cameramen. A claque of over one hundred Communist students in the front seats tried to break things up by their shouting, while the remaining two thousand or more students in the hall made matters worse by shouting back. Unable to speak, Bobby beckoned one of the Communists up on the stage to engage in a debate, but the student launched into a wild harangue. When Bobby finally got a few words in edgewise, the sound system went dead, obviously sabotaged. A hand loudspeaker was found but proved completely inadequate. A second student was substituted for the first with the same general results.

The whole thing was turning into a fiasco, and I knew the responsibility for the Attorney General's safety rested with me. I could see my diplomatic career ending suddenly and dramatically. I decided that I had better go into action to try to salvage what I could. I got up and chased the Japanese and foreign news photographers off the stage. Then I turned to the crowd and with my sternest look raised both my arms. To my amazement, the big hall fell silent, and Bobby and the student could continue with their debate, which at least the first few rows could hear. Each time the hubbub rose again, I would raise my arms with considerable though diminishing effect. Then a third student jumped on the stage. He turned out to be the school cheerleader, and he led the crowd in a thunderous rendition of the Waseda song. I slipped over to Bobby and said, "We'd better get out while we're ahead." My one consolation all along had been the knowledge that there was a rear exit to the stage and hall. Our party withdrew unobtrusively through the back way and was whisked to the quiet of the Japanese gardens surrounding the faculty club.

At the time we did not realize what a tremendous victory we had just had. Although the microphones were dead in the hall, they were operating on all the television hook-ups, so that the whole of Japan had been electrified by one of the most dramatic live TV programs in history. Bobby's calm, reasoned, even humorous presentation had come through in sharp contrast to the ranting of the Communist students. He had become in one brief moment a sort of youth hero, recognized by all Japanese, and the rest of his trip was virtually a triumphal procession. Communists continued to raise "Go Home Kennedy" signs, but their demonstrations dwindled into pathetic handfuls of extremists. To commemorate the occasion, Bobby's whole group learned the Waseda song as best they could and sang it on every appropriate occasion.

Everyone in Japan was captivated by Bobby and Ethel—Haru and I, being closest to them, most of all. Bobby's youthful energy was appealing, and the clear, steady flame of his idealism won me over completely. The President may have had the looks and charm, but it was Bobby who was unswervingly dedicated to his ideals. No one could have presented more effectively the message of a peace-loving and friendly but strong, hopeful, and vibrantly alive America, or shown more clearly our readiness for a partnership with Japan as a full equal.

Bobby and Ethel left for Hong Kong on the morning of the 10th. Just before we set off for the airport, I persuaded Bobby to give me fifteen minutes alone with him to discuss a few points I felt were important but had not been brought out adequately in his visit. Among them were Japan's normalization of relations with Korea and the Okinawa problem, which interested him greatly. I argued the need to hasten Okinawan autonomy and to return the islands to Japan in the future. He took some careful notes, which he undoubtedly passed on to the President. These probably influenced the action the President subsequently took on Kaysen's report on Okinawa and, I believe, opened the door to the ultimate reversion of Okinawa to Japan. Just before enplaning, Bobby kissed Haru and Ethel kissed me, no doubt to the surprise of the attendant Japanese officials. But we were not sorry to see them leave. We were exhausted, and I was gratified to learn that they themselves reached Hong Kong too tired to follow their schedule and had to hole up for a few days of rest.

⨾§

Bobby Kennedy's visit to Japan changed my status in Washington considerably. Henceforth I had a powerful friend there and a direct channel to the President, if bottlenecks developed further down in the Rube Goldberg machinery of government. I would confer at length with Bobby each time I went to Washington, and, during our next visit there in December 1962, he honored Haru and me with a gala dinner dance at his home in McLean across the river in Virginia. The round tables used at this dinner gave Haru and me a useful idea. Since protocol order was not clear at them, they allowed us to avoid seating a non-English-speaking Japanese between two non-Japanese-speaking Americans, as would inevitably happen at the long tables of formal dinners where everyone would be seated strictly according to rank.

Bobby and Ethel visited Japan a second time in January 1964 to meet in Tokyo with President Sukarno of Indonesia. It was still less than two months after his brother's assassination, and Bobby was reported to be benumbed by the tragedy, but the trip seems to have helped snap him out of this condition. Because meteorological conditions had disrupted communications with Washington for a week, we learned about the visit only at the last moment. On January 13 a message from Ambassador Howard Jones in Indonesia announced that he was arriving the next evening, but without saying why. Then the same day the Indonesian Ambassador called on me to tell me that Sukarno would be in Tokyo on January 15–19, casually adding that Sukarno would see Bobby then. Apparently a Sukarno–Bobby Kennedy meeting had been under negotiation for some time, and this was Sukarno's formal reply. The United States wished Bobby to impress Sukarno with its deep concern over the current military confrontation between Indonesia and Malaysia. The British Ambassador also called to pass on through me the British cabinet's attitude toward the situation.

Ambassador Jones and I joined Ikeda and the Foreign Minister on the 15th in meeting Sukarno and his party of fifty-two, then arranged with him at his headquarters in the Imperial Hotel for meetings with Bobby on the 17th and 18th. Haru and I met Bobby and Ethel on the evening of the 16th at the American air base in Yokota, far out in the western suburbs of Tokyo. They were traveling around the world in a huge windowless jet, which was like circumnavigating the globe in a high-speed submarine. Both seemed to be in fine shape, he somehow more mature than when we had last seen him but still full of vigor and she as charmingly uninhibited as ever.

The meeting with Sukarno went smoothly. Sukarno obviously liked Bobby's soft-spoken, nonthreatening manner and readily agreed to call off both his regular and guerrilla forces, if the British would do the same, and to meet with the Malaysian leaders (though actually hostilities were to continue until 1965, when Sukarno finally fell from power). Bobby met with the British Ambassador and the chief British intelligence officer from Singapore to tell them the results of his talk. It was interesting to see how touchy and provocative he was with the British— not at all like his understanding manner with the Japanese or Indonesians; in fact, Jones and I had to smooth ruffled feathers after he had left.

While in Tokyo, Bobby wished to go to Waseda University to thank the students for a special memorial ceremony they had held for his brother. Several Japanese leaders had strongly urged us to give up this part of the program, because it might seem an open challenge to the left and a provocative attempt to repeat the victory of Bobby's first Waseda speech. Since any trouble at all this time would be a serious embarrassment, we had only a narrow margin for success. But George R. Packard, III, who had become Ernest Young's successor as my special assistant and contact with youth when Young resigned the previous summer, insisted that everything would go well, so we followed his advice, setting off with Ethel, Haru, and George all in the same car with Bobby and me. (George, who was fluent in Japanese and subsequently wrote an excellent book on the Security Treaty blowup of 1960, is now dean of the School of Advanced International Studies of Johns Hopkins University in Washington.)

Our intention was to have Bobby say just a few words of greeting and thanks, then shake hands individually with the students, but our plans were derailed by the size of the crowd. Okuma Hall, where Bobby had spoken before, was crammed with more than two thousand students; at least five thousand more were standing outside in the rain. He was forced to return to the speech format, again under the full glare of nationwide television. There were a couple of "Go Home" signs in the crowd outside, and in the hall some students unfurled a large sign saying "Return Okinawa," but the crowd quickly ripped it down, and there were no other hostile acts. The students loudly applauded all of Bobby's remarks. When he concluded, the cheerleader who had led the singing two years before once again mounted the stage to lead the crowd in a thunderous rendition of the Waseda song, with Bobby and Ethel joining in. While the audience was kept in the hall, we proceeded to the steps of the building, where Bobby spoke briefly to the crowd outside and the song was again sung. Then we headed for the plane at Yokota, leaving behind a Waseda faculty and student body tickled pink at having wiped out the shame of the 1962 incident. The American newsmen who had accompanied Bobby were bug-eyed at the throngs and enthusiasm.

Haru and I were pleased to have had a chance to demonstrate how the spirit of Japan had changed during the two years since Bobby and Ethel's earlier visit. I also recorded of Bobby at the time, "One can't help but feel that he may be destined in time to succeed his brother."


# 33

# Squalls and Smooth Sailing

By THE END of our first year in Japan, both Haru and I felt quite at ease in the Embassy and well satisfied with the way things were going in Japanese-American relations, but we were also exhausted, as were many of our top officers. Edward Dougherty, the able Economic Counsellor, collapsed in the middle of a speech, and the navy doctors at Yokosuka became worried about my health. Bobby Kennedy's first visit had been quite a strain, and our schedules the whole autumn and winter had proved too heavy. But it was more than this. Japanese-American relations were climbing to a new level of intimacy, and the Embassy was simply understaffed for its increased load. Since there was scant hope of wheedling more manpower out of Washington, it was up to us to pace ourselves better. The mad dash of our early months was turning into a grueling marathon. Haru began to wish that we would be fired for some indiscretion or else could just resign with a sense of "mission accomplished"; but I felt there was still a long uphill road ahead of us.

Without a doubt, the atmosphere had improved a great deal. Protestors against American policy were still numerous, but they were pleased not to find themselves barred at the Embassy gates and allowed to send in their representatives, who could discuss their grievances in Japanese with top Embassy officers. Often they went away delighted at the courteous treatment they had received. Leonhart aptly summarized the change in spirit. My predecessor had tried to get Matsumoto Shigeharu, director of the prestigious International House, fired because of his contacts with leftist intellectuals, and Leonhart, referring to this incident, characterized the Embassy as having been like a beleaguered castle, with only a small group of faithful Japanese friends. Haru and I, he said with a quick shift of metaphor, had turned the glove inside out. Now everybody was our friend, unless he was an avowed Communist.

There was the danger, though, of coming on too hard. Toshio ("Tuskey") Tsukahira, a former American Army captain and Ph.D. from Harvard, whom I had brought out to the Embassy the previous summer to try to solve its translation difficulties, called my attention to an article in the *Tosho Shimbun*, the publishers' newspaper, entitled "Mr. Reischauer's Gift: An Intellectual and Cultural NEATO." NEATO was an acronym standing for the "Northeast Asia Treaty Organization," which was supposed to parallel SEATO (the Southeast Asia Treaty Organization), but was a pure figment of the Japanese imagination. When the term was used to Rusk, he had leaned over to me and asked "What's NEATO?" But it was frequently heard in Japan at the time. The article, which linked my activities with such things as the fellowship program of the Rockefeller Foundation, built up a picture of a nefarious cultural offensive in Japan designed to turn it into an "ideological bastion" against communism.

The left obviously was very nervous about Japan's military and political relations with the United States. There was a veritable tempest in a teapot in May when word leaked out in Washington of the movement of elements of one of our air units in Japan to Thailand because of the fighting in Laos. This produced a loud outcry by the Japanese press, which felt that the United States was not living up to its agreement to notify Japan of major changes of armament. Actually only four planes were involved, and we were well within the bounds of our agreement; but this was typical of the sort of problem that constantly came up and consumed much of my time.

The American decision to resume the testing of nuclear weapons also caused a flurry of consultations with the Japanese government and protests from it as well as from the public. The decision was announced in early April but stirred up a milder reaction than we had expected. Unfortunately, the actual resumption of testing came on April 25, 1962, while Haru and I were on a long scheduled official visit to three prefectures and were therefore away from the relative calm and security of the Embassy.

At Kanazawa on the Japan Sea coast, an incident occurred somewhat reminiscent of Bobby Kennedy's Waseda speech. The Kanazawa University authorities had seen to it that the seats in the hall where I was to speak were all occupied by not unfriendly students, but outside the hall was a much larger and somewhat unruly crowd, and a small scuffle occurred. Following Bobby's strategy, I invited the ringleaders to enter the hall; although they heckled me throughout, I was able to give my planned scholarly speech and then answer some controversial questions.

In Nagoya, we ran into more serious demonstrations against American nuclear policy. Most of the schedule, however, went quite well, including a brief speech I gave to a convention of two thousand representatives of women's organizations. The final item was a meeting with some of the faculty of Nagoya University, but we learned that large student groups were laying plans to break this up. Remembering that I had advised in the spring of 1960 that the American government should simply cancel President Eisenhower's visit to Japan when it became clear that there was going to be strong popular opposition to his coming, I decided that I should follow my own advice and go back to Tokyo, promising to return when we would be more welcome. This decision, I believe, was the dignified thing to do, and it was met with relief and gratitude from the authorities. Back in Tokyo a few hundred thousand people demonstrated against the nuclear decision, but they were steered away from the Embassy by the efficient police, causing no serious incident and occasioning us no embarrassment.

<br>

Trouble could arise on the right as well as on the left of the political spectrum. The conservative Foreign Ministry under the leadership of the Vice Foreign Minister, Takeuchi Ryuji, began to show unhappiness over my close and frequent contacts with the Prime Minister and Foreign Minister. The Japanese Ambassador in Washington in contrast got to see the Secretary of State, much less the President, only under the most unusual circumstances, normally having to content himself with the Assistant Secretary level. The Japanese were correct in seeing this as unequal, and, since I was striving for a sense of equality, I made no effort to oppose their desire to have me deal basically with the Vice Minister. I considered this attempted downgrading of the American Ambassador as a healthy sign, though actually nothing much came of it because the Prime Minister and Foreign Minister were already such close friends that they often preferred to deal directly with me.

A much more difficult problem arose in the summer of 1962 over the shift of the DCM from Leonhart to John Emmerson. Emmerson after World War II had fallen into the ill graces of Senator Bourke Hickenlooper of Iowa simply because he, as a Japanese-speaking officer, had been sent to Yenan during the war to interview Japanese Communists living with the Chinese Communists, and as a result of this experience had been assigned by MacArthur's Political Advisor to maintain contact with the Japanese Communists after the war. Emmerson actually was a mild man of very moderate political views, but Hickenlooper included him in the group who allegedly had "lost China," vowing that Emmerson would never be appointed to a post requiring the "advice and consent" of the Senate. As a result, he was twice passed over for ambassadorial positions in Africa for which he was the obvious candidate. Rusk as a gesture of compensation wished to give him the actually much more important post of DCM in Japan. I was, of course, delighted to get so knowledgeable an aide and an old friend to boot, but I felt I owed Leonhart a great deal for his invaluable help in my early apprentice days at the Embassy. I therefore told Rusk that I would accept Emmerson if he would find an ambassadorial post for Leonhart. The result was that Leonhart went to Tanzania as Ambassador, and Emmerson took his place as DCM, serving as my extremely competent right-hand man throughout the remainder of my ambassadorship.

Unfortunately, Japanese rightist activists got wind of Hickenlooper's accusations and started making objections to Emmerson's appointment even before he arrived on July 15, 1962. I was distressed to see how readily such attitudes were picked up by some responsible business and political leaders, and began to meet with many of the people individually and in groups to point out the absurdity of their fears. On some occasions I even made clear my indignation that Japanese, who as a nation were pusillanimous in their attitude toward communism and careful to avoid any hint of criticizing the Communist countries, should have the gall to attack a responsible American official for not being sufficiently anti-Communist. But I also began to see that behind "l'affaire Emmerson," as I called it, there was among older and more conservative Japanese a broad streak of lingering resentment of the liberal reforms of MacArthur's Occupation, a suspicion of the liberal policies of the Kennedy administration, and a distrust of my strategy of establishing contacts with less conservative Japanese. I even heard talk of my building up a "Reischauer Gang" of liberals at the Embassy. There was also clearly an anti-Ikeda aspect to the criticism, because it seemed a way in which more conservative factions might be able to strike at him.

The whole incident illustrated the shallowness of Japanese understanding of American thinking and how easily efforts on our part to build up a dialogue with the left could produce uneasiness and hostility on the right. But the matter blew over in the course of the summer and early autumn because of Emmerson's own sterling qualities, helped by some strenuous efforts by Leonhart on a visit to Tokyo on his way between Washington and Tanzania. Leonhart took the opportunity to point out that I had perhaps been neglecting somewhat my contacts with Japanese conservatives and the business community, and I took steps at once to start correcting this situation.

While all the brouhaha was going on over l'affaire Emmerson, the opposite end of the conservative spectrum was active in a contrasting way. Kono, the most pro-Soviet of the conservative leaders, insisted on a long conversation with me to prove how truly anti-Communist he was. This was probably part of his own maneuvering against Ikeda. A visit with a high-level trade mission of businessmen going to the Soviet Union was also designed by them to underline their basic anti-communism, while in a luncheon with Matsumura, a leading pro-Chinese conservative politician just back from a trip to Peking, he hinted at a go-between role for Japan between the United States and the People's Republic. The Japanese in general had much too high hopes for extensive trade in the near future with the Soviet Union and China, and I took these occasions to throw cold water on these hopes.

The trouble over Emmerson and these other maneuverings strengthened my belief that good diplomacy called for absolute honesty. As I recorded at the time, the old bromide that diplomats were honest men paid to go abroad to lie for their country seemed to me far off the mark. If I had said different things to the various conservative factions and to the leftist opposition, I would have tripped myself up and become hopelessly enmeshed in a tangle of lies.

ᮝ

Despite the various political squalls, 1962 passed on the whole very smoothly. Our first big event after the Kennedy visit was a trip Haru and I took to Baguio in the Philippines for a regional conference of American ambassadors.

Baguio is a lovely place in the mountains, but the conference was unutterably dull. The American ambassadors from East and Southeast Asia together with their wives and some members of their staffs were present; Bowles also had led a sizable caravan from Washington, including Averell Harriman, who, despite his distinguished career as an intimate of Roosevelt and face-to-face antagonist of Stalin, had recently taken the relatively humble post of Assistant Secretary of State for the Far East. The whole group crowded into a stuffy room to be given interminable inspirational lectures by Bowles and be fiercely reminded by Harriman that we worked for the President and no one else.

After returning from Baguio, the Bowleses and Harrimans were our house guests for several days, together with Katie Louchheim, who as a Deputy Assistant Secretary of State in charge of women's affairs was the ranking woman officer in the State Department at the time. Tired of hotels, she practically forced us to take her in, offering to sleep in a bathtub if necessary. Her insistence worked out to our great good fortune in the long run, because we became very good friends with her and her investment advisor husband, Walter; whenever we were back in the United States, their lovely old Georgetown house became our home in Washington. We shared her enthusiasm for having a women's affairs officer at the Embassy, and our combined efforts finally resulted in the arrival in October 1963 of Dorothy Robins, who performed admirably in this capacity.

The summer of 1962 proved much more restful than the year before. We even managed a nine-day vacation at our hideout at Misaki, though I spent much of my time there writing a long assessment of the situation in Japan. I put a low security classification on it in order to ensure its wide distribution in Washington but was surprised later to discover that many high-ranking officials had themselves read it despite its humble ranking.

The summer was made particularly pleasant for us by the presence of two of our children. Ann and her husband Steve came out on June 12 and Joan on July 29. Steve had just graduated from the California Institute of Technology, and, when he and Ann returned in September to the United States, it was for him to start graduate studies in molecular biology at Harvard, where they lived in our house. They went back with our first grandchild well on the way. Nathan, the eldest of their five children, was born on December 31.

Joan had dropped out of Oberlin in the spring and came to Japan for a longer stay. The pressures of publicity when we had first come to the Embassy and the complete separation from home that our stay in Japan entailed had put more of a strain on her than we had realized. In the autumn she took a job as the assistant first-grade teacher at the Nishimachi International School founded by Haru's sister, Tane. This occupied her very well until she went back to America in the summer of 1963, where she worked for a while as a secretary at Harvard before returning to college at Tufts.

Bobby had other things than a trip to Japan on his mind. He had become engaged and on October 26, 1962, married his Harvard classmate, Charlotte Scannell, a Belmont neighbor and the daughter of Dr. Gordon Scannell, a prominent surgeon at the Massachusetts General Hospital and a professor at Harvard Medical School. My father helped perform the ceremony. After graduating the following spring, Bobby went to Columbia for graduate studies, at first in Latin American Studies but eventually winning his Ph.D. in economics.

The Residence hostelry saw a steady stream of lodgers, mostly ambassadors and other high government dignitaries passing through Tokyo. Robert Murphy, who is best known for his exploits in North Africa and Europe during World War II but was briefly the first postwar Ambassador to Japan in 1952, stayed with us for ten days with his actress daughter Rosemary, and John Allison came for three weeks. Among others we entertained for meals or receptions were General Maxwell Taylor, the brilliant new head of the Joint Chiefs of Staff; Eddie Rickenbacker, the famous World War I flying ace, who proved to be a hard-shell reactionary; Yul Brynner, who had been born in East Asia of Russian parents; and Walter Reuther, the dynamic president of the United Auto

Workers. We got to know Shirley MacLaine fairly well because she came each Christmas to be with her husband, Steve Parker, a local businessman, and their daughter Sachiko, who was one of Joan's pupils. Shirley was as uninhibitedly charming as one would expect, but somewhat more sedate, at least around an Ambassador.

In June, Haru and I had dinner at the home of the famous author Mishima Yukio. The Italianate architecture of his house, its eighteenth-century European furnishings, and its Roman-style garden sculpture, all under an unrealistically full moon in a Tokyo suburb, gave a sense of fantasy which matched well the fantasy of Mishima's spectacular *harakiri* suicide eight years later. I found him a hard man to fathom even after reading the excellent biography of him by my former student, John Nathan.

The Cuban missile crisis of October did not produce any great excitement in Japan, and the Sino-Indian War, which broke out the same month, caused even less of a stir, but we had our own little incidents. In June the Embassy helped a defector from the Cuban Embassy, introduced to us by the Papal Nuncio, who called on me. Later we were to have Russian defectors as well. We became involved in such matters at the Embassy because the Japanese government preferred to turn a blind eye to them.

⋘

On November 24, Haru and I left Tokyo to attend the second meeting of the cabinet-level United States–Japan Committee on Trade and Economic Affairs, to be held in Washington on December 3–5. The meetings proved even better than those the year before at Hakone, principally because the feeling of real partnership between the two countries had matured greatly in the meantime. Counting Heller, the chairman of the Council of Economic Advisors, we had seven cabinet members at the table most of the time to six from Japan, and there were usually about fifteen persons of Assistant Secretary rank from each side. All of the American cabinet members spoke to me about what they wanted to do in Japan at the next get-together, showing their enthusiasm for the meetings.

The only untoward incident resulted from something President Kennedy said in his toast at the luncheon he gave at the White House on the first day. Having just come from a meeting of the National Security Council, where the fighting in Indo-China had been discussed, he had defense problems on his mind and stated that our bilateral economic relations and the "containment of Chinese Communist aggressiveness" were the two main problems this conference had to face. The statement was unfortunate since the Committee had been specifically set up to get away from the emphasis on military matters in Japanese-American relations, about which the Japanese public was extremely sensitive. Realizing his gaffe, the President after lunch asked me to try to correct his blunder as best I could, but representatives from both the Japanese and American press had been present, so there were limits to what I could do. In the official text released to the public, I cut out a reference to the United States and Japan as constituting a "defense chain" and made the comment on the problem of "Chinese aggressiveness" apply not to the discussions at the conference but to subjects we would have to consider "in the months ahead." The Japanese cabinet members themselves were not disturbed by the President's remarks, but there was quite an uproar in Japan. The press in particular wanted to know what was meant by "in the months ahead," but I reassured them on the vagueness of the term, and Ikeda later told me he appreciated the way I had handled the problem.

The formal discussions in Washington were strictly limited to the agenda of economic problems and went very smoothly, but on the side we had some talks with the Japanese about military matters. During the week I was in Washington before the Japanese arrived, a dispute between the State Department and the Department of Defense and the Treasury came to a head. Defense and the Treasury wanted Japan to help stem the American dollar drain in the same way Germany and Italy had done by offset purchases of American military hardware. I convinced Rusk that this was the wrong approach, for it would certainly fail and would only stir up deep fear and resentment in Japan. Finally it was agreed that the problem would be raised only at a secret meeting I would arrange with Ohira, the Foreign Minister. Subsequently, I was asked to sound out Ikeda in Tokyo about a fuller exchange of information on defense problems and needs.

In Washington Haru "took the city by storm," as I recorded at the time, being "perhaps the most publicized figure in the whole visit of the Japanese Cabinet." It was unprecedented for the wives of members of the Japanese cabinet to go on a trip of this sort, and they looked to her for guidance, as did Virginia Rusk and the other American cabinet wives. Haru was interviewed on television; *The Washington Post* paid almost more attention to the social events, especially those involving the women, than it did to the meetings themselves. The Japanese wives, who had come to Washington with some trepidation, though we had entertained them twice at the Embassy Residence to help make them feel at ease about it, were delighted with the whole trip and spoke to me of Haru being "the pride of Japan."

While in Washington, I also had a chance to discuss a number of problems of concern to me and the Embassy. One was the gradual strangulation of the Embassy because of the rising costs of rentals and the inadequate pay scale of the Japanese employees. I also had a good discussion with the President, largely about his hope of visiting Japan, and he asked me to explore the matter further with Ikeda.

One problem of particular concern to me was my own possible resignation from the ambassadorship. President Pusey of Harvard had written me already in September that my leave of absence would expire on March 16, 1963. The preciseness of the date was menacing, but I had decided to wait until this trip back to Washington to see what the attitudes toward me were before making up my mind. Staying on would necessitate resigning my positions at Harvard, which would have to be filled by other people. Since there were only a few fixed openings in my field at Harvard, I assumed that this would mean the end of my long relationship with the university. But I was prepared to do this if Washington really wanted me to stay on in Tokyo. For the most part, the other professors who, like me, had left Harvard to join the Kennedy administration returned during the next few months or moved on to positions elsewhere after leaving government.

I consulted with the President, Rusk, Harriman, and Bundy, all of whom strongly urged me not to resign. The President even wanted to write to Pusey asking for an extension of my leave, but I dissuaded him from doing this. Their attitude, together with the obvious confidence Washington was placing in my judgment on Japan and the influence I found myself able to exert, convinced me to stay on, whatever the consequences. When I subsequently told Pusey of my decision, he expressed his approval and reassuringly added that there would always be a place for me at Harvard.

# 34
# Relations with the Military

Embassy relations with the American military in Japan and the Western Pacific were often as delicate and complex as with the Japanese government. Traditionally, distrust and rivalry were the pattern, and Leonhart at first had delighted in catching the military off base on some matter and tweaking the lion's tail, as he put it. But I wished for a more harmonious relationship. So also did Air Force Lieutenant General Jacob ("Jake") Smart, who succeeded General Burns as Commander of United States Forces, Japan, in the summer of 1961.

Haru and I liked Jake immensely, and he made a special effort to get to know us well, taking us on trips to visit the outlying American bases in Japan. From the start Jake tried hard to understand my attitude about relations with Japan, which was probably quite different from anything he had encountered before. He would come to the Embassy almost on a weekly basis and we had long private talks together. At times he would get restive with my "low posture" in not demanding that the Japanese take a strong stand in backing the United States in international controversies or hastening their own defense buildup, but I would point out to him the great sensitivity of the Japanese public to such matters and explain that because of shared economic interests and political ideals our relationship would come along well enough without prodding by us.

In time, Smart became a true believer; the close relationship we developed, and the identity of views expressed by the Tokyo Embassy and United States Forces, Japan, came to be considered in Washington a model of the way things should operate in the field. I believe I won a lot of brownie points for this from both the civilian and the military authorities back in Washington, though in reality Jake Smart deserved more credit for it than I.

Jake was promoted in the summer of 1963 to be the commander of all air forces in the Pacific area at CINCPAC in Hawaii, but he passed on his warm relations with us to his successor, the delightfully witty Maurice ("Mo") Preston, and his still more humorous and artistically gifted wife Dorothy. Curtis LeMay, the hardboiled Chief of Staff of the Air Force, who was in Japan in April 1963, promised me a good replacement for Jake, assuring me that if I did not find the new commander satisfactory, I should let LeMay know and he would replace him. As I recorded at the time, this seemed like one of those promises that are easily made but rarely lived up to. But I never had to test it. Mo was more than satisfactory, and the four of us became close friends. Both Jake and Mo eventually reached the top of their profession as full four-star generals.

Another military man of importance to me was the vice admiral commanding the Seventh Fleet in the Western Pacific. Thomas H. Moorer, later the brilliant head of the Joint Chiefs of Staff, was assigned this post in 1962 and insisted that I pay him a formal courtesy call for lunch on his flagship when it came into port. As I boarded the ship, I was startled by a squeaky noise beside me, which turned out to be my being "piped aboard." I had assumed that such customs had died out a few wars back. In May 1963, Moorer invited me for a trip on the great aircraft carrier, *Constellation.* I landed on the ship on the high seas in a small plane and after deplaning suddenly found the whole section of the deck where I stood lowering to the hangar deck below, where the entire contingent of Marines was lined up for my inspection. Then Moorer had some of the planes perform an exhibition of takeoffs, bombings, and landings, and he held a second smaller display for me that night. After a night aboard while the ship ran southwestward, we were catapulted into the air in a small plane and flew to Iwakuni, the chief base of the Marines on the Inland Sea near Hiroshima.

Much more important to me than the commander of the Seventh Fleet was

CINCPAC, the commander of the whole Pacific area, Admiral Felt. He was definitely hostile to Japan because of lingering feelings about World War II, but he was gradually persuaded to take a more cooperative attitude. Going to or coming from Washington, I frequently stopped with him for talks at his headquarters at Pearl Harbor, and when he was in Japan we would sometimes hold meetings of the United States–Japan Security Consultative Committee. This was jointly chaired by the Foreign Minister and me but attended by Felt as one of my aides. The second meeting of the Committee and the first in two years was held on August 1, 1962, by which time Ohira had become the Foreign Minister.

At this meeting we decided to try to meet thenceforth twice a year. I always let the Japanese know of our interest in Japan's providing more of its own defense but avoided any hint of putting pressure on them, while Ohira made it equally clear that Japan was moving ahead in its military buildup strictly on its own volition and not in response to American demands. Actually the Japanese military budget, though increasing sharply, was not growing as fast as the budget as a whole and remained below the traditional rate of 1 percent of GNP. But Ikeda's statement during a trip to Europe that Japan now was one of the three pillars of the free world, though greeted with some derision, expressed well the new attitude the Japanese leadership was taking.

The Treasury and Department of Defense, however, continued to hope to get Japan to make up through offset purchases of American weapons the $300 million deficit in the American balance of payments caused by military spending in Japan. Roswell Gilpatric, the Deputy Secretary of Defense, came to Tokyo in February 1963 with this plan in mind; but we at the Embassy, backed up by Smart, convinced him that such an effort would be counterproductive and rewrote his talking papers so that he simply encouraged a more realistic Japanese response to its own defense problems and closer consultation with us on such matters. We had to be ever on the alert because Treasury and Defense quite regularly would attempt to revive the idea.

In contrast to the other military officers, my relations with Caraway in Okinawa remained difficult. Interest in the islands had heated up considerably in the Japanese government since my visit there in August 1961 and Carl Kaysen's report to the President that autumn. Delegations often came to see me to express their views. Periodically President Ohama Nobumoto, long the head of Waseda University and Okinawa's most distinguished native son, would lead groups of fellow Okinawans to see me, and the Chief Executive of the islands would drop in when he was in Tokyo.

In April 1962, President Kennedy finally made clear that Okinawa would someday be returned to Japan and in the meantime the Chief Executive was to be elected and there was to be an American civilian, rather than military, Civil Administrator. George McCune's younger brother, Shannon, a professor of geography, was chosen for the position, but found himself completely frustrated by Caraway's virtually ignoring him. Caraway also continued to keep Japanese aid to Okinawa and consultations as restricted as possible and limited to uninteresting fields, such as harbor construction, rather than social problems. An open clash over the aid budget took place in 1963, which came to a head in a flurry of telegrams in the middle of the night between Washington, Tokyo, and Okinawa. It was immediately resolved in our favor by Washington, but Caraway, of course, retained his ability to drag his feet.

Caraway so clearly flouted the policies the President had established for Okinawa that we at the Embassy and many people in Washington began to wonder if he should not be replaced. However, the Army Department chose to regard the problem as a matter of petty personal rivalries, though actually our personal relations always remained very cordial. Caraway stayed on as High Commissioner and for as long as he was in Okinawa remained a serious irritant in Japanese-American contacts, threatening a vastly important overall relationship by his highhanded rule in his little bailiwick. I made a serious mistake when Secretary of the Army Cyrus R. Vance made a special stopover in Japan in September 1963 to ask me to agree to Caraway's continuation as High Commissioner half a year longer than his regular term and until his retirement from the army in 1964, in order to preserve his three-star rank during retirement. I obligingly agreed to this proposal, but Caraway's uncooperative conduct during his last six months in command made me rue my soft-heartedness.

◄§

One very sensitive military matter that arose at this time was the question of the entry into Japanese ports of American submarines that were nuclear-powered but not armed with nuclear weapons. Legally, there was no reason why they should not do this just like any other ship of the Seventh Fleet engaged in the defense of Japan, but the Japanese public felt so strongly about anything nuclear that the Japanese government had hitherto reacted in horror at the very thought of nuclear-powered submarines in Japanese ports, and the American Navy had obligingly kept them out. Now the situation was changing. The Japanese themselves were experimenting with nuclear power as probably a future necessity in an energy-poor land and were also contemplating building a nuclear-powered ship (which they subsequently did, though it proved a fiasco). When I was in Washington in the early winter of 1962, I had told the navy that I felt the time had come to raise the subject, which I did with Ohira on my return. To my relief, he showed no consternation but simply said, "Let me think about this." Apparently he felt that the time had come for Japan to start overcoming its so-called nuclear allergy, and that the entrance of nuclear-powered submarines might be a reasonable first step. In late January, he suddenly announced that the United States had asked for permission to bring nuclear-powered submarines into Japanese ports—though strictly speaking permission was not needed.

Ohira's announcement gave rise to a great debate in Japan that raged along political lines and produced a considerable number of demonstrations. On one occasion forty-five thousand people demonstrated in the naval base city of Yokosuka, which is within easy reach of the huge student populations of Tokyo and Yokohama. The value of port entries by the submarines was not at all worth the political commotion they caused, but the matter was out of our hands, and Ohira and Ikeda clearly felt that the political turmoil was justified in order to get the Japanese people accustomed to the concept of nuclear power. They approached the matter with great caution, carefully studying the dangers of radiation for many months and giving ample opportunity for all sides to express their views before the first nuclear-powered submarine eventually did enter port.

A much more significant but almost unknown incident occurred on April 4, 1963. It concerned a matter of such delicacy in Japanese-American relations that I cut out the references to it in my personal notes when I left the Embassy in 1966, with the result that I must rely entirely on my memory. The United States had agreed not to install, store, or introduce nuclear weapons in Japan without prior consultations with the Japanese government. How this applied to American naval vessels that had nuclear weapons as part of their normal armament was never spelled out. I had understood that in the negotiations leading up to the revised Security Treaty of 1960 there had been an oral agreement that nuclear weapons on board naval vessels which came and went did not constitute "introduction," because it would have been entirely impractical to remove such armaments before entering Japanese ports. Recently, some of the participants in these negotiations have revealed that the matter was considered too delicate even to discuss, but that the negotiators on both sides had taken for granted that nuclear weapons would be allowed to be retained on board. In any case, it was assumed on the American side that we were within our treaty rights if nuclear weapons were on board a ship as part of its regular armaments, but much of the Japanese public came to believe that this was banned by treaty.

Under these circumstances a few of us at the Embassy became disturbed when we noticed that in interpolations in the Diet Japanese government spokesmen were replying to queries about nuclear weapons being on board American ships entering Japanese ports with the answer that they "trusted the Americans." While it was standard American practice never to affirm or deny the presence of nuclear weapons and I personally never knew if any were aboard a vessel, to a Japanese who believed that the United States was bound by treaty not to bring such weapons on ships into Japanese ports, the government's reply implied that there definitely were no such weapons and, if there were, that this was a treaty infringement by the United States. Since this was an unhealthy situation, I invited Ohira to the Residence and cautiously raised the subject with him on the basis of a paper in Japanese prepared for me by Osborn. Ohira immediately understood the problem and asked me to leave matters to him and speak to no one else about it. I do not know what he did, but the undesirable exchanges in the Diet on this matter stopped almost at once; they never were repeated during my stay in Tokyo.

Unfortunately, all this must have been lost sight of by later Japanese leaders and overlooked by subsequent American ambassadors. Under Sato and some other prime ministers, the Japanese government began again to resort to the "We trust the Americans" reply to questions about nuclear armaments on ships, and the American Embassy failed to put a stop to this as we had in April 1963. This led to subsequent emotional eruptions over the problem, the last of which was to cause me great embarrassment almost two decades later.

# 35

# The Years Stretch Out

By 1963, Haru and I not only felt completely at home in our job but had established a pace we could maintain. Although military problems loomed largest in my mind, our time was largely occupied with our diplomatic routine, public relations contacts, and various other matters. Fifteen of the top officers who had greeted us at the Embassy in 1961 had departed by summer, and the two of us had become the most knowledgeable persons on diplomatic protocol at the Embassy.

Following up on my talk with President Kennedy in December 1962, I conferred with Ikeda about a presidential visit, and he agreed that conditions had changed sufficiently since 1960 to make this possible but suggested that perhaps Eisenhower should come first as a piece of "unfinished business." Eisenhower could do this at the invitation of the Columbia Alumni Association, since he had briefly been president of Columbia before becoming President of the United States. June 1963 for Eisenhower and October for Kennedy were the dates we tentatively aimed at. The Eisenhower visit was subsequently dropped, though we still hoped to have the President visit in October.

The perennial problem of the normalization of relations between Japan and Korea had become complicated by the repressive military dictatorship of Park Chung Hee. The Japanese regarded the Korean military as being easier to deal with than the civilian politicians, but were distressed when Park's chief colleague, Kim Chong P'il, with whom the Japanese had dealt most frequently, was thrown out in February 1963. Berger tried to put strong pressure on the Koreans to return to a democratic form of government; his heavy-handed approach won him the animosity of most Korean groups, as was reported to me by Korean leaders and personal friends. I myself felt that democracy could be built in Korea only slowly, perhaps starting with the growth of local democratic institutions. The situation seemed to me not unlike the early days of Japanese democratic development between 1880 and 1918, when local democratic institutions had been the first step. But I had no way to get these ideas considered except by suggesting them to Berger, who did not agree, and to various Korean leaders, who professed to agree but did nothing. Meanwhile, Japanese-Korean negotiations made virtually no progress, though one bright spot was that when a bad harvest induced Berger to suggest that I approach the Japanese for a gift of 5,000 to 10,000 tons of grain for Korea and I suggested the 10,000 figure to Ohira, the Japanese responded with 40,000 tons of rice, wheat, and barley to be given through the Japanese Red Cross.

Naturally I kept up my heavy speaking and publishing schedule. One of the unusual speeches I gave was at the celebration of the twenty-fifth anniversary of Diet membership of Nishio, the secretary general of the Democratic Socialist Party. The other speakers were the Prime Minister and the heads of the other parties, putting me in the rarefied atmosphere of high politics. Haru also started writing a weekly column for a series called "Stained Glass," which ran in Japan's leading paper, the *Asahi,* and was designed to help prepare people for the 1964 Olympics in Tokyo.

Haru and I made several prefectural visits. In Kyoto, we attended the 1,100 year anniversary of the death of Ennin, to whom I had devoted so many years of study. It was held at the great central monastery of the Tendai Sect, the Enryakuji on Mt. Hiei above Kyoto, of which Ennin had been the third abbot. I was struck by how much the ceremonies were like those which he described in his diary of his travels in China. The only clear departures were Haru's presentation of flowers and my donation of copies of my two books on Ennin and a lecture I delivered after the ceremony. A follow-up to this occasion was a luncheon party held in Tokyo in June to celebrate the publication of a Japanese translation of my *Ennin's Travels in T'ang China,* which was attended to my surprise by three hundred people, including many prominent old friends.

One unusual experience was occasioned by the visit to Tokyo of President Sukarno of Indonesia in May. A crisis had developed between Sukarno and the international oil companies, and Washington wished to arrange a meeting between him and special representatives of President Kennedy, including Abe Chayes, a Harvard Law School acquaintance then serving as Legal Advisor to the State Department. I arranged with Sukarno for the meeting, and all went well. Sukarno had as his third wife a beautiful former Japanese show girl who went by her Indonesian name of Dewi. Because of her interest in Haru and me, he too became interested in us and, when in Tokyo, would invite us to breakfast with the two of them. He always took over the whole second floor of one of the forward projecting wings of the old Imperial Hotel, which could be easily defended because it could only be approached by a single long corridor along which his bodyguards were stationed. He usually was very jovial at these breakfasts and would merrily insult his surrounding bevy of cabinet ministers, who had to grin in meek submission. I always felt on these occasions as if I had stepped back into the court of a seventeenth-century French monarch.

The "Reischauer Hotel" was busy most of the time. Our most engaging house guest was Colonel John Glenn, the first American to orbit the earth in space and now a senator from Ohio. He and his delightful family were with us the last two weeks of May, and four hundred and fifty people turned out for the reception we gave for him. When the Glenns were leaving, he did something I had always wanted to do but had never dared: He slid side saddle down the balustrade of the long, curving stairway from the second floor.

During these years, economic problems were rising rapidly in importance and complexity. Herbert Passin, a sociologist colleague from Columbia, wrote me that my good friend President Ohara of the Kurashiki Textile Company felt that he had been threatened by the American Consulate General at Kobe-Osaka because of his company's plan to export a vinyl plant to China on credit. I asked Ohara to call on me and assured him we would not dream of standing in the way of his proposed move. The line between discouraging actions that would help strengthen the threat posed by Communist countries and discouraging the natural Japanese desire for trade with the whole world was a thin one. The major point I always stressed with the Japanese government and public was that in extending credit they should, if possible, favor non-Communist over Communist countries. I also began to point out to the Japanese that, since they carried such a light military burden, they should make their contribution to world peace by assigning larger sums to economic aid to less developed countries. Where the advanced nations had set a goal of 1 percent of GNP for grant aid, I saw no reason why Japan should not aim at 2 percent. I said these things purely as my own opinion, without authorization from Washington, but various American leaders gradually began to say the same sort of thing, though to little avail. Even today, Japan and the United States remain near the bottom of the list of advanced nations in the proportion of their GNP devoted to nonmilitary grant aid.

A bigger economic issue in the first half of 1963 was Japanese outrage at American proposals in January to slap restraints on thirty-six items which accounted for 93 percent of Japanese cotton textile exports to the United States, on the grounds that they threatened to disrupt trade. Since Japan had been carefully observing voluntary restraints for some time, there was naturally a strong public outcry. The issue was largely political rather than economic, because cotton textiles no longer loomed large in our trade with Japan, and it was the weakness of the industry in both countries that brought pressure on the two governments from textile-producing areas. Our case was not a good one, and I felt that we should show more flexibility. Fortunately we eventually backed away from our original position, but the problem was expanded to include all trade issues by the visit to Tokyo in April of Christian A. Herter, the former Secretary of State and the President's special representative on trade matters, who stayed with us. He was starting in Tokyo the first of a series of bilateral negotiations he was conducting in preparation for the so-called Kennedy round of tariff reductions to be held in Geneva. His visit drew huge interest in the Japanese press, quite overshadowing the concurrent visit of Maurice Couve de Murville, the first French Foreign Minister ever to come to Japan.

Herter's visit induced me to urge Washington to drop the obviously specious argument that Japan's "voluntary controls" of textile exports were in fact voluntary and to emphasize instead that such controls should be regarded as a normal element of "orderly marketing." I also argued to Washington and the Japanese authorities that more emphasis should be placed on American exports to Japan of agricultural products and certain industrial goods such as airplanes, and on the liberalization of Japanese travel abroad, in which the potential for dollar earnings was much greater than in textile controls. When I mentioned to Ohira how helpful it would be to the United States if Japan obtained more of its wheat imports from us, he asked me not to talk about the matter to anyone, but I noticed that American wheat exports to Japan increased by $500 million the following year.

◄§

By the summer of 1963, Haru and I had been on the job in Tokyo for well over two years and were due a home leave, for which we were more than ready. We flew back to the United States on July 20, accompanied by Joan who was coming home for good, and we did not return to Tokyo until the end of August.

While in Belmont, we concluded the sale of our house and I did most of the work on the revision and updating of what became the 1964 edition of *Japan Past and Present.* I made three visits to Washington, meeting with the President each time to discuss plans for his visit to Japan. We settled on the tentative dates of December 6–8, forgetting that this would inappropriately include Pearl Harbor Day. After returning to Japan, I discovered that Ikeda was thinking about a general election in the late autumn, which would make these dates inconvenient in any case, and Ikeda and I ultimately settled on February 1964 as the time to aim at.

Other official business in Washington included plans for American military redeployment in Japan to save expenses. With Dillon's aid, I persuaded Deputy Secretary Gilpatric of the Department of Defense to promise Ohira that we would keep the Japanese informed in advance of any changes we intended to make. I also got the air force to shift its plans on the use of bases in Japan. To my horror I had discovered on my return to Washington that it was planning to put our Misawa base on standby basis, while keeping Itazuke next door to Fukuoka in full use, even though Itazuke was a terrible political liability and Misawa, located in an economically depressed area, a definite asset. When I protested, I was told it was too late to do anything about it because the President had already approved the plan, but eventually I got the decision reversed. A few years later Itazuke was reactivated because of the pressures of the Vietnam War, but with disastrous results. An American plane crashed into a building at Kyushu University, and the base had to be closed again because of the resulting public uproar.

While in Washington, I testified before a Senate committee chaired by Senator Henry M. Jackson and in response to some questions quite unconnected with the rest of the hearings spoke my mind frankly about American relations with the Soviet Union and China. I had thought the session was off the record, but it was fully reported, surprising people both in the United States and Japan by my daring and causing quite a stir in Japan. The reactions in Japan, however, were favorable, and I received no criticism in the United States, so apparently no harm was done.

After returning to Japan, I found the general mood to be somewhat downbeat, since there was apprehension about the American "interest equalization tax" proposed for imports and dissatisfaction with the cotton textile agreement which had been arrived at. I also learned to my distress that the Embassy during my absence had prepared a strong stand against Ohara's export of the vinyl plant to China. I stopped this, feeling that it was not at all certain that trying to prevent the development of Chinese-Japanese trade was in American, let alone Japanese, interests.

The biggest problem absorbing my time was American military redeployment, which was mostly the shifting around of planes but had a bearing on Japanese budget plans. I met often with Ohira at secret breakfasts at the Residence, at which I gave him our plans for changes to be made during 1964 and

1965. The Pentagon insisted that we should start on these changes on January 1, and I insisted that before this we should inform the Japanese government fully and announce our plans publicly. With a great deal of scurrying around, we just made my deadline, issuing with the Japanese the necessary announcements on December 31.

The social side of our life naturally continued to loom large. We started holding monthly open house receptions for any Americans in town who wished to see their country's Embassy, and some two hundred fifty people turned up at the first one. Among our guests that autumn were Raymond Burr, alias Perry Mason, who generously provided us with a loan of artworks from his own collection when the Museum of Modern Art's loan was recalled in 1964.

In a luncheon speech in Japanese before six hundred thirty members of the influential Naigai Josei Chosakai—a sort of Japanese counterpart of the Council on Foreign Relations—I pointed out the dangers in the racial overtones of the Sino-Soviet split and also the dilemma for the United States posed by countries like South Vietnam and Korea, for whose existence we were partially responsible and for whose autocratic regimes we therefore shared blame. In a lengthy discussion with President Horii of the Private Railway Workers Union, I was surprised to hear him speak disparingly of Marxism and display a very moderate political stance, despite the strongly leftist orientation of the Sohyo Federation to which his own union belonged.

Fukuda Hironari, a prominent commentator who had shifted from the left to the right, published a six-month series of articles in the leading monthly magazine, *Bungei Shunju*, starting with one entitled "On the Reischauer Offensive" *(Raishawa kosei to yu mono)*. In it he argued that the pragmatism underlying my various articles on modernization was unanswerable by Japan's leftist intellectuals and that was why they remained quiet. His article was so provocative that I feared he would stir up trouble for me. This was confirmed by the prominent economist Nakayama Ichiro, who, with reference to Fukuda's article, told me that few things had shaken up Japanese intellectuals in recent times as much as my "modernization" theories, and he mentioned a recent conference of Chinese, North Korean, and Japanese scholars in Peking which denounced the "Reischauer line." *Izvestia* also published quite an attack on me. Three of the universities which had invited me to talk that autumn, including my father's own Tokyo Women's University, subsequently withdrew their invitations because of threatened trouble by leftist students. This suggested that the extreme left, feeling its growing isolation, was beginning to rally to fight the "Reischauer line," which subsequently proved to be the case.

<br>

❧

The autumn of 1963 turned out to be the halfway point in our ambassadorial life. I happen to have among my notes a memorandum, dictated on January 12, 1964, surveying the year 1963. It gives a good summary of our thoughts and feelings at that time and may be worth quoting in part:

> Relations with the United States have certainly improved . . . this year. The term partnership that I launched when I first came here is now fully accepted. . . . More important, we have gotten the U.S. fairly well out of domestic Japanese politics. The Taiwan and Korean hassles have been increasingly thought of as purely Japanese problems, not involving U.S. influence; even trade relations with the Chicoms [Chinese Communists] are not thought of as being "despite U.S. pressures" but rather "despite the delicacy of relations with Taiwan." . . .
>
> I cannot help feel that we are still doing a worthwhile job here. . . . We are ready to go on so long as Washington wants us here. . . .
>
> Our attitude toward our job has gone through interesting changes over the past 2¾ years. At first it seemed like a great and amazing stage play in which we played our parts with apparent success under the able guidance of Bill and Pidge Leonhart. The great response of the Japanese public to us carried us along effortlessly as if on the crest of a wave. The centralized organization of the embassy and the Napoleonic tradition of the Ambassador's position meant that with a minimum of effort the tone of the whole embassy operations changed to accord with my views. . . . In fact we found we had to be cautious in expressing preferences, because a casual comment might be taken as a firm order.
>
> The euphoria of the first few months gave place to a more serious buckling down to the job by the autumn of 1961, but . . . much of the feeling of being actors in a play survived at least that long. With the change to the Emmersons we found that we had to get down to running more of the details of the embassy. . . .
>
> Haru and I also found ourselves increasingly the "old hands," knowing more about how the embassy should run and what would or would not be proper from a protocol point of view than any of our advisors. . . .
>
> As a result of all this we have completely lost the play-acting feeling and the self-consciousness that goes with it. We are used to being what we are here, and the various things we do and the attitudes people take toward us just seem part of our routine life.

The autumn of 1963 to which this summary applied was perhaps the high water mark of our stay at the Embassy. Within the next few months two events occurred which substantially changed the situation for us, and then the Vietnam War began to cast a dark shadow over all Japanese-American relations.

## 36

# From Kennedy to Johnson

H<small>ARU AND</small> I were prepared for a busy day on November 23, 1963, but it turned out far differently from what we had expected. We were to participate in a television program at 8:00 a.m. about the first broadcast that morning of the trans-Pacific telestar and then go to the airport at noon to meet the American delegation to the third cabinet-level Economic Conference. At 4:30 a.m. I was awakened by a phone call from Fahs conveying "bad news." I immediately envisaged that the plane carrying the delegation had crashed on takeoff in Hawaii. Instead, it was news of the President's assassination in Dallas only an hour earlier, where it was still November 22. The delegation's plane was then an hour and a half out of Hawaii; Rusk had ordered it swung around and headed for Washington.

We were soon deluged by phone calls and people. A Japanese newsman had managed to get into the Residence by five. Ambassador Takeuchi, back from Washington for the conference, turned up before seven and Ohira before eight. By six I had assembled the chief Embassy officers for some hasty decisions and then made a broadcast to the Japanese people in English and Japanese, stressing that "our policies are durable policies," and that under President Lyndon B. Johnson we would continue to move ahead toward world peace. It was rebroadcast several times, and about twelve hours later we received instructions from Washington to pursue exactly this line. I was afraid that the Japanese people so identified all that was best in American policy with Kennedy and had so little knowledge of Johnson that the President's death might produce a cooling of their goodwill toward the United States. I therefore continued to emphasize the continuity of our policies in all my speeches and writings, of which there were a great many in connection with Kennedy's death and also the beginning of the new year.

The Japanese response to the assassination was overwhelming. We were inundated by letters of condolence and presents for the Kennedy family, including strings of folded paper cranes, usually arranged in units of 1,000 (semba-zuru), and used, as I have said, as a vague talisman for good health, peace, or other good wishes. I was struck by the warmth of the letters I received from the ambassadors of some of the Communist satellite countries. A low requiem mass held on

November 26, the day after the funeral ceremonies in Washington, was attended by five hundred but with a throng of three thousand standing outside. The final memorial service was held on December 17 in Hibiya Hall in downtown Tokyo, packed with 2,300 people, at which former Prime Minister Yoshida, representatives of the three leading political parties, various other prominent Japanese, and I all spoke. But the most moving ceremony for me was a memorial speech I gave in the same hall in Waseda University in which Bobby Kennedy had spoken. Again it was packed with more than two thousand students. But this time there was no heckling, and at the end the audience, which in Japan normally gives only perfunctory applause to speeches, gave an eight-minute ovation to the memory of John F. Kennedy.

I was instructed by Washington to discourage any high-level attendance at the funeral in Washington, but I knew how deeply Japanese feel about such things and therefore agreed with Ohira after much negotiating that he would go. Then de Gaulle refused to honor the American request and decided to attend himself. Ohira called me at five in the morning of November 24, and I happily agreed that both he and Ikeda should go. I telegraphed Washington, urging that Ikeda be given every attention possible and be treated on a level with our chief Western allies in order to emphasize that our increased closeness to Japan would not change. Johnson and Rusk, whether responding to my message or not, did exactly this. Johnson held a special session with Ikeda, as he did with de Gaulle and Prime Minister Pearson of Canada, and Rusk, somewhat to my dismay, promised the early rescheduling of the Economic Conference. Ikeda was much moved by Kennedy's death as well as the treatment he himself received in Washington. He spoke most warmly with me about these matters on his return. In a television broadcast he displayed a degree of emotion over Kennedy's death rarely seen in Japan in public and even urged all people to carry on in the "Kennedy spirit."

◆§

When a new President comes to office, it is customary for every ambassador to submit his resignation, but Johnson, who was hoping for as much continuity as possible, sent express orders not to do this. Haru and I were personally devastated by Kennedy's death, and like the Japanese public found little appeal in Johnson's cruder and less cosmopolitan ways. Haru began arguing that now that Kennedy, who had appointed me, was gone, we had no further obligation to stay in Tokyo; I countered with the argument that without Kennedy we were all the more needed in Japan. But our pleasure in our job, which was already wearing thin, was now further eroded.

Bobby Kennedy's second visit to Japan in mid-January 1964 somewhat overshadowed the rescheduled third cabinet-level Economic Conference, held on January 27–28. Only four of the principal American members of the Committee were able to attend, and the meetings were held this time in Tokyo, where the extremely efficient Japanese bureaucracy and police and our Embassy staff could handle everything with ease. As I recorded at the time, discussions were easier, franker, and fuller than ever before; in contrast to the first meeting only a little over two years earlier, when we had "strained cautiously for complete frankness, this time it came as a matter of course. Then we had been forced to stress to [the] public that we were only talking about economic affairs—not nasty political or military matters. This time [the] public was chiefly interested in political talks . . . and would have been much disappointed if they had not taken place."

Our other official activities continued much as usual. I remained in close touch with Ohira and various other Japanese leaders, but my contacts with Ikeda were largely through phone calls from him. He found this the best way to confer with me, because face-to-face meetings would stir up embarrassing press speculation. The Republic of China on Taiwan had been rankling over the Japanese sale of the vinyl plant to Peking, and its irritation was heightened by the case of a Communist Chinese deserter in November. The man slipped away from a Chinese mission, and, failing to find the Taiwanese Embassy, ended up by climbing the wall into the Soviet Embassy. The Soviets in consternation handed him over to the Japanese authorities, who allowed him to be interviewed by representatives of both Peking and Taiwan. In the end he decided to go back to the mainland, and the Government of China on Taiwan then burst forth in angry denunciations of Japan. Our Embassy in Taipei wanted us to bring pressure on the Japanese government; Washington, however, backed me up in my feeling that we should stay out of this dispute and do no more than urge the Japanese to take their time in arriving at a decision and to make other conciliatory gestures to patch up the ill feeling with Taiwan.

The Japanese-Taiwanese crisis was muted somewhat by France's sudden decision to recognize Peking. Washington asked for my views as to how we should handle this development with the Japanese, and I advised keeping them informed of all we knew and promising not to take any steps ourselves regarding China without informing them first, since they were terrified that we might suddenly make a deal with Peking and leave them out on a limb. (Actually this is precisely what President Nixon and Kissinger did do in 1971, with very adverse results for our relations with Japan.) The Japanese government accepted the French action with great irritation but outer calm. The attitude of the Japanese government in this incident made the government in Taiwan less hostile to Japan, and a détente was sealed by a visit by Yoshida to Taipei in late February.

The Japanese government also showed an encouraging interest in playing a useful role in the settlement of the conflict between Indonesia and Malaysia and actually had to be discouraged from trying to join in Bobby Kennedy's talks with the Malaysian leaders following his visit to Tokyo. This marked a great shift from the negative isolationism Japan had previously displayed. On the other hand, Japanese relations with Korea deteriorated again. Ambassador Pae and other Korean officials called several times to confer with me, but I began to realize that we could not expect a normalization of Japanese-Korean relations before 1965 (which is when it actually did occur). Caraway continued to drag his feet over cooperation in Okinawa, but the Japanese government proved understanding and tolerant. It even suppressed at my suggestion a proposal in the Diet to include empty seats for Okinawa in an election law revision.

Our usual social events picked up once again. We made three brief trips to nearby prefectures, one of them to Tochigi, which included visits to two places that claimed to be the birthplace of Ennin. The presence of the Belgian king and queen in Tokyo required two white-tie affairs, one at court and one at the Belgian Embassy, which I described at the time with some irritation as "the really silly side of diplomatic life." Though the winter months were in general a quiet period, Haru figured that we had fifteen hundred guests in the Residence in the month of February alone, and a stretch of ten weeks went by in which we were so busy even on weekends that we could not make a single visit to Misaki.

Despite Johnson's request that all ambassadors stay on, he fired the ambassadors to Malaysia and the Philippines in January. This on top of the forced resignation a few months earlier of the ambassadors to Vietnam, Burma, and Thailand—the last two old friends of mine—so impressed me with the precarious position of ambassadors that I dreamed three nights running of being fired myself. Before long the Joneses and Bergers were to depart Indonesia and Korea, leaving me the only Ambassador in that part of the world who dated back to 1961. In fact, when I finally resigned in 1966, I believe I was the longest lived of all American ambassadors then in the field. The tenure of assistant secretaries for the Far East was even more uncertain. In early March, William Bundy, the older brother of Mac Bundy, became the fifth Assistant Secretary for the Far East while I was in Tokyo. Bill Bundy, whom I characterized at the time as being "less like a computer" than Mac, stayed on for the rest of the Johnson administration, becoming one of the chief whipping boys for American popular discontent over Vietnam policies.

## 37

# The Hazards of Life in the Limelight

DURING checkups at the American Navy Hospital at Yokosuka, my physician, Navy Captain Ralph E. Faucett, frequently admonished me that I would have to go at a slower pace if I did not wish to shorten my normal life span. I would reply that I was more interested in doing all I could in my present job than in extending my old age. Now that I have reached old age, I still feel the same way, but the reason why my life may be shortened is not overwork in Tokyo but because of an entirely unpredictable incident that happened on March 24, 1964.

Exactly at noon that day I started to leave the Chancery for a luncheon engagement with Kim Chong P'il, the ousted Korean military leader. Normally the Marine guard would jump up from his desk and salute me at the door of the Chancery, but he happened to be on the phone. As I was passing through the doorway, I bumped into a small, slightly built Japanese in a seedy-looking raincoat who seemed decidedly out of place in the Embassy. I turned to the people in the lobby and said something like "Where is this man going?" He looked up at me, his face lit up, and he lunged at me with a long kitchen knife. Because we were so close and he so small, he did not have time to raise the knife—if he had this book would never have been written—but plunged it straight into my right thigh, where the tip broke off against my thigh bone. Luckily the bone protected my main nerve, saving me from being a cripple for the rest of my life. I shouted "Grab that man!" and a young Embassy officer, John Ferchak, seized him and pinned him to the floor.

Looking down, I saw a small pool of blood around my feet rapidly growing into a lake on the marble floor. Remembering that it had been loss of blood from a leg wound that had killed my brother Bob in Shanghai twenty-seven years earlier, I called for a tourniquet, but the flimsy scarf provided by a woman in the lobby had no effect. I lay down on a bench for a moment, then Ferchak, the Marine, a Sergeant Macek, and my Economic Minister, Arthur Gardiner, carried me to my car, which was already waiting at the door of the Chancery. It was a gory scene, with the three men and the inside of the car soaked in blood. Luckily the Toranomon Hospital, one of Tokyo's best, was only a couple of blocks away, and the nervous, jumpy driver rushed me there though I kept urging him to take it easy.

At the hospital I was whisked into an emergency room for a brief examination, then taken up to the operating room, seeing Haru on the way in the crammed hospital lobby and giving her an O.K. sign with my fingers. I apparently was in the operating room for about four hours, not regaining consciousness until after 4:00 p.m. in my hospital room. The surgeon had repaired nerves and arteries and searched for the tip of the knife, which was never found. Later I discovered that they had made a curving cut in my thigh, twenty inches long, which stretched most of the way from my waist to my knee.

This was before the recent spate of attacks on diplomats and embassies throughout the world made such incidents seem commonplace. The news of the assassination attempt swept the nation, creating a sensation, and was repeated around the world. The last time a foreign dignitary had been injured in Japan had been in May 1891, when a policeman had attempted to cut down with his sword the ill-fated Russian Czarevich, who as Czar Nicholas II was to meet his end in 1917 at the hands of a Bolshevik firing squad.

Flowers, messages, and presents started pouring in, and a longer bed was brought for me from Yokosuka. The Emperor and Empress sent a box of fine fruit, and the Crown Prince and Princess and their young son, Prince Hiro, sent flowers which the little boy had picked himself. Ohira turned up at the hospital within the hour. Pae, the Korean Ambassador, and many prominent Japanese soon followed. Ikeda was delayed by a session of the Diet, but by the time he arrived, the lower floor of the hospital was so crowded he could not get in and had to be received by Emmerson at the Residence. Among the presents were many strings of a thousand folded paper cranes. One ingenious lady made hers from red, white, and blue paper and mounted them on a number of strings attached to a board in such a way that, when viewed from the right angle, they formed an American flag.

Three American Navy doctors flew up at once from Yokosuka by helicopter, and a fourth Japanese-speaking American doctor was brought in to help translate. But the Japanese doctors, who were excellent, remained in charge under the supervision of the distinguished head of the hospital, Dr. Okinaka Shigeo, and the nurses were wonderful. As I dictated in a letter home, "To have one's ailment somehow an international affair puts a strangely heavy burden on one." I did, however, find it amusing to learn from the newspapers what my temperature was and that I had consumed 100 cc. of soup.

Haru had been up at the Residence receiving busloads of high school students and Girl Scouts from American military schools for dependents, who were on spring vacation trips up to the big city to see the sights, when she heard of the stabbing. She immediately rushed down to the hospital, where she was to spend almost all her waking moments for the next three weeks. We were lucky that the hospital had an open room for me and equally fortunate that across the hall from it was an empty store room, which Haru made her command post. It was fixed up with phones, typewriters, coffee, snacks, and a cot in the corner, where George Packard spent the first several nights. At seven-thirty each morning Haru would come down from the Residence with our housekeeper, Yamagata-san, and at eight three Japanese members of the Embassy staff—one to man a reception desk in the lobby—would arrive, together with an American officer and secretary. In this way, order was brought into the process of receiving callers, expressing thanks for flowers and gifts, and a myriad of other chores. Haru usually stayed until ten-thirty at night, then returned to the Residence exhausted for some sleep. The hospital swarmed with uniformed and plainclothes policemen especially detailed to protect me, because an incident like this is likely to draw the attention of unbalanced persons. Actually, some seven or eight men were apprehended trying to reach my room.

I meanwhile was kept in virtually complete isolation. Almost no outsiders were allowed to see me, except for Ohira on the second day and Ikeda on the third. Among my later visitors was Richard Nixon, who occasionally turned up in Tokyo in those years, ostensibly as a Pepsi-Cola representative, but more for the purpose of keeping alive his image and competence as a world statesman. I had always looked on Nixon with abhorrence, but in the flesh he was much larger, better looking, and more pleasantly spoken than one would gather from television. In calls he later made on me at my office, he would speak forcefully of the desirability of recognizing Peking, sounding for all the world like John Fairbank. I had felt that the American public had been ready for this for some years, and when as President he finally did do it, I was in no way surprised.

Among the many letters I received, the one which impressed me most was a warm handwritten note from Sukarno. I do not recall similar personal notes from Johnson or even Rusk, nor did I receive a Purple Heart which I felt I deserved for my close brush with death in the service of my country.

◆§

Copious transfusions of blood and plasma got me through the first few dangerous hours, and then I did quite well for a few days. When I was first stabbed, I did not feel the slightest twinge of pain, either because of the shock or because my nerves were severed; but once ensconced in my hospital bed, I became very uncomfortable. The injured leg was entirely immobile, and my two arms, loaded down with tubes for blood, plasma, and intravenous feeding, were not much better, leaving only one foot on which I could wiggle my toes. I slept hardly at all the first several nights and would have had a hard time of it if the resident, a sweet young man called Dr. Takayanagi, had not sat by my bed and talked with me for hours each night.

On March 28 my condition suddenly worsened because of serious internal bleeding. A major operation seemed necessary, which I felt quite sure I could not survive in my weakened condition, but fortunately the problem turned out to be a self-mending ulcer, and the damage was restored through massive new transfusions of blood. I was forced to cut down on my earlier efforts to keep in touch with the Embassy's activities and forego checking on important telegrams.

My chief worry while in the hospital was that some harm would be done to Japanese-American relations. The Japanese government and people were mortified by the whole incident, though the culprit had had no political motivation whatsoever. He was a mentally unbalanced youth, who had clambered over the Embassy wall at a low spot and stumbled on me by chance. Not being mentally responsible for his act, he was confined for only a relatively short period, being released even before I retired as Ambassador. His problem was that he suffered from serious myopia, which he felt had not been properly treated by the American Occupation or the Japanese government, and he wished to draw attention to his cause by some spectacular act. That he had selected me for the object of his assassination attempt, rather than the Prime Minister or some other prominent Japanese, I have always regarded as a sort of backhanded compliment.

My very first evening in the hospital, I issued a reassuring statement to the Japanese public, stressing that the incident in no way affected my attitude or that of other Americans toward Japan, and Johnson and Rusk issued appropriate statements along the same line. Fortunately, there was never the slightest anti-Japanese reaction in the United States over the matter. The Japanese government picked up all my medical expenses in Japan and insisted on having Hayakawa Takashi, the chairman of the National Public Safety Commission, assume responsibility for the incident and resign. I protested against this but was told that since Hayakawa was a relatively young man, his resignation would do his career no harm. Ikeda was pleased to be able to transmit Japan's apologies directly to the American public by telestar. After my second round of transfusions, I issued another statement to the effect that I felt all the closer to Japan because I now was of "mixed blood," which pleased the Japanese public. My fear that the whole incident might cause an irrational backlash in Japan, making the Japanese feel I was somehow a troublemaker, proved unfounded. Jamie Fahs wrote in a letter to my father and the children, "Every paper here says that Ed is the best and most beloved American Ambassador that Japan has ever had . . . and this happening will only serve, in the end, to cement the esteem in which he is held."

A more realistic fear was the reduction of our personal freedom. Clearly, I would no longer be allowed my early Sunday morning walks alone around the palace precincts or any wandering unattended on the streets of Tokyo. Henceforth I was accompanied everywhere in Tokyo by a personal bodyguard; since I did not want to break up his one day of rest for my Sunday palace walks, I gave them up. I was afraid at first that our Misaki trips too would have to be dropped, but fortunately we were still allowed them, though security was increased both at Misaki and everywhere else I went. It was irritating always to have a bodyguard at my elbow and often a whole phalanx of guards when I went outside the Embassy grounds, but I must admit that for several months I felt an involuntary wariness of any individual in an old raincoat who approached me and would keep a weather eye out until he was safely beyond striking range.

◄§

After three weeks in the Toranomon Hospital, the doctors judged it safe to move me but insisted I go for recuperation directly to some place far away from my work. The upshot was that on April 15 Haru and I flew to Hawaii on Mo Preston's plane to stay for a while at Jake Smart's roomy, comfortable home at Hickam Field in Hawaii, while Jake was away on a protracted tour of inspection in the South Pacific. Our departure from the hospital was as complex as a Broadway opening. About a hundred policemen crowded the hospital lobby; I shook hands all around with those to whom I owed my life; I rose from my wheelchair to read statements of appreciation in English and Japanese to the assembled newsmen; then behind screaming patrol cars Haru and I whizzed out to Tachikawa Air Base, making the trip in about half the normal time because the police had blocked off every side street as we streaked along. Dr. Faucett and George Packard accompanied us on the overnight trip to Hawaii.

The first few days in Hawaii went smoothly, except that the lower half of my right leg was partially paralyzed, and inadequate blood circulation made it very painful. Still I could hobble around with a cane, and I started rehabilitation exercises at Tripler Army Hospital, a pink-colored mass on the slope above Hickam Field. On April 21, however, I began to run a fever and two days later was placed in Tripler, where I remained for most of the next two months. I was given the fine VIP suite on the top floor, where I was the only resident, and when I began to recuperate I would gaze out by the hour from the top floor balcony at the planes landing and taking off at Hickam Field and the Honolulu International Airport beside it. Ever since I have thought of Tripler as being "my hospital" and have never landed at Honolulu without looking at it from afar and thinking about my days there.

The doctors were baffled by my ailment. The incubation period was too short for hepatitis, which I was likely to contract from the contaminated blood used at that time for transfusions in Japan. I had been warned about this and shot full

With the Crown Prince at President Kennedy's memorial service,
December 17, 1963.

EOR at the premiere on December 2, 1964, of the film commemorating President John F. Kennedy's presidency and death entitled 'Year of Lightening, Day of Drums.'

Recovering at Toranomon Hospital with Haru, holding some of the strings of a thousand folded paper cranes that poured in as a symbol of good wishes, April 1964.

Introducing the new commander of CINCPAC, Admiral Sharp, to Prime Minister Sato, 1965.

Calling with Burton and Jamie Fahs on a venerable Buddhist abbot. Knees no longer bend as easily as in youth.

In Japan's "snow country," 1965.
*(Yamagata Shimbun)*

During a visit to India in 1966, dressed
to visit the Golden Temple at Amritsar.

University students demonstrating outside the Embassy against America's Vietnam policy in the spring of 1966. *(Leonard Nadel)*

At Misaki.

With front line troops in Vietnam, 1966.

Closeted with President Johnson, July 1966. It was time to return to America.

With Yoshida before the farewell luncheon of the Japan-America Society,
August 1966.

of gamma globulin to lessen the severity of the disease. An uproar in Japan over the contaminated blood given me stimulated a reform effort, which eventually fizzled out, but when I was again kept alive by Japanese blood in 1983, I noticed that the problem had been cleared up and the blood was safe. The exact nature of my ailment was never fully ascertained, though there was a marked deterioration of the liver. Each morning the specialists would gather at my bedside looking dejected because their latest efforts to determine the cause of my problems had failed and they were running out of hypotheses. One of their theories that proved wrong was that I was suffering from cancer of the bone marrow. The experiments for it proved particularly harrowing, but I remember feeling guilty and almost sorry that I had disappointed the doctors once more.

I believe I was near death's door a good bit of this time. My chief comfort was Haru. She visited me daily with food she had prepared, which was more appealing than the hospital fare, and she read to me by the hour when I felt up to it. Gradually I began to improve and in late May was released for a couple of weeks, staying with Haru in Jake's house. My blood tests and general condition, however, began to worsen a second time, and I was put back in Tripler on June 4. This time I believe it was the expected case of hepatitis arriving on schedule. It further damaged my liver but seemed trivial compared to what I had already been through. In fact, during the latter part of my recuperation, I undertook what was to become the 1965 revision of *The United States and Japan* and did some work on *Japan: The Modern Transformation* with John Fairbank, who was passing through Honolulu with Wilma.

I was again released from the hospital on June 23, and Haru and I spent a final week at one of the Waikiki hotels. On July 1 I made a farewell call on Admiral Felt, just a couple of hours before he gave up the biggest military command in the world and reverted to being an ordinary citizen, driving his own little car away from the ceremonies marking the transfer of command. We had become quite fond of the Felts for all his imperious ways and felt very sorry for him in his traumatic change of status.

Arriving back at Tachikawa in the early morning of July 3, we were whisked to the Embassy, which we found in fine shape under Emmerson's experienced and conscientious care. But I could resume my duties only gradually. Dr. Faucett insisted that I limit myself to half a day of work at first. My digestion improved only slowly and, in fact, never returned to normal. My right leg, though no longer painful, was mostly numb, and at first I needed a spring placed in my shoe to keep my foot from dragging. But we didn't consider resigning. To have done so would have made the Japanese public feel all the more remorseful, so we decided we would have to stay on for at least another year.

## 38
# Back in the Saddle

Fortunately the summer of 1964 was a time of relative calm for us. At first we stayed away from all afternoon receptions and evening affairs and only slowly slipped back into our regular work schedule and social activities. I was sorry to see Ikeda drop Ohira as Foreign Minister when he reformed his cabinet early in July and was never able to establish as close a relationship with Ohira's successor, Shiina Etsusaburo, who lacked his influence and charisma and was at first quite unsure of himself. In our early meetings he would read everything he said to me from little slips of paper.

In compensation for Ohira's loss, Caraway retired at last on August 1, and his successor, Lieutenant General Albert Watson, II, was a tremendous improvement. Watson had been carefully selected, having served in the ticklish political post of American Commandant in Berlin. The Watsons broke all precedent by proceeding to Okinawa by way of Tokyo, where they stayed with us and I took him for calls on Ikeda and other Japanese leaders. The Japanese were delighted with this recognition of their interest in Okinawa, and Watson proved a most pleasant, sensible, and efficient High Commissioner, fully committed to Kennedy's policy statement of March 1962. At the meeting of the Consultative Committee on the Ryukyu Islands on September 16, the Japanese asked to raise their aid commitment to Okinawa to over $7 million, and for the first time we were able to accept their figure at once with no objections from the High Commissioner.

One of the earliest problems I faced on returning to Tokyo was the Japanese desire for the right to fly their commercial planes to New York and beyond to Europe in order to circle the globe. I backed them in their request, and eventually the right was given, but they gave up the trans-Atlantic option after only a brief trial, though the route by Alaska to New York proved a great success. A more serious problem was the announcement by the Japanese government that it would permit the entry into Japanese ports of nuclear-powered submarines. This caused large demonstrations, which became worse when the Japanese public learned that American subroc (submarine rocket) missiles were equipped only with nuclear warheads. This item of news had been revealed in Washington nine months earlier and had no connection with the entry of nuclear-powered submarines into

Japan, but nonetheless stirred up strong repercussions. The tearing down of a Japanese flag by American soldiers in Okinawa and the crashing of two American military planes within forty minutes of each other with the resulting death of five Japanese civilians but only one American airman further aroused feelings.

As I wrote in a letter at the time, "Haru sometimes feels that the burden of such incidents . . . the protests over nuclear subs, complaints over U.S. policies in Southeast Asia . . . dissatisfaction over our economic policies such as the interest equalization tax, North Pacific fisheries and the like as well as unending personal attacks on me and my 'ridiculous' historical theories by leftist intellectuals and the Communist press is more than she can take." I pointed out to her that it was our job to absorb some of the shock of criticism so that Japanese-American relations could continue to develop smoothly.

The regular Security Consultative Committee meeting was held on August 1, with Admiral U. S. Grant Sharp, Felt's successor as CINCPAC, present as my chief aide. This meeting was followed by a huge assemblage of the International Monetary Fund. Douglas Dillon, with his wife and daughter, came out at the head of a large American delegation; in addition, 155 top American bankers were on hand, 85 with their wives. One pro-Goldwater banker was heard inquiring anxiously if Haru and I would be willing to stay on if Goldwater were elected President in the autumn. I was flattered by this and also by the Japanese Finance Minister meeting with me in secret to ask if he could safely make certain points with Dillon, whom he was seeing the next day, and how best he could present these matters, finally requesting me to explain his points in advance to Dillon.

Arthur Goldberg and his wife came out late in September, staying with us at the Residence, and I accompanied him on a round of discussions with labor leaders. It was in a way a repeat performance of his visit almost three years earlier, except that then he had been the Secretary of Labor and now he was a Supreme Court Justice. As I wrote to my family, the change in spirit between the two times was "astounding." In 1961 he had held "the first tentative talk between Americans and the real left and there was a great deal of hostility; this time we met as old friends with a large area of recognized common interests." I noted a comparable change in meetings Bill Bundy had with leaders of the three major parties when he came out the following week. Contrasting these discussions with those Harriman had held three years earlier, when bilateral problems had taken at least three fourths of the time, I found that the Japanese now wanted to talk almost exclusively about our mutual problems in other parts of the world, such as Korea and Vietnam.

We gave a "thank you" buffet supper for thirty-five doctors and nurses of the Toranomon Hospital and twenty-five members of the Embassy staff, which was a most pleasant occasion. At an awards ceremony, I had the pleasure of giving a special plaque to John Ferchak, who on March 24 had disarmed my assailant.

Because of our long absence, there were one hundred sixty persons at the new-comers reception we held in July. We held a reception for sixty artists and art critics to unveil the loan of paintings Raymond Burr had provided the Embassy. A farewell reception for the Economic Minister, Gardiner, and his wife drew five hundred people. Haru noted that, while in previous years we had averaged about one thousand guests a month at the Residence, we had had that number that one week. A luncheon talk I gave to a record crowd of three hundred at the Foreign Press Club, though a success in numbers, was an embarrassment in results, because the reporters twisted my remarks to convey almost the opposite of what I was saying, presumably to make them more newsworthy. We had two Russian defectors—jazz musicians from a visiting Bolshoi Variety Show—whose cases we handled smoothly and correctly with the full cooperation of the Japanese government. Our many guests and callers ran from Arthur Godfrey, the old-time radio and television star, and Paul Nitze, the Secretary of the Navy, to "Miss U.S.A." and "Miss Universe," a beautiful Greek girl.

We were not able to get down to Misaki for a weekend until October 2. We needed the break badly because we felt all the more cooped up in the Embassy in Tokyo, with several new police boxes built at strategic points around its walls, a Marine guard accompanying me up and down the hillside between the Residence and the Chancery, and a personal bodyguard always at my shoulder whenever I left the Embassy. The added security, however, was obviously necessary. Dubious characters had always hung around the Embassy gates, and after my stabbing several apparent would-be assassins were picked up. Such is the power of suggestion to the unbalanced mind. Even at Misaki we were greeted by a police delegation of eight men, a policeman dropped by our little house every hour or so, and police details kept watch from shore when I rowed my boat around. We had indeed lost much of what little privacy we had once enjoyed.

✥

Life in the limelight, however, has its privileges as well as its drawbacks. The early autumn of 1964 was enlivened by the Tokyo Olympics, held on October 10–24, and our ambassadorial position gave us a chance to see them with ease. They were magnificently staged by the Japanese, whose national pride was at stake, and everyone agreed they were the most glorious and best run Olympics ever held. Frantic preparations had been going on for years, with the completion of new subway lines and the building of a whole new system of elevated highways. The Japanese had worked on a twenty-four-hour schedule, and two or three times the construction activities produced huge traffic tie-ups, freezing the movement of all cars over several square miles in Tokyo for hours at a time. The police had to pick these traffic snarls apart car by car, working carefully in from the edges.

But all the work was miraculously completed a day or two before the Games started, and the traffic chaos we had been living through suddenly disappeared.

I had become involved in the Olympic planning early in my stay in Tokyo. The Japanese had agreed with the American military to use part of an American residential area called Camp Drake in the northwestern suburbs of the city for the Olympic Village, and a portion of Washington Heights, a similar housing area beside the Meiji Shrine nearer the center of the city, for a new NHK (national television) building and the spectacular Olympic swimming pool and basketball facilities, designed by my friend, the world-famous architect Tange Kenzo. This was the exact spot where I had played baseball in high school, when it was known as the Yoyogi Parade Grounds. I was strongly opposed to the dividing of both Camp Drake and Washington Heights between Olympic facilities and American military areas, because this would call the attention of visitors to Japan to these symbols of the American military presence and could easily produce adverse publicity.

I started meeting with Governor Azuma of Tokyo in September 1961 and assumed a firm position that the Japanese should take back all of an American military installation or none. My idea was that Camp Drake should continue as an American military establishment and that all of Washington Heights should be returned and used for the Olympic Village as well as the other Olympic facilities planned for it. Since road construction and land prices in the Camp Drake area had already been affected by the earlier plan, there was strong resistance to my proposal in some quarters; but the plan was obviously much superior because it would cut down greatly on the travel time for the athletes to most of the sites for the contests. Eventually the Japanese cabinet swung around to my plan, and it was adopted, working efficiently during the Games.

The Japanese government generously provided all the ambassadors and their wives with two nontransferrable tickets for all the competitions they chose, and we spread ourselves quite widely. We went several times to the swimming and diving events, in which our American athletes piled up medals, and we thrilled at the close American triumph over the Soviet Union in the basketball finals, where Bill Bradley, a recent Princeton graduate and today a senator from New Jersey, proved a star. At the various events Haru and I were often placed by the police for security reasons in the normally empty box reserved for the imperial family, making us stand out rather conspicuously. Since the box at the swimming events was opposite the main television cameras, we were frequently shown with accompanying commentary during lulls in the competition. We were unaware of this until Haru's sister, Tane, admonished her for yawning at the television cameras, and the Residence staff one evening gathered at the doorway to greet us home, having seen us on television leaving our seats.

We managed to crowd all these Olympic activities and accompanying festivities into our days without disturbing our regular diplomatic routine and Embassy duties very much and had time left over for unusual events, such as the predictable appearance of two Soviet defectors. All in all these two weeks were an exhilarating experience that marked the end of my period of recuperation from the misadventure of the previous spring.

◄§

The Olympic Games were the start of an extremely busy autumn and winter for us, made all the harder by the departure in November of the Emmersons for a two-month home leave. Though still feeling somewhat weak, I was now back to a full schedule, but Ikeda meanwhile had developed a terminal case of cancer of the throat. His death shortly thereafter was a great loss for us personally as well as for Japan.

The day after Sato replaced him as Prime Minister on November 9, Sato drew me aside at the annual Imperial Garden Party in the Shinjuku Gardens for a lengthy tête-à-tête on various matters, and I cleared with him the possibility of bringing in that week the first nuclear-powered submarine. It had been almost two years since Ohira had announced that this was being considered, and in the meantime all the problems of possible nuclear accidents had been studied meticulously. Among the steps taken had been to bring Admiral Hyman G. Rickover, the venerable father of nuclear submarines, out to Tokyo to consult with the local specialists. Although his visit was kept entirely secret from the public, he stayed with us at the Residence for several days, regaling us with amusing stories of his earlier days in the navy, which he seems to have hated from the start. Despite his reputation for irascibility, he was extremely affable with us.

The dates for the entry of nuclear submarines depended on their general schedules, but the exact timing was left in my hands. The Japanese government did not want to know more than twenty-four hours in advance for fear word would leak out and allow extremist elements to build up massive demonstrations. Therefore up until twenty-four hours before a submarine came in, I could always cancel the visit if I felt there was some political reason that made it unwise just then. Considerable excitement was generated by the first visit on November 12, but less than we had expected, and the public response diminished with each succeeding visit. Ohira and Ikeda's gamble that this would be a useful step in getting the Japanese public accustomed to nuclear power had paid off. It was only later, long after my departure, that the rising excitement over Vietnam and the unwise entry of a nuclear-powered aircraft carrier into a Japanese port caused protests to build up to dangerous proportions.

Haru and I made only one trip within Japan that autumn, going to the Kyoto-Osaka area for the better part of a week at the beginning of November.

This was our seventh visit to the region, but since we had not been there for a year and a half, we went through the regular prefectural visitation routine, this time also including Shiga Prefecture around Lake Biwa.

Nihon University invited me for a major speech on November 11, which I delivered in Japanese, daring for the first time to say quite clearly that anyone who was for democracy was inevitably against communism. This is, of course, a truism but was never said at that time in Japan, where to be anti-Communist was considered to be "feudalistic" and not intellectually respectable. Nihon University awarded me an honorary degree on the occasion, which was unusual, not being part of the Japanese academic tradition, though I do have two or three other Japanese honorary degrees. Among other speeches I gave was one to the National Newspapermen's Association (Shimbun Kyokai), but two speeches scheduled at universities were canceled because of threats from Communist students, showing that these tactics were still being used against weak-kneed college authorities.

In November, a new Korean Ambassador succeeded Pae and turned out to be a much more vigorous and influential man than Pae had been. He often kept me better informed on conditions in Seoul than our Embassy in Seoul was. In December Haru's cousin, Ushiba Nobuhiko, who was then the Deputy Vice Foreign Minister, was placed in charge of the Korean negotiations on the Japanese side. He was an extraordinarily energetic and capable man and later became the Vice Foreign Minister and then for several years the Japanese Ambassador in Washington. I took heart at the strong new team working on the Korean normalization problem and met often with them individually, determined to help get the Japanese-Korean problem settled once and for all.

Sato in his new capacity as Prime Minister was eager to meet with President Johnson as soon as possible, but Washington found it difficult to schedule a visit by him before June 1965. I sent a strongly worded telegram in November urging an earlier date; perhaps in part because of this, a time was found for the visit on January 12. I planned to go in advance to pave the way and persuaded Washington to include Haru in the trip. She would not only be helpful with Mrs. Sato in Washington but was badly in need of the break herself.

As we later looked back on those days, it seems that the double blow of Kennedy's death and the ordeal of my stabbing set Haru off on a gradual downward spiral of depression. From the start she had found her position more of a strain than I, being less accustomed to public speaking and popular attention and feeling herself in a more ambiguous position because of her Japanese background. When faced by a crisis or unwelcome task, she always rose to the occasion magnificently, but not without paying an emotional price. After we returned from my convalescence in Hawaii, she became increasingly insistent that we must resign soon, and, though she stuck it out for another two years, the effort took a toll on her.

Before leaving for Washington, I had a two-hour session with Sato at which among other things we decided to expand the scope of the military Consultative Committee to include all military matters. I also met with the Korean Ambassador and with Miki, the Secretary General of the LDP, who was accompanying Sato, and invited Watson to come up from Okinawa and Preston and the other senior American admirals and generals in Japan for discussions.

Then after the annual New Year's reception at court on January 1, 1965, Haru and I left for Washington. There at a luncheon at the Louchheims' we met for the first time Walter ("Fritz") Mondale, the new senator from Minnesota and later Vice-President and presidential candidate, who is the husband of my eldest cousin's daughter, Joan.

Sato's visit went very well, and he apparently gave me much of the credit for its success. Before the big White House dinner, the Satos, the Rusks, and we were taken by the President to the second floor, where the Satos and Johnsons exchanged presents. Then we all swept regally down the staircase, while the military band struck up "Hail to the Chief." After this bit of shared glory, the rest of the group proceeded grandly to the head table, while I was ushered to table No. 5, in accordance with my lowly protocol status when in Washington. After dinner the President dutifully danced with the ladies, including Haru. Because of his imposing bulk, they made an incongruous pair. After punctiliously going once around the floor with her, he virtually flung her into my arms. Haru felt we handled the social amenities more graciously at the Residence and had the satisfaction of deciding that our cuisine was much better than that at the White House.

The first few weeks after our return to Tokyo in early 1965 were broken up by a series of trips. It had been decided to broaden the scope of the United States–Japan Consultative Committee on the Ryukyus beyond mere economic matters; before I started negotiations over this, however, I wished to consult at length with General Watson. Haru and I flew down to Okinawa on the morning of February 18 and spent four very busy days there. My talks with Watson went well, but since the local people had high hopes that the expanded focus of the Committee would lead to early reversion of Okinawa to Japan, my public talks and press interviews, as I noted at the time, were like "walking on eggs." The subsequent negotiations with the Japanese government on the new duties of the Committee went smoothly, and the Committee held its first meeting under its new mandate on May 16.

On March 2 Haru and I left for a six-day trip to the heart of Japan's "snow country," visiting for the first time the three prefectures of Fukushima, Yamagata, and Akita in northern Honshu. We deliberately chose winter for the trip, because we had heard so much in other parts of the west coast "snow country" about the debilitating influence of the heavy snowfall that we wished to experience it for ourselves. The countryside was extremely beautiful under six feet of snow. We felt the people were more exhilarated than depressed by their surroundings. Since ambassadorial visitations of any type to this area were rare, our visit drew great attention.

Two days after we got back, I flew down to Manila where a conference of American ambassadors from East and Southeast Asia had been called to discuss the deepening involvement of the United States in the Vietnam War and its repercussions on the whole area. Averell Harriman and Bill Bundy had flown out from Washington, and all the regional ambassadors were there, except for Maxwell Taylor, the former chairman of the Joint Chiefs of Staff and current Ambassador to Vietnam. He was represented by U. Alexis Johnson, an old acquaintance of mine, who was his Deputy Ambassador and later was to occupy the post of Under Secretary of State for Political Affairs before succeeding me as Ambassador to Japan. The conference was interesting but shallow, concentrating too much on the immediate situation and failing to look far enough ahead to be enlightening. I felt it typified the weaknesses of American foreign policy and, with the encouragement of some of the younger aides from Washington, tried a few times to open up the discussions to broader considerations, but Bill Bundy determinedly kept the talks in their narrow channel.

Haru gave the most notable speech during this period, going to Kobe on June 5 to speak before 10,000 women, who were said to be representatives of 400,000 women in women's organizations in Hyogo Prefecture. The federation had been put together and led for twenty years by a remarkable Mrs. Hirose, who was then well up in her seventies. By comparison my speech at about the same time to three thousand women from Kyoritsu Women's University was small potatoes, even though it was the largest all-feminine audience I ever addressed. On her Kobe trip Haru received the full police protection I usually got, even to the point of having several policemen standing on the platform outside her window at each station where her train stopped.

Diplomatic negotiations continued apace. A trip by the Japanese Foreign Minister to Korea, where he made a statement that implied a Japanese apology for the colonial past, at last broke the log jam holding up the normalization of relations. It started a flurry of talks, and the Japanese leaders, as well as the Korean Foreign Minister and other cabinet members when in Tokyo, conferred with me a great deal, though I carefully limited myself to encouragement and sympathetic listening, avoiding any involvement in the negotiations themselves. A general agreement was worked out between the Japanese and Koreans by the beginning of April, though it was not finally signed until the end of June, and ratification still lay ahead. The agreement was a significant step forward, bringing increased stability to the area and making possible South Korea's start toward rapid economic growth.

The solution of one problem, however, was always followed by the emergence of another. As I wrote in February,

> The trouble with this sort of diplomatic job is that one never reaches a smooth stretch of water. If one gets through one difficult problem successfully (let's say the Interest Equalization Tax problem of two weeks ago) then one runs smack into fish, and when they calm down Okinawa, textiles, dumping charges, a military base incident, excitement over nuclear bombs or something is sure to flare up. It's like walking on hot coals. You have to move fast not to burn your feet, but the next place you put your foot down is another hot coal. The only comfort is that some aren't quite as hot as others.

# 39

# Vietnam to the Fore

THE MOST remarkable thing about my list of problems in February 1965 is the lack of reference to Vietnam. In August 1964 I had noted for the first time popular demonstrations against our policies there in connection with the Gulf of Tonkin incident, in which American and North Vietnamese ships allegedly fired on each other; but now attention to Vietnam picked up rapidly. On February 17, 1965, three old family friends—Mrs. Uemura Tamaki, a leader of the Presbyterian-affiliated church in Japan, Mrs. Komyo, the dean of Tokyo Women's University, and Miss Watanabe Michiko, the president of the Japanese YWCA—called on me to discuss the situation in Vietnam, and by the end of March I was recording that "Vietnam is giving me lots of worries" and Japanese "emotional reactions are building up" over American involvement there. On April 14 Ichikawa Fusae, the grand old lady of the Japanese women's suffrage movement and an old friend, led a delegation of nine top women leaders, bringing a plea for world peace, and Mrs. Uemura, together with another old friend, Kaya Seiji, the recently retired president of Tokyo University, were among the so-called

Committee of Seven who came on April 23 to deliver a letter of protest to President Johnson against America's Vietnam policy.

By then American actions in Vietnam had grown to be the major newspaper story and the main cause of friction between the Japanese public and the United States. The Japanese for the most part sided with the North Vietnamese, identifying American bombing of them with the bombing they themselves had suffered from Americans only two decades earlier. Most of my discussions with Japanese now centered upon this subject, as did many of my speeches, in the question period if not in the main presentation. I talked endlessly to newspaper editors and reporters, politicians, and groups of all sorts. Several American groups also came to me seeking guidance on how to reply to the questions and criticisms they were receiving from their Japanese friends and colleagues.

I had been against our involvement in Vietnam from the start, as is clearly shown in my earlier book, *Wanted: An Asian Policy*, but by this time we had become so deeply enmeshed that I was ready to accept the administration's argument that the quickest and easiest way to end the war was to force North Vietnam by military might to desist from trying to conquer the South. In discussing the matter with Japanese, I did not insist that we were right in all our actions, some of which I privately regarded as deplorable; rather, I tried to get them to look at the situation more realistically by eliciting from them ideas as to how the problem could best be resolved and encouraging them to think about constructive contributions Japan could make to its settlement. I was appalled at the lack of knowledge about the fundamental facts in Vietnam and the failure to understand what the real alternatives were. It was easy to demand that the Vietnamese be allowed to settle their future peacefully by themselves, but there was no way to get a peaceful outcome. No matter what course the United States followed, a military resolution of the situation seemed the only possibility and was in fact the eventual outcome.

It was most distressing to see the great progress that we had made in improving attitudes between the Japanese public and the United States being eroded by our involvement in Vietnam. This situation alone would have been good reason for the United States never to have gotten entrapped in Vietnam. In April, for the first time in three years, there were popular demonstrations directed against the Embassy and the Japanese police felt it necessary to increase their guard, until by June we looked like a besieged camp, with several new police boxes erected around our walls and trucks full of riot police stationed around nearby corners. Through public and private talks, my colleagues and I did our best to minimize the damage to Japanese-American relations, but it was an uphill battle.

I met with Sasaki Kozo, the left-wing chairman of the Socialist Party, and other leaders of the opposition parties, and stayed in close touch with the leaders of the ruling LDP. Sato himself continued to find it more politic to talk with me by phone or in brief asides at social events rather than in formally scheduled calls, which would have required explanations to the press. Visiting American dignitaries also afforded me chances for unnoticed talks with Sato and other leaders. In late April Henry Cabot Lodge, the Republican vice-presidential candidate in 1960, and his wife stopped with us on their way to taking on the ambassadorial post in Vietnam for a second time. Walt Rostow, formerly McGeorge Bundy's chief assistant at the White House but by then the head of the policy planning section at the State Department, also spent ten days with us, meeting with Japanese leaders, holding discussions, and giving speeches, mostly on the Vietnam problem, though the three universities that had planned to have him speak all canceled their invitations because of fear of student protests.

Meanwhile press reports of testimony before a Senate committee in Washington created an uproar. Under Secretary of State Ball and Assistant Secretary MacArthur, my predecessor as Ambassador, were reported to have implied that the reason the major Japanese newspapers were so critical of America's Vietnam policy was because they were infiltrated by Communists and therefore mirrored the Communist line. I assume that some of MacArthur's feelings about the Security Treaty troubles of 1960 became confused with testimony about the existing situation, but in any case the Japanese press exploded in fury, accusing the United States of having slipped back to the McCarthy period when all critics were called Communists. The papers argued, not unreasonably, that if we were so uninformed on Japan, how could they believe our assertions that the Vietcong were Communists and not merely people who did not agree with us.

Because of the excellent relations our Embassy had established with the press, we were able to persuade the papers to hold off printing their Washington stories in their evening editions. This gave me time to have a session at the Residence with the editors to assure them that these reports did not reflect our views at the Embassy and also to draw up a statement of denial to be printed simultaneously in the morning with the news stories. This was a difficult document to draft because we did not wish to imply that the Under Secretary was a liar, but we had no other choice than to take independent action, since Washington was deep in sleep at the moment. We did, however, get off some hard-hitting telegrams to Washington and by morning had a flood of denials and apologies to pass on to the press.

I believe that we managed to avert a major blowup in Japanese-American relations by our quick action at the Embassy. It was incidents like this that made me feel that my presence in Japan was still worthwhile. But the whole affair was very depressing. It revealed how careless Washington could still be in its relations with Japan, and the failure of the American press to take much note of the incident showed how poor our news coverage of Japan was. Abe Rosenthal of *The New York Times* and Frank Gibney, an able writer very knowledgeable about

Japan, who came out to Tokyo a couple of weeks later, were both amazed to discover the depth of feeling about Vietnam in Japan, which they said was not being reported at all adequately in America. Their statements inspired me to send a very strongly worded telegram to the State Department about the extremely adverse reactions in Japan to the American bombing of North Vietnam.

The Vietnam situation had a clear impact on our next prefectural visit on May 11–15 to four prefectures in Kyushu. For three of the prefectures—Saga, Miyazaki, and Oita—this was our first visit, and we did all the usual things. Everywhere we were met by thousands of friendly welcomers, but the Communist Party had decided to go all out to break up our trip. They managed to get all the universities which had invited me to speak to withdraw their invitations, and wherever we went we found groups of noisy Communist demonstrators, sometimes numbering in the hundreds and provided with sound trucks and megaphones. I remember one woman who replied to my smile by trying to spit on me. For Japan this seemed truly shocking. The authorities were obviously nervous and surrounded us with platoons of bodyguards, while larger formations of police were drawn up around the corner. When I suggested that we did not need so much protection, I was given the cheerful response, "Oh, this is less than we gave Mikoyan." That was scarcely comforting. Being compared with an unfriendly Soviet leader helped make up our minds that this was not the time for further goodwill trips, and we decided to abandon them for the time being. Actually we never resumed them, falling short by seven of our resolve to visit all the forty-six prefectures.

The various unpleasant incidents occasioned by the excitement over Vietnam made Haru all the more eager for us to resign and return home, and Ann and Joan joined her in urging this, reflecting the souring attitude toward Washington on American campuses. I pointed out that we could scarcely run out on our job when understanding of the Japanese and ability to communicate with them had become all the more important. At the same time, I realized that the moment was approaching when we should leave Tokyo. Haru and I were growing stale in the job, no longer finding much pleasure or amusement in it, and this was hurting our effectiveness. More important was the growing incongruity of my role in Japan. I had from the start emphasized the desirability of an equal partnership between Japan and the United States, but the very fact that I preached this doctrine to the Japanese public was an example of inequality. No Japanese Ambassador would dream of trying similarly to preach to the American public. Japan was no longer the self-doubting country needing advice and encouragement it had been when we had arrived. As a private citizen I could say what I wished to the Japanese, but it was no longer proper for me as an Ambassador to play the role of *sensei* (teacher). The Japanese public, however, expected that of me and would not have let me change roles. The only thing we could do about it was to leave; we therefore started making plans to resign in about a year, postponing a final decision to the autumn after a second home leave during the summer.

Early in May, Sato and I had agreed on July 12–14 for the fourth cabinet-level Economic Conference, and Haru and I scheduled our biennial home leave to follow it. As was usual in preparation for the conference, I held long talks with Sato and other Japanese leaders, sent off detailed policy reports to Washington, and called together General Preston and the other senior American generals and admirals in Japan for a discussion of the local military situation. Haru and I also held a dinner party for the seven cabinet ministers and their wives who were going to Washington, and then flew back to America on July 1, making a two-day stop on the way with Admiral and Mrs. Sharp in Hawaii. In Washington I had talks with Rusk, Harriman, McNamara, and many others, while Haru met with Virginia Rusk and the other American cabinet wives.

On July 8 we flew out to San Francisco in one of the presidential planes to meet the Japanese delegation and take them the next day to the Grand Tetons in Wyoming for a brief rest and a trip by a big rubber raft down the Snake River. Then we all flew to Washington for the start of the conference on the 12th. Everything went very smoothly, but both the meetings and the White House social events seemed merely routine to us by this time. The only memorable incident was that at a White House luncheon President Johnson asked that some Stetson hats be brought to the table and started clamping them on the heads of the embarrassed members of the Japanese cabinet, to the consternation of Haru, who as usual was seated among the ministers at the head table. It was incidents like this, as well as memories of Johnson's earlier cavorting through South Asia, inviting a camel driver in Pakistan to visit him in Washington, that made me resolve to lay my head on the block if necessary to prevent him from visiting Japan. Fortunately the necessity never arose because the President became much too engrossed in the frustrating war in Vietnam to think of making diplomatic visits.

By July 17 Haru and I were free of our duties in Washington and could go to Lavalette on the New Jersey shore, where Hugh Borton had lent us his beach cottage; we were joined by my father, Ann, her husband Steve, and their two boys. At the end of the month we all drove up to Massachusetts, where Haru and I, joined by Joan, stayed at Ken and Kitty Galbraith's large and comfortable house on Francis Avenue close to Harvard while they were away. To have their home as a base whenever we returned to Cambridge was a great convenience for which we were very grateful. Our home leave was most satisfactory, and our only disappointment was that we did not see Bob and his wife, Charlotte, who were off on a trip to Central America. Talks with Pusey and others at Harvard helped incline us toward returning the next summer.

We arrived back in Tokyo on August 22 after speeches in Boston, Chicago, and Los Angeles and a one-day stop with Admiral Sharp in Hawaii. He proved to need reassurances on my thinking because of reports he had seen about statements in my speeches about Japanese attitudes toward the Vietnam War and the damage it was doing to Japanese-American relations. I found that my speeches had been widely reported in Japan too and had produced strong repercussions, mostly quite favorable. The Japanese were pleased to see that their views were being brought to the attention of the American government and public. The reports had also given rise to rumors that I was about to resign in protest. I laid these speculations to rest in a big press conference and a television broadcast a few days after our return; but in our minds we were clearly beginning to head down the home stretch.

On our return to Tokyo, we were caught up at once in one of the busiest periods we experienced in our whole Embassy stay. I was determined to try to broaden the current Japanese-American dialogue beyond Vietnam by getting Japanese to think more deeply about the future of our relations and the world in general. I hoped to get them to understand more clearly our shared national interests and to give more thought to ways by which these could be achieved. For this purpose I held long individual talks with many Japanese political leaders, such as Kishi, Fukuda, Tanaka, and Miki, prominent members of the business community like Ishizaka of Keidanren and Iwasa of Sumitomo, and many others, including Ikeda Daisaku, the head of Soka Gakkai, the politically powerful religious group, which seemed internationally very naive. I even took a five-hour trip down to Oiso to talk with former Prime Minister Yoshida, who still exerted a great deal of influence; but my talk with Sato was very disappointing, because he had the looming battle over ratification of the normalization treaty with South Korea too much on his mind to be much concerned with other matters. Word from Washington, however, was that my proposals for rethinking and deepening our relations with Japan, which I had talked about while there during the summer, were receiving top-level support.

On his way back from Vietnam, Deputy Ambassador Alex Johnson stayed with us for two days in the middle of September and delivered a fine speech to seven hundred Japanese leaders. It was well reported in the English-language press but typically all but ignored by the Japanese papers, which did, however, report Sato's somewhat equivocal introduction of Johnson before he himself left the meeting. The Japanese a week later similarly ignored the presence in Japan of Quat, a former South Vietnamese Foreign Minister, and his very cogent remarks on the situation. At the same time, the press was drawing extensively on North Vietnamese propaganda handouts, as if they were verified facts, while reporting from Saigon only the seamier side of the situation as dug up by its own reporters. It seemed to me that the Japanese public was being given a biased view of Vietnam, in which propaganda statements from Hanoi were equated with muckraking from Saigon, with no effort to point out to the uninformed readers the difference between the two contrasting types of "news." I decided, therefore, to make use of a speech to the America-Japan Society in Osaka scheduled for October 5 for an uncharacteristically hard-hitting statement on the need to work actively for peace, not just wish for it passively, and also to find an opportunity to point out the imbalanced nature of Japanese reporting on Vietnam.

I carefully prepared a written text for my Osaka speech, which seemed to be well received, as were discussions I had with local leaders, but at a press conference I committed what I consider my worst blunder during my whole ambassadorial career. I had been angered by a particularly egregious series of stories from Hanoi then running in the *Mainichi,* which accepted North Vietnamese propaganda statements at face value. It probably would have been impossible to verify them, but I felt that the writer, Omori Minoru, should have made clear to his readers the suspect source of his materials. In reply to a question at the press conference, I mentioned the *Mainichi* and Omori by name and, if I remember correctly, also the *Asahi* correspondent, Hata Shoryu, as having used these materials more cautiously. For an Ambassador to criticize by name a newspaper and reporter is inexcusable, and the moment I made the remark I realized what a gaffe I had committed. In retrospect I can see that I had become too relaxed and self-confident in my ambassadorial role.

The speech and still more the press interview really shook up the Japanese press, and the repercussions lasted for more than a month. In fact, Omori for a while practically made a career of the incident, writing books and articles about it for some years. There was considerable speculation that my speech and remarks represented a "get tough" with Japan policy coordinated between Washington and me, although Washington actually was quite innocent of any complicity. It was also suggested that my change of tone indicated that I was planning to resign soon. On the whole, however, the Japanese press, though irritated, treated me very fairly. The *Asahi* in a big editorial of self-justification ended by saying it would accept my statement as a "warning from a close friend" and take occasion to "self-reflect" on the problem.

At the annual meeting of the press association later in October, my statement was one of the major subjects of discussion, and there were some efforts to have the body officially rebuke me, but the majority view apparently was that my remarks were "friendly criticism." In fact, the same week the editor-in-chief of the *Mainichi* called on me, virtually apologizing and asking that we still be friends. Outside the newspaper world, the reactions were even better. Many people expressed support of my statement, and Sato at a speech to the Foreign Press Club praised me for my "daring." Finally, on November 9, I had a dinner meeting with the top editors of the nine largest newspapers at their request to discuss my Osaka remarks and later had a similar session with some thirty-five of the top men in broadcasting. The American news media, which were characteristically slow in picking up on the incident, were mostly supportive of my action, and the authorities in Washington were clearly pleased.

◈

On December 5, I left for a trip to Vietnam. Pleased by what I had been saying in Japan, the military wished to give me a chance to see the situation in Vietnam for myself. I was accompanied by two members of my staff, Owen Zurhelen, who had become the Political Counsellor, and Edward J. Nickel, the Public Relations Officer, and we flew by way of Okinawa and the Philippines in a small four-seater air force jet. Mo Preston had apparently set up VIP treatment for me: I was met everywhere by the local air force commander and a small honor guard.

Our first evening in Saigon we dined as the guests of General William C. Westmoreland, the American commander in Vietnam, with the chief American civilian leaders there, including my old high school friend Gordon Jorgensen, who, I suspect, was the local head of the CIA. I stayed with the new Deputy Ambassador, William Porter, an Englishman by birth, who lived in the former Ambassadorial Residence, which Lodge had abandoned for more secure quarters. Armed Marines guarded the house inside and out, and it was provided with iron coverings for the windows and surrounded by elaborate barricades. The whole city swarmed with soldiers of all descriptions armed to the teeth. Despite the heat, we had to keep the windows of our car up while driving around town in order to discourage terrorists from tossing in hand grenades. Thus even Saigon was something of a battle zone, but there were no major incidents while we were there.

On the 6th we flew up to the American supply base at Cam Ranh Bay, one of the greatest natural anchorages in the world. Though the perimeter of the base was guarded by Korean troops, I noticed in our helicopter flight from the airstrip to the supply area that we had soldiers at both doors aiming downward at the ground, although we were inside the base the whole time. From Cam Ranh we flew further north to Da Nang, where the Marines had carved out a small area around a major air base; from the air, one could see shells exploding all around the perimeter. We flew in a helicopter to some of the front-line posts, with a heavily armed second helicopter riding shotgun, as it were, above us. At one post the young officer in command proved to have taken my Rice Paddies course in 1959–60, and the major in charge of relations with the civilian population had been in the course a few years earlier. In the evening we flew back to Saigon in time for a big reception given for us by Deputy Ambassador Porter.

The next morning we flew out to a place called Vung Tao on the coast near Saigon where we inspected a program being run by an enthusiastic young Vietnamese officer to train South Vietnamese to be cadres in support of the government in their native villages. It was an effort to counter Communist techniques with the same sort of ideological warfare and was by far the most interesting and hopeful thing I saw in Vietnam, but in the end nothing seems to have come of it. Our last trip in Vietnam was to Tay Ninh, which was the center of the Cao Dai religious sect. It was a small, pro-government island precariously surrounded by the Communist supply area in Cambodia on one side, major Vietcong base areas on two other sides, and guerrilla-infested territory on the fourth. This so-called liberated area was so small that the little plane carrying us had to spiral down to land and similarly spiral up on takeoff in order to avoid flying low over enemy territory, which reached to within a half mile of the town.

After these trips we received thorough briefings in Saigon, and I had a press interview with the thirteen local Japanese correspondents, who formed the largest national press corps next to the Americans. Then we flew back to Japan by the way we had come, with a twenty-four-hour stopover in Okinawa. Our arrival there happened to be an hour ahead of schedule, giving rise to press charges that I had "sneaked" into Okinawa, an accusation I tried to clear up at a press interview the next day. Our plane got us back to Japan by 5:00 p.m. on the 10th; by 7:00 p.m. I was standing in black tie with Haru in the receiving line of the annual dinner and ball of the American Chamber of Commerce in Japan, where I presided as usual at the installation of the new president for the year.

My Vietnam expedition was interesting but not very encouraging. I retained my original view that the whole American involvement in Vietnam had been a terrible mistake from the start, though I continued to accept Washington's contention that the quickest way to get out of it was through a military victory. In my weekly letter home I summarized my impressions as follows:

> Vietnam was as confused and confusing as I had been led to believe. I was happy to see that the reporting I had been getting from all sorts of people, but particularly Henry Kissinger, fits in exactly with what I saw. The problems, as in any less developed country especially after six years of war, are mountainous. Progress in any direction is at a snail's pace. The dangers of some sort of collapse are not inconsiderable. The assurance of any sort of rapid

success very slight. . . . I'm basically confirmed in my very pessimistic view of the future of the less developed half of the world. The easy optimism since the war [World War II] both by Communists and free world people about its development is the greatest miscalculation of our times.

While 1965 was dominated for me by popular Japanese opposition to America's Vietnam policy, we also had our full share of usual activities. The Security Consultative Committee met in September with Admiral Sharp from Hawaii there in a support capacity to me. General Watson in Okinawa proved to be worried about the implications for Okinawa of some of the things I had said in my public speeches in the United States during the summer, but we cleared up his misunderstandings during a long, pleasant visit he made at the end of September. One problem I faced with him was that the State Department would solicit my views on details of administration in Okinawa, which I was reluctant to give, not wishing to seem to interfere in Watson's own bailiwick, because I felt our overall trust and friendship was more important than my views on such minor matters. On November 2 a meeting of the Consultative Committee on the Ryukyus was held, and aid from Japan of $16 million was accepted quite smoothly, in contrast to the constant haggling over $2 or $3 million during the Caraway period. The Japanese-Korean Normalization Treaty was finally ratified by the Japanese Diet on November 12, while endless negotiations with the Japanese over civil air routes, which had taken a good bit of my time all autumn, were wound up with the signing of an agreement on December 28.

As usual I wrote several articles, but the most interesting writing of this period was done for Haru by a woman writer, Akimoto Ryuko, who produced an "autobiography" of Haru under the title *Watakushi no ayunda michi (The Path I Have Trod)*. It was published serially in the popular women's magazine *Shufu no Tomo (The Housewife's Companion)* and subsequently in book form. We both felt that Mrs. Akimoto's text was very well done. She was a delightful person; several years later we had the pleasure of entertaining her and her husband when he spent a year as an exchange professor in Ohio.

There were one hundred newcomers to the Embassy at our monthly newcomers reception in September. We were impressed by the length of our own stay in Japan when we noticed that quite a few of our guests had been in Japan in our early Embassy days and were now returning after a two-year tour of duty elsewhere. That autumn we also had an unusually large salmon run of senators and congressmen—I estimated more than a hundred. Among our most memorable house guests were Edward and Joan Kennedy, who stayed for several days in November. My impressions of Teddy Kennedy had not been very favorable because of the publicity about his college escapades, but I found the young new senator from Massachusetts to be not only able to handle himself well in his discussions with the Japanese leaders but also very modest and eager to learn. Joan was shy but charming, telling Haru she did not have Ethel Kennedy's energy and was more like the former President's wife, Jackie. We could see how the strains of public life would weigh on her and sympathized deeply with both of them in their later troubles. I accompanied Teddy in his various meetings with Japanese leaders and discussions with groups representing the intellectual community, organized labor, and the LDP and Socialist Party. We also gave a luncheon for the Kennedys and a reception, at which the sudden appearance of Cary Grant, as handsome and charismatic in the flesh as on the screen, rather stole the show.

Just after my December trip to Vietnam, Senator Mansfield turned up as the head of a five-man delegation from the Foreign Relations Committee. Mansfield's visit proved to be quite unusual. When I seated myself at the head of the conference table in the Chancery to start a briefing of his group, I found he had seated himself at the opposite end, from where he completely reversed the normal procedures, making me in effect a witness at a Senatorial committee hearing. He had a complete transcript made of his detailed questioning of me regarding my views on Vietnam, and I spoke out quite frankly about my pessimism and basically negative feelings, to the consternation of my staff. They obviously feared that my deviation from the administration's line in speaking with senators might bring dire consequences, but Mansfield was clearly in general agreement with my point of view; if anything, my "testimony" enhanced my standing with certain groups in Congress.

The 1965 Christmas season, our last at the Embassy, proved the busiest and most successful of all. Not counting the usual Japanese New Year's postcards, we received over eight hundred Christmas cards, most very elaborate, despite the fact that we had not sent any cards ourselves for five years. In addition to our usual parties, Haru held open house at the Residence for several days from 10:00 a.m. to 4:00 p.m. for those who wished to see our Christmas decorations, and she was on hand to greet them. On one day some fifteen hundred and on another some thirteen hundred people streamed through the Residence; the total she estimated at five or six thousand.

Our most interesting house guests were Vice-President Hubert Humphrey and his wife, Muriel, who arrived on relatively short notice on the night of December 28. Despite a twenty-seven-hour trip from Washington, they joined with apparent enthusiasm our annual Embassy ball already in progress at the Residence. Humphrey gave a rousing speech, shook hands all around, and the two of them danced until well past midnight. That was the sort of energy, I noted, that a successful politician needs. They spent the night with us, and the next morning I took them for an audience with the Emperor and Empress in the Emperor's own limousine, lent as a special mark of honor. To the best of my memory, this was the first time an American Vice-President had been in Japan, but we did not have enough time to make much of this fact. Humphrey proved so good in talking with the Japanese and so congenial to my way of thinking that I resolved to try to get him back for a longer stay, but this never happened.

Our heavy year-end schedule lasted up through the annual court reception on January 1, after which I expected a restful break while Japan relaxed during its New Year's holidays, but the vacation shrank to a couple of days at Misaki because of the arrival on the 6th of Harriman for a series of talks with the Japanese. I could not complain because his visit was at my original suggestion. Harriman came with two young aides in a presidential plane—three men in a plane that could seat well over one hundred. He had good talks with Sato and Shiina and a big session with leaders of the four main political parties (all but the Communists) and the labor federations, except for Sohyo on the far left. It was held at the Residence and was the first time, I believe, that such a wide spectrum of Japanese political leaders had sat down informally together. The Japanese were much impressed by the authority, sincerity, and frankness of this man who had dealt directly with Roosevelt and Stalin. After Humphrey's visit I had persuaded the Japanese government to issue a fairly supportive statement on Vietnam, but now on their own initiative they put out a much stronger statement. Harriman sent a number of long telegrams back to Washington, largely about Vietnam and the Japanese reactions to the situation there. Since he was a rather slow drafter himself, I did much of the work, getting a good chance to insert some of my own thinking.

# 40
# Coming Down the Home Stretch

By THE beginning of 1966, our thoughts had turned mainly to leaving Japan and returning home. We both felt that we had accomplished everything we had set out to do. The dialogue with the Japanese had long since been restored; both government and public relations between Japan and the United States had become relaxed and intimate; a sense of equality and partnership was being established between the two countries; and the Japanese were awakening to their need to take a more positive role in world affairs. A continued large role by me as the American Ambassador threatened to do more harm than good. The time had come, I felt, for a regular Foreign Service Officer to take over as Ambassador and perform the duties in a more routine way.

We aimed at June to make the transition back to Harvard, where a position had already been created for me. This remained secret, since Johnson was extremely touchy if any announcement concerning his appointees did not come first from him. I decided, however, to stop giving public speeches, writing articles, and holding discussion sessions with leaders, though of course some activities of this sort continued right up until our departure.

My chief problem was to get the State Department and President to accept my resignation. Some of the younger activists in the White House and State Department wanted me to become an Ambassador at Large in charge of China policy or assigned to giving shape to America's Asian policies as a whole. Actually nothing would have been of greater interest to me, but I refused even to consider these ideas, in part because I was too tired but more basically because I realized that my lack of rapport with the President and disagreements with Rusk would make any such role merely an exercise in futility. While Rusk was a strong and competent Secretary of State and I agreed with his attitudes on many things, I felt he was too inclined to take a military approach to matters, and I did not like his somewhat military chain-of-command style in personal relations. I sensed a lack of compatibility between us, and he bore out my feelings by showing little interest in having me take a high post in the Department. In early April he sent me a telegram, marked "literally eyes only," meaning that only I was to see it, in which he promised to let me return to Harvard by September but said that the President was reluctant to announce a change in an important job like mine at this delicate moment.

Meanwhile word of my intended resignation had leaked out in Washington at the end of March, making front-page news in Japan, and there was another flurry of such news in the latter part of April. Johnson issued irritated denials, and Haru and I were forced to resort to saying that only the President could speak on such matters. The situation was reminiscent of the anomolous position we had found ourselves in prior to my official appointment. There were gratifying cries of protest at our rumored departure, not only from Japan but also from the United States. Mansfield made a public statement urging me to stay on, and in June he and Senator George D. Aiken of Vermont stated flatteringly in the Senate that I was "indispensable." I was also tickled by a reference to me by a group of missionary boards in the United States as a "towering public figure." But our minds were made up. In a letter home on April 9, I wrote:

> The type of special approach to the job that we brought is no longer needed here, in fact it would be a liability if we were to continue it too actively at this stage; we have succeeded in cutting down the special sensitivity of

Japanese to America to tolerable proportions and have helped the Japanese government and public to shift to looking at world problems around them in terms of Japan's own interests and not simply as reactions to what American policy may be. . . . So we are not fed up with this job in disgust, but rather in a spirit of having finished it successfully. With our minds made up to go, all the problems and irritations of this work become harder to take with each passing week, and we are eager to start making the very difficult transition back to a more normal mode of life.

Meanwhile our regular ambassadorial life went on much as usual. I had frequent consultations with many Japanese leaders such as Sato, Shiina, Naka-sone, and other LDP stalwarts, the leaders of the opposition parties, and Ikeda Daisaku, the head of Soka Gakkai, whom I found much more realistic than in earlier talks but distressingly inclined toward the heavy rearmament of Japan. Shiina told me in detail about the various efforts Japan was making on its own initiative to get negotiations going for a settlement of the Vietnamese situation. I also met with many newspapermen, intellectuals, and such people as the leading economists Nakayama Ichiro and Okita Saburo. Despite my resolve, I gave several speeches, one to four hundred prominent politicians of the LDP, wrote quite a few articles, and had even more interviews for publication.

I was offered honorary degrees to be granted in June by Harvard, Yale, and Princeton, all of which I refused, though I was much amused by this clean sweep of the big three of the Ivy League. The Harvard Club of Tokyo was resurrected, with my old friend Tsuru Shigeto as president. Admiral Rickover came as a secret house guest in late April in order to hold further consultations regarding his nuclear-powered submarines. He was his usual brilliant, opinionated, and entirely fascinating self, and we greatly enjoyed his stay, which went by again completely unnoticed by the Japanese public. At about this time Richard Halloran of *The Washington Post,* who was doing a profile on me, laughingly accused me of being "a great 'con' man" in having convinced both the Japanese and the American publics that I was taking a "low posture," whereas in reality I had from the start "made statements and taken strong stands that no other Ambassador anywhere in the world could have gotten away with."

Our most interesting visitors were McGeorge and Mary Bundy. He had just given up his White House position in order to assume the presidency of the Ford Foundation, and this gave him the opportunity at last to respond to my oft-repeated urgings that he visit Japan. They stayed with us from May 7 to 21, with a side trip to the Kyoto area, where they joined Haru when she spoke in Kobe, as in the previous year, to ten thousand representatives of women's federations. Mac had come out with the firm idea that Japan was a very important country, so I had no difficulty in "brainwashing" him. We greatly enjoyed their visit, and they seemed to have a fine time too, right down to the highly competitive croquet matches we played together in our garden. Both Mac and Mary commented on Haru's being the most wonderful Ambassador's wife they had ever heard of.

~§

My most notable experience in early 1966 was a trip I took to India from January 30 to February 6 at the invitation of Bowles, who had succeeded Galbraith as Ambassador and wanted to discuss with me the prospects for closer relations between India and Japan. I stayed with the Bowleses in their small pleasant house with only a single guest room, which they preferred to the sumptuous new Embassy Residence. Bowles arranged an interesting side trip up to the Punjab and Haryana, where I had not been before. I was flown up to Amritsar, the holy city of the Sikhs near the Pakistan border, and then motored to the Bhakra Dam, said to be the largest in the world, to Chandigarh, where Le Corbusier's massive state capital buildings stood starkly amidst a virtual desert in what seemed to me the height of dysfunctionality, and then on back to Delhi. The Vice Foreign Secretary and the Japanese Ambassador gave lunches for me, and the Bowleses held an eerie reception lit by candled lanterns out of doors among the ruins of Mughal Dynasty tombs. Life in Delhi seemed much more relaxed than in Tokyo—the atmosphere around the embassies in New Delhi like that in an overgrown American small town.

I did not see Indira Gandhi, who was not in the capital, but I met with the President, Foreign Minister, and various other high officials and scholars. Unlike my last visit to India in 1960, I found the leaders to be extremely bitter toward China and intensely interested in making stronger ties with Japan, although I sensed that the Indians, like the Japanese, were still put off by what they felt was the arrogance and indifference of the other country. Despite Bowles's optimism, significant cooperation between the two seemed a long way off. I also found depressing the terrible gap in India between grandiose government structures and projects on the one hand and the impoverished lives of the people on the other. The three universities I visited had better campuses than anything one could find in Japan, but each was surrounded by a sea of backwardness. Villages, except for swarms of bicycles, seemed little changed from antiquity. This great chasm between government and people struck me as perhaps an old characteristic of the country. Judging from the remains of the British Raj and the Mughals before it, the gap must have been even greater in those days.

Shortly after my return to Tokyo, the air force flew me down to the Philippines, where another gathering of the East and Southeast Asian ambassadors was being held at Baguio from February 25 to March 2. These meetings were much more interesting than the year before, largely because Bill Bundy, perhaps as a result of my efforts the last time, had widened their scope to include more long-range problems. I returned to Tokyo to find the third United States–Japan Cultural Conference already under way. Hugh Borton and Ambassador Howard Jones, formerly in Indonesia but by then retired and serving as the head of the East-West Center in Honolulu, were our house guests.

In mid-spring a most disturbing incident occurred over nuclear matters. By accident I discovered that there was a craft at Iwakuni, the Marine base on the Inland Sea, which held a store of nuclear weapons. I erupted in outrage, because I felt this was an entirely different case from the transit of nuclear-armed ships through Japanese waters and was a violation of our understanding with the Japanese government. I was determined to resign at once in protest if the situation were not corrected immediately. Rusk told me that he thought I had known about the vessel and promised to have the weapons removed at once from Japan. The presence of the weapons until 1966 was revealed by some former American officials and military men in 1981, but by then it was ancient history and caused no particular excitement, though in 1966 such a revelation would have produced a dangerous political explosion.

In the middle of May I made a quick trip to Okinawa to work out some differences of opinion with General Watson before a meeting of the Consultative Committee on the Ryukyus. These meetings had to be scripted almost as carefully as a Kabuki performance. In mid-June, however, a serious disagreement flared up between us when Watson was in Washington and his staff failed to coordinate certain important matters with the Embassy. I had to send a violent blast to the Pentagon, which greatly angered Watson. By this time I was becoming increasingly tough in my dealings with the military, which I felt had to be brought up sharply from time to time. In any case, the whole relationship between American Army rule in Okinawa and the position of the American Embassy in Tokyo cast the High Commissioner of the Ryukyus and the American Ambassador to Japan as inevitable adversaries, as Caraway had fully demonstrated. Considering everything, my relations with Watson were in fact surprisingly good.

An important innovation at this time was a "policy planning conference" between Japanese Foreign Ministry officials and six members of the State Department, under the chairmanship of Henry Owen, Walt Rostow's successor as Chief of Policy Planning. Owen had been in my Chinese history course at Harvard before the war. The conference was held over the weekend of June 18–19 at Hakone and proved a very useful working-level discussion.

By this point, however, my thoughts were largely on resigning, and I was becoming very irritated at the President's failure to act on it. I was, in fact, steeling myself to brave Johnson's wrath by announcing it myself and just coming home. But there was a good reason why we could not leave in June, as we had originally planned. Rusk wanted me on hand at the fifth cabinet-level Economic Conference, which was held in Kyoto on July 5–7. Of all the top people present, only the Rusks and ourselves had attended the four previous meetings. In all, 36 people came from Washington for the meeting, our Embassy supplied 106 assistants, and some 500 newsmen were present. The conference was held in the magnificent new International Convention Hall built in the hills north of Kyoto and looking from the outside curiously like a battleship. The occasion stirred up sizable protest demonstrations because of the outrage in Japan over the American bombings of North Vietnam and the fact that this was the first big official Japanese-American event held in the populous Kyoto-Osaka-Kobe area, providing leftists of this Kansai region a significant target for the first time. Some three thousand people turned out to protest the arrival of the Rusks with Haru and me at the Osaka airport on the evening of July 4, and on another evening in Kyoto seven thousand demonstrated; but, though hundreds of police were in evidence, we saw almost nothing of the demonstrators themselves.

The meetings seemed to me the best we had held, and they attracted great attention in Japan. Together with Haru's cousin, Ushiba Nobuhiko, then the Deputy Vice Foreign Minister, I was assigned the undesirable task of briefing the press at the end of each session, except the last, which was handled by Rusk and Shiina.

₰

Rusk's visit gave me a chance to tell him we were determined to leave Tokyo that summer whatever the circumstances, and he said that he would get Johnson's approval the following week on his return to Washington. After the delegation had departed, Haru and I started sorting our goods and papers for departure, and I virtually stopped work at the Embassy. In mid-week we went down to Misaki for what we hoped would be a prolonged vacation, but it was suddenly interrupted on July 17 by a telegram ordering me back at once to Washington for consultations with the President.

I was furious at what seemed to me an entirely unnecessary trip, which took exactly a week and left me exhausted. I arrived back in Washington on the evening of July 19, but the State Department had not arranged a meeting for me with Johnson until the 22nd. On that day I spent more than an hour closeted with him in a small room, while his Japanese-American photographer angled around for shots of the two of us. I tried to use my time with the President to talk about China policy, but he conducted a monologue most of the time, complaining of criticism of him in the Senate. Despite this domination of the conversation, the photographer managed to get one shot of me with finger uplifted seemingly lecturing Johnson, which he subsequently sent me. The President urged me to stay on as Ambassador, as Rusk already had, or else to return to Washington to become either the Assistant Secretary for the Far East or the Deputy Under Secretary. Yet I sensed that he was not really much interested in my continued services but simply was afraid of the criticism he might receive from some of the senators if he let me go. I do not think it was mere happenstance that during our conversation Mansfield called him up to inquire about my plans. Johnson talked with him for a while and then shoved the phone at me, saying, "Here, Ed, *you* tell Mansfield I have tried to get you to stay." Our talk and the whole trip only confirmed me in the feeling that it was time for me to leave government service. The ambassadorship I had found fulfilling because it allowed me to concentrate on a field of endeavor of much interest to me, but as Assistant Secretary and still more as Deputy Under Secretary I would have found my focus of activity so enlarged and constantly changing as to be frustratingly superficial.

While in Washington I had one small press interview and a good long talk with Vice-President Humphrey. Mansfield reactivated a subcommittee of the Foreign Relations Committee, which no one else knew existed, and asked me to testify before it. Along with some nonmembers, he brought together a group that included Fulbright, Aiken, Muskie, Inouye, Morse, and Claiborne Pell of Rhode Island. He dismissed the State Department officers who had accompanied me in a rather peremptory fashion, then settled down to a pleasant, intimate discussion over coffee of Chinese and Asian policy, in which I spoke very freely about my views on these matters, and the senators all urged me to stay on. I also had a long phone conversation with Admiral Rickover, in which he urged me to fight tooth and nail to retain my position. He seemed unable to comprehend that it was I who was doing the resigning.

The morning after my arrival back in Japan on July 25, all the newspapers were blanketed with the news released in Washington of my resignation and the appointment of Alex Johnson as my successor. The next day the papers all ran editorials on me and human interest stories about Haru and me. The news coverage was so extensive that the United States was even accused of having timed the announcement to blot out attention to the simultaneous visit to Japan of Andrei A. Gromyko, the perennial Soviet Foreign Minister. There obviously had been no such intent, but when the Soviet Embassy gave a big reception for Gromyko, all the papers printed as their main picture one of him shaking hands with Haru.

Neither Haru nor I had any doubts that we were doing the right thing in resigning and that this was a good time for us to leave, when almost everyone was still wanting us to stay. But we had sunk our roots deeply during our five and a half years at the Embassy, and it was very upsetting to have to wrench ourselves free. We were suddenly struck by a wave of emotion. It was hard to pull down the curtain on what had been such a tremendous experience for us. The fact that we had accomplished everything we had hoped to and a lot more, together with all the plaudits that were being heaped on us, made it all the harder to write *finis* to this phase of our lives. Even *The Times* of London devoted an editorial to my departure, which was unprecedented according to my friends in England. The editorial judged that I had been "one of the most effective ambassadors in American history," and that I, "with a Japanese wife and a deep knowledge of Japanese history . . . was living proof that the telephone and the airborne Prime Minister have not entirely diminished the importance of ambassadors."

The pause in our work following the Economic Conference dissolved into a whirlwind of activity after I got back to Tokyo from Washington. Less than a month remained before our departure, scheduled for August 19. Haru faced the huge task of getting us packed, while I devoted myself largely to television appearances, newspaper interviews, essential formal calls, and the social engagements that were absolutely necessary. Our resolve to avoid all other engagements was aided by the shortness of time, which made it quite impossible for us to accept more than a small fraction of the many parties and activities pressed upon us.

I finished up my last manuscripts for publication, held innumerable interviews for publication, and made many television broadcasts, some of them with Haru. I also drove down to Oiso for a farewell luncheon with Yoshida and a big televised discussion with him. This turned out to be a harrowing experience, because Yoshida at eighty-eight was unpredictable. At one point he called the Japanese people "fools" *(baka)*, and I, of course, had to rise to their defense. It must have seemed absurd for an American Ambassador to be defending the Japanese people on television from the criticism of their own most famous Prime Minister.

We were inundated with gifts from all sorts of people, including a beautifully crafted eight-foot model of a premodern coastal junk, which we brought back with us and donated to the Peabody Museum in Salem, Massachusetts. Sato very thoughtfully found us a magnificent scroll of calligraphy by Haru's famous grandfather, Prince Matsukata Masayoshi. Matsuoka, the Chief Executive of the Ryukyu Islands, came up to Tokyo to transmit the farewells and thanks of the people of Okinawa. Keidanren and four other major business organizations jointly gave us a big reception. Some twenty-six women's organizations banded together to give Haru a farewell tea party in the giant Heian Room of the Okura Hotel, where she shook the hands of five hundred ladies, and a luncheon was held for her by both the conservative and opposition women members of the Diet. Haru's impact on Japanese women was unquestionably one of the biggest achievements of our stay in Japan; many of the women told her how impressed they had been that she and I worked as a team and that she went everywhere with me.

The great publicity we received during these final weeks was not all favorable.

Leftist magazines complained that the big fuss being made over our departure was like tributes "to a national hero who has just died" and showed that the Japanese public was immature and Americans patronizing. There was something to what they said. In fact, one of our basic reasons for resigning was to remove ourselves as a continuing aspect of the imbalanced relationship between Japan and America. Still worse was a series of garbled accounts of some of the statements I made. Another sour note was struck at the farewell dinner given by the Foreign Correspondents Club, not for me, since they did not want to set a precedent of farewell dinners for departing ambassadors, but for Haru as a departing former officer of the club. I came merely as her spouse, though, of course, I had to give the main speech. It was a very jolly gala affair but was somewhat marred by a group of vociferous young Americans and Japanese standing at the entrance to the building shouting protests against America's Vietnam policies. Among them was an acquaintance from Boston, Professor Howard Zinn of Boston University, who had earlier called on me for a long and impassioned discussion. I shall never forget him wildly beating on a drum in an effort to spoil the party given in Haru's honor.

We could not escape giving a few farewell parties and making a great number of formal calls of farewell. In a very cordial long audience with the Emperor and Empress, he said to me with a chuckle that, now that I was concluding my work as the political Ambassador of the United States to Japan, he hoped I would serve as a cultural Ambassador of Japan to America. This was a joke that was currently popular, and it did fit the situation, since I was returning to my old metier of teaching about Japan at Harvard.

We hosted a formal diplomatic reception of farewell and then a much larger reception for politicians, bureaucrats, prominent businessmen, university presidents, intellectuals, artistic figures, newsmen, and others not included in the diplomatic event, dividing the roughly nine hundred people who attended into three one-hour waves. In a reception for the members of the Embassy staff, including the wives of the Americans, we handled the twelve hundred people who came in the same way in three forty-five-minute waves. We were lucky to be making our farewells in the middle of summer when travel abroad and vacations had greatly reduced the number of those who were on hand in Tokyo.

I held a final big press interview, and then on the evening of August 19 we went to Haneda Airport, where the main VIP room had been reserved for us and our special friends. After making a farewell statement in Japanese on television, we boarded the plane and flew off into relative obscurity. The next morning the daily political cartoon in one of the major papers showed a high-flying plane with the caption: "Goodbye, Mr. Reischauer." The following day there was a photograph of me loading my suitcases myself in the trunk of my brother-in-law's car in Los Angeles. The ambassadorial glory days were over.

In retrospect, both Haru and I were quite content with our experience at the Embassy and our decision to end it when we did. We sacrificed six years of our pleasant, quiet academic life and I six years of my scholarly career as well as a goodly portion of my health, but our achievements in bettering Japanese-American relations seemed well worth the price. The Vietnam War was later to worsen Japanese-American relations for a while, and Japan's extraordinary economic success created endless frictions between the two countries. Yet the increased understanding between the two governments and two publics that we helped build during our stay unquestionably laid solid foundations for what is today probably the most important as well as unusual international relationship in the whole world. As we look back, there is little that we would wish to change in what we did in Japan. Admittedly we played a very unconventional role, far from that of a typical Ambassador and his wife, but the situation and our backgrounds called for this. We were given unusual latitude and trust, and we acted with a degree of independence that would not be suitable under most circumstances. We responded to the needs of the time; our style of operation, however, was not appropriate for the future. It was high time for us to withdraw from public life, and we have never had any regrets that we did.

# PART SIX
# WINDING DOWN
# 1966-

The final meeting with Prime Minister Ohira before his death in June 1980.
*(Courtesy of Consul General)*

# 41
# Reentry

Rᴇᴛᴜʀɴɪɴɢ from public service to one's usual private activities is often referred to as "reentry," implying as it does a drastic and difficult deceleration from the high-flying orbit of political affairs to the slower pace of ordinary life. The term fits my experience well, and reentry was followed for me a few years later by an even greater slowing down caused by age and failing health. The final section of my memoirs covers this process of winding down.

Haru was fifty one and I fifty-five when we returned from Japan, and a good bit of our lives still lay ahead of us. Some people who have been in positions of prominence are reluctant to revert to their former more obscure posts, seeking stimulating and challenging new careers instead, but we were eager to slip back into our old, less taxing life, in which I could continue to concentrate on my major interests of deepening knowledge about East Asia in America and strengthening understanding and cooperation between the United States and Japan. From my point of view, Harvard was the perfect place to be. I might no longer have the direct influence on national policy I had exercised at the Embassy, but I could speak more frankly and effectively on a wider range of topics and to a broader audience.

Much progress in Japanese-American relations had been made during my years abroad. In fact, they could now be said to be over the hump. Many scholars also had matured during these years to help carry the message. In this sense, my voice was less needed than before, yet my experience as Ambassador did lend my opinions more weight. And freed from the routine of diplomatic life, I could take a broader look at world problems. I came to see that mutual knowledge, understanding, and cooperation would not suffice in just a few key countries like the United States and Japan; they were becoming worldwide necessities if humanity was to survive in the age of vast global complexities and horrible destructive power it had created. My interests and efforts increasingly turned to this broader problem.

When we returned from Tokyo in the latter part of August 1966, we were processed through Washington in surprisingly quick order. There were no formalities, except for Rusk's presenting me with the large ambassadorial flag that had stood with the American flag behind my desk in the Chancery. I was not called on for any extensive debriefings, which were clearly not needed in view of my voluminous reporting from Tokyo. I was pleased to learn from Richard Sneider, who once again was in charge of the Japanese desk at the State Department, as he had been when I went to Japan, that a committee had been set up between the State Department and the International Security Affairs section of the Defense Department to look into alternative ways of handling the Ryukyu Islands, showing that my initiatives on the reversion of Okinawa to Japan were beginning to bear fruit. I had expected a careful medical checkup because of continuing physical problems from the stabbing and subsequent diseases of the liver I had undergone during my service in Japan, but there was none except for a rather cursory examination at the Chelsea Naval Hospital after my return to the Boston area. We stayed for about a week in Washington only because I was appearing on August 28 on CBS's "Face the Nation."

Back in Cambridge, Haru and I again had the use of the Galbraiths' comfortable house while they remained at their summer place in Vermont. We had expected to be able to find a house to buy before they returned, but a frantic search proved unsuccessful. Any place one of us liked would inevitably be vetoed by the other, so we finally rented a house in Belmont, deciding to take our time in finding a satisfactory permanent home. Though quite small and not very convenient—our six foot five inch son, Bob, had to stoop when he went upstairs —it served our purposes for a transition year. My father, sister, daughters Ann and Joan, and Ann's husband and now three small boys, all of whom lived in my father's two-family house, would come over to our little place for Sunday dinners, and Bob and his wife visited us occasionally from New York. It was a pleasure to be surrounded by family once again, and we reveled in our role as grandparents. We found it as satisfying as it was reputed to be, with all the fun of having small children around and little of the hard work and worry that inevitably accompany them.

I was determined to avoid administrative work of all sorts, having had my fill of such activities, and to concentrate on teaching, public speaking, and writing. At Harvard I refused all administrative posts and turned down the position of master of Eliot House. It would have been attractive in some ways, bringing us both into the mainstream of undergraduate life, but I realized that it would draw me too far away from my Japanese interests, and some of its duties, particularly the writing of endless letters of recommendation, would have proved irksome. I did, however, renew my ties with Adams House and found myself still a member of the History Department and the Department of East Asian Languages and Civilizations, as the old Department of Far Eastern Languages had been renamed, though I soon gave up attending meetings of either department.

Both within and outside the university I became a member of various committees but always resolutely refused any chairmanship. I also turned down without hesitation several invitations to take on university presidencies, some from very prestigious institutions. I have always thanked my lucky stars that, in the half-dazed condition in which I returned from Japan, I was not beguiled into this precarious path.

The process of reentry was not without its difficulty and pain. Suddenly I found myself driving round and round to find a parking place, forced to stand in lines to do a bit of banking or make a purchase, and having my time consumed by a thousand petty details of daily life. My efficiency seemed to fall to 1 or 2 percent of what it had been in Tokyo. Intellectually I could comprehend that this was because I no longer had scores of able aides and hardworking servants who devoted themselves to saving me time and facilitating my work, but emotionally it was extremely frustrating to find my seeming greyhound speed reduced to a snail's crawl. Fortunately Haru, whose life at the Embassy had remained closer to everyday reality, suffered no such frustrations and adjusted smoothly to being once again a housewife and *mater familias.*

One disappointment was to find that the field of East Asian studies at Harvard had lost much of the pleasant coziness it had enjoyed when I left in 1961. This was largely the result of growth. There was a whole new group of young professors whom I did not know, and the scholars in the various different branches of the field seemed no longer to have much contact with each other. The graduate students were more numerous but also more restless and dissatisfied. They were distressed by American policy in China and Vietnam, worried about their own future, and jealously competitive over grades. The professors in the Japanese field were indignant that John Fairbank had vigorously built up Chinese studies while letting the Japanese field languish. The blame, of course, lay with them for not having been as enterprising as John, but they counted on me to help redress the balance and get more funds channeled into the Japanese field. In any case, the old *Gemütlichkeit* of the East Asian field had definitely evaporated.

Returning to my teaching duties also presented some difficulties. Since I had ignored scholarly publications in my field for six years and was mentally and physically exhausted, I felt quite unprepared to resume teaching at once. Fortunately this was not necessary. I had been appointed one of the seven or eight University Professors, who are free to determine their own schedules, devoting themselves to research if they wish or teaching whatever courses they choose in any part of the university. It was the most desirable status in the whole university, though it often caused me difficulties when people would say, "Yes, I know you are a university professor but what is your title?" Free to do as I wished, I made my first year back at Harvard a sabbatical for retooling, and then salved my conscience by carrying a full load of courses for most of my remaining years at Harvard. Retooling meant a heavy schedule of reading and attending many conferences and extracurricular seminars. My focus of interest had shifted from ancient Japan and China to modern Japan, especially its recent political development, on which I concentrated my reading because the Government Department asked me to offer a course on the "Government and Politics of Modern Japan."

The spotlight of attention which had shone on Haru and me while in Tokyo faded with distressing slowness. Some people continued to regard us as notables, and we were inundated with phone calls, letters, and visitors. Many people invited us to dinners, in some cases probably to repay us for receptions and other entertainment we had given them in Tokyo. In any case, we allowed these contacts to wither away for the most part by not reciprocating. A heavy social life was the last thing we wished to become involved in.

I was also deluged by offers of honorary degrees and "Man of the Year" type awards. Harvard gave me an honorary degree in June 1967, and, when the planned speaker for the post-Commencement festivities suddenly had to drop out, Pusey asked me to fill in. I felt no inspiration for this big undertaking but did my best to sound impressive, though I felt very inadequate when I thought of General Marshall's first presentation of the Marshall Plan on a similar occasion. That same spring I received honorary degrees from Yale, Chicago, and a number of other less illustrious universities, and the following year another batch when Commencement season rolled around. In between, in October 1967, I received an honorary degree from the University of Michigan in connection with the celebration of its 150th anniversary. On this occasion I had the honor of sharing a lecture platform with Dean Acheson, whom I consider to have been our last great Secretary of State. A year later, Haru received an honorary degree from Western College for Women in Ohio, an institution that later was absorbed into neighboring Miami University, which I am told keeps the degree alive.

After two years of collecting honorary degrees, I came to the conclusion that this was not a very productive activity. Frequently the degrees were tied to giving Commencement addresses, but the audiences on such occasions were normally not what I wanted. Instead of being persons who were interested in hearing what I had to say, they would be made up of proud parents and friends who had come to see Tom or Beverly graduate and were not at all concerned with my message. To save my time and strength, I decided to make a strict rule against delivering Commencement addresses or accepting honorary degrees. By the time I came around to this decision, invitations for both had begun to taper off, but there were a few later occasions when special circumstances induced me to relax my self-imposed limitation. In all, I must have accepted well over twenty honorary degrees.

Among other honors I received were duly inscribed decorative clocks, plaques, and pieces of Steuben glass. The Thomas A. Dooley Foundation, which was an organization engaged in refugee work in Southeast Asia, presented "Splendid American" awards to Danny Kaye and me on November 30, 1966, at a formal banquet for about a thousand people at a large hotel in New York. Shirley MacLaine was slated to be the master of ceremonies but for unexplained reasons was in Paris that night. Danny Kaye and I both spoke, but the highlight of the evening was a phone conversation between the two of us and Shirley, broadcast to the whole audience. I, of course, knew her from our contacts in Tokyo, but the "How are you darling?" sort of conversation, especially when it is being trumpeted around a crowded banquet hall, is hardly my style, and I died a thousand deaths of embarrassment in trying to live up to being a Hollywood type "splendid American."

One of the best aspects of reentry into normal life was the chance for vacations and activities unrelated to my work. Our first winter back, some friends lent us their seaside home in Grenada, which had not then attracted worldwide attention as the scene of a glorious American military victory over no opposition but was simply the most remote, backward, and least known of the Lesser Antilles. Starting in January 1968, we sailed almost annually for more than a decade with Haru's childhood pen pal, Prestley Blake, in Florida waters in his 47-foot teak ketch built in Hong Kong. One year we varied our usual routine by sailing with him from Antigua to the Virgin Islands on the replica of the yacht *America,* which he owned for a while—the original *America* had been a mid-nineteenth-century craft from which the America Cup race derived its name. In 1971 Press married Setsu, the widow of Haru's only brother, Mako. Although the marriage did not last, it made our relations with him even closer, and he continues to treat Haru's only nephew, Nao, as a surrogate son.

⋅⋅§

The "reentry" process was not complete until Haru and I had established a permanent home. Unable to find a house we could both agree on, we ended up building a new one. A large wooded tract on Belmont Hill had been given to the Audubon Society for a bird sanctuary, but a small strip of it was devoted to a few housing plots of close to two acres each, and we were given first choice among these. The area is a lovely one, where Concord Avenue, the old road leading from Cambridge to Concord, suddenly changes from a city street into what appears to be a country lane, with woods on both sides. The old stone walls, which New England farmers built to surround their fields and pastures before they themselves pulled up stakes and moved out to the more fertile lands of the Midwest, run romantically through the trees. I had admired the spot ever since I had first come to Massachusetts in 1931, but we would never have dared build our own home if it had not been for our neighbor, Carl Tobiason. His experience and the fine craftsmen he employed produced for us a modest but beautiful home which has been our pride and joy ever since. Made of California redwood and built into the side of the gently sloping hill, it fits harmoniously into its forest setting. We kept its lines so simple that Japanese commonly take it for "modern Japanese architecture." We centered its internal decor around wide windows, which virtually bring its forest environment into the house, as well as a lot of warming sunshine in winter, as is done in Japan.

Because of late lingering spring snows, construction on the house did not start until early May 1967, but Tobiason had it completed in time for us to move in ahead of schedule in September. The building took a lot more work and decisions than I had anticipated, and the garden around required never-ending labor. This Haru provided for the most part, together with the farming skills she had acquired during World War II. She enriched the poor, thin soil and surrounded the house with rhododendrons, mountain laurels, forsythia, azalea, Japanese maples, dogwoods, pines, firs, and a wide variety of other decorative trees, bushes, and flowers, as well as a very productive vegetable garden and raspberry patch. I supplied the ax work in the forest and several years' worth of wood for the fireplace.

We built our house larger than the two of us needed in order to match the large plot of land on which it stood. In the lower floor we made a semi-separate apartment to house my father and sister, Felicia. Unfortunately, Felicia had a nervous breakdown just at this point. Her deafness had tended to cut her off from friends, and she had developed the habit of living her own independent life in a somewhat unreal world of her own making. In her present condition she proved quite incapable of being with her father, so I found her a separate apartment nearby where she stayed quite contentedly until my own failing health persuaded me in 1983 to move her to a home for the elderly deaf in the Los Angeles area, where she appears to be quite happy and Ann, by then settled in La Jolla in the San Diego area, can take responsibility for her. My father, however, lived in the apartment we built for him for three years, wielding his ax to clear up our woods and build our woodpile, until his failing strength made it advisable to move him in February 1970 to a home for retired missionaries in the Los Angeles area, where he died peacefully the next year, just short of his ninety-second birthday.

After his departure we gave the apartment free to a series of young couples usually engaged in postgraduate studies, in return for the added security of their presence in an isolated area and some help with the heavier garden work. Our experiences with these young couples were uniformly pleasant. They kept us in touch with the attitudes of a younger generation between our own children and grandchildren in age, and they themselves often became almost our surrogate children.

The move to our new house, coinciding as it did with my resumption of teaching in September 1967, marked the end of our period of transition as well as a reshuffling of our family arrangements. Joan found a suitable place in Cambridge. Meanwhile Ann and her family had transferred to Palo Alto in California, where Steve became a postdoctoral fellow at Stanford University for a few years before moving to La Jolla to take over a laboratory in the Salk Institute. Haru was already well reestablished in running a normal American-style household, and I plunged back into the regular teaching duties of a Harvard professor.

# 42
# Getting Back to Work

TEACHING at Harvard after 1967 was not very different for me from what it had been before I left for Tokyo, except that I no longer had any responsibility for language instruction or advanced courses in premodern Japanese history and in their place had assumed new duties in modern Japanese government and politics and American relations with East Asia. I resumed with pleasure my old place in the introductory Rice Paddies course, though it was now divided into one semester on China and one on Japan. The two halves at first drew roughly the same number of students, always well over one hundred each, but gradually the Japanese half began to draw ahead, reflecting the soaring American involvement with Japan. By 1985, some 700 applicants to the course had to be limited to 480 because of lack of seating space.

My new course on "Government and Politics of Modern Japan" initially took a lot of work to prepare. In size it varied between about 40 and 110 students. My course on "The United States and East Asia" was also new, but I shared it with several others, giving only the lectures on Japan. Together with Jim Thomson, who returned from government service at the same time I did, and later Peter Stanley, who became the dean at Carlton College, I gave an undergraduate seminar on American East Asian Policy, in which we read and discussed a number of books and the students, who were limited to twenty, wrote major term papers.

I frequently gave guest lectures in other professors' courses, and in the autumn of 1973, Roger Revelle, the creator of the University of California at San Diego, who was then teaching at Harvard, joined with me in organizing through Adams House a nondepartmental undergraduate seminar, which we labeled "The Future of the World." With such a title, we were mobbed by students, of whom we accepted sixty. The course, however, was a little chaotic, and we chose not to repeat it.

There was a noticeable falling off of graduate students as the employment situation for scholars worsened in the 1970s but a decided pickup in general interest in the study of East Asia, particularly Japan, which suddenly began to loom large as America's major economic partner and rival. With my enthusiastic support, we started an undergraduate concentration in East Asian Studies, which rapidly won a place of respect and prominence, attracting not just would-be specialists but students who saw in the study of East Asia as valid an approach to a liberal education as the study of the classics or American history. Today East Asian Studies is one of the larger fields of undergraduate concentration at Harvard. Under these circumstances the supervising of undergraduate senior theses and individual reading courses began to take more of my time than directing the dwindling number of Ph.D. students. I was content with this change of emphasis, because I felt there was more valuable teaching to be done at the undergraduate level, where students need to have their interest aroused and their energies channeled, than at the graduate level, where students are already well motivated and better able to guide themselves.

My course schedule was quite flexible, and I adjusted it to permit a large number of outside activities. In fact, I spent a major part of my time giving public speeches to various types of groups all over the country and from Montreal to Mexico City. Between speeches and different meetings, I made countless trips to New York City, often twice in a single week, and only slightly fewer to Washington and Chicago. Television appearances were also frequent, many of them from New York or Washington but increasingly through tapes made in Boston television studios or in my own home. Many of these taped interviews were for Japanese television, but a surprising number were for the official British network, the BBC, and some for the corresponding CBC of Canada and German and other European networks. At first, my speeches and television appearances tended to be reports on Japan, but gradually China policy became a major focus and then Vietnam. Eventually my main theme became the future of international relations as a whole and the need for more knowledge about the rest of the world.

I joined several committees which met more or less regularly. At Harvard, one was to plan the further development of East Asian studies there and another to organize and supervise the activities of the Institute of Politics, which ultimately became a part of the Kennedy School of Government. In time I also became a member of the executive committee of the Center for International Studies and joined a group in it which was studying Japanese defense problems, making occasional visits to Japan under the able direction of Ben Brown for discussions with Japanese scholars. A more lasting activity for me was service on the board of trustees of the Harvard Yenching Institute, which had played so large a role in my life before I went to Tokyo. I became a member of the board in 1968 and the chairman in 1970. During my chairmanship, John Pelzel, who had succeeded me as director in 1963, resigned and was followed by Albert Craig. Both were extremely able administrators who made my duties as chairman of the trustees quite easy.

Away from Harvard I participated in the work of the National Committee on United States–China Relations, chairing a huge meeting held in a New York hotel in March 1969. I became a regular member of the U.S. delegation to the United States–Japan Cultural Conference and its panels, attending meetings held in various places such as Washington and Hawaii. In 1972, the Japanese government created the Japan Foundation to further the study of Japan in other countries. Breaking my own rule, I took on the chairmanship of an American Advisory Committee, which met periodically in Washington to advise on general policy regarding the United States and to help decide on research and study awards made to American scholars. Another committee I joined was the Joint Committee for Japan of the Social Science Research Council and the American Council of Learned Societies, which under Jack Hall's chairmanship held periodic meetings at various interesting places, such as Estes National Park in the Rockies.

<sub>ᢌᢒ</sub>

After my return to Harvard, a constant stream of people came to interview or consult with me. Curiously, there were relatively few my first academic year, but they increased to a torrent the next year and flowed strongly for the next several years. Many Japanese scholars and younger bureaucrats and businessmen spent short periods of a year or more at Harvard. One of the most interesting was Sato Seizaburo, a young professor from Tokyo University who has since become a prominent member of Prime Minister Nakasone's personal "think tank." The Japanese Ambassador during these years was Haru's cousin Ushiba Nobuhiko, and we naturally saw quite a bit of him and his wife. An unusual member of the Harvard community during October 1970 was Lee Kuan Yew, the extremely capable, iron-fisted, but democratic president of the city-state of Singapore. He repeated his Harvard "sabbatical" in October 1977, and both times we had him for dinner.

An intriguing South Korean visitor was Sun Myung Moon, the now well-known head of the Unification Church and the so-called Moonies, who called on me twice. He somehow seemed to be less like a religious leader than a retired general, which is what I mistook him for when I once ran into him on a flight from Seoul to Tokyo. Kim Yong Sam, the democratic political leader, called on me more than once, and the leading Korean newspaper, the *Dong-A Ilbo*, interviewed me from time to time and asked me for articles which they would feature as a means, I suspect, of expressing a more unequivocal advocacy of democracy and human rights in Korea than they dared print as their own opinion.

My most frequent and interesting Korean visitor was Kim Dae Jung. In 1971 he won 46 percent of the vote as a democratic candidate for the presidency, though running against the incumbent military dictator, Park Chung Hee. Between 1971 and 1973 he conferred with me several times about what he should do to help establish a democratic system in Korea. I offered to arrange for him to spend a year at Harvard, doing research and writing; but the main question on his mind was whether he should return to Korea and almost certain imprisonment and possibly death or fight for democracy from outside the country. It is difficult to advise a man when his life is at stake, while you yourself are in a position to stand without danger on principle. He decided to go to Japan to confer with his supporters there and while in Tokyo was kidnapped the day after I had met with him and taken to Korea, apparently by the Korean CIA. The Japanese government, I have always felt, showed shameful weakness in not insisting on his immediate return since he had been seized by foreign agents on Japanese soil.

On one of my subsequent visits to Japan, I made a one-day trip to Seoul to see him. He was under house arrest at the time, but he and a group of his supporters were allowed to meet me at the airport, where we were surrounded by a wild scramble of newsmen and cordons of police. We had a chance to talk in his car driving to the city from the airport, and he turned up the radio very loud in his house so that we could talk there without fear of being bugged. The normal police guards around his house were greatly reenforced for the occasion. Little of course can be accomplished in a hurried trip of this sort, but its purpose was to demonstrate to the military dictatorship that Americans were concerned about Kim's fate. In December 1982 he was finally released from long imprisonment and allowed to come to the United States for recuperation from the many ills he had incurred during his seizure and imprisonment; but he returned again to Korea in early 1985, despite a suspended death sentence hanging over his head.

Between classes, hordes of visitors, many speaking engagements, and the meetings of various committees in and outside of Harvard, I was extremely busy and did not have as much time for scholarly reading and research as I would have liked, but I still managed to get in a great deal of writing. In the spring of 1967

I started a book published that autumn by Knopf, which I called *Beyond Vietnam: The United States and Asia*. It drew on the bitter lessons of the Vietnam experience to bring up to date the basic concepts I had already expounded in *Wanted: An Asian Policy*. These were that nationalism would protect the less developed countries from domination by the Soviet Union or China far better than our military power could and that in the less developed parts of the world we should rely first on local nationalism and the attractiveness of our own ideals of national independence and democracy, secondly on economic development, and only as a last resort on military power. At the end of the book I analyzed the problems of formulating an Asian policy and stressed the need for more knowledge of Asia on the part of the American public and improved education about Asia and other foreign areas in our schools—a theme I was to develop more fully in later writing.

In a way it was too early for me to have undertaken this book, for I was still too much influenced by my long period in government service and believed that the Vietnam War, however mistaken, could be won—a view I changed completely not long afterward. Though I may have rushed into writing the book too soon, I did have the good sense not to succumb to pressure from various publishers to write an account of my period as Ambassador. I was still too close to that experience to have much perspective. In addition, many of the chief actors were still involved in political life, and the issues of that time were extremely sensitive, making it impossible for me to have written about many of the things of most interest.

# 43
# Contacts with Washington and Japan

Dʟ URING these years, I was called to Washington from time to time for congressional hearings on problems involving Japan, China, and Korea, and once President Johnson invited me and three or four other scholars to confer with him about China policy. We sat together around the cabinet table in the White House, and I could see that he was trying to win understanding from the academic community. Nothing came of this meeting except an embarrassing incident in which Johnson mistook his own White House advisor on East Asian affairs for a member of the visiting group. It showed how disgracefully little the poor man was consulted.

Bill Bundy organized a more formal advisory panel on East Asia at the State Department, but this proved to be almost a complete failure. The group met only once, on April 26–27, 1968, and though I was asked to be chairman of the panel, even I was not included in any of the preparatory work. The purpose of the panel seemed more to win the support from its members for the administration's already determined policies than to seek our advice. Abe Rosenthal, the editor of *The New York Times,* who was one of the few nonacademic members of the group, showed his good sense by dropping out after the first day. However, we did accomplish one worthwhile thing. When informed that, in returning the Bonin and Volcano Islands to Japan, Iwojima would be retained by the United States because of the intensity of feeling about this island on the part of veterans organizations, the panel unanimously objected on the grounds that this would serve merely to perpetuate old animosities on both sides. The State Department apparently was won over, and Iwojima together with the other islands was restored to Japan later that year without a single voice of protest being raised.

I attended a great number of conferences made up of scholars, senators, congressmen, government bureaucrats, and top military figures, organized by the Brookings Institution of Washington and other organizations. One series of meetings at Brookings in the late autumn of 1968 was designed to produce a volume to serve as a policy guide for the new Washington administration. Kermit Gordon, the head of Brookings, was the editor, and Henry Kissinger was one of the contributors. The book was called *Agenda for the Nation,* and I wrote the chapter on "Transpacific Relations."

I also conferred individually with many senators from both parties who had become friends during my days at the Embassy. One was Teddy Kennedy, who one snowy day even sought me out in my office at Harvard. More frequently Jerome Cohen of the Law School organized strategy sessions at which a group of us from the Harvard faculty would meet with Teddy at Cohen's home.

On January 21, 1968, Bobby Kennedy and I were part of a panel discussion on CBS in Washington, after which he took me back for lunch at his home in McLean in Virginia. Then he persuaded me to join him, Ethel, and General Maxwell Taylor, the former Chairman of the Joint Chiefs of Staff, in a game of tennis. It was the first time I had held a tennis racket in my hand for close to a decade, but I handled myself creditably and was urged by Bobby to take up tennis again. Fortunately a Belmont Hill Club had been formed within a five-minute walk of our new house, and it had indoor and outdoor tennis and swimming facilities. For the next several years I became a faithful twice-a-week tennis player, though too ambitious exertions once put my right hand in a sling for almost a month with a broken bone and another time embarrassed me at a speech I gave in Texas, where I turned up with a shiny black eye from a collision with my huskier partner on the tennis court, making me look more like a prizefighter than a professor.

On March 31, I was in Los Angeles speaking at the Modern Forum between engagements in the Central Valley at Fresno, Modesto, and Sacramento, and one at San Diego State University. That was the night President Johnson announced his decision not to run for reelection. I listened to the broadcast of the news in my hotel room and as a result turned up a little late for the speech. Naturally the talk I gave was quite different from the one I had planned.

With Johnson out of the race, I felt that Bobby was perhaps the only person who could hold the nation together during this period of violent divisiveness over Vietnam. I realized that he was deeply hated by some elements in the country, but it seemed to me that only he could keep the outraged younger people and other disaffected elements securely on board and, with his charismatic appeal, carry enough of the people with him to form a solid majority in support of his liberal, anti-Vietnam policies. I therefore joined the host of people who were urging him to run for the presidency.

I had no intention of participating in Bobby's campaign myself, never having thought of myself as being involved in politics. When he faced a crucial final primary in California, however, he called me up, saying that I had urged him to run and now should follow through with some real support. The primary was on June 4, and I had only a little time between a speech at Connecticut College on June 2 and a scholarly conference being held at the University of Chicago on June 4–5. I caught a plane late on the 2nd which got me into San Francisco the same night, spoke there in behalf of Bobby the next morning, then engaged in a curious threeway presentation at a dinner meeting in Los Angeles that evening. Alan Cranston spoke in behalf of his own candidacy for the Senate, which turned out to be successful and launched him on his distinguished career. Myrna Loy, who had been one of my favorite film stars in my youth, spoke for the Republican cause, and I much admired her for her well-preserved good looks and the sincerity and patriotism of her political effort, though I felt she was not a serious match for me in a political debate. I, of course, pressed Bobby's cause.

The next morning was the primary election itself; since no electioneering was permitted, I headed for the conference in Chicago. At about 5:00 a.m. the following morning I was awakened in my hotel room by a phone call informing me of Bobby's assassination in Los Angeles and demanding my comments. I do not know what I said in my combined state of shock and sleep-drugged confusion, but several people later told me they heard my remarks repeated several times on national radio. I do not know of any event which so discouraged and saddened me. The meeting at the University of Chicago was held under a pall of gloom, and I mourned to see what seemed to me the end of the last good chance for a peaceful passage through a troubled time.

I did not take much part in the campaign after that, though on July 24 I joined a small group to draft a speech on Vietnam for Humphrey, who was the Democratic nominee for President. We produced a good document, clearly breaking with Johnson's past policies but not seeming to repudiate him. It was the sort of statement, I felt, that could win the presidency for Humphrey. He was pleased when he read it, but then mused, "I wonder who will clear this for me with the President?" My heart sank, for if he were not willing to beard Johnson himself, no one could do it for him. The speech was never given, and Humphrey lost to Nixon.

&

It is an unwritten rule that ex-ambassadors stay away from their country of service for a period of time to allow their successors to become fully entrenched. Haru and I were careful to absent ourselves from Japan for the first two academic years, but by the summer of 1968 it seemed safe for us to return. Perry Wolff, who was in charge of special features at CBS, had approached me on the possibility of doing an hour-long TV program on Japan, and the idea intrigued us. From September 5 to 17 we went out to Japan with Wolff, Igor Oganesoff, and their wives. Oganesoff, whom we had known in Tokyo as the correspondent of *The Wall Street Journal*, was the producer under Wolff as executive producer and was in charge of the camera work. In Japan we found ourselves still recognized by most of the people we encountered in the streets, and we had a chance to see many of our old friends. The Ohiras invited us for dinner, and Sato in his official residence conferred on me the Order of the Rising Sun, First Class. It is the highest award that can be given a foreigner, but I had been unable to accept it while still in government service.

This trip was sheer pleasure, freed as we were of Embassy duties and protocol, and the filming of the two of us at various places around Japan was not an arduous task. The real work came the next winter during repeated trips to New York, where I soon discovered that in television the picture overpowers the spoken word. I served as my own commentator, using a text drawn by Wolff from my various writings. Unfortunately much of the footage had been shot and edited by Oganesoff, who had a very different, more sensational view of Japan than I. I constantly felt as if I were trying to swim upstream against the powerful current of his pictures. In my frustration, I suggested abandoning the whole project several times, but Wolff, who was a genius of compromise as well as careful writing, managed to save the situation. The program was finally worked out to my satisfaction and was shown in prime time in April 1969 and again later that year. A member of the Federal Communications Commission remarked to me that more Americans learned something useful about Japan during that one-hour presentation than in all the lectures and college classes to date in American history. The program was well received and won a handful of Emmies. I personally was given a special one as "Commentator" in the "Cultural and Documentary Programming" category. Still suffering from a surfeit of formalities, I did not go to receive it at the awards ceremony in New York, but the somewhat tinny Emmy itself stands proudly, if a bit incongruously, among the books in my study.

Once the ice had been broken, Haru and I made frequent trips back to Japan, commonly going twice or more a year. In January 1969, I attended a Japanese-American meeting organized indirectly by the Japanese government and held at the International Conference Center in Kyoto. The purpose was to sound out the American side informally on the possibility of the return of Okinawa to Japan. Irredentist sentiment was at last beginning to become a serious problem for the Tokyo government, but it was reluctant to broach the subject openly for fear of an American rebuff, which would leave Tokyo in an embarrassing squeeze between popular Japanese clamor for reversion led by the opposition parties and the irritation of the United States government, whose goodwill and cooperation were necessary for Japan. Though contingency plans for the reversion of Okinawa had been worked out in Washington, the American military saw no reason to act on them unless the Japanese government demanded the return of the islands, but this the Japanese were too nervous to do. Meanwhile the situation grew progressively more explosive. On more than one occasion I had told Japanese officials, including Okawara Yoshio, later the Japanese Ambassador in Washington, that if Japan requested the return of Okinawa, I believed the United States would comply on terms acceptable to Japan, which meant with all nuclear weapons removed, as in the American military installations in Japan, a condition defined as *hondo-nami*, "the same level as the main islands."

I shared the chair of the 1969 Kyoto meeting with Takeuchi, whom I knew well as a former Vice Foreign Minister and Ambassador to the United States, the usual two crowning posts for the top men in the Japanese Foreign Ministry. The Japanese were not much interested in my views on the future of Okinawa, for they knew them well, but they were concerned about the opinions of the two retired military figures in the American delegation, General Maxwell Taylor and Admiral Arleigh Burke, a former head of the navy as Chief of Naval Operations. When they discovered that the two of them agreed with the scholars and others in our group in favoring the reversion of Okinawa, they were relieved and as a result, I believe, were emboldened to ask formally for the return of the islands. In any case, the communiqué issued by Sato and Nixon following their summit meeting in Washington in November 1969 promised the reversion of Okinawa within a few years, meaning after the war in Vietnam had calmed down; the islands did revert to Japan on the *hondo-nami* basis on May 15, 1972, becoming Japan's forty-seventh prefecture once more.

I was out in Japan again at the beginning of September 1969 to attend one of the early meetings of the Japan-American Assembly, held at Shimoda, the beautiful little port on the tip of the Izu Peninsula which was opened by Perry in 1854. The whole series of conferences came to be known from this first meeting place as the Shimoda Conferences. Both the discussions and the setting of this particular meeting were excellent.

Four months later, in January 1970, I was again in Japan, this time as a member of a five-man OECD (Organization for Economic Cooperation and Development) commission to study Japanese education. The OECD regularly made studies of various aspects of the economy or society of member nations by commissions made up of one person each from five or six of the other member states. Such studies were for the purpose of exchanging ideas and making recommendations when needed. We had a congenial group. Berry Hayward, an American member of the OECD secretariat, was our cheerful and able organizing officer, and we elected as our chairman Edgar Faure, who had twice been the French Prime Minister. He was a jovial man and in uncharacteristic style for a Frenchman was soon on a first-name basis with the rest of the delegation. I was told that he had been initially afraid that I would wish to be the chairman, but this was the last thing I wanted, while the position apparently meant something to him politically. Our interests, therefore, coincided perfectly, cementing our friendship. The most interesting member of the group was Ronald Dore of England, the brilliant student of Japanese society and in my judgment the outstanding scholar in the Japanese field in all Europe. He is in addition a delightful person, and it was a real pleasure to get to know him well on this trip.

We traveled around a bit, braving the frigid January weather in an inadequately heated though beautiful inn in Kyoto. One day on our travels we divided into two groups, and I noticed that the group I was with, unlike the other, was surrounded by policemen and patrol cars everywhere it went. I was puzzled until I later realized that we had that day passed through Mishima in Shizuoka Prefecture, the home of the youth who had stabbed me in 1964. The local authorities, I presume, were determined that there would be no embarrassing repetition of that incident.

In the summer of 1970 the Institute of International Education of New York held the first of a series of conferences between American and East Asian university presidents on the model of a similar series held by American and Latin American university presidents. The Institute asked me to be an advisor to the project and included me as one of the American members of the conferences. We all took our wives with us and had a very jolly as well as instructive time. The

Asian members of the group, several of whom were old friends of mine, came from Japan, South Korea, Taiwan, the Philippines, Hong Kong, South Vietnam, Thailand, Malaysia, Singapore, and Indonesia. We usually had trouble finding a suitable Japanese representative, because few of the presidents of leading Japanese universities spoke adequate English, and in any case they lacked the authority in their own institutions that most other East Asian and American presidents had. We met in June 1970 in Hong Kong, and in subsequent years at Nara; at Jogjakarta in Indonesia, near the magnificent medieval Buddhist monument of Borobudur; and at Chiengmai in northern Thailand, where I came down with a painful attack of shingles.

During June 1970, Haru and I were guests for four days at the Osaka International Exposition (Osaka Bampaku), since I had been selected to be the American representative in a series of lectures given by one person each from a number of foreign countries. In November 1972 I spoke in Kobe at a conference of PEN, the international club of writers, which looms large in Japan. I went somewhat against my will, having unintentionally become obliged to attend, and made the visit as quickly as I could, leaving Belmont on a Friday morning and returning in time for dinner the next Monday. The trip had been so quick my internal time clock never changed and for once I did not feel the ill effects of jet lag.

I took the occasion of a visit to Japan in 1971 to take a tour of inspection to Korea, Malaysia, Singapore, and Indonesia in the capacity of a trustee of the Asia Foundation, returning home by way of Australia. Haru and I also often went to Hawaii for meetings, sometimes in transit to or from East Asia, and we frequently visited Ann and her family in La Jolla on the way. In her typically unconventional style, Ann had moved her brood from Stanford to La Jolla in the summer of 1970 driving by way of Alaska. By the summer of 1971 when we stopped with them, the family had just reached completion with four boys and one girl—Nathan, Danton ("Danny"), Thadden ("Tad"), Eden ("Edey"), and Quentin.

In our many trips to Japan, Haru and I both noticed that the longer we stayed, the busier we became. We would arrive unnoticed except by the few who were connected with the specific reason for our coming, but gradually word would spread that we were there, and people would flock around in increasing numbers. Appointments and activities proliferated, until we were in a mad dash from morning to night. Only our departure could save us, but the last few hours before we left were likely to be a whirlwind of frenzied activities. We always boarded the plane with a sense of relief and the feeling that we did not want to return to Japan for a long time. In this and other ways, the aftereffects of our ambassadorial experience lingered on for many years.

# 44

# A Time of Troubles

Wᴴɪʟᴇ ɪ was in Japan in January 1970, Haru called me to say that some Harvard professors wanted me to be a candidate for election to the Faculty Council, which was being newly organized. This was exactly the sort of activity I wished to avoid, but I was embarrassed to admit it at a time of crisis, when the university was facing serious problems of student and faculty unrest. In any case, I was sure I would not be elected and therefore need have no fear of agreeing to be a candidate. Unfortunately, things did not work out that way. Unknown to me, a large part of the faculty had divided into radical and conservative factions, and I was being put forward by the conservative group as a person who would stand a good chance of election. Actually my name, I was told, was the first to clear the complicated electoral process.

Shortly after I returned to teaching at Harvard in September 1967, the situation had begun to turn sour, as it did all over the country. Unrest over Vietnam was the root cause; to it were added civil rights issues, the draft, the women's liberation movement, the proposal for Black Studies, historical revisionism, and the challenging of all authority and anything that could be classified as the establishment. The unrest overwhelmed campuses everywhere and concern over Vietnam policy was all-pervasive. As early as September 1968 I had argued against continuing the war in a hotly debated panel discussion on Vietnam at the annual meeting of the American Political Science Association held in Washington, and I spoke at a similar meeting held by Common Cause in Washington in March 1971, together with John W. Gardner, the founder of the organization, and General James Gavin, who led the parachute attack on Normandy in World War II. In October 1969 I participated in a huge open air gathering in front of the State Capitol building in Providence, Rhode Island. I was distressed by the revolutionary zeal of some of the speeches but comforted by the presence as a fellow speaker of Jerome B. Wiesner, the provost and later president of MIT.

The following May I spoke on Vietnam to an overflow audience in a big hall at the University of California at Berkeley. In view of the violence that the university was then experiencing, my hosts were extremely nervous; except for the temporary interruption of my talk by someone pulling out the wires of the broadcasting system, however, the evening went very well, and the crowd remained in a good mood. The only truly unpleasant incident I encountered during any of my speeches was at Union College in Schenectady, New York, when a young member of the faculty became abusive of me personally.

Campus violence first broke out at Columbia and Berkeley, then to everyone's surprise spread even to sedate Harvard. Administrative buildings were seized by student activists, and there was some vandalism. The Center for International Affairs, which then occupied the old Semitic Museum and was locally known as the CIA, was trashed, probably under the misapprehension that it was connected with the more famous institution with the same abbreviated name. The Center hastily changed its abbreviation to CFIA, as it is still known. ROTC was dropped from the university, and an Afro-American Studies program was inaugurated after several stormy faculty meetings. I myself approved of the concept of Afro-American Studies but was opposed to the way it was being set up as a special and therefore inherently inferior sort of department. Haste, I felt, would indeed make waste in the long run, which, I believe, is what did happen.

I found the student radicalism of the time most distressing, for I was all too familiar with it in Japan. It was understandable there because of the large depersonalized nature of the universities, the rigidity and lingering tradition of rote memory work in education, and the tremendous social and psychological upheavals Japan had been through. Somewhat similar conditions could explain student radicalism in Latin America and much of continental Europe. But there seemed less reason for it in the socially more stable and educationally freer and more personalized atmosphere of American education. I had assumed that American students would see that in a relatively free society evolution was a far more certain road to progress than revolution and that violence would produce more chaos than reform. But the pressures of the Vietnam War apparently swept typical American moderation away, and a generation of college students espoused the belief that they could create instant perfection through their own intransigence.

A college generation, however, is of brief duration. I had for long witnessed the mood on campus shift markedly about every six years, and I had no doubt that the radicalism of the Vietnam days would pass in due time, as in fact it did as soon as the war itself began to fade, leaving only a small and largely beneficial residue in a Harvard that was otherwise little changed. Regulations concerning student life were permanently relaxed, and new institutions permitted more student participation in decision making. Dress became very much more informal, going to extremes of sloppiness—even dirtiness—before swinging back to an aesthetically more desirable balance. Student demands for the abolishing of grades, as I argued at the time, were shown to be quite impractical, since this undermined the value of any academic record and threatened to push the need for the evaluation of skills off to the much less fair system of one-shot entrance examinations to postgraduate schools or avenues of employment, as is the situation in the much criticized examination system of Japan. The attack on the grading system did leave one unfortunate legacy in the considerable devaluation of grades, as intimidated professors got in the habit of handing out many more A's and B's than before. On the whole, however, the political radicalism of the time swung back like a pendulum toward apathy or conservatism, going for a while too far in these directions in recompense for the extremism of the earlier radical swing.

The most distressing aspects of the time of trouble for me were the ill will shown by both the student body and faculty and the wishy-washy confusion and timidity of much of the faculty. When Adams House held a discussion session between students and faculty, I was surprised to find myself the only faculty member present who was ready to discuss the problems rationally with the students and still more surprised to be praised by some of my colleagues for my "daring." Differences in scholarly interpretation are to be expected and encouraged, but it was upsetting to find some students engaging in acrimonious criticism of their teachers. I remember one of the assistants in the Chinese half of our Rice Paddies course exploding at a final discussion session in an emotional denunciation of the professors in the course and their ideas. An eloquent rebuttal by the Indian head tutor in the course, who had studied for several years in Communist Peking, was all that saved the situation. Differences of opinion in the faculty gave rise to similar personal attacks, and faculty meetings turned from rational debate to political maneuvering, which I feel should have no place in academic life.

In my own field of modern Japanese history, the whole radical movement was accompanied by an attack on previous interpretations as the "conventional wisdom." I did not mind that the "conventional wisdom" being held up to ridicule was often the ideas I had expressed in my books. Scholarly progress is normally made by new generations rejecting or refining the concepts of their immediate predecessors. But I did regret to see this process take the form of a return to Marxist interpretations, from which my earlier students and I had attempted to liberate American analysis of Japanese history. Not unexpectedly, this wave in turn has passed, and historical interpretations have returned to a better balance in which ideologies play little part.

The large and frequent meetings of the Faculty of Arts and Sciences faced a great increase in complicated issues to be handled and an even greater rise in the heat of debate. It was for this reason that a Faculty Council to serve as a sort of steering committee had become necessary. During most of my service at Harvard before and after that time the problem was always to muster enough participants in faculty meetings to make a decent showing. Now the problem was to steer necessary legislation through an excited and unruly body of scholars cramming a much larger meeting place.

I did not in the least enjoy my work on the Faculty Council, but I could not complain, having allowed myself to be entrapped. The first meeting I have recorded in my appointment book was on March 25, 1970, and my term of membership apparently expired in the summer of 1972. I do remember having determinedly refused to run for reelection. To be considered a member of the conservative "party" was a new experience for a lifelong liberal like myself, but the tenor of the times, just like the atmosphere in Japanese politics, had placed my type of moderation on the conservative side. I feel more comfortable now that subsequent shifts in political opinion have restored me to my accustomed position somewhat left of center.

John T. Dunlop, of the Department of Economics and one of the leading labor negotiators in the country, served as the extremely skillful and judicious dean of the Faculty of Arts and Sciences during this time of trouble, and a change in the presidency of the university also took place. Nathan Pusey, who had borne the main brunt of the student onslaught, retired at the end of the academic year in June 1971. Much of the faculty had turned viciously against him, accusing him of undue rigidity, and failing to appreciate his effort to stand by his principles. At the last meeting of the Faculty of Arts and Sciences over which he presided on May 18, there was no general effort to mark the occasion appropriately, but some people suggested to me that I should offer a resolution of appreciation. This is not the sort of thing I am very good at, but *faute de mieux* I complied, hoping to show that there were many of us who appreciated Pusey's good intentions and sterling character. Derek Bok, the dean of the Law School, was officially installed as his successor the next October; he appointed my former student, Henry Rosovsky, as the new dean of the Faculty of Arts and Sciences.

While the university and nation were having their time of trouble, our family too was passing through a difficult period. Haru suffered what we felt was a delayed reaction to the overwork and strain of our Embassy days and the special burdens imposed on her by my stabbing. Ever since that incident, she had felt a decided decline in spirit. When she developed back troubles in 1969 from working too hard in the garden and was as a consequence deprived of one of her chief pleasures, she slipped into a prolonged state of depression. It had become pronounced by the beginning of 1970 and lasted about three years. Professional aid proved of little value, because no one else could possibly comprehend her background or the strains of her Embassy experience. Among her friends, Ed Wagner's Korean wife, Nam-hi, was the most understanding and helpful, getting Haru to take up pottery making. Still more helpful was some work she began to do outside of our home. John Pelzel and I persuaded her to take charge of the housing for the Harvard Yenching Institute's Visiting Scholars. This involved her in menial chores, such as scrubbing out dirty apartments, as well as more managerial work like devising a system of permanently rented apartments. It was a curious situation to have me at the top of the Institute's hierarchy as the chairman of the board of trustees and Haru at the other end as hourly wage labor. But it was effective; slowly she came back until she was fully restored to her usual efficient, hardworking, and cheerful self.

Haru was completely well by the summer of 1973, when we had a glorious family reunion on Cape Cod during the month of August. Katie Louchheim had a pleasant summer home at Chatham, one of the loveliest parts of the Cape, and a mutual friend there lent us a splendid big summer house on seven choice acres of land, situated between the waters of an inlet and a swampy piece of land she had donated to the Audubon Society as a bird sanctuary. The house itself was close to two hundred years old, with the distinctive broad wood floorboards of that period. To the original home had been added a large kitchen and pantry area and servants quarters, providing ample room for our whole family. Ann, Steve, and their five children drove from California in their truck, and Bob, his family, and Joan were also with us.

Joan was still living in Cambridge at this time, having taken several jobs in Boston after graduating from Tufts, ending up in the publicity side of the publishing business. We naturally saw her quite often throughout the year, and the same was true of Bob and his family. After completing his Ph.D. in economics at Columbia, he had gone to Washington, where he was a member of the research staff of the Brookings Institution. Before leaving New York, he and his wife Charlotte had had a daughter, Alyssa, in February 1969, and in the autumn of 1972 they had adopted a Korean baby boy, who arrived by plane in March. On the plane he had been referred to as "Ambassador Reischauer's baby," probably raising some speculation and eyebrows among the people in charge. By coincidence, before giving a speech in Cincinnati a few days later, I happened to sit at dinner beside the woman who had just served as the baby's escort to the United States, and she was quite eager to find out who "Ambassador Reischauer's baby" really was. Bob and Charlotte named him Tae to preserve some of his Korean heritage, but he has since changed his name to Peter and is an all-around American boy.

With Ann's family of seven and Bob's of four, we numbered fourteen in all, which rose to fifteen when my sister, Felicia, joined us for a week, or Haru's then widowed mother visited us from Japan. We had a glorious month together, and in 1974, when we were again lent the house, this time for two months, we had an even more wonderful time. Unfortunately our benefactrice sold the house the next year. For this and other reasons, there was no general family reunion in 1975; but in 1976, 1977, and one final time in 1980 the family rallied around again in

Belmont, with the grandchildren camping out in tents in the woods behind our house. After that Ann's older children grew too mature for family summers, and it became impossible to assemble the whole brood at one time. But those were wonderful summers while they lasted, and pictures of them line our kitchen wall as reminders.

# 45
# New Activities

OCTOBER 15, 1970, was my sixtieth birthday, and four of my close associates and former students—Al Craig and Don Shively of Harvard, Jack Hall of Yale, and Marius Jansen of Princeton—organized a surprise banquet for me. Suggested to me as a black-tie dinner at Don's house, it turned out to be a big affair at the Faculty Club, attended by many of my former students and friends.

One's sixtieth birthday, known as *kanreki* in Japan, marks in East Asia the traditional end of one's active career, being the completion of a cycle of sixty years, which is the way time was formerly figured in that part of the world. We had noted Elisséeff's *kanreki* with some special publications, and a big dinner had been put on for John Fairbank's. Now it was my turn. I find such occasions horribly embarrassing—I always feel for those who are coerced into coming—but I appreciated the thought and the handsome volume prepared for the occasion, which was entitled *Personality in Japanese History* and was dedicated to me. It had been edited by Craig and Shively and contained chapters by them and a large number of my former students.

Despite this reminder that my career was nearing its end, I found myself busier than ever and even became involved in several new activities. I had already made one television program in 1968–69, but during the 1970s I got more deeply into television work. At the CULCON subcommittee meeting at Hilo, Hawaii, in June 1973, D. B. ("Woody") Varner, the president of the University of Nebraska, who was a member of the American delegation, proposed to me that I take the lead in preparing a television course on Japan for the University of Mid-America, which was a consortium of Great Plains state universities organized to make television programs for isolated schools in that area. They had marvelous facilities at Lincoln, Nebraska, but their first course on mathematics had not proved very popular, and their second on the culture of the Great Plains, organized under the famous American historian Henry Steele Commager, sputtered out. The jump to Japan seemed a big one, yet it was an interesting challenge. I agreed to take on the task, but only if I could obtain the aid of Jackson Bailey of Earlham College in Richmond, Indiana. He had been one of my students and had proved a remarkable organizer of programs on Japan in the small private colleges of the Midwest. Bailey agreed, and in September we all met in Lincoln to plan the project. On the plane on the way out, I drafted an outline for fifteen half-hour shows. My draft was enthusiastically received, and, at the suggestion of some obscure member of the project who soon disappeared from it, we casually agreed to double it to fifteen full hours.

We did not realize what we were getting ourselves into. The task stretched out over the next five years, proving much harder than I had ever imagined. I went out to Lincoln repeatedly for three- or four-day periods, working on scripts and sometimes doing on camera presentations myself. But the bulk of the load fell on Bailey, who, with his talented wife Caroline, devoted great chunks of time to it, including whole semesters. He had to wrangle incessantly with the directors and cameramen selected by the University of Mid-America, who knew nothing about Japan and constantly kept changing, and he also had to worry about collecting the necessary funding, a good bit of it from Japan. He deserves infinitely more credit for the success of the project than I. The fifteen hour-long programs covered a brief sketch of Japanese history, outstanding aspects of Japanese culture, and a survey of the situation in contemporary Japan. The first half was completed by the spring of 1976 and the remainder by September 1978, when it was first tested out in public showings in New York and Washington. The programs are still used fairly extensively in high schools and colleges, especially in the Great Plains states and North Carolina, and sometimes on public television.

Another less taxing television undertaking came up early in 1974. I was approached by an enthusiast for Japanese films named Sheldon Renan to be the commentator—the Alistair Cooke role—for thirteen well-selected Japanese films with English subtitles to be shown on the Public Broadcasting System. The financial backers of the project wanted serious sociological commentaries by someone like myself to ensure the intellectual value of the undertaking. Japanese films are scarcely my field of competence, but Renan assured me that Donald Richie, the well-known authority on the subject, would prepare suitable texts for me to deliver on camera at the beginning of each film and again at a break in the middle. We worked on the project in May and June 1974, doing the filming of my appearances at WGBH, the local PBS station in Boston. Once again the undertaking proved much more difficult than I had expected. Richie had prepared long, rambling essays, which were entirely unsuitable for television, so I had to write my own texts for each of the films, merely drawing in places on Richie's material. For publicity purposes, I attended the openings of the programs in early January of 1975 in San Francisco, New York, Washington, and Chicago. The whole project was very successful, and the series was shown extensively and repeatedly on PBS stations. I learned a great deal about Japanese films and came to the conclusion that Kurosawa Akira's *Ikiru (To Live)* was the most moving film I had ever seen.

An undertaking of a very different sort was the founding of the Trilateral Commission, which was designed originally to bring Japan more fully into the activities of the industrialized democracies and to strengthen its ties with Western Europe. America's contacts with Japan on the one side and Western Europe on the other were intimate and strong, but the bonds between Japan and Western Europe were weak. David Rockefeller, the banker, stood behind the effort, and Gerard C. Smith, the former chief American negotiator at the Strategic Arms Limitation Talks (SALT), acted as the chairman of the American Executive Committee; but Zbigniew Brzezinski, later President Carter's chief advisor on security matters, was the prime mover in organizing the Commission and served as its dynamic first executive secretary. I had known Zbig since his days at Harvard, and I had been much impressed by his perspicacity in spotting the rising importance of Japan and spending a half year there in 1971, from which experience he produced a quite creditable book entitled *The Fragile Blossom: Crisis and Change in Japan.* I served as a member of the organizing group and the American Executive Committee, together with such people as Cyrus R. Vance and Paul C. Warnke, the chief negotiator at the SALT talks under Carter.

In the winter of 1974–75 I was requested by some prominent Japanese to write a letter of support for the nomination of Prime Minister Sato for a Nobel Peace Prize. I had earlier done the same for former Prime Minister Yoshida, though without success, but I was later told that my letter for Sato was one of two that had the most influence in inducing the committee to select him for the award. His choice mystified people everywhere, not least the Japanese themselves; but if the committee did in fact follow my reasoning, there was plenty of justification for it. I argued that the Japanese people as a whole had been staunch supporters of peace ever since the end of World War II and that, since a group award could not be made, Japan's long-term Prime Minister was a suitable recipient as the representative of the Japanese people. I felt that awarding the prize to Sato certainly made more sense than the awards the preceding year to Henry Kissinger and Le Duc Tho of North Vietnam, who had escalated and prolonged a senseless war and had achieved a peace that was clearly only a respite before a final military dénouement.

An unpleasant new task which occupied much of my time in the early 1970s was the raising of funds for Japanese studies at Harvard. By then universities all over the country were running into financial difficulties, and aid from both the government and large foundations for special fields of study, such as East Asia, was beginning to dry up. Meanwhile inflation was increasing costs alarmingly. Harvard faced a particularly serious problem in the East Asian field because it had such a large library, the costs of which kept going up at a dramatic rate. The university authorities made it quite clear that it was up to us in the field to fi..d the new resources we needed to maintain or expand our area of scholarship.

Faced with this challenge, we created a Council on East Asian Studies to coordinate the work in the field and raise new funds for it. The Council never did much coordinating, but it did spark some money-raising efforts. Despite my determination to avoid administrative work, I found myself forced to play a leading role in organizing the Council and seeking funds. Fairbank and I were called on to make many speeches around the country and approach possible sources of money, largely, I am afraid, without success. However, an unexpected gift by the Mitsubishi interests in Japan through Jerome Cohen for the establishment of a chair of Japanese legal studies in the Law School suggested to me that Japan might be a fruitful source of support. Japanese business was booming, and knowledgeable Japanese saw that a well-informed American public was of vital interest to Japan. Such attitudes made me feel that some Japanese might respond to an appeal for financing for Japanese studies at Harvard.

In order to make our proposals clearer in Japan, we created a Japan Institute, of which I was forced to be the director, though the detailed work was undertaken by Don Shively as the executive director. The Institute planned to build a Japanese wing for the library, underwrite the increased needs of the library in the Japanese field, establish several new professorships, and expand research and other activities. All this we explained in a well-illustrated glossy pamphlet with texts in both English and Japanese. I suspect that this was the first bilingual effort of this sort that had ever been attempted by Occidentals. Armed with this pamphlet, I made a series of calls on the captains of Japanese industry in the summer of 1973. I was accompanied by Professor Michael Y. Yoshino of the Business School, who carried the ball during most of our presentations. Since Mike Yoshino was a relatively young man, I was amazed by how well he knew the business leaders of Japan, and still more by how well they seemed to know him. He deserves a great deal of the credit for our achievements that summer.

Early on, we enlisted the crucial support of Keidanren, the powerful Federation of Economic Organizations, sparked by Hanamura Nihachiro, the jovial and extremely able controller of Keidanren's financial dealings. The great automotive companies, Nissan and Toyota, came forth largely on their own to give us $1 million each. I remember the president of Nissan asking me to his office and almost casually handing me a check for the sum. In all, we asked the Japanese for $10 million, assuring them that we would find matching funds in the United States, a promise which to my shame still remains unfulfilled.

The Japanese came through with most of the $10 million they had promised, but the other hoped-for sources of funds provided very little. This necessitated a cutback in our plans for the Institute; it was, however, gratifying to see that Japanese Studies at Harvard were underwritten for some time into the future, even if at a more modest level. The raising of the funds I had found a most distasteful experience. Many of the Japanese business leaders I approached had responded with such statements as, "Since it is you, Mr. Reischauer, who asks, we, of course, must give." This always made me cringe, and I resolved never to get involved in a money-raising venture again.

Several other American institutions which faced similar financial straits were dazzled by Harvard's success and sent out expeditions to find more gold, but they had missed the bus. In the meantime the first oil shock had struck the world, throwing the Japanese business community into consternation. The mendicant American academician holding out his begging bowl became a familiar figure in Tokyo, but the bowls remained largely empty.

The Japanese donors to Harvard had been very insistent that they wanted their money spent exclusively for Japanese studies, not for China or other East Asian areas. They had the justifiable fear that their contributions might be used by Harvard to defray regular costs in the Japanese field, thus freeing funds for use for China and other countries. To see that this did not happen, I insisted on strict agreements governing the use of the money and made certain that the Japan Institute would have an unusual degree of independence in controlling the funds.

An entirely new type of activity for me was the joining of the boards of a few business firms. I started this in the autumn of 1970 by becoming a member of the board of the General Reinsurance Corporation, later renamed General Re, which was located in New York City and later in Greenwich, Connecticut. I took this step into business with some misgivings but was urged to do so by R. Keith Kane, a member of the Harvard Corporation, the ultimate controlling body of the university, who made the initial introductions. Having joined one board, adding a second in 1974 was a less difficult decision. This was the board of the Brunswick Corporation of Skokie in the suburbs of Chicago. In 1976 I joined a third board for a small investment fund for Japanese stocks, operated first by Nomura Securities, the biggest Japanese securities company, and later by Merrill Lynch of New York under the name of the Pacific Fund.

I initially knew nothing about the three different lines of business represented by these three companies. Reinsurance is an arcane art at best, and the gyrations of stocks puzzle even the experts. Only the activities of the Brunswick Corporation, which, though originally known as a firm specializing in bowling equipment had become a broadly based manufacturing company, were relatively easy to understand. I never had much to offer these companies and was involved in only four to seven meetings a year for each of them, yet I derived a great deal from my association with them. I came to know a side of American life I had never encountered before and had a chance to see business from the point of view of the big corporations. I often wished that I had had this experience earlier in my career, particularly before my service at the Tokyo Embassy. There were also some perquisites such as meetings sometimes held with wives present at interesting places like Hilton Head, South Carolina, and Scottsdale, Arizona. The Nomura–Merrill Lynch Board had an annual meeting in Japan, but I was already surfeited by trips there. The pay scale of these businesses was a personally gratifying surprise, but the discrepancy between it and government and academic wages seemed to me a shocking anomaly.

وهي

After seven years of uninterrupted teaching, I decided to take the autumn of 1974 off as a sabbatical. Haru and I went out to Japan in October, and I proceeded on to Hong Kong for what was known as the Williamsburg Conference IV. The first Williamsburg Conference, which I had attended, had been organized by John Rockefeller at Williamsburg, Virginia, in April 1967 and had given its name to the whole series. The conferences were attended by intellectual leaders from the West Pacific—from Japan to Australia—and also from the United States. In Japan I gave numerous speeches and Haru and I appeared several times on television. Among the friends we saw were the Crown Prince and Princess, who invited us to their private quarters in their palace, where he had a tank of fish and she her harp. Ostensibly the invitation was for tea, but in actuality we had a very nice Japanese supper.

The most interesting aspect of our stay in Japan in 1974 was its coinciding with the visit on November 18–22 of President Gerald Ford, the first President to visit Japan while in office. The sensitivity over President Eisenhower's aborted trip in 1960 and the Vietnam War now lay safely in the past. I was touched to discover that at a large luncheon for Ford held at the Prime Minister's official residence, except for the President's official party, the only foreigners included were the dean of the diplomatic corps, who represented all the ambassadors, and myself. I was obviously there not as a foreigner but as a prominent semi-resident of Tokyo. Before we sat down to lunch, I ran into Donald Rumsfeld, who insisted that I come into a smaller adjoining room where a select few were being introduced to Ford. As I approached, Kissinger, who was standing beside Ford,

Back in America with the family: (from left) Joan, Tad and Haru, EOR, Nathan and Ann, great-grandfather, Bob, Charlotte, Danny and Steve, 1966.

Lifelong friend and colleague Hugh Borton, 1966.

Flanked by Governor Volpe and President Nathan Pusey, EOR delivers the post-Commencement address at Harvard after being awarded an honorary degree, 1967.

The grandchildren (Peter, Quentin, Alyssa, Edey, Tad, Danny and Nathan) dressed in Hapi coats brought them by Haru's mother, at Cape Cod, 1974.

Momentary calm in Belmont garden, 1980. From left: Steve Heinemann, Quentin, Peter, Charlotte Reischauer, Haru, Bob, Alyssa, EOR, Joan, Danny, Bill Simon, Edey, Nathan, Ann, Tad. (Harvard T-shirts, kindness of Haru.)

With Albert Craig in Harvard office.

With Joan's children, Katie and Richard, 1984.

glowered at me with the fiercest look I have ever seen. This was because on the day Ford's party had arrived the papers had carried prominently a statement I had made criticizing Kissinger's foreign policy. Exactly the same thing had happened the last time Kissinger had been in Japan. Both times it was mere happenstance, since I was continually attacking his policies, especially his having recognized China without informing the Japanese in advance; but he was furious that a fellow American and friend should be criticizing him, the Secretary of State, while abroad. I felt differently about it, because as a private citizen I considered myself as free to criticize the American government in Japan as in the United States.

New activities occupied much of my time in the early 1970s, but my more regular work went on as usual. In addition to my teaching and outside lecturing, I did a great deal of writing, especially for Japanese publications. I made such extensive revisions in my *Japan Past and Present* series that I gave a new name to the 1970 edition—*Japan: The Story of a Nation*. This I further revised and brought up to date in 1976. The two-volume *East Asia* history which John Fairbank, Al Craig, and I had written together, we rewrote and brought out in 1973 as a single handsome volume of close to 1,000 pages.

In 1968 I had been asked by the Harvard University Press to serve as editor of their American Foreign Policy Library series, in which my own *The United States and Japan* had been published. I did not prove much good at finding authors for the series, but I did enjoy passing on the acceptability of manuscripts and sometimes helping to shape them. The works covered such diverse lands and areas as Germany, Italy, Poland, Ireland, Scandinavia, the Balkans, various groups of Latin American countries, China, India, Burma, Malaysia, and the Arab world. I found it stimulating to turn my attention even briefly to such different areas, and enjoyed writing Introductions for the various volumes.

I brought out only one entirely new book during these years. This was a small work entitled *Toward the 21st Century: Education for a Changing World*, which was published by Knopf in 1973. In my public speaking I had been gradually moving toward a broad brush analysis of the mounting international problems, particularly the growing frictions among the advanced industrialized democracies and between them and the Communist nations and the less developed Third World. Ultimate worldwide catastrophe seemed to me all too likely. The only long-term solution I could see was a great deal more understanding and cooperation within the group of advanced democracies, and the gradual incorporation of the other two groups into the community of free trading nations that the advanced democracies were building.

To achieve these goals, the people of all countries, I concluded, would have to develop a less parochial attitude toward international relations and come to see themselves as world citizens. For this, a profound restructuring of education would be necessary. The emphasis in education could no longer be just on the glorious traditions and history of one's own nation but should be on the achievements of mankind as a whole. The advanced democratic nations like the United States and Japan, I felt, would have to lead the way, since the problems of international relations were most pressing for them as worldwide economic powers and their opportunities for showing leadership were the greatest. This sermon I had given orally countless times, but now I tried to put it down in brief written form. The book caused no sensation, receiving only a few tepid reviews, yet the response I have gotten to it over the years shows that it did have a wide impact among groups interested in education and world affairs.

# 46

# Slowing Down

My YEARS after returning to Harvard in 1966 were not only very fulfilling but also extremely busy. I remember marveling that I seemed more vigorous as I approached my mid-sixties than I had been in my thirties and forties. There were limits, however, especially because of the liver ailments incurred from my stabbing in 1964. A breaking point came suddenly on February 20, 1975. I had just returned from a week's trip, speaking for Jay Rockefeller at West Virginia Wesleyan College, of which he was then president, spending two days working on the television course in Nebraska, speaking in Chicago, and addressing the National War College in Washington. I had ten out-of-town speeches and meetings lined up for the next two weeks. But just after lunch on February 20 my speech became slurred and my right arm went numb. My secretary rushed me to the hospital, where it was discovered that I had suffered a stroke.

Recovery was slow. Although my mind cleared within a few days, the partial paralysis of my right side took longer to pass, gradually merging with the numbness of parts of my right leg from the stabbing and leaving a permanent stiffness in my right hand, which made my manuscripts all the more of a challenge for my long-suffering secretaries. The continued impairment of my speech was a more serious problem. It took a conscious effort to articulate my words at all clearly, and the slightest fatigue would show up in noticeable slurring. I found it almost impossible for a few years to pronounce words like "literature" which had more than one "l" or "r." This together with greatly increased difficulty in finding the name or word I was seeking would force me to clumsy circumlocutions. My whole rate of speech slowed down markedly. Previously I had found myself inadvertently supplying words to slow speakers, probably to their great irritation, but now it was I for whom others supplied words. This was all intensely bothersome, and my public speaking skills never recovered to what they once had been. It was distressing to have one of my chief assets greatly impaired. Equally distressing was the loss of my competence in foreign languages, including even Japanese. The greatly increased effort required for proper articulation threw off my rhythm of speech, and I lost confidence to such an extent that in time I all but abandoned efforts to speak Japanese, though of course I retained my comprehension of it.

After my stroke I clearly had to curtail my activities. I was forced to abandon my classes for the remainder of the semester, returning only for the final lecture on April 30 in the Rice Paddies course on Japan, and I canceled my speaking and meeting schedules until late April. Thereafter I slowly began to return to some of my activities, especially television appearances and interviews with newsmen, as well as my tennis games, but I never resumed the frantic pace of the earlier years. Many activities I terminated permanently, resigning from several committees and organizations. I returned to my normal teaching schedule in the autumn, though I shared my course on the "Government and Politics of Modern Japan" with another younger scholar from then on. The first year, Nathaniel Thayer of the School of Advanced International Studies of Johns Hopkins in Washington and my former Press Attaché in Tokyo, came up to Harvard for a semester to join me in the course and offer others himself. In subsequent years Terry MacDougall usually shared the course and in some years Kent Calder.

I was still rather shaky and unsure of myself when the Japanese Emperor and Empress visited Washington at the beginning of October 1975 on what was the first trip to the United States of a reigning Japanese monarch. Haru and I were invited by the President and the Emperor to the white-tie banquets each gave. I felt quite emotional about these occasions because I knew how much the trip to America meant to the imperial couple, and had prepared a flowery statement of greeting to the Emperor in Japanese, but it evaporated when upon seeing me he smiled broadly and said *"Shibaraku,"* which is the standard colloquial greeting for a friend one has not seen for some time. After the President's banquet there was a musical presentation and then dancing, at which we ran into Kissinger and he flashed his ready wit with, "Well, you can tell I didn't make up the guest list."

Slowly I got back into the routine of making out-of-town trips, principally to give speeches. I also began to attend again the board meetings of the firms I was connected with. In January 1977 I went for a conference as far as Hawaii for the first time since my stroke, and in May I went to Japan for some lectures in Nagoya.

My close friend Ohira Masayoshi became Prime Minister in December 1978 and made a visit to Washington the next May. Fearing that the Carter administration might not fully appreciate his fine qualities and solid friendship for the United States, I wrote a detailed letter about him to Fritz Mondale, the Vice-President and my cousin's son-in-law. I never received a reply, but the letter was obviously taken seriously by someone. When Haru and I went to Washington to attend the President's dinner for Ohira, I was informed that Ohira was anxious to see me at Blair House, the official guest house across Pennsylvania Avenue from the White House. He told me that Carter had mentioned the letter to him, and he seemed to credit it with some of the warmth of his reception in America.

Haru and I went to Japan again in June 1979 for speeches in Kobe at Kwansei Gakuin University, which provided us with as plentiful police protection and patrol car escorts as we had ever had even in our days at the Embassy. On this trip or perhaps on our next one in May 1980, I made a special point of calling on Ohira at the official residence of the Prime Minister, just for the pleasure of seeing him in this position, which I had always felt sure he would occupy some day. Shortly after my second trip, however, on June 12 Ohira suddenly died. It was a tragic loss for Japan and the world, for he was a man who had the wisdom, strength, and political skill to be a great leader.

Although my stroke had greatly impaired my speaking skills, my ability to write continued little changed. The Harvard University Press wanted an update of *The United States and Japan,* but this book had become like a layer cake, with writing reflecting the highly diverse conditions in Japan in 1949, 1956, and 1964. Since adding another layer based on the situation in the mid-1970s would risk having the whole compilation collapse from its many inconsistencies, I decided to begin afresh and write an entirely different book. I started in the summer of 1974, then threw away this beginning as being too lengthy and made a fresh start again the next summer after my stroke.

Called simply *The Japanese,* this was, I believe, the best of all my writings. The Harvard University Press was pleased and, instead of bringing it out in the American Foreign Policy Library series, selected it for special, very handsome publication as one of the Belknap Press series. The book contains a short section on Japan's geographic setting, a somewhat longer but still very brief outline of its history, then three lengthy sections on the nature of Japanese society and the psychology of the people, the modern Japanese government and the political process, and finally Japan's place in world affairs. *The Japanese* got good reviews and sold extremely well, making the best-seller list in Washington for several weeks, and it did even better in Japanese translation as *Za Japanizu.*

A smaller writing project was a long chapter on Japan for Karl W. Deutsch's *Politics and Government: How People Decide Their Fates.* In this chapter, which was also used in his *Comparative Government: Politics of Industrialized and*

*Developing Nations,* I emphasized that, while the Japanese political system differed in some respects from those of the other major democracies, particularly the presidential system of the United States, it was every bit as democratic and efficient in translating the popular will into government policy. Fairbank, Craig, and I also split up our large *East Asia* book into separate volumes on China and Japan, and in the spring of 1981 I brought out a thorough revision and updating of *Japan: The Story of a Nation,* which best expresses my interpretation of Japanese history. A publication of a different sort was the nine-volume Kodansha *Encyclopedia of Japan,* completed in 1983, for which I served as the chairman of the American Advisory Committee and wrote an Introduction. My corresponding figure on the Japanese Advisory Committee was my old friend Tsuru Shigeto.

꒛

During these years I became deeply involved in Henry Rosovsky's plan for a "core curriculum" for undergraduates at Harvard. I was a member of several different bodies which worked on this plan, and I believe that a strong appeal I made to the main steering committee in November 1976 for an international element in the core curriculum was in part responsible for this aspect of the project, though Rosovsky's own background as a specialist in Japanese economic history was of course a key factor in its adoption. The plan for a requirement in "foreign cultures," as it was called, specified a half-course on the history, society, or culture of some alien area. The English-speaking countries were ruled out as being too similar to the United States, and courses on lands with the more familiar European languages were to have the reading done basically in the native language. The important point was that hereafter no student could graduate from Harvard without having had some sophisticated exposure at the college level to the civilization of some very different area. This had been a goal of mine all my career, though at first it had seemed entirely unattainable in my lifetime.

In 1977, I served as a member of a Summer Working Force to draw up specific plans for the core curriculum, being assigned with another professor to work on the foreign cultures element. I had the Rice Paddies course in mind as a model, because it was ideally suited to meet not just the foreign cultures aspect but also part of the historical studies requirement. This sort of killing two birds with one stone was promised by the advocates of the core curriculum as a means of lessening its burden. Once the whole scheme was approved and set into motion, I joined a committee under Ezra Vogel to supervise the administration of the foreign cultures requirement.

When the final vote on Rosovsky's core curriculum was taken in the faculty, Henry asked me to be the person to defend the foreign cultures component. I was all primed for the occasion, but the natural scientists and the scholars in the humanities were so busy fighting over their respective shares in the core curriculum that the question of foreign cultures was never brought up. I noted also that it was the one aspect of the plan that drew no student criticism. The inclusion of the study of foreign areas as part of a college education was becoming accepted as a matter of course.

In 1978, I was asked by Washington if I would be willing to head up a Presidential Commission on Foreign Languages and International Studies. I declined in view of my health but agreed to serve as a member. The Commission first met in Washington in October of that year under the able and vigorous chairmanship of James A. Perkins, the former president of Cornell. Among its members was Congressman Paul Simon of Illinois, who has since been elected to the Senate and was, I believe, the prime mover behind the creation of the Commission. The project was designed to foster the type of educational reforms I had advocated in *Toward the 21st Century,* but the times were not propitious. Efforts at cutting the budget made Washington unreceptive to any suggestion that might require money, and I doubt that President Carter was much interested despite the loan of his title for the Commission. At the start of its deliberations, he even failed to give us his blessing in person, substituting Zbig Brzezinski for himself at the last minute. We met diligently several times in Washington and at hearings around the country and submitted our report in November 1979. It was full of fine ideas but produced no great results.

The usual stream of visitors continued during these years, and the number of advanced Japanese scholars working temporarily at Harvard grew rapidly. Among the more interesting brief visitors was Asukata Ichio, who was the first chairman of the Japan Socialist Party to visit the United States. He and the delegation he headed did not receive much attention in Washington; the discussion I arranged for them at our home on November 18, 1979, with a group of prominent Harvard professors was said to have been virtually the high point of their visit to America.

My pace of activity had gradually increased over the years following my stroke, until I was once again overdoing. Following a family reunion with our three children and their families in early August 1980, Haru and I went for a few days to the Louchheim summer home at Chatham on Cape Cod. There on August 24 I played tennis too long in the hot sun, took unwisely heavy doses of aspirin the next day at the suggestion of a local doctor, persisted in going through with an unusually long television taping for a Japanese network, and then collapsed on the kitchen floor early the next morning with serious internal bleeding. A team of paramedics from the local fire department managed to get me by ambulance to a small hospital in Hyannis, where my condition was stabilized enough by evening to permit my transfer by ambulance to a hospital in Boston.

The hospital room soon became so buried in elaborate bouquets of flowers that I felt I was attending my own funeral.

The impression of participating in my own last rites was heightened by various honors that followed my brushes with death. Shortly after my stroke in 1975 I had been elected an honorary member of the Japan Academy, which had only ten non-Japanese honorary members, of whom only two others were Americans and most were famous natural scientists. In 1975 I was also given the Japan Foundation Award as the fourth individual so honored. I had been delighted when my old mentor, Serge Elisséeff, had been the first in 1973, and later I was gratified to see old colleagues and former students added to the list: Jack Hall in 1976, Burton Fahs in 1979, Hugh Borton in 1980, and Donald Keene in 1983. An honor of a different sort was bestowed on me in 1984 when Johns Hopkins University named its center for East Asian studies at its School of Advanced International Studies (SAIS) in Washington the Edwin O. Reischauer Center. The fact that George Packard, my former personal aide in Tokyo, was the dean of SAIS helps explain this development. My colleagues at Harvard followed suit the next year by renaming the Japan Institute the Edwin O. Reischauer Institute of Japanese Studies. Now whenever I enter either place I feel that my black-draped picture on the wall would be more appropriate than my ambulatory presence in the flesh.

All these honors were reminiscent of what Japanese facetiously call being made an *o-mikoshi*, the portable Shinto shrine and deity traditionally carried around the streets by boisterous young men on the festival day of the local shrine. In Japan, being called an *o-mikoshi* is the equivalent of our less courteous phrase of being "kicked upstairs." Having already had more than my share of flowers and honors, I wrote clearly into my will an old resolve that when the time did come there should be no funeral or memorial service for me of any sort.

Following the internal bleeding incident in August 1980, I was forced to cut back still more on my activities. There was a further dimunition of strength and also a deterioration of speaking abilities, because my vocal cords began to wear out, perhaps in retribution for my overuse of them for so many years. I took a leave of absence for the autumn semester, shifting my Government course to the spring term, which started at the beginning of February. By October, I was able to attend a few meetings in Cambridge and out of town, give an occasional talk, and participate in a few television interviews; but my activities remained far below the already lowered level I had established after my stroke. I gave up tennis permanently, stopped going to almost all social occasions, and resigned from most of the remaining committees and organizations to which I belonged, becoming in many cases an inactive "honorary" president, chairman, trustee, or the like. My career was clearly drawing to a close.

# 47

# Retirement

I TURNED seventy on October 15, 1980, which meant I had to retire from Harvard the following June. I did so with some relief, after a final semester of a heavier than normal teaching load. My colleagues gave a very congenial small farewell dinner party and voted me a lifetime office and secretarial aid, which were the best farewell presents I could imagine.

It is the custom at Harvard for one's colleagues and friends to attend one's last lecture at the university. I actually had three last lectures in my courses on American-East Asian Relations, Modern Japanese Government, and the Japanese side of the Rice Paddies course, but I chose the third of these for sentimental reasons to be my symbolic last lecture, although it happened to be scheduled first. To my embarrassment, NHK decided to record it for television broadcast in Japan—a procedure I had never heard of happening at Harvard before. The lecture hall was already mostly filled on April 22 before the regular students in the course began arriving and in some indignation were forced to sit on the floor or crowd around outside the entrances. I spoke extemporaneously and very informally about my past experiences and my hopes for Japanese studies and Japanese-American relations. At the end, two little Japanese girls in beautiful kimonos came up with large bouquets of flowers. Later I learned that their father was a hopeful candidate for the Japanese Diet and this act was designed to be part of his campaign. The lecture was broadcast in Japan on prime time on May 26 and again in the summer. I have never received more favorable comments on a single television appearance than I did about this one from a great variety of people from taxi drivers to university professors.

This glorious finale to my Harvard career was followed by a fiasco of much greater proportions. A *Mainichi* reporter, Komori Yoshihisa, was doing an in-depth study of Japanese-American strategic relations but had postponed a long-planned interview with me until May 9 because of the visit to Washington of the Japanese Prime Minister, Suzuki Zenko, and the seventh seven-power economic summit conference in Ottawa. I noticed that Komori was particularly interested in what I told him about my discussion with Ohira in 1963 regarding nuclear weapons on American naval vessels in Japanese waters. I thought nothing of this at the time, because I had referred to it in general terms in my 1981 edition of *Japan: The Story of a Nation,* which had recently appeared, and other people, including a retired American admiral, Gene R. Larocque, had revealed the situation publicly some years earlier. The Japanese public, however, had become aroused by some statements about the defense relationship Suzuki had made in Washington, and the papers chose to feature my account of the incident that had happened eighteen years earlier.

My remarks, called the "Reischauer Statement" *(Raishawa hatsugen),* were greatly sensationalized and subjected to all sorts of absurd interpretations. Actually, the Japanese government had painted itself into a corner by allowing the Japanese public to assume for two decades that American vessels entering Japanese waters never carried nuclear weapons. This was something no expert in the military field could possibly believe, but the government was nonetheless furious with me when the Japanese public accepted what I had said without question and accused the government of lying to it. Our telephone rang off the hook on May 17 and 18, and we were deluged by Japanese newsmen. Fortunately, George Packard happened to be our house guest for a meeting of the Harvard Yenching Institute board of trustees. He took some of the burden off my shoulders, arranging for all the representatives of the Japanese press and television to come to a single press conference before the trustees meeting on the 18th. The sensation over my so-called revelation lasted for some time, and bitter things were said about me by members of the Japanese government; but Komori, who had written the original article, tried to calm the situation by giving a very accurate account of the circumstances surrounding my remarks. Throughout, the public remained as friendly as ever, commenting to me more about my last lecture at Harvard than about the "Reischauer Statement." After the affair had calmed down, I came to the conclusion that I had inadvertently gotten rid of a bothersome gray spot in Japanese-American relations.

Because of my retirement from Harvard and the "Reischauer Statement" incident, there was a flood of television and press interviews in May and June, mostly for the Japanese media, but by summer my schedule had become much freer. This permitted me to resume a project with NHK that had been temporarily shelved because of my collapse in August 1980. When Haru and I were in Japan in 1979, representatives of NHK had suggested making a multi-part documentary of my life, and the next March two of their directors, Naya Yuji and Hotta Kingo, spent a week with us in Belmont taping long interviews and collecting pictures from our family albums. Naya, who had originated the idea, had read my books about Japan and come to the conclusion that a biography would serve as a good framework for the presentation of my interpretation of modern Japanese history, about which he felt Japanese were woefully ignorant and confused. Thus, the biographic element was to be the sugar coating for what was essentially a lesson in history.

When our family gathered in Belmont in the summer of 1980, NHK did some filming of all of us disporting ourselves in the backyard, but then my physical collapse intervened, and the project had to be shelved. We picked it up again in the autumn of 1981. Haru and I met a NHK team of five—Naya, Hotta, another director, a cameraman, and a sound man—in Amsterdam on September 5 and spent the next two weeks filming in Leiden, Vienna, Salzburg, and Paris to cover my days of study in Europe. We found not a single one of my old teachers or associates in Europe, with the sole exception of Professor Elisséeff's younger son, Vadim, by then a leading figure in Chinese and Japanese art studies in Paris, with whom I had a long recorded conversation. From Europe we returned with the NHK crew to the United States, where we did some filming, mostly in Cambridge and Washington. NHK recorded talks between me and John Fairbank and also with Hugh Borton at his home in western Massachusetts. One particularly interesting session was with a group of six of my former wartime students, now mostly senior Harvard professors, who gathered at our home in Belmont to reminisce about the days at Arlington Hall. It was the closest thing to an Arlington Hall reunion we ever had.

On October 6 we went out to Japan, where Haru and I stayed until November 24, except for a one-week trip to China with the NHK crew and three days in Okinawa. In China we visited Peking and Xian, the ancient capital, where Ennin had spent five years. It was Haru's first trip to China and my first to Xian, and we got in some simple sightseeing on the side. As I have recorded before, the beggars and starving people of my prewar days in China were all gone, but so also were the walls of Peking and much of the charm of the old China. Peking was scarcely recognizable, with its high-rise hotels and apartment buildings, hardly visible in the smog, and its wide boulevards clogged with bicycles. I mourned the loss of the calm of the old slow-paced city. But it was good to see that everyone seemed to be adequately fed and clothed, and the throbbing energy of the people and their rugged cheerfulness were encouraging. The hoary antiquity of China was as impressive as ever, especially after the bright shiny newness of Japan and the United States. Yet everything seemed depressingly drab. It was a dusty, grimy country, and talking with its people soon revealed what constrained lives they lived. We had been assigned a Red Flag car, a sort of cross between a Cadillac and a light tank, which is the top of the line in China; the disregard its driver showed for all traffic rules—Red Flags cannot be arrested—revealed how strongly preserved were the lines of hierarchy, or perhaps one might say "class." We enjoyed our visit to China immensely, but we were intensely thankful that we were not among the more than one billion people locked away in its totally inadequate environment. The trip confirmed my already strongly held opinion that because of its huge population China would make progress only slowly and unevenly.

We developed a close friendship with the five-man NHK crew, working as we did so long together. They were a most attractive and jolly group but at the same time were real professionals. The chief difficulty we encountered was that my stroke and subsequent illness in 1980 had left my articulation of Japanese so impaired that I could not speak effectively for many of the Japanese segments. I ended up doing most of these in English, extemporaneously rather than with teleprompters, because the NHK experts felt that I was more persuasive in that format. A running Japanese commentary carried the main story, and superimposed Japanese texts translated my little commentaries on the background of Japan's modernization and its recent development.

The project ran to five one-hour programs, which concentrated on my childhood in Japan; my studies in Europe and China, which gave chances for historical comparisons and contrasts with Japan; my wartime service; and my days at the Embassy. The program was shown in successive weeks on prime time during the spring of 1982 and again that summer. On the whole it seems to have been considered a success, though I deeply regretted that I had not been able to do it all in Japanese as originally planned.

An interesting spinoff was a well-illustrated book published by the Nihon Hoso Shuppan Kyokai (Japan Broadcasting Publishing Society), an affiliate of NHK, which unlike NHK itself is a profit-making company. It based the book on the NHK program and on unused materials in the interview tapes made in March 1980. It was called *Nihon e no jijoden (My Autobiography for Japan)*. I objected to the title, since the book was written not by me but by the publishers, but they assured me that it had just the right ring in Japanese. I went over the first galleys very carefully, correcting the numerous errors and pointing out the distasteful boastful tone, which they promised to correct. The book was written in an informal, chatty style, reflecting its oral origins in the tapes, and it sold very well.

~§

Although I had dropped most of my outside activities after my illness in 1980, Haru and I did pick up a new one which came to loom large in our lives. During a trip to Japan in May 1978, an attractive youngish Japanese woman named Mrs. Momoko Izu had introduced herself while I was eating breakfast in the Okura Hotel. She was the vice-president for international affairs of a small, high-technology company called Energy Conversion Devices, located in Troy, Michigan, in the suburbs of Detroit, and she wished me to meet with the president of her firm, Stanford Ovshinsky, which I agreed to do. This led to a call by Ovshinsky, his wife Iris, and Momoko on Haru and me in November.

Stan Ovshinsky had been the pioneer in converting sunlight into electrical energy through the use, not of silicon crystals, but of cheaper amorphous glasslike materials. Lacking a university education, he had long been looked on askance by the scientific community, but his discoveries were just beginning to win recognition and were soon to be seen as one of the most promising routes to the commercial utilization of sunlight for energy. Stan Ovshinsky was moved by a strong idealistic urge to bring the fruit of his efforts to the less developed parts of the world, and he was convinced that the Japanese would be good partners in doing this. Momoko felt that my contacts with Japan and my international ideals matched well with Stan's interests and that I could serve as a useful support to him in his efforts.

Although I repeatedly protested that I was neither a scientist nor a businessman, both Haru and I were excited by the prospect of making electricity available to remote Third World villages so as to allow the people to have electric lighting, run radios and television sets, and operate pumps for irrigation. We were persuaded eventually to become consultants to ECD, as it is generally called; I became a member of the board of directors and the two of us served as the chairman and vice-chairman of its Tokyo affiliate, Japan ECD. The Ovshinskys became close friends, and Momoko, who had reverted through divorce to her maiden name of Ito, became virtually a younger sister to Haru. ECD board meetings took us periodically to Detroit or New York, and our work with the company also took us out to Japan fairly frequently. Even when I dropped most of my other activities in 1981, we did not give up our ECD connection.

Retirement brought a decided shift in our pattern of life. Starting in 1982, we spent the winter months of January, February, and March in a little house we had bought in La Jolla on the outskirts of San Diego. During a three-day stopover at Ann's home on our way back from Japan in 1978, Haru had become curious about houses in the neighborhood, had made up her mind to buy one, and had gotten me to close the deal before we flew on to Belmont. I was somewhat dubious about this hasty action, but she argued that the house was a good investment and would come in handy after I retired. She was right. We never had any trouble renting it, at first by the year and then for the nine months we were not there, and it proved an excellent retirement refuge for winter. We preferred being in Belmont the other nine months, watching the beautiful change of season in the woods around our house, but we felt the New England winters were just too long and snowy to suffer through if we didn't have to. In La Jolla I could sun myself almost daily on the beach, and it was pleasant being close to Ann and her family. Bob often dropped by on speaking engagements to the west coast, and he and Joan sometimes brought their families out for brief vacations.

Bob, who now lived in the Washington suburb of Bethesda, had left the Brookings Institution some years earlier to become, under Alice Rivlin, the second in command of the Congressional Budget Office, a position of considerable influence which he greatly enjoyed. Later he became the executive vice-president of the Urban Institute, an economic think tank in Washington, before returning again to Brookings. He went to meetings and lectured all over the country, being a very articulate and amusing speaker. Joan had moved several years earlier to New York, where she continued to work in the book publishing field and married a young attorney, William Simon. They subsequently moved to the Westchester suburb of Larchmont, where they had a daughter, Katharine ("Katie"), in 1981 and a son, Richard Danton, in 1984. This brought the number of our grandchildren to nine, a pleasingly symmetric increase from three children.

The whole family, minus Ann's two eldest sons, gathered in Belmont in August 1982, and Haru and I went out to Japan in March, July, and September of that year and again in April 1983. This last trip was in order to take part in a so-called College of the Young Presidents Organization. Haru had strongly opposed doing this because of my health and I had my doubts, but the large body of eager young leaders, mostly from the United States, offered an educational opportunity I could not resist. Haru and I successfully completed our four hour-long sessions of answering questions, but the strain obviously was too much for me. On the morning after the last session, which was April 15, I had another serious attack of internal bleeding. I was rushed to a hospital and a few days later moved to the more adequate facilities of the hospital attached to Tokyo University.

For more than a week I was in a coma most of the time and, after regaining consciousness, I was still unable to speak for several days and could not take anything by mouth except cracked ice for some time after that. I remained in a state of semi-trance, not really aware of my surroundings but envisioning myself as sleeping on a marble couch in a Chinese palace surrounded by rivulets of clear flowing water and looking out over a broad valley lush with green rice plants. I even had a vision of floating in a stone boat down a stream a few inches deep and passing below the towers of Angkor Wat. During this vision, I actually held forth semi-consciously in an oracular sermon on world brotherhood, delivered in reasonably fluent Japanese to my bewildered nurse. She had had the experience of being a prisoner of the Russians for several years in Sakhalin so she may not have been as open to my message of world brotherhood as I would have wished.

My nurses were all wonderful, giving me endless and untiring tender care, and I owe my life, I believe, to the special attention of two doctors, Endo Yasuo and Inoue Noboru, whom we had come to know through Momoko and who had been supplying me for some time with a newly developed but still unmarketed medicine for my liver ailments. By May 4 my mind was completely clear, and the doctors felt that I could be safely flown back to the United States. Dr. Endo and a younger doctor accompanied us, and we took a whole block of first-class seats to accommodate our party of four and my stretcher and medical equipment. Bob met us in New York and supervised my transfer by ambulance to a Boston hospital, where I remained off and on into the summer.

Remembering the problems of publicity she had suffered from during my collapse in 1980, Haru kept my illness secret in Japan with the cooperation of the Japanese Foreign Ministry and the American Embassy. I had been transferred to the Tokyo University hospital incognito, and the name on the door of my room read Mr. Edo Rai. "Edo" is the original name for Tokyo, and "Rai" the Japanese pronunciation of the surname I use in China. An announcement had to be made, however, when we left Japan. A brief statement was released, and I appeared before a group of newsmen and cameramen at the airport. As a remarkable gesture of personal friendship, Mike Mansfield, who had been the incomparably prestigious and competent American Ambassador since 1977, drove all the way out to Narita Airport with his wife Maureen to see us off. Back in Belmont, Haru changed our phone number and installed a recording machine to save herself from the deluge of calls that had almost drowned her in 1980.

I slowly regained my strength during the autumn of 1983, and we were able to spend our usual three months at the beginning of 1984 in La Jolla. I did not accompany Haru, however, when she went out to Japan in late February and early March because of her mother's failing health, nor when she went again in June at the time of her mother's death at the age of ninety-two. I cut back my outside activities almost to zero, giving up all public speaking and virtually all social engagements. I even resigned my chairmanship of the board of trustees of the Harvard Yenching Institute, being replaced in the autumn of 1983 by Henry Rosovsky, who himself retired from the Harvard deanship in June 1984 and was later made the first faculty member of the Harvard Corporation in exactly a century.

I limited myself for the most part to occasional interviews, some television appearances if they could be filmed at home, a few callers, my work with ECD, and also my writing. A brief history of the Japan Society of New York, entitled *Japan Society 1907–1982: 75 Years of Partnership Across the Pacific,* which I wrote on the basis of materials provided me by a research worker, had appeared briefly before my collapse in 1983. Thereafter I still wrote occasional articles, primarily for Japanese and Korean publications, worked on this not inconsiderable tome, and continued editing Haru's book on her two grandfathers and some other relatives. (It was published by the Harvard Press in the spring of 1986 under the title *Samurai and Silk* and is far more interesting than anything I have ever written.) All in all the drastic curtailment of my activities after 1983 seemed much more like retirement than had the termination of my Harvard teaching duties in 1981.

# 48

# Epilogue

EVER SINCE the stabbing in 1964, my stroke in 1975, and still more after the bleeding incidents in 1980 and 1983, I have felt that I was living on borrowed time, to say nothing of borrowed blood. According to my doctors' estimates, I received 268 units of blood and plasma in Japan alone in 1983 and still more after returning to the United States. My coma and visions during my hospitalization in Japan also gave me a strong sense of being reborn. Having survived more than once only through the heroic efforts of others and the contributions of the life blood of so many people, I have felt all the more a strong compulsion to do whatever I can for Japanese-American cooperation and for world peace.

I realize, of course, that there is little I can accomplish at this stage, though I have the seeds of another book rattling around in my brain. In any case, I can at least hope that my life has made some contribution. It has been a good life for me personally. In Adrienne and Haru I have been blessed with two wonderful companions. No one could have had a more loyal and satisfying family. But I trust that my life has had some broader significance beyond myself and my family. It has been a varied, broken-up life, yet it all hangs together around a few central themes. My upbringing in Japan, my worldwide travels as a student, my three separate periods of teaching at Harvard, my government service in Washington, in the army, and at the Embassy in Tokyo, and my extensive writing and speaking have all centered upon better understanding between the United States, Japan, and the rest of East Asia. More broadly speaking, all phases of my life have been focused on world peace and understanding.

No one can deny that in many ways the world is worse off today than it was when I was born in 1910. The tremendous increase in man's capacity for self-destruction is certainly the gravest new problem, though by no means the only one. There is also the vast increase in global population, the degradation of the human environment, and the fantastically increased complexity and confusion of everyday life. These are problems that fresh generations will have to face and solve if mankind is to survive.

The voices of doomsday ring in our ears, but there are probably more ways in which the world has improved than worsened during the past three quarters of a century. Great progress has been made in the broad areas of health and affluence, and also in the field of international relations, which has always concerned me most. Imperialism, which then was taken for granted, has all but disappeared. Attitudes of racial inequality, which once held unchallenged sway, are now in retreat. International consciousness has become incomparably more widespread. Knowledge in the United States about Japan and the rest of East Asia and the recognition of the importance of these areas to us have spread much more than I had dreamed possible in so short a time. Democracy has become stronger in the few lands where it already existed in 1910, has extended vigorously to a few more, and is at least paid lip service almost everywhere. Japan itself has become a firmly based, healthy, and extraordinarily egalitarian democracy. It and the other advanced democracies, some of which were mortal enemies in the two world wars, now form a closely knit community of trading nations between whom war has become unthinkable. Perhaps in time the presently hostile Communist states and the chaotic, discontented less developed lands will be drawn by this already existing community of trade to join it in a single peaceful worldwide community.

Most gratifying to me is the strong, equal partnership the United States and Japan have forged. Since they are the two greatest of the world's democracies, they stand at the heart of the community of democratic nations. And since their partnership is the one great alliance that bridges major cultural and racial cleavages in the world, it is a model for a future worldwide community. The Japanese still find it hard to feel at ease with outsiders or to play the full international role their economic strength and technological advancement demand of them, but they are moving toward overcoming these weaknesses. Cooperation between the United States and Japan is constantly shaken by economic bickering, yet their alliance stands firm. This is one of the main reasons one can have hope for the future of the world.

Today I have the satisfaction of seeing that the causes which meant most to me throughout my life have progressed much faster and farther than I had ever expected to witness in my lifetime. But this does not mean that many serious problems do not remain. In addition to the terrifying nuclear balance of destruction and the great domestic problems all complex modern nations face, we have much more to achieve even in the areas where we have had relative success. A great deal must still be done to educate people in the United States, Japan, and everywhere else for peaceful participation in a world community. The Vietnam War did not teach Americans adequately to avoid unwise military and political involvement in less developed countries. Our handling of the problems of human rights is still far from satisfactory, especially in countries like South Korea, for whose very existence we are in large part responsible.

I also have some personal regrets. In my involvement in public affairs, I failed to achieve some of the things I had set my heart on. I never got around to writing a comprehensive history of Japan, beyond the various short accounts I essayed. I never attempted a balanced world history that would be more satisfactory than the still largely Western-oriented works of Spengler, Toynbee, and William A. McNeil. I failed to produce a major television presentation of Japan which would fully mirror my views. But these disappointments are small when compared with my satisfaction with the progress I have witnessed in the areas of my major interest, or the realization that a whole army of vigorous young scholars now stands trained and eager to carry the causes I believe in far beyond what my limited abilities and energy could ever achieve.

Looking back on the past three quarters of a century, I can see that my droplet of life, falling where it did, has had a long, sometimes tumultuous flow, but always in the main stream of world events. It has followed an exciting and satisfying course. Now it slows as it nears the river's mouth and prepares, in the Buddhist metaphor, to merge in the great sea of infinity. My greatest remaining regret is that of the historian. I wish the wheel of time would speed up so I could see how things turn out. I have no doubt, however, about one aspect of the future. Japanese-American relations will continue to stand on a very solid base of shared interests and ideals. There can be no repetition of the great tragedy that once engulfed my two homelands in war with each other.

# Index

Page numbers in *italics* refer to illustrations.

Journey's End. (Twilight at Misaki) *(Leonard Nadel)*

## About the Author

Born in 1910 in Tokyo, Japan, to American missionary parents, Edwin O. Reischauer has spent his whole life involved in Japanese-American relations. He grew up in Japan, and at a time when other attitudes prevailed, he developed a keen sense of the equality of all peoples and the importance of East Asia in the world.

After graduating from Oberlin College and studying at Harvard, the Sorbonne, and in Japan, Korea, and China, he joined the Harvard faculty, specializing in ancient Chinese and Japanese history. He was determined to help make East Asian studies a significant part of university activities in the United States. With the cooperation of his colleague, John K. Fairbank, he succeeded spectacularly in this at Harvard, developing the famous "Rice Paddies" course and establishing a thriving center of East Asian studies. He also wrote and spoke prolifically.

In the meantime, he served in the American Army during World War II, supervising the processing of intercepted military and diplomatic messages, which proved extremely helpful to the American cause. He also spent a year at the State Department helping in the planning for postwar Japan and Korea.

From 1961 to 1966 he was unexpectedly drafted to be the American Ambassador to Japan. After the death of his first wife, he had married a Japanese, Haru Matsukata, who was of aristocratic descent but happened to have a strongly American cultural heritage. The two were extremely popular in Japan, and Reischauer, given an extraordinarily free rein by Washington, pioneered in establishing the sense of "equal partnership" between Japan and America that has characterized their relationship ever since.

After resigning from the foreign service, Reischauer returned to Harvard, this time in the special position of University Professor. He resumed his extensive speaking and writing, including his well-known book *The Japanese*, and after retiring from Harvard in 1981 he still continues his writing as well as his close contacts with his three children and nine grandchildren.